Inductive
BIBLE
STUDY

Inductive
BIBLE
STUDY

A Comprehensive Guide to the
Practice of Hermeneutics

David R. Bauer
Robert A. Traina

Foreword by Eugene H. Peterson

B
Baker Academic
a division of Baker Publishing Group
Grand Rapids, Michigan

Published by Baker Academic
a division of Baker Publishing Group
P.O. Box 6287, Grand Rapids, MI 49516-6287
www.bakeracademic.com

Printed in the United States of America

Library of Congress Cataloging-in-Publication Data

Bauer, David R.
    Inductive Bible study : a comprehensive guide to the practice of hermeneutics / David R. Bauer, Robert A. Traina.
       p. cm.
    Includes bibliographical references (p.   ) and indexes.
    ISBN 978-0-8010-2767-3 (cloth)
    1. Bible—Hermeneutics. 2. Bible—Study and teaching. I. Traina, Robert A. (Robert Angelo), 1921– II. Title.
    BS476.B39 2011
    220.601—dc22
                                            2010034320

11 12 13 14 15 16 17   7 6 5 4 3 2 1

This book is dedicated to the memories of
Wilbert Webster White and Howard Tillman Kuist,
pioneers, teachers, interpreters,
men who loved God and God's Word

Contents

List of Figures

Foreword

Fifty-six years ago I drove into New York City, negotiated my way through the traffic of midtown Manhattan, and enrolled in a seminary on East 49th Street. Later that week I sat in a classroom led by a professor who over the next three years would profoundly change my perception of the Bible, and me with it, in ways that gave shape to everything I have been doing for the rest of my life. This is not an exaggeration.

A couple of years before I entered his classroom, Professor Traina had written the book *Methodical Bible Study*, which was used throughout the seminary as a text. The book that you hold in your hands, *Inductive Bible Study*, is an expansion of that early text by Professor Traina and his colleague Professor Bauer. As I read this sequel, memories of my first reading come alive again. I am giving witness to that early but never-diminishing delight.

I grew up in a Christian home and from an early age was familiar with the Bible. I read it daily, memorized it, and on entering into adolescence argued with my friends over it. But quite frankly, I wasn't really fond of it. I knew it was important, knew it was "God's Word." To tell the truth, I was bored with it. More often than not, it was a field of contention, providing material for "truths" that were contested by warring factions. Or it was reduced to rules and principles that promised to keep me out of moral mud puddles. Or—and this was worst of all—it was flattened into clichés and slogans and sentimental God-talk, intended to inspire and motivate.

It only took three or four weeks in Professor Traina's classroom for me to become aware of a seismic change beginning to take place within me regarding the Bible. Until now I and all the people with whom I associated had treated the Bible as something to be *used*—used as a textbook with information about God, used as a handbook to lead people to salvation, used as a weapon to defeat the devil and all his angels, used as an antidepressant. Now incrementally, week by week, semester by semester, my reading of the Bible was becoming a conversation. I was no longer reading words—I was listening to voices; I was observing how these words worked in association with all the other words on the page. And I was learning to listen carefully to these voices, these writers who were, well, *writers*. Skilled writers, poets, and storytellers who were artists of language. Isaiah and David were poets. Matthew and Luke were masters of the art of narrative. Words were not just words: words were holy.

I employ the term *seismic* to describe what I was experiencing. Here is another term for what happened: *paradigm shift*—a totally different way to look at and interpret and respond to what I have been looking at all my life. Like the paradigm shift from Ptolemy to Copernicus. The shift from the world of Ptolemy to the world of Copernicus totally changed the way we understand the cosmos. Ptolemy told us that the sun revolved around the earth, and that made perfect sense for a long time. Copernicus told us that the earth revolved around the sun, and suddenly we were "seeing" things, the same things that we had been seeing all along, but now in a far more accurate and comprehensive way.

When I entered Professor Traina's classroom, I had a Ptolemaic understanding of the Bible: I was the center (my will, my questions, my needs) around which the Bible turned. After three years in that classroom, I was a thoroughgoing Copernican: the Bible was the center (God's will, Christ's questions, the Spirit's gifts) around which I turned.

The experience was not merely academic. The passion and patience that permeated that classroom instilled in me an inductive imagination: fiercely attentive to everything that is there and only what is there, alert to relationships both literary and personal, habitually aware of context—the entire world of creation and salvation that is being revealed in this Bible. And always the insistence that I do this firsthand, not filtered through the hearsay of others or the findings of experts. His faculty colleagues shared the work, but it was Professor Traina's intensity and comprehensiveness that penetrated my mind and spirit in a way that shaped everything I would do and am still doing as a pastor, professor, and writer. And not just my vocational life—also my personal life, my marriage and family, my friends and community and church. The inductive imagination continued to develop into a biblical imagination.

And not only for me. My sense is that this way of reading the Bible—and *living* the Bible—has been transformative for thousands; probably by now the number must run into the millions.

Eugene H. Peterson
Pastor Emeritus, Christ Our King Presbyterian Church, Bel Air, Maryland
Professor Emeritus of Spiritual Theology, Regent College, British Columbia

Preface

Our intention is to present rather comprehensively our understanding of the approach to the study of the Bible known as *inductive Bible study*, and to direct this presentation primarily to seminary students and those engaged in Christian ministry. But we anticipate that this volume will be useful also to scholars who are engaged in advanced study of the Bible and who are conversant with contemporary hermeneutical discussions. Moreover, we hope that it will be serviceable as a textbook for certain college and university courses. Though this book is based on serious hermeneutical reflection and will at points engage current hermeneutical issues, its primary purpose is to provide practical guidance in original, accurate, precise, and penetrating study of the Bible.

This book serves as a sequel to *Methodical Bible Study*, by Robert A. Traina, which many have used as a reliable introduction to inductive Bible study. We are gratified by the influence and popularity of *Methodical Bible Study* and are encouraged that it continues to be used as a textbook in numerous seminaries and colleges around the world; yet that book is somewhat dated, for it has not been revised since its appearance in 1952. Moreover, whereas *Methodical Bible Study* was intended to be a general description of inductive Bible study, arranged topically in terms of major components, this book offers a specific, orderly process that readers can apply directly as they work with particular biblical texts. In addition, it reflects significant developments in the presentation of method that have come about as the result of years of classroom instruction, further reflection, and new insights into hermeneutics that have emerged since 1952. Together we have a combined sixty years of seminary teaching of inductive Bible study since *Methodical Bible Study* first appeared.

A number of clarifications in the area of inductive Bible study have emerged over the years, many of them related to developments in hermeneutical reflection among biblical scholars in general. This volume cites and interacts with contemporary literature. For the inductive study of Scripture to have any future, it must converse with the major issues and considerations that are surfacing in the burgeoning discipline of hermeneutics.

In addition, we are convinced of the necessity for a fuller treatment of the principle of induction, the implications of induction, and the importance of an attitude of induction. Although inductive Bible study involves certain steps that are performed, it is not solely a matter of techniques. It involves, above all, a commitment to an inductive posture, which means radical openness to the meaning of the text, wherever a study characterized by radical openness might lead.

This book is the result of collaboration between Dr. Robert A. Traina, a graduate of The Biblical Seminary in New York (now New York Theological Seminary) and for many years a member of the faculty of that institution, and later academic dean and F. M. and Ada Thompson Professor of English Bible at Asbury Theological Seminary, and Dr. David R. Bauer, a student of Dr. Traina at Asbury and currently dean of the School of Biblical Interpretation and Proclamation and the Ralph Waldo Beeson Professor of Inductive Biblical Studies at Asbury Theological Seminary. In personal and communal study, we have found that the inductive approach as set forth in this book has caused the Bible to come alive in ways that far surpassed our greatest expectations. Through this process we have consistently encountered the God to whom the biblical text bears witness. We hope that all who read and use this book will find the assistance that will enable them to experience the same kind of excitement and encounter.

We gladly thank those who have played a role in the production of this book. We are grateful to Mrs. Judy Traina Seitz, who assisted greatly in its editing and organization. We are indebted to many students and colleagues who read early drafts of the manuscript and offered helpful suggestions. And we are grateful to Mr. James Kinney, director of Baker Academic at Baker Publishing Group, for his encouragement and meticulous care in bringing this book to publication.

David R. Bauer
Robert A. Traina

Abbreviations

AB	Anchor Bible
ABRL	Anchor Bible Reference Library
BDAG	W. Bauer, F. W. Danker, W. F. Arndt, and F. W. Gingrich. *A Greek-English Lexicon of the New Testament and Other Early Christian Literature*. 3rd ed. Chicago: University of Chicago Press, 2000
BDB	F. Brown, S. R. Driver, and C. A. Briggs. *A Hebrew and English Lexicon of the Old Testament*. Oxford: Oxford University Press, 1907. Reprint, Peabody, MA: Hendrickson, 1979, 1996, with *Strong's* numbering
BLS	Bible and Literature Series
FOTL	Forms of the Old Testament Literature
GBS	Guides to Biblical Scholarship
Hermeneia	Hermeneia: A Critical and Historical Commentary on the Bible
IBC	Interpretation: A Bible Commentary for Teaching and Preaching
IBT	Interpreting Biblical Texts
ICC	International Critical Commentary
Int	*Interpretation*
JBL	*Journal of Biblical Literature*
JSOT	*Journal for the Study of the Old Testament*
JSOTSup	Journal for the Study of the Old Testament: Supplement Series
LCBI	Literary Currents in Biblical Interpretation
LEC	Library of Early Christianity
LXX	Septuagint
NASB	New American Standard Bible

NICNT   New International Commentary on the New Testament
NIGTC   New International Greek Testament Commentary
NRSV   New Revised Standard Version
NT   New Testament
NTL   New Testament Library
NTS   *New Testament Studies*
OT   Old Testament
OTL   Old Testament Library
SBLDS   Society of Biblical Literature Dissertation Series
TDNT   *Theological Dictionary of the New Testament.* Edited by G. Kittel
             and G. Friedrich. Translated by G. W. Bromiley. 10 vols. Grand
             Rapids: Eerdmans, 1964–67
TDOT   *Theological Dictionary of the Old Testament.* Edited by G. J.
             Botterweck, H. Ringgren, and Heinz-Joseph Fabry. Translated by
             J. T. Willis et al. 15 vols. Grand Rapids: Eerdmans, 1974–2006
WBC   Word Biblical Commentary

Introduction

Meaning of Inductive Bible Study

We should begin by indicating what we mean by *induction*. The term *inductive* is used in both a broader and a narrower sense. In the broader sense, it involves a commitment to move from the evidence of the text and the realities that surround the text to possible conclusions (or inferences) regarding the meaning of the text. In this sense, *inductive* is practically synonymous with *evidential* over against *deductive*, which is presuppositional, involving a movement from presuppositions with which one approaches the text to a reading of the text intended to support these presuppositions.

This broader sense of inductive, with its stress on the movement from evidential premises to inferences, implies an emphasis on inductive, inferential reasoning: one examines the evidence in order to determine what may properly be inferred from the evidence for the meaning of passages. This broader sense of inductive also involves the attempt to help students understand and process the critical interaction between their preunderstandings, including theological creeds and doctrinal commitments, and the witness of the biblical text.

In the narrower sense, *inductive Bible study* pertains to a movement in the history of hermeneutics that traces its beginnings to the work of William Rainey Harper, of Yale and the University of Chicago, and his associate Wilbert Webster White, a Yale-trained Hebraist and the founder of The Biblical Seminary in New York.[1] These scholars were concerned that the almost exclusive attention paid to higher-critical issues—such as trying to reconstruct sources that presumably lie behind the final form of the text, which focused on more or less speculative elements behind the biblical text rather than on the text itself—rendered the

---

1. The authoritative resource for the life and work of Wilbert Webster White is still Charles R. Eberhardt, *The Bible in the Making of Ministers: The Scriptural Basis of Theological Education; The Lifework of Wilbert Webster White* (New York: Association Press, 1949).

study of the Bible lifeless and devoid of clear significance for Christian faith and ministry. Consequently, they insisted that students should give priority to examining the scriptural text in its final form, although eventually they should consider evidence from historical and even historical-critical examination of the text. This procedure involved (1) direct study of the biblical text in the student's mother tongue,[2] with the hope that students who had opportunity and ability would supplement the study of the Bible in the vernacular with original-language analysis; and (2) special attention to the ways in which the immediate and broader-book context of passages and the literary structure of passages themselves inform students' understanding of their meaning.

Although the origin of inductive Bible study in the narrow sense is associated especially with the founding of The Biblical Seminary in 1900, this approach had precursors in the history of interpretation and has, since the beginning of the twentieth century, enjoyed widespread dissemination. Over the years it has been part of the instruction in such institutions as Princeton Theological Seminary, Union Theological Seminary in Virginia, Fuller Theological Seminary, the Associated Mennonite Biblical Seminaries, Columbia Theological Seminary, Dallas Theological Seminary, and Azusa Pacific University, to say nothing of the hundreds of schools outside North America that have adopted the inductive study of the Bible. In addition, inductive Bible study has significantly influenced the work of several scholars of global reputation.

Inductive Bible study is probably best known, however, in its lay-oriented forms. For example, it has become central in the discipleship development program of InterVarsity Christian Fellowship; and it has been introduced to millions through the writings of popular authors. One of the advantages of inductive Bible study is that it can contribute to the most sophisticated and serious biblical scholarship while also equipping laypersons to study the text for themselves.

Emphases in Inductive Bible Study

This more narrow sense of *induction* involves a number of emphases that reflect both the convictions of Harper and White and the ways in which induc-

---

2. Thus inductive Bible study was often called "English Bible," as reflected, for example, in the curriculum of The Biblical Seminary in New York. This nomenclature accurately represents the emphasis that was given to the study of the Bible in the vernacular but was problematic in that (1) it assumed an English-language environment and was insufficiently global in its reference; (2) it gave the impression that inductive Bible study was limited to vernacular translations, whereas from the beginning it was acknowledged that inductive Bible study would be ideally executed with texts in the original languages; and (3) it seemed to suggest that the use of the vernacular was the central concern when actually the principle of induction was the operative issue, and the role of the vernacular was understood to be a tactical concession to the limits of linguistic equipment on the part of most students as they pursued their inductive work in the Bible.

tive Bible study has developed over the years. First, it emphasizes the meaning of the *final form* of the text. This attention to the final form arises from two considerations. The first consideration is that this final form is, in fact, the only text that actually exists today. All earlier sources or redactional (editorial) processes that may lie behind the text and could have contributed to the development of the text are more or less speculative in terms of whether they ever existed or their specific character or shape. In any case these earlier stages of the tradition no longer have a material existence but are scholarly constructions. As we shall see, an inductive approach recognizes that source theories and redactional reconstructions might at times be helpful in the interpretation of the final text and should be employed in interpretation, with the proviso that their tentative character and their limitations must be kept in mind. But it is both unwise and unrealistic to focus on entities that do not (presently) have an existence independent of the minds and judgments of scholars and about whose (past) existence scholars themselves disagree. The second consideration is that the church has accepted this final form of the text as canonical Scripture.[3] Indeed, when one talks about the Bible, one assumes a canonical collection and one implies a canonical form. Thus inductive Bible study gives priority both in emphasis and in sequence to the direct study of the text in its final form. Subsequently, the use of background knowledge, considerations of the developments of traditions that lie behind the final form of the text, the history of interpretation, and so forth are incorporated into an overall process that has as its starting point the examination of the text itself and has as its goal the meaning of the text in its final, canonical shape.

3. The implications of the canon of Scripture for the centrality of the study of the final form of the text are most thoroughly and vigorously set forth by Francis Watson. See esp. his *Text, Church, and World: Biblical Interpretation in Theological Perspective* (Grand Rapids: Eerdmans, 1994), 15–17, 60–63, 70–77, 221–40. See also Robert W. Wall, "Canonical Context and Canonical Conversations," in *Between Two Horizons: Spanning New Testament Studies and Systematic Theology*, ed. Joel B. Green and Max Turner (Grand Rapids: Eerdmans, 2000), 165–82. But the view that the final form is the proper focus for the study of the Bible as the church's canon is universally identified with the "canonical approach" of Brevard S. Childs. See esp. his *Introduction to the Old Testament as Scripture* (Philadelphia: Fortress, 1979). In this regard, Childs's approach should be distinguished from the "canonical criticism" of James Sanders, who insists that the notion of canon points not to the centrality of the final form, or canonical shape, of the text, but rather to the dynamic process of the readaptation of traditions within the community of faith, both as reflected within the Bible itself and as carried on within the interpretive practice of the church throughout its history. See James Sanders, *Torah and Canon* (Philadelphia: Fortress, 1972); idem, *Canon and Community: A Guide to Canonical Criticism*, GBS (Philadelphia: Fortress, 1984); idem, *From Sacred Story to Sacred Text: Canon as Paradigm* (Philadelphia: Fortress, 1987). For a helpful comparison of the canonical approaches of Childs and Sanders, see Frank Spina, "Canonical Criticism: Childs versus Sanders," in *Interpreting God's Word for Today: An Inquiry into Hermeneutics from a Biblical Theological Perspective*, ed. Wayne McCown and James Massey, Wesleyan Theological Perspectives 2 (Anderson, IN: Warner, 1982), 165–94.

A second emphasis of inductive Bible study is the *form* of the text, giving serious attention to the ways students can identify for themselves literary structure and can show how such structure informs the meaning of the text. It also pays attention to the ways in which literary genre has a bearing upon construal of meaning. This emphasis upon structure and genre is supported by the consideration that communication never comes as pure content but that form and content are always inextricably bound together in the communicative process.

The concern with the final form of the text leads to an emphasis upon the *study of the biblical book* as, in most cases, the basic literary unit in the Bible's final form. As G. Campbell Morgan suggests, the Bible is not so much a book as it is a library of books.[4] Consequently, an inductive approach insists that students recognize both the importance of interpreting individual passages in light of their function within the world of the book in which they stand and the importance of grasping the message of books-as-wholes.

Inductive Bible study involves an emphasis upon students *developing their own skills* in the study of the Bible. This development of skill is accomplished through students' consistent and constant firsthand study of the text itself, using background information, critical approaches, commentaries, and other secondary sources in the process of an overarching program that focuses—in both its starting point and goal—upon their ability to construe the meaning of the final form of the text. Students can best understand hermeneutical principles and can most effectively learn how to study the Bible as they themselves pursue an experimental practice of actually observing, interpreting, and appropriating the biblical text.

Inductive Bible study also emphasizes practicability, with a concern for adapting the methodological program to realistic expectations of what readers of the Bible, including those preparing for and involved in Christian ministry, can reasonably achieve as they seek to incorporate the principle of induction into their own useable process. This emphasis arises out of the conviction that inductive Bible study seeks to tailor a methodical approach to all aspects of the existence of the biblical text, which includes the relationship of the reader/interpreter to the biblical text and to the dynamic study of that text. Thus an inductive approach attends not only to the nature of the biblical text but also to the nature of the student and to the realities that exist in the situation of most students.

Inductive study of the Bible likewise emphasizes a *broad methodical process* that involves particular orderly steps or phases. Inductive Bible study should not be considered as one specific exegetical approach that can be set alongside

---

4. G. Campbell Morgan, *The Study and Teaching of the English Bible*, rev. E. D. De Rusett (London: Hodder & Stoughton; New York: Fleming H. Revell, 1910), 30–31. Also available online at http://www.gcampbellmorgan.com/studyteach.html.

other exegetical approaches, such as form criticism, redaction criticism, or narrative criticism.[5] Rather, it is a holistic program that seeks to incorporate the values of the various specific exegetical approaches or procedures within it, and it is methodical in recognizing that the practical reality of the actual study of the Bible requires serious attention to certain steps performed in a certain sequence.

A further emphasis of inductive Bible study has to do with the *dynamic interrelation* between the various specific steps or phases in the study of the Bible over against a rigidly linear model that understands these phases to exist in isolation from one another or that assumes the possibility of completing a certain phase and never returning to it. Rather, an inductive approach is *spiracular*: it is characterized by a spiral in the sense that once students move from observation to interpretation, they will see the need to correct some of the observations they have made and will make additional observations. When students move from interpretation to contemporary appropriation, they will recognize additional aspects of interpretation and perhaps correct some dimensions of their interpretation. In other words, although one can and should differentiate among the various specific steps, these steps constantly impinge upon one another in the actual practice of inductive Bible study. Thus the issue is emphasis rather than mutual exclusion.

Finally, inductive Bible study emphasizes the development of a *holistic and integrative* process that seeks to be comprehensive in the following ways:

1. It tries to incorporate within its model all legitimate evidence, wherever it is found, including insights from critical approaches and every appropriate exegetical operation in the study of the text, but it seeks to do so at the most effective point in the process and in the most effective fashion.
2. It tries to deal with the text at its various levels: the book, the division, the section, the segment, the paragraph, the sentence. Inductive Bible study also provides for studying the canon-as-a-whole so as to assist in tracing the meaning of themes throughout the Bible and the relations between the two Testaments.
3. It tries to address the range of the hermeneutical concerns, which includes initial observation of the text,[6] interpretation, considerations of

---

5. For helpful discussions of these specific exegetical (and esp. critical) approaches, see John Barton, *Reading the Old Testament: Method in Biblical Study*, rev. ed. (Louisville: Westminster John Knox, 1996); I. Howard Marshall, ed., *New Testament Interpretation: Essays on Principles and Methods* (Grand Rapids: Eerdmans, 1977); David Alan Black and David S. Dockery, eds., *Interpreting the New Testament: Essays on Methods and Issues* (Nashville: Broadman & Holman, 2001); Joel B. Green, ed., *Hearing the New Testament: Strategies for Interpretation* (Grand Rapids: Eerdmans, 1995).

6. Including interrogation, that is, raising questions of these observations in an attempt to probe their interpretive significance.

contemporary appropriation and proclamation, and the correlation of the teachings of individual passages and books into a biblical theology and a biblically based theology. This approach rejects a textual atomism or disjunction that would fail to take connections within the text seriously. And it also rejects a methodological atomism that would present various approaches or steps in exegetical work as self-standing and as functioning in isolation from one another.

Although we have just described major emphases that have come to characterize inductive Bible study, we acknowledge that those who practice inductive Bible study, even in the more narrow sense of the tradition of Harper and White, do not adopt an absolutely monolithic model; rather, in a variety of ways practitioners have developed inductive Bible study within certain broad parameters.

Our present work emphasizes the comprehensive and synthetic dimension of inductive Bible study so that it may be methodical, spiracular, holistic, and integrative. As explained, *holistic* and *integrative* describe a comprehensive approach that at the most effective point and in the most effective way incorporates every legitimate exegetical operation of the study of the text, including critical methods. Indeed, one of the purposes of *Methodical Bible Study* (1952) was to relate inductive Bible study, as it had been practiced, to mainstream exegesis: established interpretive techniques employed by scholars around the world. This emphasis upon comprehensiveness and integration is not a departure from the vision of Harper and White but a development of their vision and an articulation of some of their basic concerns. We contend that inductive Bible study is essentially *a comprehensive, holistic study of the Bible that takes into account every aspect of the existence of the biblical text and that is intentional in allowing the Bible in its final canonical shape to speak to us on its own terms, thus leading to accurate, original, compelling, and profound interpretation and contemporary appropriation.*

Two Significant Clarifications

At this point we raise two important issues to clarify the presentation that follows in the remainder of the book. First, we recognize that one of the chief features of an inductive approach is tentativeness and open-endedness; therefore we present our discussion in this book as a working hypothesis, which we invite readers to consider and to judge regarding its legitimacy, appropriateness, practicality, and helpfulness. The method itself should submit to this hypothetical character of induction. We do not claim that this is the last word on induction; the principle of induction requires that a person subject one's understanding of induction or of the inductive process to correction and development. Indeed, we are open to suggestions of improvement and correction: if we become convinced on evidential grounds that the process as a whole or any specific feature of it is problematic and justifies change or alteration, we are prepared to make the necessary adjustments.

Second, the process we are about to describe is presented in its ideal form. We recognize that readers will need to adapt these principles and procedures to their own abilities, interests, and time constraints. Readers will want to consider what types of modifications and shortcuts they can incorporate to make the process workable for them. We present the process in the large and with significant detail because readers will be able to decide how to adapt and abbreviate only if they have a sense of the entire procedure. Indeed, the full-blown process we discuss is especially relevant for critical and difficult passages in the Bible; many passages will not require the kind of full implementation of method described here.

Overview of Presentation

Part 1, "Theoretical Foundations," is the first of the book's five parts and presents the hermeneutical bases for the inductive approach as set forth in the remainder of the book. It deals with such issues as the meaning of induction over against deduction, the relation between induction and presupposition, and the major characteristics of an inductive approach.

Part 2, "Observing and Asking," begins the presentation of the actual implementation of an inductive approach to the biblical text. This part, along with the remainder of the book, uses 2 Timothy 3:16–17 as an example of each of the stages discussed along the way. We will also include many additional specific examples from the Bible. Observation involves the discipline of being attentive to all elements within the text and serves as the basis for raising questions, the answering of which constitutes interpretation.

Part 3, "Answering or Interpreting," discusses in depth the various kinds of evidence used in the process of interpretation. This part also gives careful attention to the process of reasoning inferentially from evidential premises to inferences.

Part 4, "Evaluating and Appropriating," explores the process of examining the teachings of passages, as derived from interpretation, to determine which of these teachings can be legitimately appropriated directly in other times and places (including our own) over against those that are so closely bound to the original situation as not to be directly applicable. This part also gives attention to the process of examining contemporary situations so as to understand them in depth and to determine if, and to what extent, the passage might pertain to a given contemporary situation. Additionally, this part explores the specific creative and constructive process of relating the teaching of a biblical passage to contemporary situations.

Part 5, "Correlation," discusses the movement from the teaching of individual passages and books to the construction of a New Testament or Old Testament theology, and then to a biblical theology. This part also discusses ways in which all of these elements relate to, and might contribute to, a biblically based systematic theology.

Suggestions for Reading

In anticipation of some of the problems that commonly arise in this process—and because an ounce of prevention is worth a pound of cure, as the saying goes—here are a few suggestions that we hope will prepare readers for better understanding and using the forthcoming material.

First of all, readers should try to see the methodical process of study as a whole before trying to apply any of its parts. Such perspective is necessary because of the interrelatedness of the various steps. They are so interdependent that understanding the purpose and function of any one of them is impossible without knowing its relation to what precedes and follows. Consequently, we urge readers to peruse the entire book before trying to use its suggestions or even before making a serious attempt to fully understand any of its parts. Further, readers should take advantage of the introductions and summaries that precede the various sections in order to note carefully their contents and organization. In these ways readers will be able to see the interrelations between the steps and thus to apply each individual step more intelligently.

We also suggest that when readers are ready to apply the material they use either the exercises given throughout the book or comparable exercises. The inclusion of exercises suggests certain similarities between developing a methodical approach to biblical passages and developing a strong physique. Both are accomplished primarily through actual practice, and both are gradual and consequently demand patient perseverance. Just as a strong body cannot be realized by merely reading a discussion on the subject or by taking a few easy lessons, a mere perusal of this book will not produce the ability to do inductive Bible study. This discussion will prove of real worth if it indicates certain lines of action that readers may pursue and in that pursuit they teach themselves how to do inductive Bible study. Such a process will take years if not an entire lifetime. The exercises pertain to Jonah and Mark, thus offering students an opportunity to apply the principles to both Old Testament and New Testament texts. Readers may also find our own work and the work of others on the passages at www.inductivebiblicalstudy.com.

We encourage those who use this book to look up examples in their Bibles and to make a serious attempt to discover the ways those examples illumine the ideas to which they correspond. Finding one's own illustrations for the various points is helpful.

Readers should utilize at least some of the bibliographic suggestions because the following presentation by no means exhausts the vast field of Bible study.[7] The discussion must of necessity be in the form of an outline guide that should be used in collaboration with other books in the field. Some of these books will be indicated in the course of the discussion and others in the footnotes.

In addition, readers should test for themselves the statements made. We do not expect readers to accept them unquestioningly. On the contrary, we urge readers to pursue their own inductive study. And if in so doing they arrive at conclusions that contradict those of this book, they have not only the privilege but also the obligation to embrace what they have found.

Readers are likewise encouraged to practice suspended judgment. They are urged neither to accept nor to reject statements immediately upon reading them. Readers should give the ideas some time to take effect. If, for example, some readers are unable to see the purpose of certain suggestions, and if the suggestions appear to be superfluous or even ridiculous, readers should leave room for the possibility that the suggestions may have a necessary function and that, given time, that function may become clear. Also, readers should have specific and sound reasons for accepting or rejecting certain ideas. And even after readers have formed conclusions, they need to be willing to change those conclusions if and when new data come to light that would necessitate such a change. These suggestions are true to the inductive approach.

Readers should also remember that this book is intended to present a comprehensive view of hermeneutics and is primarily designed for those who are preparing for a Christian professional vocation. However, we are not saying that readers can make no adaptations or simplifications. Average laypersons, for example, must employ a simpler version if they are to study the Bible for themselves.[8] But the most important point is to realize that one cannot begin with abbreviated studies, for abbreviating what is not first understood in a more complete way is impossible. In other words, a more or less ideal conceptualization is requisite for a valid abbreviation.

Readers should also be aware that repetition is purposely employed in this book as a necessary pedagogical device and in order to insure thorough presentation. We have tried to conceive of ourselves as personal tutors of everyone who reads this material. Therefore our primary concern has not been to use the fewest possible words to describe inductive Bible study but to think

7. For a relatively comprehensive guide to resources in biblical studies, see David R. Bauer, *An Annotated Guide to Biblical Resources for Ministry* (Peabody, MA: Hendrickson, 2003).

8. A number of fine books or manuals are intended to introduce laypersons to inductive Bible study, including David L. Thompson, *Bible Study That Works*, rev. ed. (Nappanee, IN: Evangel Publishing House, 1994); Oletta Wald, *The Joy of Discovery in Bible Study*, rev. ed. (Minneapolis: Augsburg, 1975).

in terms of effective communication. Repetition is one of the most effective means of imparting ideas.

Readers should also keep in mind that mechanics are a necessary part of any worthwhile activity. Einstein became a great physicist because he first learned the laws of physics. Paderewski had to spend hours practicing finger exercises before he developed the ability to interpret the spirit of great composers. Neither of these men could have reached his position without so mastering the mechanics of his field that they became second nature to him and thus the means by which he could delve into the mysteries of the universe or capture the emotional quality of great music. Eliminate the mechanics of physics and piano playing, and you eliminate Einstein and Paderewski. Indeed, every child who has ever learned to play the piano knows that learning tedious scales is a prerequisite for the enjoyment of masterful performance.

The same principle should be applied to Bible study. As much as one might like to avoid the mechanics of Bible study, one must realize that they cannot be eliminated, for there is no mystical or purely intuitive means for arriving at scriptural truth. One cannot bypass the techniques of exegesis and expect to become a profound interpreter of the Bible any more than one can expect to become a great pianist without mastering the techniques of fingering the keyboard.[9] Some students believe that mechanics and the Spirit are irreconcilable because mechanics necessitate self-discipline and at times are tedious. One should be careful, however, not to equate the tedious with the unimportant, for such a mistake would be just as fatal to a Bible student as to a pianist. Or more positively, one should gladly discipline oneself to master the mechanics, knowing that though the necessary road might be hard, the joys to be found at the destination are well worth the difficulties of the journey.

Furthermore, a methodical process should not be made an end in itself. This points to a real danger because the mechanics might loom so large as to hide their purpose. As Christian believers, we are convinced that the development of a methodical, inductive approach is the means of training the mind to become a more fit instrument for the operation of God's Spirit. Because biblical interpretation involves a rational process, the mind must function properly if interpretation is to be valid. But the mind's proper function is not automatic; therefore the mind needs to be trained, or it might become the means of negating God's Spirit. A methodical approach involves a description of how the Spirit works through the mind and how one might cooperate with the Spirit so that the Spirit might function freely.[10]

9. We recognize that effective Bible study cannot be reduced to technique but also recognize that technique is the necessary concretization of attitude, perspective, and theory.

10. This thought introduces the vexing issue of the role of faith in biblical interpretation, an issue that will be addressed in part 1.

The ultimate purpose of mechanics and certainly of this manual, then, is that readers might through their use in studying the Scriptures come to know the real author of the Scriptures, the only true God, and Jesus Christ, whom he has sent. We have recorded the suggestions found on these pages only because in our own experience the application of this process has enabled us to realize a more intimate relationship with God through Jesus Christ. Additionally, a methodical, inductive process may also have value for unbelievers. As such, it can be utilized to make possible a better understanding of the biblical text even without a prior faith commitment.

Finally, readers should avoid conceiving of this book as an attempt to dictate a precise and rigid formula for Bible study. We make this suggestion for the following reasons:

- The very nature of thought processes makes coercing the mind into an inflexible pattern or an intellectual straitjacket infeasible. For example, one might indicate that certain steps should be taken before the interpretive phase of study begins. But at times one's thoughts will naturally move to interpretation, especially when the meaning of what is noted is self-evident. Such elasticity is intrinsic to the mind and should be respected.

- Individual differences also make it impractical for one person to force a stringent formula for Bible study upon others. Now certain basic principles might be laid down as essential, ones that cannot be transgressed if one's approach is to be inductive; but in the precise application of these principles, individuals must be left to determine what is most suitable and effective for them.

- Even in relation to the general pattern and concrete steps suggested, one must make allowance for interplay. The various phases of study are interdependent: The first phase contributes to the second, and the second in turn contributes to the first. We shall have occasion to call attention to this principle frequently in the forthcoming discussion. Furthermore, none of the individual aspects of a study process is ever fully completed. Therefore, if finishing the first phase were needed before moving to the second, the latter would never be reached.

For these and other reasons, the contents of the following pages should not be construed as an exact formula to be followed page for page every time one studies a given passage. Rather, they primarily involve an analysis of Bible study that might be used as a basis for formulating a methodical, inductive approach to biblical passages. Readers must understand this fact if they are to use the following material. This manual tries to dissect the study process to discover its component parts. It might therefore be likened to the exercises used to teach typing, which represent an analysis of the typing process. No

Part 1

Theoretical Foundations

At the very outset, any discussion of biblical hermeneutics should address the issue of method. Hermeneutics deals with the way one thinks about and executes the practice of studying the Bible. Thus the concern for practice or performance poses the fundamental question as to *how* it is to be done, which is essentially the question of method. This present study of hermeneutics begins, then, by exploring the meaning of method and the ways in which method illumines the practice of Bible study.

Our English word *method* is really a transliteration of the Greek *methodos*, which literally means a "way of transit," a way of moving from one point to another or from where we are toward our destination. The following brief definitions capture the essence of *method*:

- *Webster's II New College Dictionary* defines *method* as "a manner or means of *procedure*, especially a *systematic* and regular way of accomplishing a given task, . . . *an orderly and planned arrangement*."[1]

- John Dewey, perhaps the most prominent educational theorist in the twentieth century, said, "Method at bottom is but the *way of doing things* followed in any given case, . . . the *main steps* that have to be taken . . .

---

1. *Webster's II New College Dictionary*, s.v. "Method." In this and the two representative definitions that follow, emphasis has been added.

and the crucial points where conditions of growth have to be carefully maintained and fostered."[2]

- In his careful reflection on the ways in which *method* has been defined and used, Howard Tillman Kuist concludes: "Conceived in its widest possible scope, method is procedure. And the primary consideration in procedure of any kind is that it be suited to the end in view. Experience teaches men that when anything is to be done, some ways are *better*, certain movements more effective, than others. . . . Method is the conscious accommodation of one's powers to the *requirements of the situation*."[3]

To summarize these definitions, *method* has

- character—is orderly, systematic (Webster)
- content—has certain specific steps (Dewey)
- criterion—what is the best way or most suitable to the task (Kuist)

The basic meaning of *method*, then, is "the best specific procedure for doing anything," where "best" is determined by what is suitable to the task. Hence, central to the notion of method is the principle of suitability. A requisite characteristic of method is that it should correspond in nature with its objective, for it is the means by which the objective is reached. For example, method applied to throwing a baseball would include, among other things, gripping the ball firmly, cocking the arm back, and propelling the ball by a forward flip of the arm. These steps are true because of the very nature of throwing a baseball. In pursuing any significant activity one should always ask, What is the nature of the task, and given the nature of the task, what is the best, most suitable, most effective way to proceed?

The application of the principle of suitability to Bible study involves reflecting upon the three major factors involved in the study of the Bible:

1. The Bible
2. The student/reader/interpreter
3. The relationship between the Bible and the student/reader/interpreter

The operative question is, Given the nature of the Bible in all aspects of its existence, the nature of the student, and the relationship between the Bible and the student, what is the most suitable way to proceed?

2. John Dewey, "Method," in *Cyclopedia of Education*, ed. Paul Monroe (New York: Macmillan, 1913), 4:204–5.
3. Howard Tillman Kuist, *These Words upon Thy Heart: Scripture and the Christian Response* (Richmond: John Knox, 1947), 47–48.

We devote the remainder of this part to the presentation of the major characteristics of proper Bible study. These characteristics stem from our convictions regarding the nature of the Bible, of the student, and of the relationship between the Bible and the student. We will sometimes make these convictions explicit, but at other times they will remain implicit. However, these convictions consistently stand behind all that will be presented in this enumeration of major characteristics and, indeed, in the presentation of Bible study throughout the remainder of the book. We emphasize, however, that these characteristics and the underlying convictions from which they stem are presented as a working hypothesis. We recognize that they do not possess anything like a stamp of divine imprimatur but are set forth for the thoughtful consideration of the reader, who is invited to accept them or reject them, yet hopefully always on the basis of reasonable and evidential considerations.

1

Inductive Study

Meaning of Induction and Deduction

The present discussion employs the term *inductive* synonymously with *evidential*: that is, a commitment to the evidence in and around the text so as to allow that evidence to determine our understanding of the meaning of the text, wherever that evidence may lead. *Deduction* is used synonymously with *presuppositional*: that is, a commitment to certain assumptions (whether stated or implicit) that we allow to determine our understanding of the meaning of the text.

The importance of adopting an inductive approach to the study of the Bible is based on the principle of suitability, which stands at the center of the very notion of method. Induction best suits the nature of the Bible, which stands outside of ourselves and has its own message to speak to us, a message that has its basis in, and emerges out of, its own social, linguistic, and historical context. The Bible, as we personify it, beckons us to hear its message on its own terms; it wishes to speak a new word to us, challenging our presuppositions over against conforming to them. Induction is the method of history and the humanities, including literature, whereas deduction is the method of mathematics, which assumes a self-established closed system. But an inductive approach is appropriate for exploring realities that have an existence of their own and cannot be contained by a system that we bring to them.

Essential Aspects of Induction and Deduction

An inductive approach to Bible study has two essential aspects: an inductive spirit, or attitude, and an inductive process that implements such a spirit and attitude. Ideally an inductive attitude precedes an inductive process, but at any rate, both must be present and are indispensable for genuine inductive Bible study.

The test of the inductive spirit is whether one's approach is characterized by *radical openness* to any conclusion required by the biblical evidence. This attitude is the inner dimension of the inductive approach, while any specific process that might be considered inductive is its outer expression and implementation.

The deductive spirit and the inductive spirit are mutually exclusive. The deductive spirit is dogmatic and authoritarian, absolute and categorical, characterized by a closed mind. It amounts to hermeneutical absolutism. It does not entertain the possibility of being in error and therefore is unwilling to change. It is not open to challenge or dissent. It is resistant to the discussion of differing views. It is often concerned with seeking supportive proof texts for a position already held. This dogmatic mentality is well expressed in the saying "My mind is made up; don't confuse me with the facts."

The deductive attitude may be motivated by the fear that cherished traditions are subject to challenge. Such traditions, often based on the acceptance of what a person has heard preached or taught, may not have been examined critically in the light of the biblical text. They are sometimes viewed as foundational to one's belief system, and the fear exists that an open-minded scrutiny of them might cause the belief system to crumble.

Persons with this mentality try to control the outcome of Bible study by indicating in advance the interpretations that should result from the process. Accordingly, certain creedal presuppositions, including various theological systems or particular doctrines, are brought to the Scriptures and inevitably predetermine the outcome of the interpretation of texts.[1] The process is circular and self-confirming. In such cases, instead of hearing the text on its own terms, the interpreter tells the text what it should mean.

Still others have problems with the biblical worldview and consequently try to interpret the text so that it conforms to their own contrasting worldview. Thus, instead of focusing at the interpretive phase on the message being communicated through the text and leaving value judgments until later, they begin by imposing their own views on the text and reading it accordingly. For example, some people make an a priori assumption that the universe is closed and that miracles cannot happen, so they interpret miracle stories as "myths." Others begin with the assumption that transcendent divine revelation

---

1. See James Barr, *Fundamentalism* (Philadelphia: Westminster, 1978). See also the discussion in appendix B below.

is impossible; therefore they understand the text exclusively in terms of the history of religions, as a record of merely human thinking and striving after the Divine. Even social and political agendas—such as feminism, liberation theology, capitalism, or socialism—have been brought to the hermeneutical process in order to predetermine its outcome. Among the major concerns of the leaders at the beginning of the inductive Bible study movement were the so-called assured results of biblical criticism, which those who taught inductive Bible study recognized to be actually a set of assumptions (some of them better grounded than others, but all of them speculative) that often served as a prism through which to view the biblical text. One could cite many other examples of more or less unexamined views that have been used by those with a dogmatic, deductive spirit.

In contrast, the inductive spirit and the process by which it is implemented seek to be undogmatic. The inductively minded person welcomes discussion and even challenges; this eagerness is based on the desire to hear whatever the text has to say, whether one agrees or disagrees. Such an inductively minded person recognizes that at a later point one will have opportunity to make value judgments concerning the message communicated by the text. Furthermore, one who has this inductive spirit is willing to acknowledge one's own fallibility and to begin any interpretation with the statement, "I may be wrong, but this is my understanding and the evidential reasons for it." Such a person is open to changing one's view if the evidence warrants it. In fact, the person with a truly inductive spirit will actively seek differing interpretations and the reasons for them. Even if one does not find grounds to justify a change in one's own understanding of the text, at least one will have a better understanding and perhaps a better appreciation for differing points of view.

If what has been said above about the character of induction is valid, some of what passes as inductive Bible study is not truly inductive because this kind of spirit is lacking. One can mimic particular techniques of the inductive process while harboring a deductive spirit, thereby giving the appearance of induction without its reality. In such cases the deductive mentality takes over and becomes dominant at some point in the process.

Fortunately, one can begin with a deductive spirit and eventually adopt an inductive spirit through a direct study of the text. This transformation often happens when the inferential process—the process of reasoning from evidential premises to possible conclusions, which is often used subconsciously—is brought to the level of consciousness and the tests for its soundness are applied.

Conversely, one can begin with an undogmatic spirit and go awry because of the absence of a proper process to implement it; having a radical openness to the text is not sufficient. It is essential to identify a process that truly allows the text to speak for itself, which is the goal of the person with an inductive spirit. One must avoid divorcing an inductive spirit from an inductive process if one hopes to genuinely engage in inductive Bible study.

The discussion now turns to a focus on the second component of inductive Bible study—*the inductive process*. This process is the attempt to implement an inductive spirit. The reader must not lose sight of the indispensability of the inductive spirit, which gives rise to the process. Otherwise the process will become form devoid of the spirit that gives it meaning and purpose.

The inductive process is the test as well as the expression of the inductive spirit or attitude. In general, the inductive process is whatever is most effective and efficient in determining the meaning of the text and thus effectuating or implementing an inductive attitude. In the following pages, we propose a specific inductive process by which we intend to accomplish this goal. We set forth this process in an undogmatic, inductive spirit because this process too should be open to discussion and challenge. Readers do need to implement this process in order to understand it, but once they understand it, we urge readers to determine for themselves the inductive process that in their judgment best implements the inductive spirit.

Both the deductive spirit and the inductive spirit are expressed in a process of *inferential reasoning* that flows from them. Inferential reasoning—drawing conclusions from premises about the meaning of a passage—is inevitable and unavoidable in any understanding of the biblical text. The inferential reasoning may be subconscious or conscious, presuppositional or evidential, dogmatic or hypothetical, illogical or logical, invalid or valid. One thing is certain: inferential reasoning is always present when interpretation occurs.

One does not need to become skilled in proper inferential reasoning to gain what the community of faith considers to be a saving knowledge from the Scriptures; however, those who aspire to leadership in the community of faith should develop skills in inferential reasoning in order to gain a more accurate and profound grasp of the scriptural message.

In the process of inferential reasoning, some constants or essentials flow from both induction and deduction. Both deduction and induction contain two major components: one or more *premises* followed by an *inference*, sometimes called a conclusion. A premise is a statement or assertion from which one may causally derive an inference or conclusion. Thus "therefore" or its equivalent stands between one or more premises and an inference.

In deductive inferential reasoning, one or more deductive premises (which are presuppositional and absolute) are employed. In inductive inferential reasoning, by way of contrast, inductive premises that are evidential and conditional are employed. Deductive inferences are, like deductive premises, absolute and unchangeable; on the other hand, inductive inferences are hypothetical and probable, therefore open to change.

We have been describing the constants or essentials of inferential reasoning that exist in both induction and deduction. But the process of inferential reasoning also has variables, whether that reasoning is inductive or deductive. What is variable in both deduction and induction is that in both cases the premises as well as the inferences may be either general or particular.[2] Definitions of induction often describe inductive reasoning as the movement from particular data to general inference, and some definitions of deduction describe deductive reasoning as the movement from general premises to particular conclusions; yet such definitions tend to be limited in their perspective and overlook the different ways deduction and induction can be used, as appendix A indicates. Although in some cases inductive reasoning involves the movement from particular premises to general inferences and in some cases deductive reasoning involves the movement from general premises to conclusions regarding particulars, all of this concern with general and particular is not essential to induction and deduction as such. Both deductive and inductive premises and inferences may be either general or particular, depending on what is appropriate or suitable in individual cases.[3]

2. This point is well made by Joel Rudinow and Vincent E. Barry, *Invitation to Critical Thinking*, 5th ed. (Belmont, CA: Wadsworth/Thomson, 2004), 147–48.

3. Two factors determine whether the premises and inferences of deduction and induction are general or particular. One is the nature of the task and of the goal of their use in a given task. In some cases deductive premises that are general as well as presuppositional and absolute are required, as is true of mathematical logic, which often begins with general axioms such as that of Euclid: Things equal to the same thing are equal to each other. To the contrary, the deductive use of general premises in approaching literary texts, such as the Bible, is inappropriate and unsuitable because of the differences between mathematics and literature. Literature consists of particular texts, and any reasoning about them must begin with particular premises based on those particular texts, not general statements about them.

At the same time, deductive reasoning may begin with particular premises based on particular literary texts and assume a meaning that is incorrect, thereby leading to unsound inferences. The issue in this case is not whether the premises are general or particular but whether they are presuppositional and absolute, or evidential and conditional. Thus deductive premises may be either general or particular; in addition, as will become evident, both deductive and inductive inferences may be either particular or general.

The second factor that accounts for these variations is the stage of the reasoning process. Inferential reasoning is cumulative; it has initial stages, which in turn become building blocks for subsequent stages. Though initially, in examining literary texts as in the scientific endeavor, the premises are necessarily particular, at subsequent stages, when the inferences drawn are in turn used as premises for further inferential reasoning, the inductive premises may be more general, though always evidential and provisional. For example, in science the observation of various episodes of the gravitational pull of the earth may lead to a general inference regarding the pattern of gravitation, which may then be used as a premise to do further inductive inferential reasoning in relation to phenomena not previously observed. Similarly, in the Synoptic Gospels one finds that Jesus repeatedly refers to himself as "the Son of Man." On the basis of particular premises based on this evidence, one may infer that this self-identification is, in general, Jesus's favorite way of describing himself and his role. This general inference may then be used at a subsequent stage of inferential reasoning as a general premise on which to draw further inferences as to the NT's presentation of Jesus's self-consciousness and self-understanding, depending in part on the meaning of "Son of Man." (The prime examples of the later stages of inferential reasoning

To reiterate, what is always constant is that the premises of deductive reasoning are presuppositional and absolute, whereas those of inductive reasoning are evidential and conditional. Accordingly, what is always constant is that deductive inferences, like their premises, are certain and absolute, whereas the inferences in inductive reasoning are probable or hypothetical and open to correction as necessary. Induction and deduction are diametrically opposed in relation to these constants.

The great danger in the process of inferential reasoning is that it often begins subconsciously by deductively embracing one or more premises as axiomatic assumptions, for which adequate evidence is not cited or perhaps cannot be cited. Often such premises are based upon incomplete or partial evidence, or upon general impressions, or upon traditions that one has assumed to be valid. The antidote is to raise one's reasoning process to the level of consciousness.

The wise action, then, especially in relation to very important passages and at least some problematic passages, is to write down one's process of inferential reasoning. Such an objectification of the process will not only make a person conscious of what is occurring but will also enable one more effectively to discover whether one is bringing unrecognized assumptions to the study process and then to test those assumptions.

Inductive reasoning consciously tries to avoid assumptions (or at least tries to test assumptions), hidden or otherwise, because it intends to develop premises solely on evidential grounds. Such premises are always open to change and correction if this is warranted by evidence not previously observed or used. The inductive person does not seek only evidence that supports one's point of view, but rather attempts to observe all of the evidence, whether it agrees or disagrees with one's views. Only after such an endeavor is a premise seriously proposed, although various possible premises may be tested in the process. The critical question is always, What is the evidence?

As to the inferences, deductive reasoning aims at absolute certainty. Thus its inferences, like its premises, are dogmatic. Certainty leads to certainty. Sometimes a valid logical process is followed, though at times inferences are drawn on the basis of logical fallacies. But even in the case of a valid logical

---

are found in "correlation"; see part 5.) So both deductive and inductive premises may be either general or particular. Whether they are one or the other does not itself determine whether they are deductive or inductive.

What is true of deductive and inductive premises may also be true of deductive and inductive inferences. They may be either particular or general, depending on what is suitable to the nature and goal of the task at hand and to the stage of the inferential reasoning process. To state unequivocally that deductive inferences are always particular and that inductive inferences are always general is to miss the point of these distinctive lines of reasoning. Again, the issue as to whether the movement is from general to particular or from particular to general is not essential to either induction or deduction but is contingent upon the nature and goal of the task at hand and upon the stage of the inferential reasoning process.

process, one cannot assume that all of the relevant evidence has been found or is being used properly; thus absolute inferences tend to be problematic. The deductive interpreter will refuse to acknowledge that inferences are sometimes unreliable and therefore should not be treated as certain.

Inductive inferences, however, are not only subjected to the test of valid logic; they are also considered hypothetical and therefore always open to change. Such inferences may be accepted as "belief" statements; but they are not necessarily "truth" statements. This distinction is critical because of our fallibility as human interpreters, including fallibility in knowing when we are fallible. In addition, whereas deductive reasoning results in stagnancy and prevents growth in the understanding of the biblical text, inductive reasoning allows room for growth because it makes possible a change in understanding the meaning of the text when appropriate.

These changes do not necessarily involve basic creedal affirmations, such as the belief that God created human beings in God's image and likeness, or that Jesus is the Son of God. Rather, a person may need to change one's understanding of the meaning of the biblical statements and the creedal affirmations based on them. An accurate and profound understanding of the meaning and significance of these realities should be the goal of the biblical student.

Illustration of Inductive and Deductive Inferential Reasoning

The litmus test of the presence and practice of the inductive spirit is the willingness to gather evidence fully and openly for and against the premises stated and to accept them as conditional (when necessary), along with the acknowledgment that the inferences drawn are hypothetical and changeable.[4] Resistance to applying such a test may indicate that the requisite spirit for genuinely inductive Bible study is lacking. Unless and until such a closed attitude changes to one of radical openness, no amount of supposedly inductive procedures will avail. However, the use of these so-called inductive procedures may have some value for the deductive person. But under such conditions, inductive procedures will not have the full value of a truly inductive approach to the text.

Here are several examples of inferential reasoning that may be used, properly or improperly, in interpreting the texts mentioned in the premises for each example. We encourage readers to attempt to identify which of these arguments are inductive and which are deductive.

4. At times inductive premises could, admittedly, be both evidential and absolute, as is the case when premises are formulated that contain pieces of raw data whose presence is self-evident (e.g., in direct or virtual quotations from the biblical text). However, even here the possible discovery of additional text-critical or other historical data may render absoluteness problematic.

Example 1

PREMISE 1	If God covenanted to give all the physical land of Canaan to the ethnic descendants of Abraham (Gen. 17:8),
PREMISE 2	and if the Jewish people are Abraham's ethnic descendants,
INFERENCE	it would follow from the text that the Jewish people will ultimately and eternally possess all the physical land of Canaan.

Example 2

PREMISE 1	If Genesis 1:3–2:1 states that God created all things in six "days,"
PREMISE 2	and if a "day" as used here is not a twenty-four-hour period,
INFERENCE	it would follow that this text does not mean that God created all things in six consecutive twenty-four-hour periods.

Example 3

PREMISE 1	It is absolutely certain that God by nature is immutably righteous and faithful,
PREMISE 2	and if God made a covenant with Abraham (Gen. 15),
INFERENCE	therefore either it was impossible for God to commit an unrighteous and unfaithful act by breaking this covenant or if he did break the covenant, God's violation could not and would not be unrighteous and unfaithful.[5]

Example 4

PREMISE 1	It was necessary for the Son of God to die in order to satisfy God's wrath.
PREMISE 2	Jesus was the Son of God.
INFERENCE	It would follow that Jesus's death satisfied God's wrath.

Example 5

PREMISE 1	If Jesus's mission is to *fulfill* the law and the prophets and not to abolish them (Matt. 5:17–18),
PREMISE 2	and if *fulfill* means something other than to obey all of the commandments that are found in the Law and the Prophets,
INFERENCE	it would follow that Jesus's mission, according to this passage, was not necessarily to obey all of the commandments in the Law and the Prophets.

The inductive premises in the previous examples are set forth conditionally, though some readers might be inclined to view at least some of them as absolutes. In the final analysis, however, the issue is not whether premises are presented in conditional form ("if") but whether they are set forth in the attitude of openness regarding their validity. Thus, an inductive premise may

5. We take this to be a deductive argument since the first premise is presented absolutely, even though the second premise is presented conditionally and is clearly evidential. If even one premise of an argument is deductive, it renders the entire argument deductive.

be stated unconditionally, but with the recognition that the premise may be wrong. The inductive issue is whether they can be supported by sufficient evidence or whether the converse premises could receive more evidential support, as well as whether they are are presented with the recognition that the premises *may* be wrong. Because the inductive premises expressed are conditional, the inferences would also need to be considered conditional, although again some might be inclined to view them as dogmatic. In addition, the logical test would need to be applied to the inferences: if one accepts the premises and if the inferences are validly drawn from the premises, they are unavoidable.

The Community of Faith's Role in Induction and Deduction

The previous discussion has focused on the individual's use of induction; however, induction also has communal implications. The church should be a community of biblical, theological, and moral discourse. Often such discourse is discouraged because those with a deductive, dogmatic spirit will not allow it. In such communities anyone who challenges views held by some or perhaps most of the members is made to feel unwelcome and even heretical; thus churches may lack the openness that should characterize true community.

The key to finding true community and unity is not to avoid issues that may carry different views; rather, it is to have open discussion and the freedom to challenge all premises and inferences on the basis of an evidential approach to the biblical text. This practice should be especially true for those who presumably subscribe to the supreme authority of the Scriptures for faith and practice.

Often a fallible person or group of persons control authoritarian communities. These leaders posit an ever-widening list of doctrines that one must hold if one is to be considered orthodox, with no questions asked. The so-called authorities stand between the reader and the biblical text, much as the hierarchy of the Roman Catholic Church did in the period immediately preceding the time of the Reformation.

The inferential process that lies behind the dogmatic positions taken is seldom exposed to the inductive tests of evidence and logic. Such a posture practically contradicts the claim made by these persons of Scripture's ultimate authority. The so-called authorities who stand between the individual and the biblical text, whatever their tradition, have become the ultimate authority. The call for an inductive spirit is a challenge to such a deductive, dogmatic, authoritarian approach.

Communities of faith, however, should not be completely latitudinarian. Christians can agree on many basic and vital biblical issues on the grounds of an inductive spirit and process. And room should always be left for communities with distinctives. At the same time, an inductive spirit is a call to exhibit love and respect while hearing the views of others, especially those who are members of the community of faith. It is an acknowledgment that all have blind spots in relation to which the help of others is needed. Persons within particular communities should listen to others within and outside the particular communities of which they are a part, and specific Christian communities (traditions or denominations) should engage in conversation with other communities around the biblical text.

Principles Related to Induction

Two critical principles of inductive study as applied to the Bible are of particular significance for those who want to better understand and practice it. First, at the center of induction is the *principle of probability* over against absolute certainty; in an inductive approach, one must always speak in terms of degrees of probability.[6] This consideration is due to the evidentiary and inferential character of induction. For one thing, evidence is sometimes ambiguous; it will not always clearly lead to a specific conclusion. Moreover, evidence is sometimes conflicting; one piece of evidence may point to one conclusion, while another piece of evidence may point to a different conclusion. Further, evidence is often limited; more evidence may surface (one can think here of the massive amount of new evidence for biblical interpretation that came with the discovery of the Dead Sea Scrolls or the Nag Hammadi library). Finally, our understanding of evidence may be limited; we need to realize that our construal of the meaning of evidence should be open to new insight.

This claim that an inductive approach to the study of the Bible involves probability should not lead students to a sense of interpretive agnosticism, that is, the suggestion that we really cannot speak confidently about the meaning of any biblical passage. One can arrive at an interpretation of at least the basic sense of almost all passages with a degree of probability so high that one can talk of virtual certainty. But some biblical passages do have a lower level of probability for interpretation; in such cases the student must acknowledge that the interpretation is relatively more provisional. Indeed, in some passages the evidence is inconclusive, with the result that students must suspend judgment regarding their meaning.

Second, students who adopt an inductive approach should embrace the *principle of reality*, which acknowledges that in fact pure or absolute induction does not exist. All of us have presuppositions. What is required is that we do all we can to become aware of our presuppositions and then intentionally expose these presuppositions to the biblical evidence with a willingness to change if the evidence requires. As Adolf Schlatter says, "We are freed from our presuppositions and lifted above them only when we are keenly con-

---

6. Rudinow and Barry, *Invitation to Critical Thinking*, 212: "Inductive strength is relative, which means it *admits of degrees*" (emphasis original).

scious of them."[7] This attitude of radical openness to the evidence, wherever it leads, is the essential character of induction; we might call this attitude the *inductive spirit*. Clark Pinnock describes it well: "The lesson to be learned here is allowing the Bible to say what it wants to say without imposing our imperialistic agenda onto it; our exegesis ought to let the text speak and the chips fall where they may."[8]

In practice, of course, identifying all of the presuppositions that impose themselves upon our interpretation of a passage may be difficult, but two processes can assist. The first helpful process is to write out explicitly the lines of inferential reasoning. As we set forth our evidential premises and draw possible conclusions from these premises, we should be able to identify untested and previously unacknowledged presuppositions that have crept into our articulation of the evidence or our inferential reasoning toward conclusions. The second helpful process is, at the proper time, to engage in dialogue with others, including the use of commentaries. Others' interpretations will often present us with alternative interpretive possibilities and the evidence for these other possibilities, forcing us to confront the ways in which our own presuppositions may have intruded into our understanding of the evidence or our inferential reasoning toward conclusions.

7. Adolf Schlatter, "Atheistische Methoden in der Theologie," in *Zur Theologie des Neuen Testaments und zur Dogmatik, Kleine Schriften*, ed. Ulrich Luck, Theologische Bücherei 41 (Munich: Kaiser, 1969), 142, quoted in Peter Stuhlmacher, *Historical Criticism and Theological Interpretation of Scripture* (Philadelphia: Fortress, 1977), 47.

8. Clark Pinnock, "Climbing out of the Swamp: The Evangelical Struggle to Understand the Creation Texts," *Int* 43 (April 1989): 155.

2

Transjective Study

The description of induction, with its emphasis on a fair appraisal of the evidence of the text without the determining intrusion of one's own presuppositions, may lead to the conclusion that inductive Bible study is concerned only with the object of study (the biblical text) and gives no serious attention to the role of the subject, the reader, who actually engages in the process of study. Such a conclusion would be erroneous, for inductive Bible study is certainly concerned with all aspects of the study process, including the vital role the reader plays as an active observing and inferring subject. The principle of suitability, which is central to the whole notion of method, requires that consideration be given not simply to the nature of the biblical text, but also to the nature and functioning of the student/reader and to the relationship between the text and the student/reader. Examining the realities of the study of texts, including the biblical text, reveals that the relationship is neither wholly objective nor exclusively subjective, but *transjective*.

Dialectical Character of Bible Study

The word *transjective* reflects the fact that the relationship between the Bible and the student involves the dynamic combination of objective and subjective dimensions. On the one hand, the Bible is a *witnessing object*. It arose from outside of us, bears witness to realities outside of us, and exists outside of us. As such, its otherness must be embraced, and a healthy distance between the biblical text and us, its readers, should be maintained for the sake of perspective.

The danger in examining or studying a reality that has its own independent existence is in imposing our own views, biases, or preconceptions upon it.

On the other hand, we encounter the Bible also as a *beckoning subject* that addresses the deepest dimensions of the human spirit and hence calls for the subjective response of empathy and personal involvement. The distance that is appropriate for our relationship to the Bible as witnessing object does not mean detachment, for the necessity of subjective involvement must also be kept in mind. This necessity of subjective involvement is based on three considerations.

First, the Bible's character as literature requires this subjective or personal involvement to understand the biblical message. The study of all literature requires a kind of suspended disbelief, as Samuel Taylor Coleridge states.[1] Thus Mark Allan Powell says,

> As readers, we must accept the implied author's evaluative point of view even if it means suspending our own judgments during the act of reading. We may have to accept the notion that cowboys are good and Indians are bad. We may have to believe in talking animals or flying spaceships. And even if we are atheists, we will have to become Christians for a while if we are to read Bunyan or Dante. Readers are free, of course, to critique the point of view a narrative espouses. An initial acceptance of that point of view, however, is essential as preliminary to such criticism, for without such acceptance the story can never be understood in the first place.[2]

Thus, if one is fully to understand any piece of literature, one must, at least during the process of reading, sympathetically connect with the thought of

1. Samuel Taylor Coleridge, *Biographia Literaria: Biographical Sketches of My Literary Life and Opinions and Two Lay Sermons* (London: Bell & Daldy, 1880), 145.

2. Mark Allan Powell, *What Is Narrative Criticism?* GBS (Minneapolis: Fortress, 1990), 24. Although here Powell is speaking specifically of narrative, his comments pertain to the study of all types of literature. Francis Watson, *Text, Church, and World*, 60–61, aims unfair criticism at Powell's statement when he claims that Powell's position involves "a poor phenomenology of reading," in that no one can fully suspend one's judgment, and a "refusal to engage in serious critical analysis of the rhetoric of oppression." Powell does not claim that such a suspended judgment is perfectly possible or that readers should refuse to go on to pursue critical judgment, but simply that an attitude of suspended judgment should be the essential stance that one adopts in the initial reading process. Thus also Kuist, *These Words upon Thy Heart*, 58–59, 96, 107, distinguishes between "re-creative criticism"—the process of understanding a text, as it were, from the inside through personal engagement—and "judicial criticism"—the process of assessing the value of the text or of what is presented therein. To engage in critical assessment before reaching a significant measure of understanding of the text itself, through sympathetic engagement, is to violate the rights of the other (in this case, the author as we encounter the author in the text) in social communication, especially the right to be heard without interruption and the right to expect an initial openness on the part of the addressee. See also Kevin J. Vanhoozer, *Is There a Meaning in this Text? The Bible, the Reader, and the Morality of Literary Knowledge* (Grand Rapids: Zondervan, 1998), 374–75, 392–401.

the text to such an extent that one imaginatively and subjectively inhabits the world of the text.

All literature exists for the purpose of having an impact on the reader, and often this purpose involves more than a cognitive, or intellectual, impact. Literature often involves an appeal to the emotions, and through the emotions, to the will. This transcognitive purpose is especially pervasive in the Bible, where one constantly encounters emotive language, poignant and moving rhetoric, with the view toward winning personal agreement and commitment on the part of the of the addressee. Thus the very character of the text requires a personally engaged, subjective involvement in the process of reading.

Second, not only does the Bible's literary character require a subjective participation in the reading process, but the Bible's content requires the same. For the Bible itself presents its content as witness[3] to the revelation of the one God to his people and ultimately to the entirety of his human creation. The Bible's very content, then, confronts humans in the depth of their existence as creatures addressed by their Maker and/or as a community called by its Lord. A personal decision to accept the revelatory claims of the text or a subjective commitment to faith is not necessary for a basic understanding of the meaning of biblical texts; yet a full and profound understanding of the text does require that, at least during the process of reading, one adopt as much as possible a sympathetic openness to the personal, subjective, experiential dimensions that the reader encounters within the text.

Third, as recent hermeneutical discussions that have sought to clarify this objective/subjective dialectic in biblical interpretation have shown, subjective involvement is necessary to approximate objective understanding of the text. Scholars have often observed that a central concern of hermeneutics over the past two hundred years has been this issue of objectivity/subjectivity.[4] During this period the definite tendency has been to opt for one or the other: Either our interpretation of texts (including the biblical text) should be completely or essentially objective, detached, and disinterested, so as to capture the pure, objective meaning of texts without any influence from our own perspectives, or our interpretation is (or at least should be) completely or essentially subjective. Indeed, many have recently rejected the notion of stable meanings in texts and have insisted that texts cannot properly be said to mean anything in themselves: meaning inheres in the reader, they say, and any meaning that readers believe they draw from texts is actually brought by them to the texts.[5]

---

3. The Bible's character as witness has often been pointed out, but perhaps most forcefully by Brevard S. Childs. See specially his *Biblical Theology of the Old and New Testaments: Theological Reflection on the Christian Bible* (Minneapolis: Fortress, 1992).

4. E.g., N. T. Wright, *The New Testament and the People of God* (Minneapolis: Fortress, 1992), 3–46.

5. Ben F. Meyer describes this view by citing Northrop Frye: "Early in his career the late Northrop Frye recalled a comment on Jacob Boehme: 'His books are like a picnic to which the

The reader's preunderstanding—whether a matter of the reader's own psychological or spiritual experience or a matter of the reader's community (and the ethos, expectations, and reading strategies proper to that community)—is thus ultimately determinative for meaning.

But this standard is a false either/or, for a hermeneutic that operates on the basis of the principle of suitability, as previously described, will seek to account for all of the dynamics involved in the Bible and the study of the Bible, both the objective and the subjective. It is, first of all, misleading to speak of *the text* as though it were an isolated reality about which one could legitimately make claims regarding the presence or absence of meaning. Obviously inkspots on a page do not in themselves possess either the ontological or functional capacity to contain meaning. But texts are more than marks on a page: they are part of a broad act of interpersonal communication that extends from the flesh-and-blood author (or authors) through the text as mediator to the actual flesh-and-blood audience.[6] In other words, our encounter with texts is a matter of our participation in a comprehensive literary-social matrix within which the text plays a central role. Thus the question, stated precisely and most properly, is not, Is there meaning in this text? but, How do we derive meaning from this interpersonal communication in which the text plays a central role?

Most recent literary theory is dependent on the simple yet compelling communication model of Roman Jakobson.[7] In this model, which involves basic speech-act theory,[8] every communication involves three elements: a sender (author), a message (text), and a receiver (reader):

Author ——————▶ Text ——————▶ Reader

In their relation to one another, all three of these realities are involved in the communication of meaning. And indeed, intention is necessarily involved: the

author brings the words and the reader the meaning.' This, said Frye, may have been intended as a sneer at Boehme, 'but it is an exact description of all literary works without exception.' And Frye lived to see this conception of reading adopted almost universally among North American theorists" (*Reality and Illusion in New Testament Scholarship: A Primer in Critical Realist Hermeneutics* [Collegeville, MN: Michael Glazier, 1994], 2).

6. Vanhoozer, *Is There a Meaning in This Text?* 201–80.

7. See Roman Jakobson, "Linguistics and Poetics," in *Style in Language*, ed. T. A. Sebeok (Cambridge, MA: MIT Press, 1960), 350–77. Although some scholars (e.g., Powell, *What Is Narrative Criticism?* 9) consider Jakobson's model to be an exclusive alternative to the historical-critical approach, we do not so conceive it; instead, we are convinced that the development of traditions such as those that are appropriately explored in historical criticism can be employed, within limits, to illumine certain aspects of author, text, and reader in the service of the meaning of the final form of the text.

8. For a critique of speech-act theory, especially as espoused by John Searle, Anthony Thiselton, and Kevin J. Vanhoozer, see Stephen E. Fowl, "The Role of Authorial Intention and the Theological Interpretation of Scripture," in Green and Turner, *Between Two Horizons*, 71–87; idem, *Engaging Scripture: A Model for Theological Interpretation* (Malden, MA: Blackwell, 1998).

intention of the author to communicate meaning, the intention of the reader
to derive meaning, and the role of the text as the mediator of intentional communication.[9] Both the role of the author and text, which involves the objective
dimension in that they exist independently of the reader, and the role of the
reader, which involves the subjective dimension, must be given proper weight
in the interpretive process.

Critical-Realist Hermeneutics

These dynamics of the communicative process have led several scholars, such
as Ben F. Meyer and N. T. Wright, to apply to the interpretation of the Bible
what has been called in philosophical circles "critical-realist hermeneutics."[10]
These scholars insist that one can reject the reality and importance of objective
knowledge or objective textual communication (reality or meaning that exists
outside of and independent of ourselves) only by denying the obvious; yet they
argue that one can approximate an objective construal of the meaning of the
biblical text only through subjective involvement. Thus Meyer says:

> At the heart of critical realism is the theorem that the way to objectivity is
> through *the subject, operating well*. The objective element in successful acts of
> reading is—what? It is not the writer's meaning (which might be inept, menda-
> cious, dead wrong), but the *accurate recovery* of whatever meaning the writer
> has managed to objectify in words. That meaning is mediated, communicated,
> recovered, only if the reader reads *well*, only if he or she attends to an exact
> decoding of signs, to the particularities of the word-sequence that emerges, to
> how every element in it works with every other. . . . *Objectivity is not achieved*
> *by the flight from subjectivity nor by any and every cultivation of subjectiv-*
> *ity, but by an intense and persevering effort to exercise subjectivity attentively,*
> *intelligently, reasonably, and responsibly.*[11]

Advocates of critical realism insist that philosophical and literary discussions
about objectivity and subjectivity throughout the modern period, and now into

9. Vanhoozer especially emphasizes the role of intentionality in the communication model,
although he stresses the intention of the author almost to the exclusion of the intention of the
reader. See Vanhoozer, *Is There a Meaning in This Text?* 201–80. Cf. Meyer, *Reality and Illusion*, 49, 53; note especially Meyer's notion of the reader's "drive for meaning" or "drive for
truth," which stems from a sense of wonder, or "drive to reality," over against Nietzsche's "will
to power"; see viii, 5, 7–8, 22–23, 51, 116.

10. See Ian Barbour, *Issues in Science and Religion* (London: SCM, 1966); Andrew Louth,
Discerning the Mystery: An Essay on the Nature of Theology (Oxford: Clarendon, 1983);
Colin E. Gunton, *Enlightenment and Alienation: An Essay towards a Trinitarian Theology*,
Contemporary Christian Studies (Basingstoke, UK: Marshall, Morgan & Scott, 1985); Bernard
Lonergan, *Method in Theology* (New York: Herder & Herder, 1972).

11. Meyer, *Reality and Illusion*, 3–4, emphasis original.

the postmodern period, have taught us that we must reject the claim of the objectivists ("naive realists") that we can know certain things *straight*, that is, exactly as they are. All data that we encounter must be processed through our subjective consciousness and thus necessarily bear the imprint of our preunderstandings. But these advocates also claim that the same philosophical and literary discussions have taught us that we must likewise reject the claim of the subjectivists that neither objective reality nor meaning exists, or that if it does, we cannot know it; and therefore such objective reality/meaning[12] is irrelevant for us.

Over against both of these positions stands critical realism, described by Wright as

a way of describing the process of "knowing" that acknowledges the *reality of the thing known, as something other than the knower* (hence "realism"), while also fully

---

12. This claim of the "subjectivists" is actually the position of existentialism, which N. T. Wright dubs "phenomenalism," a reaction during the period of modernity against the radical objectivist position of positivism. According to Wright (and many others), both positivism and phenomenalism were part of the Enlightenment epistemological project aimed at arriving at a certainty of knowledge (*New Testament and the People of God*, 32–33). The positivists believed that there were *some* things that we could know straight, with absolute objectivity, particularly empirical observations of the natural world that come to us by sense perception; all else they considered to be not knowledge but opinion or feeling. In response, existentialism insisted that the only thing we could know with certainty is our own experience, that is, our own subjective consciousness. Thus the entire modern epistemological project, in both its positivistic and phenomenalistic forms, was an attempt to find some basis or sphere of *absolutely certain knowledge*. In some respects, *deconstruction* is an answer to this quest for some foundation of absolutely certain knowledge, since deconstruction insists that no such foundation exists, and therefore we *postmoderns* should abandon any search for transcendent meaning and embrace a world of self-contradiction and incoherence. Indeed, deconstructionists such as Jacques Derrida, Roland Barthes, and Michel Foucault insist that the proper reading of texts should lead us to this deconstructionist conviction, for texts actually do not *construct* meaning but *deconstruct* it through their own inconsistencies and dissonances. In their view, any meanings that readers believe they find in texts are actually construals of meaning that they unconsciously themselves impose upon texts. Since deconstruction is not so much a hermeneutic as it is an antihermeneutic, it is not explicitly addressed in the present volume. But it can prove helpful, in an indirect way, to constructive hermeneutics. Vanhoozer, *Is There a Meaning in This Text?* 52, suggests that deconstruction is "a positive technique for making trouble." See the trenchant comment by Mark Allan Powell, "What Is Literary about Literary Aspects?" in *Society of Biblical Literature 1992 Seminar Papers*, ed. Eugene H. Lovering Jr. (Atlanta: Scholars Press, 1992), 48: "What I am suggesting is that the concerns of deconstruction might not be with *literary* aspects at all. . . . In fact, deconstruction (in the forms in which I have encountered it) questions the potential for texts such as the Gospels and Acts to communicate or to convey meaning in any sense at all. If this is the case, then what role can the deconstructors possibly play in an interpretive community committed to explicating communicative functions? Are they destined to occupy the place of the agnostic at a prayer meeting, challenging and annoying the faithful with their irreverent perspective? We might find their presence useful. They may keep us honest by continually exposing the assumptions in our research and the inadequacies of our conclusions." For the application of deconstruction to biblical texts, see Stephen D. Moore, *Literary Criticism and the Gospels: The Theoretical Challenge* (New Haven: Yale University Press, 1989).

acknowledging that the only access we have to this reality lies along the spiraling path of *appropriate dialogue or conversation between the knower and the thing known* (hence "critical"). This path leads to critical reflection on the products of our enquiry into "reality," so that our assertions about "reality" acknowledge their own provisionality. Knowledge, in other words, although in principle concerning realities independent of the knower, is never itself independent of the knower.[13]

Applied to the study of the Bible, these insights mean that it is appropriate to aim at a knowledge of the objective dimensions of the communicative act, such as the intention of the author, as it has been encoded in the text and can thus be inferred by us from the text.[14] But these insights also mean that such a knowledge is always tentative and provisional: we can never be absolutely sure we have captured the meaning of these objective realities, and such knowledge always comes through the grid of our subjective consciousness, which influences our understanding of these objective realities and imbues it with elements of our own subjectivity.[15]

Role of Presuppositions

Thus our subjective presuppositions or preunderstandings (what Thiselton, following Gadamer, calls the "horizon of the reader"[16]) are inevitable and

13. Wright, *New Testament and the People of God*, 35.

14. This statement introduces the notion of the *implied author*: the author as a construct of the text, which we must infer from the text. This concept will be discussed in chap. 4.

15. Here we have employed insights from critical realism because these insights accord with hermeneutical convictions we had embraced even before we became aware of critical realism. Thus for many years these critical-realist perspectives have been at least an implicit part of the teaching of inductive Bible study in some circles. Perhaps we should not be surprised to find some coalescence at points between the hermeneutical insights of inductive Bible study and critical realism: both try to describe and analyze what actually happens in communication over against coming to the question of meaning from prior ideological commitments. Of course, no one can be free from one's own ideological preunderstandings as one thinks about hermeneutics and interpretive method; see Edgar V. McKnight, "Presuppositions in New Testament Study," in Green, *Hearing the New Testament*, 278–300. But both inductive Bible study and critical realism are intentional in deriving an understanding of meaning in communication from an analysis of the experience of communication itself, with a view toward arriving at a nonideologically driven hermeneutic. Critical realism, especially as expressed by Meyer, *Reality and Illusion*, 142, captures also the general components of the hermeneutical process as we have pursued it in our work in inductive Bible study over the years: "The hallmark of critical realism is its insistence on the empirical (data), the intelligent (questioning and answering), the rational (the grasp of evidence as sufficient or insufficient, the personal act of commitment) as—all of them together—entering into true judgment." Yet the agreement with certain insights from critical realism does not mean that we necessarily embrace all of the specific elements of critical-realist hermeneutics as developed by, say, Meyer or N. T. Wright.

16. Anthony C. Thiselton, *The Two Horizons: New Testament Hermeneutics and Philosophical Description* (Grand Rapids: Eerdmans, 1980); Hans-Georg Gadamer, *Truth and Method*

actually necessary for us to grasp the objective realities/meaning within the communicative process.[17] They are necessary because some commonality between the perspectives of the text and those of the reader must be present for communication to occur, and presuppositions are the provisional concretizations of the impulse that readers naturally and necessarily have to grasp the sense of a text on the basis of their own experience and prior understandings. Presuppositions represent the reader's first attempt to understand a text that places demands or expectations upon the reader, and to do so with the only resource that the initial reader has: the reader's own preunderstandings.[18]

These presuppositions are thus necessarily present, but they are not necessarily correct; they may not actually coincide with the perspective of the text (what Thiselton calls the "horizon of the text"). Therefore they may prove to be ultimately unhelpful and even debilitating in grasping the sense of the text. Precisely because presuppositions are not necessarily correct or helpful, readers are obliged to engage in constant critical interaction between their presuppositions and the data of the text.

Specifically, such critical interaction involves the attempts both to identify what these presuppositions are and to temporarily suspend these presuppositions, to constrain them from effectively determining our construal of the text. The purpose of this suspension is to recognize how the perspective or message of the passage may differ from, and indeed challenge, the presuppositions with which one comes to the passage.[19] As Thiselton says, "To hear the Bible speak

---

(New York: Crossroad, 1988). They speak of the horizon of the reader, the horizon of the text, and the importance of the "fusion of horizons" for interpretation. See Vanhoozer, *Is There a Meaning in This Text?* 389–90.

17. Preunderstandings and presuppositions can be distinguished in this way: *preunderstanding* refers to one's sense of the meaning of universal realities, based on one's humanity and human experience, while *presupposition* refers to specific ideas regarding particular aspects of these universal realities. For example, one's experience of the death of others may provide a preunderstanding of the reference to "death" in 1 Cor. 15, while a conviction that death is final and that no reasonable person believes that it could be followed by resurrection would be a presupposition with which one might come to the reading of 1 Cor. 15. But in fact such a distinction between preunderstanding and presupposition is often nebulous, and they function in similar ways within the interpretive process. Therefore, in the present discussion these terms will be used together.

18. Meyer (*Reality and Illusion* , 69), in citing Lonergan, speaks of the "fallacy of the empty head": the notion that we can, and should, approach any writing with absolute neutrality, a tabula rasa. This notion is sometimes also called the "Baconian Fallacy." See David Hackett Fischer, *Historians' Fallacies: Toward a Logic of Historical Thought* (New York: Harper & Row, 1970), 4. But Francis Bacon himself speaks of the "idol of the den," which acknowledges that everyone interprets reality from one's own angle of perspective; cf. his *Novum Organum*, "Aphorisms" (1620; repr., Oxford: Clarendon, 1888), bk. 1, nos. 38–44.

19. Joel B. Green, "The Practice of Reading the New Testament," in Green, *Hearing the New Testament*, 416, helpfully lists three advantages of reading the NT while recognizing our presuppositions in our own "life-worlds": "First, beginning in this way self-consciously helps us to come clean on the interests and commitments that help to shape our reading of Scripture—

in its own right and with its due authority, the distinctive horizon of the text must be respected and differentiated in the first place from the horizon of the interpreter. This is not only a theological point; . . . it also arises from general hermeneutical theory."[20] The critical issue, then, is how a reader causes these presuppositions to function within the interpretive process. As emphasized in the discussion of induction in chapter 1, readers must do all they possibly can to *avoid making these presuppositions part of the inferential process* they employ in interpreting the text. Readers interested in a fuller discussion of the role of presuppositions in recent hermeneutical discussions should consult appendix B.

Spiritual Experience

At this point we acknowledge a moral and spiritual factor residing in the individual and in the community that inevitably enters into the process of interpretation. Although it is intangible, it may be just as real as, and probably is more important than, some of the more "objective" and tangible and technical elements involved in interpretation. Paul had this principle in mind when he wrote, "Those who are unspiritual do not receive the gifts of God's Spirit, for they are foolishness to them, and they are unable to understand them because they are spiritually discerned" (1 Cor. 2:14). Jesus was utilizing the same principle when he said to the Jews who marveled at his teaching and wondered as to its source: "My teaching is not mine but his who sent me. Anyone who resolves to do the will of God will know whether the teaching is from God or whether I am speaking on my own" (John 7:16–17).

In view of these considerations, biblical exposition should never be conceived as a purely mechanical or intellectual process, for it engages the spirit of persons as well. Thus, given the same aptitudes with regard to the techniques of exegesis, two persons may well differ in their ability to understand scriptural truth proportionately to their possession of spiritual sense. So important is the spiritual factor that one sometimes finds individuals who, though deficient in the skills of interpretation, far surpass in insight those who have had the best training in exegetical procedures. Nevertheless, even as technical expertise is not a substitute for spiritual experience in the pursuit of the fullest and most penetrating interpretation, so also spiritual experience cannot be a substitute for technical and methodological expertise.

---

interests and commitments that are operative even when they remain unacknowledged. Second, appreciating as fully as possible the self-identities and experiences from which we interpret opens further the potential for our own experiences and commitments to come under critical scrutiny. We bring to texts pre-understandings that may require emendation, that may be judged in the reading task as parochial, egocentric, and so on. Third, this approach allows us to engage self-consciously in critical reflection on our lives in the world."

20. Thiselton, *Two Horizons*, xx.

Spiritual sense is made possible by the presence of certain characteristics. Among them are teachableness, sincerity, and an intimate knowledge of God.[21] The more one possesses these, the more profound will be one's insight into biblical truth. They make it possible for one to be receptive to God's Spirit, who has motivated and guided the experience of the scriptural authors and is (according to the Scriptures) their best interpreter.

In addition, people in the community of faith do have a clear and undisputable advantage in terms of contemporary application of the meaning of the text over against those who approach the Bible without a faith commitment.[22] The Bible is most directly relevant to the faith community and to persons within it; for the most part at least, the Bible is addressed to those in the community of faith with a view toward forming their lives within that community and as members of it.[23] It is incumbent upon those within the church always to relate their interpretation of the Bible to their own faith and life within the Christian community, for the purpose of allowing the Bible to shape, correct, and confirm their theology and their broad spiritual experience.

21. Vanhoozer, *Is There a Meaning in This Text?* 367–452.

22. Bruce C. Birch and Larry L. Rasmussen, *Bible and Ethics in the Christian Life*, rev. ed. (Minneapolis: Augsburg, 1989), 179.

23. Green, "Practice of Reading the New Testament," 413.

3

Intentional and Rational Study

Intentionality of Biblical Study

Process necessarily involves method, and method by definition includes specific steps intentionally chosen based on their appropriateness for meeting certain objectives. Clearly, then, Bible study involves conscious decision regarding specifically what to do and careful deliberation as to why each step is appropriate and why each is pursued in the fashion in which it is pursued, in the overall attempt to arrive at the most effective study of the Bible.

We have observed that, as performed by both laypersons and those in professional Christian ministry, much Bible study is haphazard, with those who study the Bible not knowing exactly what they are doing or why. One telling anecdote has to do with a former student who went on to do further graduate study at one of the premier theological seminaries in the United States. He reported that when he asked master of divinity students who were approaching graduation what was the one thing they thought their seminary experience failed to give to them, their answers across the board were something along the lines of "a clear method for studying the Bible for ourselves."

Of course, effective study of the Bible cannot be reduced to method or process. To make such a claim would be to commit what we might call "the mechanical fallacy," the notion that effective interpretation is reducible to technique. Effective Bible study involves, fundamentally, an attitude or perspective in relation to the Bible. We recognize that reality, which is why we began part 1 with characteristics that involve overall perspective and attitude (inductive, transjective). But attitude in itself accomplishes nothing; a proper perspective

38

or attitude must be concretized in a process for the study of the Bible actually to be accomplished. Everyone who studies the Bible engages in process and thus has a method (broadly defined). The question, then, is whether that process, as conducted in practice, is the most effective one for achieving the legitimate goals of Bible study. We are convinced that a correlation exists between the quality of process and the quality of results.

The nature and function of the Bible call for a methodologically reflective study of it. For one thing, the *importance* of the Bible calls for careful methodological reflection on its study. The dominant role of the Bible—in the church, in Western civilization, and for that matter in the world—suggests that if one is sloppy in the way one thinks about or actually pursues the study of the biblical text, one implicitly adopts a stance of disregard for the significance of the Bible or even disrespect toward its greatness. .

For another thing, the *difficulty* of studying these texts calls for careful methodological reflection regarding how this challenging task might be pursued most effectively. These texts are difficult in that they are ancient documents. As such, their cultural context was quite different from modern Western culture, as well as from other cultures now represented in the world, and their perspectives were from the start largely countercultural. They are difficult in that they are theological texts: they deal with divine realities over against purely human realities. And indeed, the Bible presents the God who reveals himself as the transcendent one, as the God who is far beyond human ability to comprehend or understand fully, and who stands over against typical human ways of thinking and valuing (e.g., Isa. 55:6–11). These texts are difficult in that they are sophisticated and subtle literary texts, characterized by depth and richness of literary expression. After twenty centuries in which the Western world has given some of its greatest minds to the study of these documents, we continue to discover fresh depths of meaning in them through new literary insight. It is a romantic myth, entirely contradicted by all evidence, that these writings are the product of simple, untutored primitives, with the corollary that anyone can understand all that is communicated here merely by perusing them in the most casual way.[1]

Rationality of Biblical Study

In addition to being intentional, the study of the Bible ought to be *rational*. It necessarily engages the human mind. According to the perspective of the

1. Meir Sternberg, *The Poetics of Biblical Narrative: Ideological Literature and the Drama of Reading* (Bloomington: Indiana University Press, 1987), 53, speaks of the deceptive literary artistry of the Bible, a brilliant artistry that refuses to parade its sophistication: "The Bible's verbal artistry, without precedent in literary history and unrivaled since, operates by passing off its art for artlessness, its sequential linkages and supra-sequential echoes for unadorned parataxis, its density of evocation for chronicle-like thinness and transparency."

Bible itself, no necessary dichotomy exists between the mind and the Spirit of God. The Spirit often works through the human mind and certainly seeks to work through the mind, especially as the rational faculties, limited by our creatureliness and infirmed by our sinfulness, have been healed or empowered by the Spirit of God to function in a truly effective way.[2] Indeed, even the phenomenology of reading makes clear that reading itself is a rational process. Of course, one must distinguish between *rational* and *rationalism*. Rationalism is a school of philosophical thought declaring that reason is the highest or final reality and is ultimately sufficient for all things human; hence one might well, on biblical, theological, or philosophical grounds, reject rationalism. Nevertheless, the fact that reason may not be sufficient does not mean that it is not necessary.

However, many Christian readers of the Bible do have a profound distrust of the rigorous use of the mind in the study of the Bible out of an often unarticulated suspicion that any serious reliance upon the intellect is an affront to God and an impediment to hearing God's voice in the Scripture. Historically, two primary bases exist for this suspicion.

One basis is related to the Protestant Reformation and the Reformers' doctrine of Scripture's clarity (Luther's *claritas scripturae*) and perspicuity (Calvin's *perspicuitas*). Many post-Reformation Protestants have mistakenly understood this doctrine to mean that the message God wishes to express in Scripture is perfectly clear on the surface, so that no rigorous, intellectually engaging study of Scripture is needed in order to understand it. In reality, Luther employed the notion of *claritas* in his polemic against Erasmus's view that the meaning of Scripture is too incoherent and unclear to serve as an adequate basis for action. Luther responded by arguing that although certain individual passages might be obscure, the Scriptures-as-a-whole were sufficiently clear that any reasonable person could find, through the reading of Scripture, salvation in Christ and a basic knowledge of God's will so as to have a firm foundation for Christian discipleship. Thus Luther's doctrine of the clarity of Scripture involved a clarity that could lead to a *threshold* understanding of the revelation of God in the Bible, sufficient for salvation and for embarking upon discipleship, but not necessarily adequate for the strenuous demands of continuing discipleship. The latter requires exposure to the kind of intense exegetical insights reflected in Luther's commentaries and sermons.

Luther also employed the notion of *claritas* in his polemic against many medieval and scholastic writers who insisted that only they or the magisterium of the Roman Catholic Church, through a special, mysterious revelation of God's Spirit, held the "secret esoteric keys" that could alone unlock the

2. Markus Bockmuehl, *Seeing the Word: Refocusing New Testament Studies* (Grand Rapids: Baker Academic, 2006), 78–79; Wolfhart Pannenberg, *Basic Questions in Theology* (Philadelphia: Fortress, 1970–71), 2:1–64.

highest mysteries and deepest meaning of God's Word. In response, Luther insisted that God offers depth of spiritual insight to persons as they pursue a rigorous exegesis of the "literal sense" of Scripture. Thus, far from sanctioning a suspicion of serious, intellectually challenging exegetical study, Luther's doctrine of the clarity of Scripture urges a strenuous employment of the best of the rational faculties.[3]

The second basis for the suspicion that many Christians hold toward a rationally engaged study of the Bible has to do with the reaction found within some forms of pietism, revivalism, Pentecostalism, and the charismatic movement, a reaction against what is taken to be the sterile and lifeless character of a purely cerebral Christianity. The profound dissatisfaction with a purely intellectual faith has led some Christians to equate rigorous thought with dependence on the human rational faculties and the consequent deadening of the spiritual life. We can readily understand such a reaction on the part of these groups that emphasize the immediate experience of God's Spirit in the Christian life. But that reaction must not become an overreaction that largely overlooks the character of the revelation of God in Scripture. According to the Bible and the tenets of the Christian faith over the centuries, God has chosen to reveal himself in the rational discourse of Scripture, and Scripture itself regularly and explicitly appeals to reason. The testimony of Scripture, which comes to us in the form of rational and sometimes complex argument and an appeal to the intellect, describes and warrants the immanent presence of the life-giving Spirit within the Christian and the Christian community.

The anti-intellectualism just described is not a necessary or inherent characteristic of pietism, revivalism, Pentecostalism, or the charismatic movement. Some of the most committed and influential pietists were fully convinced of the necessity of rigorous intellectual endeavor, including a reasonable and informed study of the Bible. In this connection one thinks of the groundbreaking commentator and textual critic Johannes Bengel; of John Wesley, the founder of Methodism; and of Adolf Schlatter, the great pietistic New Testament scholar and systematic theologian who was extremely influential in European Christianity at the beginning of the twentieth century. In addition, much serious biblical scholarship is now being produced within Pentecostal and charismatic circles.[4]

---

3. See the fine discussion on the Reformation doctrine of the clarity of Scripture in Anthony C. Thiselton, *New Horizons in Hermeneutics: The Theory and Practice of Transforming Biblical Reading* (Grand Rapids: Zondervan, 1992), 179–85. Thiselton goes on to show that Calvin's doctrine of the perspicuity of Scripture is very similar in essentials to Luther's notion of Scripture's clarity.

4. See esp. the work of John Christopher Thomas, *Footwashing in John 13 and the Johannine Community* (Sheffield: JSOT Press, 1991); idem, *The Spirit of the New Testament* (Leiden: Deo, 2005); Roger Stronstad, *The Charismatic Theology of St. Luke* (Peabody, MA: Hendrickson, 1984); idem, *The Prophethood of All Believers: A Study of Luke's Charismatic Theology* (Grand Rapids: Zondervan, 1993).

4

Re-Creative Study

After trying to consider all the dynamics bound up in the communicative function of texts, we contend that the basis for determining the interpretation of texts is an appeal to the intention of the author, as the author can be inferred from the text itself. This conviction stems from the nature of texts themselves and the phenomenology of reading texts, including the biblical text.[1]

The most fundamental reality of the reading process is the sense of being addressed, the sense of the presence of an author. This is not simply a matter of encountering an author's *voice*, that is, the words directed to the audience;

---

1. We are aware of the vigorous and complex discussion in hermeneutical circles regarding authorial intention, with scholars on one extreme wishing to banish the notion of the author entirely from the interpretation of the text: thus Roland Barthes speaks of "the death of the author." On the other extreme, E. D. Hirsch Jr. argues that for interpretation to have any validity, it must involve appeal to the intention of historical authors in terms of their consciousness. See E. D. Hirsch Jr., *Validity in Interpretation* (New Haven: Yale University Press, 1967); idem, *The Aims of Interpretation* (Chicago: University of Chicago Press, 1976); cf. Elliott E. Johnson, who applies Hirsch's position specifically to biblical texts in *Expository Hermeneutics: An Introduction* (Grand Rapids: Academie Books, 1990). Engaging fully in this debate is outside the purview of the present study. We have decided to adopt an interpretive model that seeks to move empirically from examining the way in which communication in general actually happens—the way both authors and readers relate to texts in practice as part of their function within the broader process of communication—to considering hermeneutical conclusions. This approach is inductive in that it seeks to move from empirical data to conclusions, what Thiselton calls a "metacritical" approach. See Thiselton, *New Horizons in Hermeneutics*, 11, 15.

indeed, authorial presence includes authorial voice.[2] But it is a much broader and more profound sense of the presence of the author, who not only speaks but also is responsible for ordering the material with the result that the text, in its expression, draws forth certain constructions of meaning in the mind of the audience.

This author, insofar as he[3] is inferred from the text, is *implied* by the text and is actually a construct of the reading of the text itself. Scholars refer to this author who is inferred from the text as the "implied author."

Although the general concept of this kind of implied author has been operative in literary analysis for many years, Wayne Booth, in his book *The Rhetoric of Fiction*, first developed the idea and explored its literary significance.[4] He points out that the picture of the author we gather from the reading of a text (implied author) is not synonymous with the flesh-and-blood author who was responsible for penning the book:

> Our present problem is the intricate relationship of the so-called real author with his various official versions of himself. We must say various versions, for regardless of how sincere an author may try to be, his different works will imply different versions, different ideal combinations of norms. Just as one's personal letters imply different versions of oneself, depending on the differing relationships with each correspondent and the purpose of each letter, so the writer sets himself out with a different air depending on the needs of particular works.[5]

In fact, the implied author of a work is never completely identical to the flesh-and-blood author. For one thing, the implied author is always smaller than the flesh-and-blood author. Take the Gospel of Matthew as an example. We have every reason to believe that the historical author of Matthew's Gospel knew much more about the actions and teachings of Jesus than he was able to include, or chose to include, in his narrative. Indeed, certainly his own personal understanding of Jesus as the Christ (his Christology) included more than he was able to communicate within his Gospel. In a sense the Christology of the historical author of Matthew's Gospel thus is larger, or broader, than the

---

2. The technical expression for the authorial *voice*, at least in narrative material, is the *narrator*.

3. Most scholars consider it indisputable that all, or at least virtually all, of the writers of the biblical books were male and, insofar as one can determine, present themselves as male. Therefore not only the real authors but also the implied authors of biblical books seem to be male. Thus we use the masculine pronoun here.

4. Wayne Booth, *The Rhetoric of Fiction* (Chicago: University of Chicago Press, 1961), 71–76, 151–52, 157, 200, 211–21, 395–96. Readers should not be put off by the use of the word *fiction* here. Although Booth is concerned primarily to analyze fiction, what he says regarding the implied author applies equally to nonfiction material.

5. Ibid., 71.

Christology of the First Gospel. The author of the Fourth Gospel concedes this point explicitly: "Now Jesus did many other signs in the presence of his disciples, which are not written in this book. But these are written so that you may come to believe that Jesus is the Messiah, the Son of God, and that through believing you may have life in his name" (John 20:30–31). Later he states again, "There are also many other things that Jesus did; if every one of them were written down, I suppose that the world itself could not contain the books that would be written" (21:25).

The implied author is also always larger than the historical author. Any piece of literature, especially an extended and complex one, will communicate to readers more than the historical author consciously intended to communicate. The author we infer from the text will implicitly communicate some ideas that the historical author did not deliberately set out to advance. Even E. D. Hirsch Jr., perhaps the chief proponent of the notion that interpretation involves re-creating the consciousness of the historical author, acknowledges that authors may, upon subsequently reading their own works, recognize the presence of meanings in their texts that they had not consciously intended.[6] When an author is confronted by readers who suggest an interpretation that they have derived from one of that author's passages, the author might respond by saying, "I did not consciously intend to communicate that thought, but now that you mention it, that is the sense of my text, or at least it is in harmony with what I have written. This interpretation does not contradict what I intended to say, and I actually agree with it."[7] Thus the "intention of the (implied) author" is tantamount to the construction of the sense of the text inferred by the reader as the reader accurately attends to the literary dynamics of the text itself.[8]

---

6. Hirsch, *Validity in Interpretation*, 6–9. Hirsch actually does not refer to these unintended senses as "meaning," but rather as "significance."

7. This example reflects our conviction that the unintended meaning is typically in agreement with, and frequently an extension of, the meaning intended by the historical author. But in principle a text can mean something that stands in contradiction to what the historical author wished to communicate. In such a case, the historical author would be incompetent. Though an inductive approach is open to all possibilities, including that of an incompetent biblical writer, the evidence is solidly against the conclusion that any of our biblical writers were incompetent. At any rate, the practicalities of the interpretive process require that readers assume a competent author unless the evidence for incompetency is overwhelming.

8. Sternberg, *Poetics of Biblical Narrative*, 9, states that "as interpreters of the Bible, our only concern is with 'embodied' or 'objectified' intention; and that forms a different business altogether, about which a wise measure of agreement has always existed. In my own view, such intention fulfills a crucial role, for communication presupposes a speaker who resorts to certain linguistic and structural tools in order to produce certain effects on the addressee; the discourse accordingly supplies a network of clues to the speaker's intention. . . . [Intention] is a shorthand for the structure of meaning and effect supported by the conventions that the text appeals to or devises; for the sense that the language makes in terms of the communicative context as a whole."

Significance of the Appeal to the Implied Author

The focus on the implied author over against the flesh-and-blood author in the reading process carries several points of interpretive significance, not least of which is that speaking of the implied author of the various biblical books is more realistic simply because readers of the Bible do not have direct access to the flesh-and-blood authors. In other words, the only author that present-day readers of the Bible have is the author they encounter in, and can infer from, the texts themselves.

Furthermore, since the biblical authors are not directly accessible to us, the reader's sense of the implied authors is more reliable than the reader's reconstruction of the historical authors. In reality we know little about most of the authors of the biblical materials; indeed, in most cases they are anonymous. Thus any attempt at reconstructing the historical authors tends to be highly speculative. We often cannot be certain that a single historical author is responsible for the production of a given biblical book. We have indications that many of the books of our Bible are the result of a more or less extended process of development, making locating the historical author in one person difficult.[9]

Likewise, the focus on the implied author is more constructive than a focus on the flesh-and-blood author because the aim of interpretation is to gain a sense *of the text*. The emphasis on the implied author stems from and leads to a text-centered approach and thus contributes directly to the realization of the goal of interpretation. It also avoids what C. S. Lewis called "the personal heresy," the mistaken notion that interpretation is to be centered on the reconstruction of the life or consciousness of the historical author rather than on the meaning of the text the author has composed.[10] Thus the intention of the implied author is tantamount to Eco's "intention of the text," or "operational intention" (*intentio operis*), which ideally directs readers' construal of the text (*intentio lectoris*).[11]

The notion of the implied author leads to a more robust interpretation of the text because it yields broader interpretive possibilities than does the attempt to verify every observation or interpretation on the basis of the conscious

---

9. See the major works on OT and NT introduction, especially Childs, *Introduction to the Old Testament as Scripture*; Werner H. Schmidt, *Old Testament Introduction*, 2nd ed. (Louisville: Westminster John Knox, 1995); John Drane, *Introducing the Old Testament*, rev. ed. (Oxford: Lion, 2000); Werner Georg Kümmel, *Introduction to the New Testament*, rev. ed. (Nashville: Abingdon, 1975); Brevard S. Childs, *The New Testament as Canon: An Introduction* (Philadelphia: Fortress, 1985); Ralph P. Martin, *New Testament Foundations*, rev. ed., 2 vols. (Grand Rapids: Eerdmans, 1986).

10. C. S. Lewis and E. M. W. Tillyard, *The Personal Heresy: A Controversy* (Oxford: Oxford University Press, 1939).

11. Umberto Eco, *Interpretation and Overinterpretation*, ed. S. Collini (Cambridge: Cambridge University Press, 1992), 25.

intention of the historical author. A focus on this intention, for example, might cause a student who identifies a clearly and manifestly present contrast within a passage to worry whether this contrast was consciously intended by the historical author and to judge it to be of interpretive significance only if the reader can demonstrate that the author intended it. Making a judgment about the conscious intention of the historical biblical author is most often impossible; therefore this approach leads to a kind of interpretive supercaution or timidity. Paul Ricoeur describes the disengagement of the observation or interpretive process from appeal to the consciousness of the historical author as providing a possible "surplus of meaning" in the text.[12] Moreover, a text-centered interpretation finds meaning embedded in the text, and the operative question is whether the dynamics of the text, meaning the implied author, lead to a given observation or interpretation.

Yet another point in favor of focusing on the notion of the implied author is that it gives rise to the corollary concept of the *implied reader*—the reader whom the text envisages and projects, the sense of the reader that one infers from the text itself. The implied reader is the creation of the implied author. The author, as we infer him from the text, has so shaped the text as to offer us a given understanding, or sense, of the reader who is intended to be addressed by the text. The notion of implied reader is extremely important for interpretation because it serves to locate the kinds of expectations the text places on readers for the understanding of the text, the kinds of background knowledge, linguistic understanding, and so forth, that the text assumes the reader has and will bring to bear in the construal of the text's meaning.[13]

The hermeneutical reason for most literary theorists' enthusiastic acceptance of this distinction between the historical author and the implied author is the consideration that texts, once written, have *in some ways* a life of their own. This argument is made by William K. Wimsatt and Monroe Beardsley in their famous essay "The Intentional Fallacy,"[14] and it corresponds to the

12. Paul Ricoeur, *Interpretation Theory: Discourse and the Surplus of Meaning* (Fort Worth: Texas Christian University Press, 1976), 30.

13. For the notion of implied reader, see Wolfgang Iser, *The Implied Reader: Patterns of Communication in Prose Fiction from Bunyan to Beckett* (Baltimore: Johns Hopkins University Press, 1975); idem, *The Act of Reading: A Theory of Aesthetic Response* (Baltimore: Johns Hopkins University Press, 1978); Umberto Eco, *The Role of the Reader: Explorations in the Semiotics of Texts* (London: Hutchinson, 1981); cf. Kevin J. Vanhoozer, "The Reader in New Testament Interpretation," in Green, *Hearing the New Testament*, 301–28 (Grand Rapids: Eerdmans, 1995); Thiselton, *New Horizons in Hermeneutics*, 515–55.

14. W. K. Wimsatt and Monroe Beardsley, "The Intentional Fallacy," in *The Verbal Icon: Studies in the Meaning of Poetry*, ed. W. K. Wimsatt (Lexington: University of Kentucky Press, 1954), 3–18; cf. certain recent criticism of the intentional fallacy as proposed by Wimsatt and Beardsley, such as the critique from Anthony C. Thiselton, "'Behind' and 'In Front Of' the Text: Language, Reference, and Indeterminacy," in *After Pentecost: Language and Biblical Interpretation*, ed. Craig Bartholomew, Colin Greene, and Karl Möller, Scripture and Hermeneutics Series 2 (Grand Rapids: Zondervan, 2001), 107–8.

previous claim that implied authors are always both smaller and larger than the historical authors of works.

Yet one must be careful here, for although a distinction can and must be made between historical authors and implied ones, they are also connected.[15] We discover this principle of connectedness between the implied and historical author from the experience of reading. When readers sense that they are being addressed in a text, they do not think of this authorial presence (the implied author) that they are encountering as a textual abstraction but imagine a flesh-and-blood author.[16] The text invites the projection of a flesh-and-blood author, yet this flesh-and-blood author does not present himself *directly* to the reader but only through the mediation of the text he has produced. The implied author is the image that readers construct of the historical author, an image mediated through the text.[17]

Practical Issues Raised by Appeal to the Implied Author

We conclude this chapter by noting that these considerations regarding the connection between an implied author and the historical author raise two practical issues pertaining to the interpretation of texts, and especially of biblical texts. First, the concept of the implied author prompts the question of the relationship between literary and historical study. As one actually reads texts, one cannot construe the implied authors as timeless abstractions, with no historical context of their own, but must construe them as historical persons who occupied their own place in time, out of which historical situation they speak to others through their texts.

At one time certain scholars thought of the implied author and his intentions as the sole product of examining the literary features of the document itself, with no concern whatsoever for the historical context associated with the original writing of the document. However, such a narrow literary understanding of the implied author and his intentions, that is, of textual interpretation,

15. See Sternberg, *Poetics of Biblical Narrative*, 69, who refers to the historical author and the implied author as "the person and the persona," and as "two faces of the same entity."

16. This sense of a flesh-and-blood author is always present to some extent, but it is more prominent, and more significant, for the reading process in some works than in others. One need only compare the book of Jonah with 1 Thessalonians.

17. Ricoeur, *Interpretation Theory*, 30, speaks of the "fallacy of the absolute text," that is, of finding meaning in texts without some consideration that human intention lies behind it. See also Nicholas Wolterstorff, *Divine Discourse: Philosophical Reflections on the Claim That God Speaks* (Cambridge: Cambridge University Press, 1995), 172; idem, "The Promise of Speech-Act Theory for Biblical Interpretation," in Bartholomew, Greene, and Möller, *After Pentecost*, 71–90, where Wolterstorff draws a close connection between the author that we encounter in the text and the flesh-and-blood author without collapsing them into a single hermeneutical reality. Both Ricoeur and Wolterstorff are reacting to the claim of the "New Critics" that texts exist in absolute autonomy from their historical authors.

was not sustainable for long. All texts necessarily assume a historical context; thus the concept of implied author, as set forth here, provides a warrant for historical study and establishes a restriction (and focus) for historical study. This emphasis upon the implied author requires a text-based inquiry into historical background involving three components: (1) rejecting the practice of simply amassing all the available information on historical background and summarily dumping it into the interpretation of the text in favor of a procedure that begins with the portrait of the author and of his intentions as set forth within the text itself (the implied author); (2) identifying the kinds of historical background information this portrait of the author and his intentions invites or even requires the reader to have for a fully competent construal of the text on its own terms;[18] and (3) employing this relevant historical background with a view toward arriving at a full and rich understanding of the text according to its own agenda.[19]

But beyond the question of the relationship between literary and historical study, a second practical issue has to do with the relationship between the intention of the implied author and the views of the historical author as known through his other writings. This question is critical for biblical interpretation, for the Bible contains several bodies of writings, collections of two or more books written by the same author. One obvious example is the Pauline collection. When one is interpreting a passage from, say, Romans, one might ask about the legitimacy of considering what Paul says in Galatians or Philippians. The answer to this question is that one must acknowledge two realities. One must first acknowledge that it is important to derive our understanding of the implied author's intention from the book itself, with an emphasis on the unity and distinctiveness of what Paul is saying *in Romans*, thus giving priority in interpretation to evidence from book context. However, one must also

---

18. Max Turner, "Historical Criticism and Theological Hermeneutics of the New Testament," in Green and Turner, *Between Two Horizons*, 48–50, helpfully develops Ricoeur's concept of "presuppositional pools" (i.e., knowledge pertaining to historical background that the implied author shares with the reader envisaged by the text: the implied reader). The *text* assumes that the reader has and will bring this knowledge to bear upon its construal. Cf. Peter Cotterell and Max Turner, *Linguistics and Biblical Interpretation* (Downers Grove, IL: InterVarsity, 1989), 90–97. See also Sternberg, *Poetics of Biblical Narrative*, 13–16.

19. These matters of historical background may be either general or particular. In interpreting Galatians, for example, the text will require the reader to consider such general matters as Koine Greek as it was employed in the first-century Greco-Roman world, and the social and literary expectations associated with letter writing in that culture (epistolography). In this same letter, however, the interpretation of Paul's reference to circumcision requires a more particular historical examination of the way circumcision functioned and was understood in first-century Judaism and Christianity. Whether the background is general or particular, readers must engage in critical conversation between the information we gather from historical background and the ways the implied author suggests such information should appropriately be applied to the construal of the text. See chap. 16 on the danger of overinterpretation by the uncritical employment of historical background.

acknowledge that the implied author of Romans overtly identifies himself as the historical figure Paul; thus the book itself presents its implied author as a historical figure who functions in the church and world at large. The book invites the reader to consider what Paul is saying in Romans in light of what Paul as a historical figure thought and did. We have access to this information primarily from Paul's other epistles.[20]

20. And, one might add, from the book of Acts. Although, in employing Luke's portrait of Paul for the purposes of historical reconstruction, one should be aware of the historical-critical issues involved in the relationship between Luke's presentation of Paul and the historical person of Paul himself, and factor these critical considerations into any use of Acts for understanding the person of Paul as presented in his letters.

5

Direct Study

Because an inductive approach is evidential and is concerned especially with moving from the evidence of the text itself to interpretive conclusions, inductive Bible study emphasizes firsthand study of the text rather than the study of books about the text. We want to stress that in an inductive approach, secondary sources, such as commentaries, are used and are an essential part of the process, but one ought to give priority to the biblical text in terms of both sequence and emphasis.

The Importance of Firsthand Study

This priority on firsthand study of the primary sources corresponds to the way literature in general is studied. A course in Shakespeare or Goethe, for example, typically would involve a serious engagement with the texts of these writers. But often university or seminary courses on books of the Bible instead give priority to secondary sources. Indeed, at a major evangelical seminary in the United States, one of us took a course on the book of Acts in which a student could earn the highest possible grade in the course without being required to read even one word of the book of Acts. Really, the course was misnamed; it should have been presented as a course on the literature about the book of Acts rather than a course on the book of Acts itself.

This experience is not rare. Howard Tillman Kuist—who taught inductive Bible study at Princeton Theological Seminary before Vatican II, and before the significant changes that great council precipitated in the Roman Catholic

Church in the study of the Bible for clergy and laypeople alike—identifies the existence of something like a "re-Catholicization" of the Bible in Protestantism. Kuist describes the tendency of Christians in general, including Protestants, to act as though the people (clergy and lay) cannot be trusted to read and interpret the Bible for themselves; instead, it is thought that the people should read the Bible only with an *authorized* interpretation, which in Protestantism is provided not by the pope or the magisterium but by the professor or the commentary writer.[1] Whether Kuist's description accurately reflects the reading of the Bible by laypersons in pre–Vatican II Roman Catholicism, his assessment that persons in general are inclined toward an immediate submission to *professional interpretation* is valid.

Of course, commentaries play an important and indeed indispensable role, but the interpretation of the Bible is ultimately the happy responsibility of the reader. Scholars, and especially teachers in the church, exist to assist readers in arriving at their own understanding of the text, not to serve as a proxy for readers' direct engagement with the Bible. Indeed, scholars have a functional instead of dogmatic authority in interpretation. Any authority that scholars have is not found in the fact that they possess earned degrees or have been able to convince a publisher to distribute their commentaries and are thereby empowered to render authoritative pronouncements on the meaning of biblical texts. Rather, their authority is found in their ability to assist readers in making sense of the text for themselves.

Reasons for Emphasis on Direct Firsthand Study

As a general principle, commentaries should normally be consulted after the initial phase of firsthand study. There are a number of reasons for this. First, if one begins by going immediately to a commentary in order to "get the answer," one will find that one's thinking has been prejudiced by the interpretation offered by the commentator. In other words, consulting commentaries at the outset will tend to create blinders or parameters that will be difficult to transcend. The possibility of the reader's discovering original insights will be diminished.

Second, to begin by going to commentaries to get the answer involves a misuse of commentaries. Commentaries do not exist as an alternative to firsthand study of the text. They exist to aid readers as they struggle to capture the meaning of the text for themselves.

Third, moving immediately to commentaries to obtain the interpretation of passages robs readers of the excitement and ownership that come from personal

---

1. Kuist, *These Words upon Thy Heart*, 32–36, takes this impulse to shift responsibility to the "expert" as a reflection of the sinful craving for security and its corollary, the flight from personal responsibility.

discovery. When one grasps scriptural truth through one's own discovery, one has a deeper, more personal, and more meaningful understanding than occurs when one encounters the meaning secondhand. This kind of fuller, deeper, and more personal understanding makes possible a fuller, deeper, and more profoundly personal response to the truth encountered.[2]

Fourth, readers often need to judge between different interpretations offered in commentaries. Commentators do not always agree on the interpretation of passages, especially in the case of difficult sections. Bible readers are required to decide for themselves; to do so with integrity, they will need to make the determination based on their own examination of the text.

In sum, then, students of the Bible should give priority to the direct study of the text, which will provide impetus and perspective for the employment of secondary sources, such as commentaries.

2. Ibid., 35–36.

6

Comprehensive
and Integrated Study

The study of the Bible calls for an integrated model that incorporates every legitimate approach and every specific exegetical component into a holistic process. The terms *integrated* and *holistic* suggest a common aim or goal toward which all aspects of study should be directed, which raises a problem. The Bible can be (and has been) studied in a variety of ways with various specific goals. Some study the Bible for the purpose of reconstructing the life of Jesus, others for the purpose of tracing the historical development of the early church, and still others for the purpose of exploring the relation of the religion of Israel to the culture of the ancient Near East. The list could go on and on.

Basis of an Integrated Approach: Focus on the Text's Final Form

While all these aims of study are appropriate to be explored, and they all more or less directly relate to the Bible, one might legitimately ask whether studies with these kinds of focus and ultimate goals can strictly and properly be called "Bible study." The answer to this question involves, on one level, semantics and definition, but at a deeper level the question is substantive and central. One helpful distinction to make is between studies that have as their *ultimate* interpretive concern some realities that lie behind the text and study that is concerned primarily with the meaning of the text itself as a literary entity

53

that we encounter in its present form, which to be sure references or bears witness to extratextual realities. The word *ultimate* is emphasized because all of these pursuits may contribute to the interpretation of the text itself in its final form, thereby becoming part of "Bible study" more narrowly defined; but insofar as they focus on these behind-the-text matters as ends in themselves, they may more precisely be dubbed "studies related to the Bible" rather than "study of the Bible" or "Bible study." In this regard, Ben F. Meyer makes a helpful distinction between *interpretation* and *analysis*. For him, interpretation involves the process of discerning the sense of the final form of the text, while analysis involves the exploration of behind-the-text technical issues, such as textual criticism, historical background, sociological studies, and history of the tradition (e.g., redaction criticism). He insists that although analysis may ultimately aid interpretation, it cannot become a substitute for interpretation.[1]

At any rate, by an integrated and holistic approach, we mean one in which the various aspects of study are all directed toward, and together contribute to, the meaning of the biblical text in its final form. The final form is central to the hermeneutical task and thus provides the basis for methodological unity and coherence, because all realities associated with the Bible intersect at the final form of the text. All that lies behind the text is moving toward its final form, and all that lies "in front of the text" (the response of readers and effects upon readers) emerges from encounter with the text. The centrality of the final form means that Bible study begins with the text, and all these other realities are pursued in relation to it. Our position is that the nature of the biblical books and passages, characterized as they are by both complexity and unity, requires an approach that is both multiple and integrated around a cohering center.[2]

Importance of an Integrative Approach

Over the past century, biblical scholarship has spawned a variety of specific critical approaches to the study of the Bible. In *Reading the Old Testament*, for example, John Barton offers discrete chapters on genre recognition, literary criticism, form criticism, redaction criticism, the canonical approach, structuralist criticism, and new criticism.[3] And in *Interpreting the New Testament*, edited by David Alan Black and David S. Dockery, we find chapters on textual criticism, source criticism, form criticism, redaction criticism, literary

---

1. Meyer, *Reality and Illusion*, 99–100; Vanhoozer, *Is There a Meaning in This Text?* 328. See Green, "Practice of Reading the New Testament," 411–12, for the role of "normative aims" in interpretation.

2. So also, with some differences, W. Randolph Tate, *Biblical Interpretation: An Integrated Approach*, rev. ed. (Peabody, MA: Hendrickson, 1996).

3. Barton, *Reading the Old Testament*.

criticism, and sociological criticism.[4] In its own way, each of these critical approaches addresses key aspects of the meaning of biblical texts. But if each is used in isolation, with no regard to how it relates to the others in an integrated construal of the meaning of biblical passages, students are left with a virtual smorgasbord of approaches,[5] with the suggestion that if they choose to pursue a passage on the basis of, say, redaction criticism, they will arrive at an understanding of the passage that is peculiar to that approach. Likewise, their choice of a form-critical examination will necessarily result in a different set of interpretive conclusions.

Some may say that such a multiplicity of interpretive conclusions, reflecting the plurality of methodological options, adds richness and depth to the meaning of passages,[6] but such a situation can actually result in confusion and a sense of arbitrariness.[7] We contend that the dynamics of passages themselves, in their literary contexts, should determine which of these approaches are deemed to be most relevant and helpful in the interpretation of the passage in question, and how they can most effectively be related to one another in the process of study. The purpose is to work toward arriving at an interpretation that is deep and rich in that it reflects, in a robust way, the coherence of the various facets of a passage around a central communicated issue. By "central communicated issue," we do not wish to suggest that the meaning even of an individual passage can be reduced to one simple interpretive proposition. Quite the contrary, the kind of integrated approach urged here is coherent in that it has a center, but it is rich in that the central issue of a passage is

4. Black and Dockery, *Interpreting the New Testament*.

5. See Steven L. McKenzie and Stephen R. Haynes, *To Each Its Own Meaning: An Introduction to Biblical Criticisms and Their Application* (Louisville: Westminster John Knox, 1993); cf. Sternberg, *Poetics of Biblical Narrative*, 17. Bockmuehl, *Seeing the Word*, 61–63, describes this smorgasbord of approaches as indicative of the lack of focus or clear purpose of biblical interpretation and sees it as a crisis that threatens the discipline of biblical studies itself.

6. Thiselton, *New Horizons in Interpretation*, 549.

7. In fact, the employment of various critical methods on the same passage, used in virtual isolation from one another, may result in two or more interpretations that are contradictory and mutually exclusive. Diachronic approaches, tracing the chronological development of traditions through their various stages, often emphasize ways in which later stages of the transmission process alter or correct the earlier ones. Thus Thomas Weeden insists that Mark took pre-Markan gospel traditions that originally presented Jesus's divine sonship in terms of the triumphalistic miracle-working "divine man" and through his redactional activity "corrected" the earlier meaning of these passages in the direction of presenting Jesus now as the humble and suffering Son of Man. The same passages, then, mean one thing in their original contexts, as reconstructed through source criticism, and something quite different and even contradictory in their later manifestations as products of Mark's redactional activity. See Thomas J. Weeden Sr., *Mark: Traditions in Conflict* (Philadelphia: Fortress, 1971); cf. Jack Dean Kingsbury, *The Christology of Mark's Gospel* (Philadelphia: Fortress, 1983). Numerous examples of this same phenomenon from the OT abound in Brevard S. Childs's discussions of the development of traditions behind the "canonical shape" of OT books and passages. See Childs, *Introduction to the Old Testament as Scripture*.

7

Individual and Communal Study

Character and Importance of Individual Study

The study of the Bible ought to be individual in two particular ways. First, in terms of *process of study*, giving space in the study process to one's individual encounter with the text is critically important.[1] Individual encounter with the text should be pursued so that the possibility of originality is maintained. If one typically begins by consulting others regarding the meaning of passages (either directly in conversation or indirectly through the use of commentaries), one's thinking will necessarily be influenced by the thoughts of conversation partners. As a practical psychological matter, it will be challenging to break from patterns of thought with which one was initially confronted. As a result, the development of fresh insights will be much more difficult and unlikely. Moreover, because students will not always have a peer group with which to work and discuss matters pertaining to the text, they would do well to give attention to developing their own hermeneutical skills as they work independently with biblical passages.

The second way in which study ought to be individual is in terms of the *conclusions drawn from study*. Within limits, making allowances for individual differences in interpretive conclusions is vitally important. Given the rich and often deeply textured meaning of passages, individual interpreters may be able

---

1. Balancing one's own encounter with the communal emphasis is also vital. While students engage in individual study of the text, they do so in the full recognition that the whole of the Bible has been addressed to communities and that they must always keep issues of Christian community in mind as they read. See Green, "Practice of Reading the New Testament," 417–18.

to arrive at different (though not mutually exclusive) interpretations that are equally correct and proper. One should think of passages as having a range of possible meanings within parameters, with differences in the background or perspective of individual interpreters determining where in the range of possible appropriate construals they will land in their interpretive conclusions.

A story from the lore of Union Theological Seminary in Virginia illustrates this principle of allowing, within limits, for individual differences in interpretive conclusions. During the Second World War, two faculty colleagues at Union—John Bright, professor of Old Testament, and Howard Tillman Kuist, then professor of biblical studies—had a friendly disagreement. Bright insisted that if he took two students of essentially equal ability, gave them the same passage to interpret, provided them with the same tools, and allotted them the same amount of time, assuming they did their work with commensurate skill, they would arrive at exactly the same interpretation of the passage. Kuist disagreed. He declared that those two students, working under parallel conditions and doing their work with equal quality, might well arrive at different, though not mutually exclusive or contradictory, interpretive conclusions.[2]

We believe that Kuist has the better argument. After all, some passages are multivalent: the evidence points to two or more equally viable interpretations. Take as an example 1 Samuel 17, the story of David and Goliath. We are told in verse 40 that David "chose five smooth stones from the wadi, and put them in his shepherd's . . . pouch." But we learn from verse 49 that David killed Goliath with just one stone. Within this tightly knit narrative, with no throwaway details but where every word seems to bear weight, we have what we will later describe in this volume as the structural relationship of contrast: an emphasis on the difference between the fact that David collected *five* stones and the fact that he used only *one*.

What is the meaning of this contrast? The evidence points to two quite distinct answers. First, contextual evidence indicates that David's faith was characterized by an element of weakness in that he seemed vulnerable to the suggestion that, although God would give him the victory over Goliath (v. 37), he needed to procure some additional resources of his own to establish more securely his own safety and victory.[3] He thus picked up four additional stones for the purpose of giving himself extra backup. Conversely, other contextual

2. This account was related in private conversation to David R. Bauer by Dr. Donald G. Miller, himself a professor at Union Theological Seminary and close personal friend to both Dr. Bright and Dr. Kuist. It has not been independently verified and probably at this point, so many years later, cannot be.

3. Among other things, we note that in 1 Sam. 17:38–39 David accepted from the hand of King Saul (who throughout 1 Sam. 13–31 is pictured as depending on his own weaponry rather than placing confidence solely in God's power to deliver) Saul's armor and even his sword. David removed them only because he could not walk with them and reported that he was "not used to them." David's assumption of these military props stands in tension with his speech to Goliath in 17:45–47.

evidence indicates that David's act of gathering five stones reflected his firm belief that God would deliver to him not only Goliath but also final victory over the entire nation of the Philistines, who, elsewhere in 1 Samuel, are referred to as "the *five* cities [or 'lords']" (see 1 Sam. 6:4–5, 16–18). Thus David's act of grabbing the five stones is testimony to his confidence in God's power eventually to grant total and complete deliverance for God's people Israel through David his servant.

Whether this specific reading of 1 Samuel 17 is compelling or not, it serves to illustrate a reading of a passage in which two equally plausible, and somewhat different, interpretations might commend themselves. In their own way, both of them may be correct. The implied author may present both of these possibilities to the minds of readers. One could conclude from the passage that even the remarkable and ultimately effective faith of David can have elements of weakness. Someone else might conclude from the passage that even a stripling like David can have the kind of faith that generates expansive dreams of what God can do beyond the challenges of the present day. And each of them would be correct. Indeed, these two construals may complement each other: David's faith has aspects of both strength and weakness.

Like the principle of multivalence, demonstrated in the 1 Samuel 17 passage above, the principle of indeterminacy also supports the notion that passages may contain a range of plausible interpretations. The terms *determinate/ determinacy* and *indeterminate/indeterminacy* pertain to the fact that all passages have both a range of plausible meanings and boundaries or limits to their plausible meaning. No passage, understood in its context, can mean just anything; a passage that means anything means nothing. The recognition of *boundaries* of plausible interpretations points to the fact that all passages are determinate: they have determinacy. But within those boundaries is always some range of more specific plausible construals.[4] The recognition of a *range* of plausible interpretations points to the fact that all passages are somewhat indeterminate or have some indeterminacy.

All passages stand somewhere along what we call the *continuum of determinacy*:

◄───►
Determinate   Indeterminate

Determinate passages are those whose range of plausible interpretations is narrow:
[———]
Indeterminate passages are those whose range of plausible interpretations is broad:
[————————————————]

---

4. See Ricoeur, *Interpretation Theory*, where he discusses the "sense potential" of texts within certain boundaries. These boundaries are established by the "structure" of the text as well as by its style and syntax.

Even the most determinate passages have some range of plausible and accurate interpretations, although the range is narrow. And even the most indeterminate passages have firm boundaries, interpretations that are not correct, although the boundaries are relatively broad. Although some biblical passages stand at one extreme or the other, most passages function somewhere between these two poles. As Ricoeur declares: "Perhaps we should say that a text is a fine space of interpretations: there is not just one interpretation, but, on the other hand, there is not an infinite number of them. A text is a space of variations that has its own constraints; and in order to choose a different interpretation, we must always have better reasons."[5]

A number of factors are involved in considering the degree of determinacy/indeterminacy of passages.[6] For example, genre may play a role. Some genres lend themselves to relative indeterminacy (poetry, parable), while other genres tend to contain more determinate speech (logical discourse). It is beyond the purview of the present discussion to offer a full taxonomy of determinacy/indeterminacy. The purpose here is to alert readers to the existence both of boundaries and of range in the interpretation of any passage and to suggest that within the range of possible construals, subjective elements that readers bring to interpretation find expression. The personal experience of one reader, or the community out of which the reader comes, may cause one to embrace a particular possible interpretation within the range; the quite different personal experience of another reader, or the different community in which that reader participates, may cause one to embrace another possible interpretation. Ideally these various readers with their different interpretive predilections would converse with one another so that each could became aware of other possibilities within the range of plausible and correct interpretations and thereby come to a fuller understanding of the sense of the passage in its breadth. We now turn to the description of just such a dialogue.

Nature and Importance of Communal Study

Even as the study of the Bible ought to be individual, it also ought to be communal, giving attention to the community's role in interpretation in the

---

5. Paul Ricoeur, *A Ricoeur Reader: Reflection and Imagination*, ed. Mario J. Valdés (New York and London: Harvester Wheatsheaf, 1991), 496, quoted in Vanhoozer, *Is There a Meaning in This Text?* 436.

6. Eco (*Role of the Reader*) distinguishes between passages that are "closed," those passages whose meanings are more tightly prescribed, and passages that are "open," which allow the reader more of a participatory role in "creating" a meaning within the boundaries. Cf. Vanhoozer, *Is There a Meaning in This Text?* 139–40; Michael Fox, "The Uses of Indeterminacy," *Semeia* 71 (1995): 173–92; Charles H. Cosgrove, ed., *The Meanings We Choose: Hermeneutical Ethics, Indeterminacy, and the Conflict of Interpretations*, JSOTSup 411; The Bible in the Twenty-First Century Series 5 (London: T&T Clark, 2004).

same two spheres previously discussed under individual study: process and conclusions.

First, the study of the Bible should be communal in terms of the *process of study*. At the proper time comes dialogue with others regarding the meaning of the biblical texts, including both the sense of the text and its contemporary appropriation. Such dialogue is both direct, involving ongoing conversation with other persons, and indirect, involving consultation with what others, past and present, have said or written about the meaning of passages. As mentioned, the meaning of biblical passages is larger than the necessarily limited perspective of individual interpreters.[7] One's own interpretations can be broadened and indeed corrected through the insights of those whose background and experience are different from one's own. Moreover, the dynamic give-and-take of social interaction often leads readers to develop insights that were not explicitly mentioned by anyone else in the conversation but that come to them serendipitously as they are forced in the course of dialogue to process their perspective in relation to the perspectives of others.

Second, the study of the Bible should be communal in terms of the *conclusions drawn from study*. When one considers the "thick" character of the meaning and significance of the biblical text, the difficulty of interpreting biblical texts that arose in cultures quite different from our own and that speak of theological realities that are truly divine and transcendent, and the careful and complex literary expression employed by the biblical writers, one will recognize the importance of seeking insight from those who throughout history have committed their massive intellects and enormous amounts of energy to explaining the Bible. Thus consulting the interpretation of others, found primarily but not exclusively in commentaries, is essential in an inductive approach.

This consideration does not mean that we simply accept, on the basis of their own authority as scholars, what these persons say or write. Rather, we should take account of the history of interpretation in the sense that we critically relate our own conclusions to those of others who have studied the Bible over the centuries, judging all potential construals by examining the evidence of the text.

Here one should not conclude that such consultation should be limited to the formal study of the meaning of biblical texts as presented by scholars. In recent years a recognition has emerged that we can learn a great deal about the meaning of biblical passages by examining how these passages have been used in a broad range of forms, for example, in poetry, hymnody, liturgy, paintings, or fiction. The technical term for this kind of examination is *Wirkungsge-*

---

7. See Vanhoozer, *Is There a Meaning in This Text?* 39, where he discusses Francis Bacon's "idol of the cave" (individual prejudices) and "idol of the theatre" (community or tradition prejudices).

schichte, often translated as "the history of use," or "the history of effects," or "the history of response." It is actually a heuristic (discovery) process. A process of critically analyzing how the various ways a biblical passage has been employed can assist us in discovering aspects of the meaning of the text that otherwise might have remained hidden to us.[8]

We have seen, then, that inductive Bible study seeks a balance between individual and corporate study. Throughout the Western world at least since the Enlightenment, the emphasis has been upon the individual. But in the last thirty years, a reaction to this individual focus has resulted in an emphasis upon the communal. The Bible attends to both of these aspects, and inductive Bible study attempts to give each its due, as well as to consider the deep connection between them.

---

8. A number of the more recent commentaries take account of these insights from *Wirkungs-geschichte*; indeed, the German commentary series Evangelisch-katholischer Kommentar zum Neuen Testament intentionally emphasizes this approach. For an example from this series in translation, see Ulrich Luz, *Matthew: A Commentary*, vol. 1, *Matthew 1–7*, Hermeneia (Philadelphia: Fortress, 1989); idem, *Matthew: A Commentary*, vol. 2, *Matthew 8–20*, Hermeneia (Minneapolis: Fortress, 2005); idem, *Matthew: A Commentary*, vol. 3, *Matthew 21–28*, Hermeneia (Minneapolis: Fortress, 2005).

8

Compositional Book Study

The basic literary unit in the Bible is the biblical book. While some literary exceptions appear in the form of "nonunified books," such as possibly the book of Psalms[1] and the book of Zechariah,[2] or broader collections, such as the Pentateuch or the "Deuteronomic History,"[3] in the vast majority of

1. A significant recent movement, however, takes seriously the arrangement of the psalms within the book of Psalms and thus studies the Psalms as a unified (canonical) whole. See Childs, *Introduction to the Old Testament as Scripture*, 504–25; J. Clinton McCann Jr., *The Shape and Shaping of the Psalter*, JSOTSup 159 (Sheffield: JSOT Press, 1993); idem, *A Theological Introduction to the Book of Psalms* (Nashville: Abingdon, 1993), 25–50; James Luther Mays, *The Lord Reigns: A Theological Handbook to the Psalms* (Louisville: Westminster John Knox, 1994); idem, *Psalms*, IBC (Louisville: John Knox, 1994); idem, "The Place of the Torah Psalms in the Psalter," *JBL* 106 (1987): 3–12.

2. See, e.g., Carol L. Meyers and Eric M. Meyers, *Haggai, Zechariah 1–8*, AB (New York: Doubleday, 1987); idem, *Zechariah 9–14*, AB (New York: Doubleday, 1993); David L. Petersen, *Haggai and Zechariah 1–8*, OTL (Philadelphia: Westminster, 1984); idem, *Zechariah 9–14 and Malachi*, OTL (Louisville: Westminster John Knox, 1995).

3. Although the individual books of the Pentateuch and of the Deuteronomic history are somewhat distinct and can be, and often are, studied as separate entities, they do belong to a more or less continuous narrative of the larger collection. See Joseph Blenkinsopp, *The Pentateuch: An Introduction to the First Five Books of the Bible*, ABRL (New York: Doubleday, 1992); David J. A. Clines, *The Theme of the Pentateuch*, 2nd ed., JSOTSup 10 (Sheffield: JSOT Press, 1997); John H. Sailhamer, *The Pentateuch as Narrative: A Biblical-Theological Commentary* (Grand Rapids: Zondervan, 1992); Martin Noth, *The Deuteronomistic History*, JSOTSup 15 (Sheffield: JSOT Press, 1981); J. Gordon McConville, *Grace in the End: A Study in Deuteronomic Theology*, Studies in Old Testament Biblical Theology (Grand Rapids: Zondervan, 1993); Ter-

cases, the biblical book represents the fundamental unified literary entity in the Bible.

Importance of Book Study

This notion that the Bible is a collection of distinct books, each one manifesting its own perspective and purpose, is suggested even by the etymology of our English word *Bible*, which comes not from the Greek *ton biblion*, meaning "the book," but rather from *ta biblia*, "the books."[4] Moreover, the church recognized this multiple-book character of the Bible as it carried out its work of canonization. As the church struggled with what materials would be included within the canon of Scripture, it made its decision on the basis of books. The church did not deliberate, say, about whether what is now John 14 should be considered canonical over against the rest of the Gospel of John. They decided on the basis of including or excluding books in their entirety.[5]

The Bible itself, then, bears witness to the fact that the biblical writers produced and planned books. The literary context of any passage is ultimately the biblical book of which it is a part; thus during the process of biblical study serious attention must be given to examining the meaning of passages within their book contexts. In addition, students must attend to the meaning and message of books-as-wholes. As will be discussed later under the claim that the study of the Bible should be canonical, this insight that the Bible is essentially a collection of books has significant implications as well for a canonical reading or interpretation of the Bible.

Importance of Compositional Study

The study of the Bible ought also to be *compositional* study. This principle derives from the previous claim, namely, that the Bible is a collection of discrete books, and as such, individual passages must be interpreted in light of their literary context, which is to be understood finally as the context of the book-as-a-whole. When a writer produces a book, the writer creates, as it were, a textual world. Everything within the book relates, either directly or indirectly, to everything else within that book. Individual passages fit, wherever they are placed, within the program of the whole book. Yet books also

---

ence E. Fretheim, Lloyd R. Bailey Sr., and Victor P. Furnish, eds., *Deuteronomic History*, IBT (Nashville: Abingdon, 1983).

4. *Webster's Seventh New Collegiate Dictionary* (Springfield, MA: G. & C. Merriam Co., 1963), s.v. "Bible."

5. See, e.g., John Barton, *Holy Writings, Sacred Text: The Canon in Early Christianity* (Louisville: Westminster John Knox, 1997); F. F. Bruce, *The Canon of Scripture* (Downers Grove, IL: InterVarsity, 1988); Bruce M. Metzger, *The Canon of the New Testament: Its Origin, Development, and Significance* (Oxford: Clarendon, 1987).

typically contain within them discrete coherent units of various sizes. Thus individual passages must also be interpreted in light of their function within the division, section, or segment in which they stand.

The word *composition* comes from the Latin *com*, meaning "with, together," and *pono*, meaning "to place, to put." Thus *composition* means a putting or placing together and suggests the notion of connectedness or relationship. Words are placed in relation to other words to form sentences; sentences are placed in relation to other sentences to form paragraphs; paragraphs are placed in relation to other paragraphs to form segments; segments are placed in relation to other segments to form sections; sections are placed in relation to other sections to form divisions; and divisions are placed in relation to other divisions to form the book-as-a-whole. As W. W. White says, "Things hook and eye together."[6]

The word *compositional*[7] refers to the fact or reality of relationship, while the word *structure* refers to the specific ways things relate to one another in a given passage or book. The issue of structure involves, then, the question of how things within a literary unit relate to one another, how they are arranged.

In this chapter we have attempted to challenge two tendencies among students of the Bible. In the face of the tendency to limit the notion of context to the verses that immediately precede and follow a passage, we have insisted that context pertains to the entire book, and against the tendency to engage in "choppy" reading that construes passages in isolation from surrounding material, we have insisted that the meaning of an individual passage is fundamentally constituted by its relationship to other passages throughout the book.

6. W. W. White, unpublished papers, quoted in Eberhardt, *Bible in the Making of Ministers*, 145.

7. W. W. White's understanding of *compositional* was twofold. White held to a general compositional theory, saying that all things in the world cohere so that the study of all things in the world is bound together in a grand network of truth. One can enter this network of truth at any point and eventually, under ideal circumstances, encounter all truth in the world. Thus the study of the Bible leads to truth in all areas; and, conversely, truth in all other areas is relevant, either directly or indirectly, to the study of the Bible. However, White also adopted a specific compositional theory, saying that individual books of the Bible cohere; thus everything within a biblical book is related, directly or indirectly, to everything within that book (ibid.).

9

Canonical Study

Basis of Canonical Study

The word *Bible* itself connotes the assemblage of a number of individual books into a canonical collection—more specifically, the Jewish or Christian canonical collection. The study of the Bible must therefore take into account the fact that we are dealing not with an assortment of individual books that exist in virtual isolation but with books that come to us in the form of a body of literature. This requires that, at some level and in some sense, these books be read and understood in light of one another and in terms of their position and functioning within the canon-as-a-whole.

Moreover, the notion of *canon* involves a rule or norm. The canon of Scripture, then, points to the reality that the community of the Christian church has claimed that these books, read as a canonical collection, have normative authority within the Christian community. More specifically, the canonizing process involved the judgment of the church that God somehow reveals God's self and God's will through these writings in unique ways, with the result that taken together as a canonical whole, they function as a theological norm and as the means of Christian formation.[1] Bound up with the concept of canon, then, is the issue of the divine inspiration of these writings. An awareness of the Bible's role as canon requires that readers consider what these ecclesial

1. Wall, "Canonical Context and Canonical Conversations," 165, refers to their twofold function as "rule" and "sacrament." See esp. Barton, *Holy Writings, Sacred Text*; and Metzger, *Canon of the New Testament*, 251–93.

claims, implicit within the canonical collection, mean for the process of arriving at an understanding of the Bible, and how these ecclesial claims regarding the Bible's authority and inspiration should be assessed.

Significance of Canonical Study

These issues of canon, authority, and inspiration are extremely complex and have been, and continue to be, vigorously disputed. Engaging in a full examination of them at this stage in the present discussion is not possible. However, we must make two fundamental points regarding the significance of the canon for the study of the Bible.

First, the notion of the canon raises the issue of the relationship between the individual biblical books and the canon-as-a-whole. As previously mentioned, the basic literary unit of the Bible is the biblical book, and the canonizing process was book centered: decisions were made regarding the inclusion or exclusion of *books*. The fact that the canon involves the assemblage or bringing together of originally independent books, each of which has its own perspective, purpose, and message, suggests a dialectical relationship between the parts and the whole, between the message of individual books and the witness of the canon-as-a-whole.[2]

From one standpoint, the fact that the canon involves the inclusion of distinct books means, at least to some extent, that real diversity may exist among the various books within the canon. The perspective of one book is not necessarily that of another; therefore simply and uncritically reading the meaning or the message of one book into another is an illegitimate practice. The distinctive voice of each book must be heard on its own terms.[3]

From another standpoint, the fact that the church has collected these books with the conviction that they together bear witness to the revelation of the one God suggests, in the judgment of the community of faith at least, an underlying unity of thought and perspective among these books. Anyone engaged in the study of the Bible should not just examine these books as individual documents and leave the matter there; rather, one is required to explore how the message of one book relates to and might contribute to the message of the biblical canon-as-a-whole.

The Bible as canon, therefore, supports the reality of both unity and diversity among these books. To use a musical analogy, then: in the biblical canon we have not a simple melody but a harmony. Unity comes through

2. Trevor Hart, "Tradition, Authority, and a Christian Approach to the Bible as Scripture," in Green and Turner, *Between Two Horizons*, 201–2.

3. Wall, "Canonical Context and Canonical Conversations," 171, rightly emphasizes that a canonical reading begins with a "text-centered exegesis," concerned with the text's "original meaning."

diversity.[4] In the end, readers will decide whether they can accept this canonical understanding of the Bible and particularly this relationship of the
books of the Bible to one another. But this unity through diversity is at least
the claim that is implicitly put forward by the canonical assemblage, and
every reader, whether or not that reader is a member of the community of
faith, has the responsibility to examine this claim and to assess its viability
and legitimacy.

Second, the notion of canon raises the issue of the relationship between
the *human* author, whose voice is immediately encountered as one reads the
books of the Bible, and the *divine* author, the voice of God, who, according
to the church's canonical claim, speaks to the reader through the text of the
Bible. Again, a dialectical relationship seems to be present here.

On the one hand, no biblical book claims to have actually been written by
God. The implied author, the image of the author that the text causes the
reader to infer, is always human. The implied author, especially the implied
author of biblical narratives, may have a "God-like omniscience," presenting
information that presumably only God can know,[5] but even such authors as
these always refer to God in the third person and present God as a character
within their narratives, not as the author of the narratives themselves. These
indicators provide an implicit resistance to substituting the divine voice for
the human voice or to collapsing the human into the Divine.

On the other hand, as previously mentioned, the church at least has understood that its canonical decision reflects the claim that, in some sense,
God himself speaks through these texts. Insofar as one accepts this canonical perspective, one must say that in the Bible one is confronted by both
the human author and the voice of God. This dialectic is actually articulated within the New Testament itself. For example, 2 Peter 1:21, speaking
of the inspiration of the Old Testament Scriptures,[6] declares that "men
and women moved by the Holy Spirit spoke from God." We note that the
grammatical structure of this statement points both to human authorship
and to divine involvement. The basic assertion is found in the subject and
predicate: "men and women . . . spoke," indicating human authorship. But

4. Wall, ibid., 179–80, speaks also of a "conversation" between the various books of the
Bible. This conversation involves a "mutual criticism," which does not detract from the meaning
and witness of any one biblical book but serves to "thicken" the message of each. The notion
of a canonical conversation brings to mind the posthumously published study of NT theology
by George B. Caird, *New Testament Theology*, ed. L. D. Hurst (Oxford: Clarendon, 1994), in
which the various writers of the NT engage in a roundtable conversation.

5. Sternberg, *Poetics of Biblical Narrative*, 46–48, 89–99.

6. The wording of 2 Pet. 1:19–21 indicates that the OT Scriptures are primarily in view;
see especially the references to "the prophetic message" and "prophecy of scripture." However,
the suggestion of 2 Pet. 3:15–16 that Paul's epistles are part of Scripture raises the possibility
that the author of 2 Peter had in mind at least some of the documents that would later become
officially and formally a part of the NT canon.

divine involvement is also asserted through the subordinate clause, "moved by the Holy Spirit."

The operative question is exactly how we are to understand this relationship between human authorship and the divine voice. The issues involved are complex and cannot be developed here. We believe that the most satisfying explanation of the relationship, the explanation that best accounts for the evidence, is that God speaks through Scripture in the sense that *God, having worked mysteriously in and through human beings, makes use of their human words as these are found throughout the whole canon of Scripture in order effectively and uniquely to reveal himself and his will.* In other words, God in mysterious, various, and often recondite ways has evoked the human speech found in the Bible and takes up these human words in their dynamic relation throughout the whole canon of Scripture so as to cause them to function in a way that uniquely, reliably, and powerfully reveals the truth of himself, his purposes, and his world.

According to this view, the relationship between human words and the divine voice is *instrumental*: it involves God's using human words to accomplish his purposes.[7] It is *holistic*: God's voice is not identified finally with individual passages and books abstracted from the rest of the Bible and read in isolation from the rest of the canon; rather, God speaks through passages as they are set within their canonical context and understood within the whole flow of biblical revelation.[8] It is *paradoxical*: one can rightly embrace them as divine speech only while taking seriously the words of the Bible as human words and human communication, conditioned by the limitations of human existence, including the limitations of historical setting.

This view is, admittedly, a dynamically functional way of understanding what we take to be at least part of what is involved in the Bible's own conception of divine inspiration. We do not put forward this statement as though it contains all that might be said regarding the Bible's inspiration and divine authority. It does not seek to address, for example, the theological, metaphysical, existential, or psychological realities involved in God's inspiration of the human beings themselves as they wrote or spoke the communication that has become the content of the Bible, nor is it the final word on the subject.[9]

In the end, an inductive approach requires that one examine the evidence, especially the evidence of the biblical text itself, as the basis for one's understanding of the divine authority and inspiration of the Bible. The Bible itself—both through its claims and through its nature, through the phenomena

---

7. Wolterstorff, *Divine Discourse*, emphasizes (perhaps too exclusively) this instrumental understanding of inspiration.

8. Vanhoozer, *Is There a Meaning in This Text?* 264–65, 349.

9. We deal more specifically with certain aspects of divine inspiration while we use 2 Tim. 3:16–17 as the primary example of an inductive study of an individual passage; see parts 2–5, below.

of the text and perhaps also through its effects in the histories of individuals and communities—must be determinative in one's decision regarding what the authority and inspiration of the Bible mean.[10]

To sum up: Recognition of the canonical character of the Bible requires one to consider how the individual biblical books relate to one another and to assess the significance of the canonical theological claim that these books are uniquely authoritative and inspired.

---

10. G. C. Berkouwer, *Holy Scripture*, Studies in Dogmatics (Grand Rapids: Eerdmans, 1975).

10

Flexible Procedural Study

Principle of Flexibility

Although the nature of the readers and the reading process have many constants, no two readers are identical in the way they study and think. Readers vary in other ways as well, including their situations, their purposes, and their judgments. All of these considerations lead to the conclusion that method in Bible study should be flexible in the sense that one should make allowances for individual differences. One must be careful not to build rigidity into the process or to give the impression that there is only one way to study the Bible.

We emphasize this principle of flexibility because we realize that the discussion of specific steps in an inductive approach to Bible study, as offered in the remainder of the book, might give the impression that only one specific process qualifies as inductive Bible study. The corollary prospect might be that if students do not adopt every particular task presented, they are deficient in their hermeneutical practice.

We offer an explicit, specific procedure not because we are convinced that it is the only process or even that it is necessarily the best one for every student. We offer it because we have found that this kind of procedure has worked well for us, and most of our students over the years have testified that this kind of process has been effective in their own Bible study.

We present this procedure in a very structured and specific way because we have found that beginning students can best grasp the principles of inductive Bible study and initiate the process of putting these principles into practice if they have a rather straightforward model from which to work. But over time, students take the process that they learn in its specificity at the very beginning and adapt it to their own mental processes, time constraints, needs, and judgments. Students should ask themselves: Is this process, or this specific phase within the process, legitimate? Is it helpful? Can I introduce shortcuts that will make it more manageable and realistic for me without violating the integrity of an inductive approach to the study of the Bible?

Foundations, Characteristics, and Process

We have argued in our discussion of theoretical foundations for what we take to be essential: the notion that Bible study should be methodical, involving the principle of suitability, and inductive, involving the principle of the movement from evidence to inference. We have also presented a number of characteristics of Bible study, from transjective to flexible, that represent an attempt to apply the principles of suitability and induction to develop a list of distinguishing features of proper and effective Bible study. Thus these characteristics are presented as reflecting the nature of the Bible, the nature of the student, and the relationship between the Bible and the student—as we understand these realities. In the text that follows we suggest a specific process that builds on

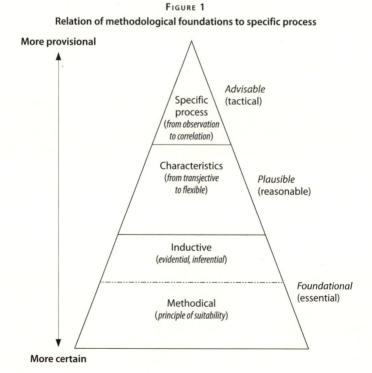

FIGURE 1
Relation of methodological foundations to specific process

the characteristics just described. Figure 1 illustrates how we understand the relationship between the foundations (methodical/inductive), the characteristics (from transjective to flexible), and the specific process presented in parts 2 through 5. All that is presented in this book is provisional and tentative, but it has an ascending *scale of provisionality* in that the foundations are relatively more certain than the characteristics, with the specific process being the most provisional or tentative.

The conclusion from this discussion of theoretical foundations is that the study of the Bible calls for an approach that is inductive, according to the description of induction given here. We maintain that *inductive Bible study* is a comprehensive, holistic study of the Bible that seeks to take into account every aspect of the existence of the biblical text and that is intentional in allowing the Bible in its final canonical shape to speak to us on its own terms. This process should thus lead to accurate, original, compelling, and profound interpretation and contemporary appropriation. As such, inductive Bible study has characteristics that are expressed in the process of study.

At this point we emphasize that although the inductive process will have certain constants, individual differences will be reflected in the precise way inductive Bible study is pursued. Throughout the following chapters, we will often say "the student should" or "the student must." We use this language for the sake of simplicity and direct expression. In all such instances, we mean, "in our opinion, the student should." We wish to maintain the tentative and hypothetical character of the process throughout.

Before moving on to examine one way in which this understanding of inductive Bible study might be made concrete in practice, we present this general outline as an overview and summary of the specific tentative process as set forth in the remainder of the book (with corresponding part numbers given in parentheses).

I. Observation (part 2)
   A. Survey the book-as-a-whole
      1. Identify the general materials of the book (biographical, ideological, historical, etc.).
      2. Locate the major units and subunits in the book and identify the main structural relationships operative in the book-as-a-whole.
      3. Ask a few interpretive questions based on each major structural relationship observed.
      4. Identify the key verses and strategic areas that provide insight into the book-as-a-whole.
      5. Identify higher-critical data.
      6. Note other major impressions relating to the book-as-a-whole.
   B. Survey individual sections or segments

1. Locate the major units and subunits within the section or segment and the main structural relationships operative in the section or segment-as-a-whole.
2. Ask a few interpretive questions based on each major structural relationship observed.
3. Identify the key verses or strategic areas that provide insight into the section or segment-as-a-whole.
4. Identify the literary form(s) employed in the section or segment.
5. Identify other major impressions.

C. Observe significant elements within individual paragraphs and verses, employing either detailed observation or detailed analysis of the passage, and ask detailed interpretive questions based upon these observations.

II. Interpretation (part 3)

A. Answer the most significant questions raised in the observation of paragraphs and verses
1. Identify the most significant questions asked based on importance, difficulty, and interests.
2. Note the types of evidence available for answering each interpretive question and employ this evidence to answer each question selected.

B. Integrate the answers to the questions in a progressive fashion so as to interpret the paragraph, next the segment, then the section, and ultimately the book-as-a-whole. This process may involve answering questions raised during the survey of sections, segments, and books.

III. Evaluation and appropriation (part 4)

A. Find the truths or principles that can legitimately be applied to contemporary times and places other than the original scriptural setting.

B. Relate these truths or principles to appropriate contemporary situations so as to inform your response to the contemporary issue or problem.

IV. Correlation (part 5)

A. Relate the book's theology to the teaching of other biblical materials by the same author.

B. Relate the book's theology to the New Testament-as-a-whole (or to the Old Testament-as-a-whole).

C. Relate the book's theology to the Bible-as-a-whole, thus developing a biblical theology.

Part 2

Observing and Asking

Because an inductive approach fundamentally entails the movement from evidential premises to inferences, students must become acquainted with the evidence, and this acquaintance is accomplished by means of observation. Observation is the act of regarding attentively (i.e., noticing, perceiving), of being alert. This action involves more than physical sight; it has to do with keen mental awareness. Through observation the mind encounters the primary data from which it draws conclusions.

Characteristics of Effective Observation

Effective observation has a number of essential characteristics that we wish to enumerate and discuss.

Perceptivity: Being Aware of What Is There

Probably the greatest observer in the history of literature is the fictional detective Sherlock Holmes. In the story *The Hound of the Baskervilles*, Sir Arthur Conan Doyle puts into the mouth of Sherlock Holmes these words: "The world is full of obvious things that nobody by any chance ever observes."[1] A blinding power of expectation is especially a problem when we try to observe

1. Arthur Conan Doyle, *The Complete Sherlock Holmes* (Garden City, NY: Doubleday, [1930?]), 683.

what is familiar to us. People have often noticed that children are in general the best observers because they have not yet learned what to expect.

This experience of the dulling effect of expecting the familiar led James Denney, the great Scottish theologian of the turn of the twentieth century, to make the following stark reflections:

> Does it ever occur to you . . . that we read our Bibles too much, and that it might do us good to read none for a twelvemonth, just as it would do some people good if for as long they read nothing else? I have sometimes felt weary of the very look and sound of the New Testament; the words are so familiar that I can read without catching any meaning, and have to read again, far oftener than in another book, because I have *slid* a good bit unconsciously.[2]

Denney's description of the problem is accurate, but his tongue-in-cheek solution is hardly viable. The appropriate response is to try to read the text as though we were reading it for the first time. This exercise involves an act of imagination that we can never perform perfectly but that is helpful insofar as we can manage it. At least we can develop the discipline of becoming aware of our lapses into the dullness of expectation and check such lapses by intentionally pausing to reflect on the wording of the text with a view toward seeing new things in familiar words and passages.

Exactness: Seeing Precisely What Is There

Precision is the key to accuracy, penetration, and depth. General or superficial observation will almost always result in superficial and even erroneous interpretation. One of the primary ways in which one can nurture exactness and precision in observation is to give specific labels to what one observes. Indeed, one is more likely to observe the various elements present in the text if one has labels or categories at hand. One psychological principle says that we tend to be oblivious to realities for which we have no labeled categories or elements. Thus George B. Caird states:

> Even our capacity for observation is closely related to the availability of names for what we perceive. We do not accurately observe anything to the point of distinguishing it from all similar objects until we can give it a name of its own. It has been remarked that classical Hebrew is deficient in words for colour, and there can be little doubt that this betokens a corresponding deficiency in discrimination, at least on the part of those who wrote the books of the Old Testament, probably also among the population at large.[3]

2. James Moffatt, ed., *Letters of Principal James Denney to His Family and Friends* (London: Hodder & Stoughton, [1922?]), 81, emphasis original.

3. G. B. Caird, *The Language and Imagery of the Bible* (Philadelphia: Westminster, 1980), 12–13.

In other words, because the Hebrew language had few words for specific colors, the ancient Hebrews were largely color-blind, unable consciously to differentiate clearly between colors. Whether or not one accepts Caird's assessment of the color consciousness of the ancient Hebrews, his point stands as an effective illustration of the principle that categories are important for exact observation.

The importance of categories for exact observation has led us to give names in aiding precise observation. Thus we give extended attention to the discussion of various categories and emphasize the labeling of these categories in the observation phase. Of course, one always faces the danger of forcing data into a Procrustean bed of ready-made categories. In other words, readers may be tempted to make use of categories simply because they have them at hand. Therefore students must be on guard to let the text speak for itself and to make use of these categories only when such use is justified by the data of the text. Silence is better than assigning incorrect or dubious categories to observed data.

Persistence: Continuing to Look for More That Is There

The biblical text tends to be "thick": it contains depth and even layers of communicative sense. Therefore one should never believe that once one has observed a passage, even if with great care, then the passage has nothing else to offer the observer.

Those who taught inductive Bible study in earlier years would typically refer their students to the story titled, "The Student, the Fish, and Agassiz," by the Student. This story recounts the experience of Samuel H. Scudder when, as a beginning student at Harvard, he first met the great naturalist Louis Agassiz.[4]

In short, the story is as follows: When the student first met the great botanist, Agassiz simply handed the new student a fish and instructed him to take a pencil and record his observations. At this point Agassiz promptly left. Over the next three days, Agassiz returned only three or four times, on each occasion just briefly, to ask Scudder what he had observed from the fish itself. Although rather soon Scudder considered that he had observed all he could possibly see, his isolation and his instruction from Agassiz forced him to continue to observe. He was amazed at how the number of significant observations grew every day. Indeed, only on the third day did he observe some of the most important features of the animal. Scudder records, "And so, for three long days, he placed that fish before my eyes, forbidding me to look at anything else, or to use any artificial aid. 'Look, look, look,' was his repeated injunction."

4. So important was this story to the teaching of inductive Bible study over the years, and so illuminating regarding the importance of firsthand observation, that we have included it in its entirety on our website (www.inductivebiblicalstudy.com).

Impartiality: Seeing What Is Truly There

Being completely free of presuppositions or being entirely impartial is unattainable; therefore students should do all possible to be aware of their prejudices in reading the text, with a view toward exposing the prejudices to the evidence from the text. Partiality can cause readers unconsciously to read elements "into the text" and thus observe things that are not really there. Partiality can also blind readers to elements that are present in the text. A helpful process is to identify one's prejudices explicitly, to name the things that one expects to find, hopes to find, or is afraid to find. After identifying these prejudices, one should compensate for them by intentionally being aware of, and perhaps even looking for, the elements that one hopes not to find in books or passages. One should engage in constant self-criticism by assessing the viability of observations that reflect what one hopes to find in books or passages.

Levels of Observation

We have tried to emphasize that an inductive approach requires the process of study to reflect the nature of what is being studied. We have seen that the basic literary unit of the Bible is the biblical book and that individual books are themselves comprised of a number of coherent units of various sizes. As such, observation should attend both to the book-as-a-whole and to the larger and smaller units one finds within the book. Figure 2 illustrates the three levels of observation entailed in the inductive approach.

FIGURE 2
Three levels of observation

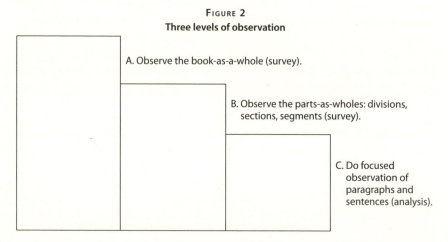

A. Observe the book-as-a-whole (survey).

B. Observe the parts-as-wholes: divisions, sections, segments (survey).

C. Do focused observation of paragraphs and sentences (analysis).

Each of these levels of observation will be discussed in the following chapters. Chapter 11 will treat the survey of the book; chapter 12 will deal with the survey of extended portions within the book; and chapter 13 will describe focused observation of individual details.

11

Survey of Books-as-Wholes

Basis of Book Survey

The study of books-as-wholes arises, first, from the literary principle that the book is the basic literary unit of the Bible. As previously mentioned, some exceptions appear in terms of nonunified books (e.g., Psalms, Zechariah). Nevertheless, the point stands that typically biblical writers produces books. They did not write bits and pieces (sentences and paragraphs here and there) and haphazardly slap them together. Every evidence indicates that the biblical writers planned books. They carefully determined what to include and how to arrange the material they included. Thus, when one surveys the whole book, one begins with the literary product as the writer that we encounter in the text, the implied author, conceived it. We begin where the writer did. We begin by getting a sense of what the writer set out to do.

The second reason for beginning with the survey of the book-as-a-whole has to do with the contextual principle. As we shall see in part 3, the most important factor in interpretation is context, especially literary context: the setting of individual passages within the book of which they are a part. When one tries to interpret a passage, one will need to have some sense of the literary "neighborhood" that surrounds the passage and that is significant for determining the meaning of the passage. In other words, interpretation of passages assumes familiarity with the literary context, which includes not just the verses that immediately precede or follow but also the entire book. Through the survey of the book, one gains such familiarity and thus equips oneself for the task of interpretation.

The third basis for beginning with book survey is the procedural principle that for most students it is advantageous to gain a sense of the entire book before moving to an examination of the details. To be sure, two broad procedures are possible for survey. The first is to begin with the details and then, through a process of synthesis and integration, move to construct some sense of the structure of larger units. This procedure is effective for many students in the observation of smaller passages (e.g., segments or perhaps even paragraphs). Some students will find this procedure the most effective for doing book survey. They first immerse themselves in the minutiae of the book and then develop a sense of the broad structure and general nature of the book-as-a-whole.

However, in our experience, by far the majority of students will find the second possible procedure more effective: beginning with a sense of the broad or general movement of the book and subsequently focusing on the details of the text. In other words, most students do better when they get a bird's-eye view before getting a "worm's-eye view." Most readers are drawn to details and can observe details much more easily than they can see the major dynamics of broad units, such as the biblical book. Those who begin by focusing upon details quite often have great difficulty in transcending the details in such a way as to see the whole. Thus most students will find that if they are ever to grasp a sense of the whole, they will do so by beginning with a focus on the broad overarching movement of the book and the book's major features. Most students move more easily and effectively from observing wholes to observing parts than they move from observing parts to observing wholes. Those who try the latter will frequently become lost in the details and not be able (to use a popular expression) to see the forest for the trees.

Seeing wholes is a difficult mental exercise. One must beware, most of all, not to become bogged down in details at the point of book survey. To do so would be *survey suicide*. We cannot focus on two things at the same time—either our attention will be focused on details, in which case seeing the broad overarching movements in the book-as-a-whole will be impossible, or our attention will be focused on the broad movement of the book, in which case we will be less aware of the individual details. Those who have experience in photography will understand this phenomenon. When taking a picture of a tree, for example, one must decide to focus the lens either on the tree as a whole or on an individual leaf. The first decision results in a picture where the tree will be clear and distinct while the individual leaves appear grainy and unclear. The second picture has clear and distinct leaves, but the tree as a whole appears grainy and unclear.

But not only is seeing wholes difficult for persons in general; it is also particularly difficult for those of us who are products of the contemporary Western educational system. Most of our education is geared toward examining parts rather than wholes. Analysis is emphasized at the expense of synthesis. Those in the current educational system are especially inclined to think that understanding, at any level, involves knowing all the details. We have a tendency to focus on details at the expense of seeing the whole.

The conclusion here is that we should be intentional in effectively pursuing the goal of observing the book-as-a-whole, and for the majority of students this goal will be most effectively realized by *beginning* with book survey. The importance of seeing the whole before analyzing the parts is illustrated by the experience of Robert Traina at his arrival in New York City as a student at The Biblical Seminary. He was met at Grand Central Station by a fellow student who walked him to the seminary. The student, trying to orient Traina to the city, pointed out individual landmarks and other pertinent spots along the way. But not until Traina went to the observation deck of the Empire State Building was he able to understand fully where these various sites were located and how they were related to each other.

Character of Book Survey

Book survey has a *broad* versus a *narrow* focus. Given the fact that book survey involves seeing the whole and taking note of general or broad features of the book, students who pursue book survey should be careful to read the book in such a way as to avoid a counterproductive obsession with details. Most students find it helpful to read through the book at several sittings as rapidly as possible, as they force themselves to keep moving through the reading process. They have two general possibilities here: (1) rapid word-for-word reading, or (2) scanning or skimming. The latter seems to work best when readers are surveying longer books or when readers find themselves struggling against becoming bogged down in details.

Ideally in book survey, students see the general features and take note of the broad overarching movement of the book while also being aware of significant details. This ideal can be realized, or at least approximated, only by reading through the book quickly many times. G. Campbell Morgan, the prominent biblical expositor whose ministry spanned the first half of the twentieth century, said that he typically read through the book at least forty or fifty times.[1] Most students will not have the opportunity for such multiple readings and must settle with the number of readings they can manage.

Although one should read through the book as many times as possible and should give all the time necessary for adequate book survey, one must recognize that the survey of the book does not exist as an end in itself but is designed to serve as the basis for later stages of study, especially interpretation. As such, one should limit one's time for book survey so as to give adequate attention to subsequent stages of study. In other words, one should not spend all of one's time on the beginning stages of study, such as book survey, with

---

1. Morgan, *Study and Teaching of the English Bible*, 37.

the result that one neglects the later stages. If one does have the opportunity to read through a book fifty times, one should by all means take advantage of this opportunity. But some students have a tendency to believe that they must do everything perfectly, no matter how much time it takes and regardless of whether they have the hours to manage it. This attitude is unrealistic and may even become paralyzing. Limiting one's time will result in reducing the likelihood of becoming bogged down in details while increasing the tendency to use the time one has more efficiently.

Book survey is *observational* versus *interpretive*. The purpose is not to arrive at conclusions regarding the meaning of passages throughout the book, or even the meaning of the book-as-a-whole, but rather to gain some sense as to the things that are present in the book and how they are arranged within the book. Of course, *pure observation* does not exist, for all observations, especially specific and descriptive ones, involve the construing of basic sense, which is minimal interpretation. Reading itself is an interpretive process, a process of making sense. But the goal of book survey is to gain a basic sense of what is here and how things are arranged rather than to identify the specific meaning of things at this stage. One should be careful, then, not to engage in unnecessary interpretation at the point of book survey, for that would require adopting groundless assumptions.

But because observation always involves some element of interpretation, even before one has specifically and intentionally pursued the process of interpretation, the observational project of book survey is *tentative* versus *final*. Observations made in book survey will often implicitly depend upon our construal of the meaning of various features throughout the book, construals that may turn out to be wrong. This provisional character of book survey is simply a part of the necessarily tentative nature of observation; it cannot be avoided. Readers should acknowledge, then, the tentative character of their observations and realize (to quote one of our former students) that in book survey it is "alright to be wrong," to make observations that may be justified at the point of book survey but will be subject to correction at later stages of study. In fact, the whole process of inductive Bible study is self-correcting. Later stages of study will correct or confirm what we do in the earlier stages.

While executing book survey has no absolutely right or wrong specific procedure, we have found the following phases effective in addressing the major issues involved in the survey of the book-as-a-whole:

1. Identifying the *general materials* of the book
2. Describing the *structure* of the book
3. Raising interpretive *questions* regarding the structural features of the book
4. Locating *key passages/strategic areas* in the book

5. Identifying *higher-critical data* within the book
6. Noting *other major impressions* relative to the book

We go on now to examine each of these phases.

Identifying General Materials

Two primary elements are involved in any unified entity: substance and arrangement of the substance, or worded somewhat differently, material and structure (the way the material is put together). Later we shall deal with structure or the arrangement of the material. Here we describe how students may handle the material content of the book by posing and (tentatively) answering the question: What is the primary emphasis of the content of this book? We have found five major possible answers to this question.

First, some books present *persons* as the primary concern of their content. In this case we say that the general materials are *biographical*. This term is not used here to suggest anything regarding the genre of the book (that it is in the form of a biography) but only to point to the primary concern of the book's content.

The book of Genesis is an example of biographical general materials, for the book moves along according to the presentation of a series of protagonists, each of whom is paired with a foil, who serves to highlight the features of the protagonist by way of contrast. Thus chapter 4 presents Abel along with his foil, Cain. Chapters 6 through 10 present Noah along with the foil of "his generation" (6:9). Chapters 11 through 26 present Abraham along with his foil, his nephew Lot; and Isaac with his foil, his half-brother Ishmael. Chapters 27 through 36 present Jacob with his foil, Esau; and chapters 37 through 50 present Joseph with his foil, his brothers.

The book of 1 Samuel offers another example of biographical general materials. The book is concerned with the reversal of fortunes of two pairs of persons, as illustrated in figure 3.

Figure 3
Biographical general materials in 1 Samuel

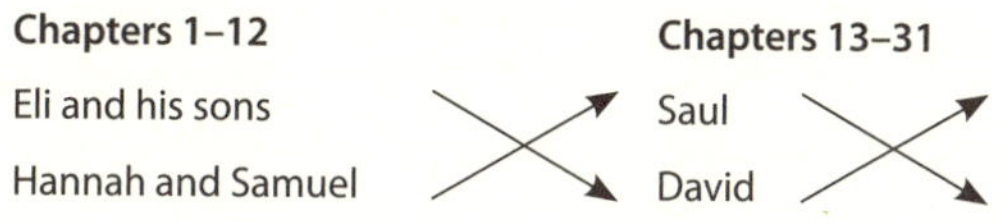

Chapters 1–12		Chapters 13–31
Eli and his sons		Saul
Hannah and Samuel		David

Second, some books have as the primary concern of their content the presentation of *events*, in which case we label the general materials *historical*. Again, this designation says nothing regarding the genre of the book. We are not necessarily indicating that the book is in the form of a history, nor are we making any claim regarding the historical accuracy or inaccuracy of the book. We are simply suggesting that the book is principally concerned with events. The book of Joel offers an example of historical general materials insofar as the book is primarily concerned with events surrounding the day of the Lord (e.g., 1:15; 2:1, 11, 31; 3:14; cf. 2:2; 3:1). Of course, other elements in addition to historical concerns are represented in the book of Joel, as are features other than the concern for persons in Genesis or 1 Samuel. As we will emphasize, the identification of general materials pointing to a concern as primary does not suggest that this feature is the only significant one within the book. In fact, most books will contain more than one of these features. The purpose of the identification of general materials, however, is to try to identify the *one primary concern* of the book-as-a-whole.

Third, the content of other books centers on the *chronological time line*, and we say that these books have *chronological* general materials. The Gospel of John is an example of chronological general materials because from beginning to end the Gospel is concerned with the "hour" of Jesus's death.[2] This *hour* comprises the whole of chapters 13–21; indeed, chapters 2–12 present a consistent time line that moves from one Jewish feast to the next, toward the hour of Jesus's death in the following chapters. Even the presentation of Jesus is largely dependent on where he is on the time line. Thus, for example, Jesus declares that he is the "light of the world" (8:12) precisely at the Feast of Tabernacles (7:2), otherwise known as the Feast of Lights because via a multitude of torches and candles the feast celebrated[3] the wilderness wanderings, when God led the people by pillar of fire (Exod. 13:21). When Jesus is at the Passover, he declares himself to be "the bread of life" (John 6:35). In other words, the very presentation of Jesus in John's Gospel seems to be subordinate to the point where he is on the time line. Thus, although the Gospel of John may seem at first blush to be biographical in its general materials, it might actually be chronological.

Fourth, still other books, in terms of their content, emphasize *geographical places or geographical progression*. These books have *geographical* general materials. The book of Joshua offers an excellent example because its content centers on the movement of the people of Israel from Transjordan (east of the Jordan River) to the land of Canaan, and recounts the people's progressive conquest and distribution of the land. The book of Joshua has a number of

2. John 2:4; 7:30; 8:20; 12:23, 27; 13:1; 16:21, 32; 17:1; cf. 4:21, 23; 16:25; 19:27.
3. See, e.g., C. K. Barrett, *The Gospel according to St. John*, 2nd ed. (Philadelphia: Westminster, 1978), 335. At the Feast of Tabernacles, a procession was made to the pool of Siloam, to draw water that was then poured out as a libation of thanksgiving to God. This may relate to Jesus's declaration in 7:37b–38: "Let anyone who is thirsty come to me, and let the one who believes in me drink. As the scripture has said, 'Out of the believer's heart shall flow rivers of living water.'" See Geoffrey W. Bromiley, ed., *The International Standard Bible Encyclopedia*, rev. ed. (Grand Rapids: Eerdmans, 1979–88), 1:535, s.v. "Booths, Feast of."

other significant features, including the person of Joshua himself; yet if one asks oneself whether in the book of Joshua the land has significance because of the person of Joshua or whether Joshua has significance because of the role he plays in relation to the land, one would be forced to conclude that the land is the primary thing. Joshua has the significance he does within the program of this book because of the role he plays in the conquest and distribution of *the land*. Thus the general materials are geographical rather than biographical. Indeed, posing just that kind of question is helpful in determining what is (and is not) the primary concern of the content in a given book.

The book of Acts offers another example of geographical general materials. Scholars have often noted that Acts 1:8 may be a virtual table of contents for the book of Acts: "But you will receive power when the Holy Spirit has come upon you; and you will be my witnesses in Jerusalem [chaps. 2–7], in all Judea and Samaria [chaps. 8–12], and to the ends of the earth [chaps. 13–28]." Thus Luke orients this book to the geographical expansion of the gospel from the beginning and carries out this geographical emphasis throughout the remainder of the book of Acts. Indeed, the primary concern with geographical content ("geographical general materials") explains why the book ends where it does.

Over the years many readers of the book of Acts have found its conclusion somewhat strange: Luke ends with Paul under house arrest in Rome, awaiting his appeal before Caesar. Some scholars argue that Luke certainly could not have wished to end his book in this way, leaving the reader hanging regarding what would happen to Paul. Therefore some suggest that Luke may have died before he had opportunity to finish the project; others have opined that the book has been mutilated so that the end of it has been torn away; and still others have speculated that Luke wished to write a third volume (beyond the Gospel of Luke and the book of Acts), in which he planned to round off the story.[4]

All of these suggestions presuppose that Luke was primarily interested in the portrait of Paul, which would be true if the book were biographical in its general materials. But given the fact that the book is geographical in its primary material emphasis, Luke would wish to conclude the book as he does with Paul in Rome, able to bear witness to the gospel in that most significant place, in a relatively unhindered fashion, while he waits to fulfill his appeal to Caesar himself. Luke brings the book to a *geographical* culmination, not a biographical one. Again, if one asks whether, in the program of Acts, the geographical spread of the gospel has significance because of Paul or whether Paul

---

4. See Mark Allan Powell, *What Are They Saying about Acts?* (New York: Paulist Press, 1991); W. Ward Gasque, *A History of the Interpretation of the Acts of the Apostles* (Peabody, MA: Hendrickson, 1975); Bruce W. Winter and Andrew D. Clarke, eds., *The Book of Acts in Its First Century Setting*, vol. 2, *The Book of Acts in Its Ancient Literary Setting* (Grand Rapids: Eerdmans, 1993).

has significance because of his role in the geographical spread of the gospel, the answer is patent: Paul is subordinate to the primary material concern of the book of Acts: the geographical spread of the gospel.[5]

Finally, some books are characterized by a primary material concern with *ideas*. In such cases we say that the general materials are *ideological*. This characterization is clearly the case with all of the New Testament Epistles, such as Romans. It may also be true of the book of Job, where the primary concern of the book's content is not the person of Job himself but the ideological issue of the suffering of the (apparently) righteous.

The identification of general materials serves a number of purposes related to interpretation. For one thing, identifying general materials enables us to recognize the features in the book that tend to be most significant for interpretation. Ideological material, for example, points the eye toward logical connectives (e.g., "therefore," "for," "because") and the development of the argument, but biographical material will cause the readers, once they reach interpretation, to focus on issues of characterization (e.g., how are the major characters developed, and how are they related to one another?).

Moreover, the general material may form a frame of reference for later study. If the book is essentially biographical, one may choose to study the book in terms of its presentation of leading persons. However, if a book is geographical, in interpreting it one may pursue the significance of geographical places and progression. The book of Exodus, for example, may be judged to have geographical general materials. When one interprets this book in depth, one may discover that the land of Egypt is not simply a place, according to the thought structure of the book of Exodus, but also represents a *type of existence*, as does Mount Sinai.

Finally, in the next section ("Describing Structure") we shall note that the identification of general materials may have a direct bearing on the reader's understanding of the book's literary structure. These identified general materials may then affect that reader's ultimate interpretation of individual passages throughout the book, and even the reader's construal of the message of the book-as-a-whole.

One last word about general materials. Some may object to insisting that we identify only *one* type of general material for each biblical book as arbitrary and unnecessary. They would argue that more than one element is almost always present in a book; therefore they should identify all of the major features of the book to be more accurate (e.g., biographical/geographical). But if one identified two or three elements together as constituting the general materials, one would actually be indicating that the primary concern of the book's content is the

---

5. Luke truly has great interest in Paul and sees Paul as playing a special role in salvation history. But Luke presents that role primarily in terms of Paul's significance in the spreading of the gospel, both geographically and (related to this geographical expansion) ethnically.

dynamic interaction between these two types of material. While that kind of creative and dynamic conversation between elements within a book is sometimes found in modern literature, it seems to be absent in ancient literature. At least we have found no biblical examples. Thus students can identify two or three types of general materials in a given book, but they should be aware that they are thereby suggesting not simply that both features are present but that the book materially revolves around their interaction.

The importance of noting just one primary material concern of a biblical book has to do with the fact that the identification of general materials involves locating the center of the book's concern: the thing that gives the book its unity and coherence. For a book to have unity, it must revolve around one main thing. The identification of the general materials is an initial attempt to locate the material center of the book.[6]

Describing Structure

As previously mentioned, every holistic entity is comprised of material and structure, of stuff and the arrangement of stuff. This symbiotic relationship between material and structure is true, for example, of houses. A house has material: lumber, shingles, bricks, nails. But a house is more than a pile of

6. Some have found it helpful to identify, in addition to the general materials, the specific materials of the book. This process involves giving a title to each chapter whereby the contents of the chapter may be recalled by association. These titles should be (1) *observational* versus interpretive, reflecting the contents of the chapter rather than a particular interpretation of the chapter's contents (e.g., one should not label Ezek. 38, the chapter dealing with invasion by Gog, as "Russia invades from the North"); (2) *distinctive*, relatively unique, so that the title given to any one chapter cannot apply to any other chapter in the book; (3) *brief*, usually no more than one or two words; (4) *simple* rather than complex: chapters that seem to deal with several apparently disparate things should not be given a title that reflects a cumbersome attempt to get everything into the title itself but should mention one prominent element in the chapter, something that will bring to the reader's mind various things mentioned in the chapter; (5) *associative*, so that the title brings to mind the contents of the chapter; (6) *memorable*, easy to recall; and (7) *personal or individual* to the reader—that is, the title that works for the reader. Whatever is effective for the individual in bringing to mind the contents of the chapter is a good title. The identification of these titles will concentrate attention upon the chapter, and anything that captures the attention aids observation. Moreover, the titles allow readers to think through the contents of the book without recourse to the text, thereby enabling readers to make connections between elements within the book even when they do not have the biblical text open before them. Quite often insights regarding connections come to us serendipitously, not when we are staring at the page but when we are engaged in other activities and are simply thinking through the biblical book or ruminating on it. Finally, they provide a handle for content by way of association, so that at least by chapter we are able to identify where things are found within a book. They may help us to recall, for example, that the conversion of Cornelius is found in Acts 10, while Paul's speech before the synagogue at Antioch of Pisidia is found in Acts 13. These titles assume the chapter divisions in our Bibles, which are obviously not original to the text. But these chapters have now become "givens" for biblical reference.

lumber, shingles, bricks, and nails. It becomes a house only when these materials are arranged in a certain way. And the way they are arranged determines the character of the house, whether, say, the house is a Tudor or modern. But a house is more than form or structure; a blueprint is not a house. For a house to exist, it must have a dynamic connection between form, or structure, and material. In this case, what is true of houses is also true for books.

We have thus far noted what is involved in the identification of material. We now explore how the materials of a book are arranged. That exploration involves the description of structure. The structural analysis of biblical books has two major components: (1) the division of the book according to its linear development, and (2) the identification of major structural relationships operative in the book-as-a-whole. At this point we discuss the linear division of the book. We will then go on to describe structural relationships.

Determining Units within the Book

The *division of the book* involves identifying the main units and subunits. These units should be as broad as possible. We have already mentioned that a real danger in book survey is to become focused on details so that one is unable to see the broad overarching movement of a book. The tendency to focus upon details in book survey comes to expression, among other things, in prematurely breaking the book down into small units. Rather, the overarching themes covering usually larger areas of material should determine the major units. If one is ever going to identify the large units that exist in a book, it will most likely take place here at the point of surveying the book.

Although alerting students as to what to expect can be somewhat problematic, as a general rule they will find that most books have approximately three major units. Of course, one must avoid imposing a foreign unity upon the literature and allow books to have as many units as the material warrants. But if one finds that in a book survey one locates, say, ten major units, such a breakdown should give the reader pause and lead the reader to consider whether two or three of these units might be combined to form a larger one. The principle, then, is that *units and subunits should be as broad as the material allows.*

We have two ways of determining units within the book. The first involves *looking for major shifts of emphasis within the book.* As one reads (quickly) through the book, one should note points where the writer moves from a dominant concern with one issue or theme to another one.

At this stage two things should be kept in mind: (1) As already mentioned, units (and subunits) should be as broad as the material allows—one should look for the *major* shifts of emphasis in identifying the main units.[7] (2) One

---

7. These shifts often indicate that an element in one unit ceases to recur and that another element begins to be used recurrently. Thus the use of the structural relationship of recurrence provides a specific clue in identifying main units. Other relationships are sometimes used to

should remember that the substance, or material, of the book and the book's linear structure (the arrangement of material) have a profound relationship. One cannot ultimately separate form and substance. Therefore the major shifts of emphasis should correspond to the kind of general materials one identifies. Thus, for example, if one identifies the general materials as biographical, one would look for the major shifts of emphasis in the presentation of *persons*. On the other hand, if one identifies the general materials as geographical, one would expect the main units to reflect major shifts in the presentation of *geography*, or *geographical* progression. At first, readers might identify the general materials as, say, biographical, only to find that the book does not seem to break down naturally in terms of the presentations of persons. In such a case, readers will reconsider their choice of general materials and in the end might determine the general materials of the book based on what appear to be the most natural major shifts of emphasis.[8]

The different assessments of a book's linear structure are often demonstrably the result of implicit differences in judgments regarding the general materials of the book. In other words, differences in understanding the breakdown of a book often stem from varying decisions made implicitly about the general materials. And given that one's understanding of the linear structure of the book frequently affects one's understanding of the book's message, clearly a line may extend from the identification of general materials through the decision about the linear structure or breakdown of the book, and finally to the construal of the book's message or theology.[9]

---

indicate coherence of main units within a book, such as climax. Note, for example, how Peter's confession of Jesus in Mark 8:27–30 may point to the unity of 1:16–8:30. Of course, one would only identify these relationships as major relationships in the survey of the book if they controlled more than half of the material in the entire book.

8. This scenario is a fine example of the self-correcting nature of the process.

9. This phenomenon is clearly seen, for example, in the history of examination into the structure of the Gospel of Matthew. Benjamin Wisner Bacon—in "The 'Five Books' of Matthew against the Jews," *Expositor* 15 (1918): 56–66; and *Studies in Matthew* (New York: Henry Holt, 1930), 80–90—worked with the implicit assumption that the contents of the Gospel of Matthew are primarily concerned with presenting ideas, or teachings, that Matthew delivers to his audience through the mouth of Jesus; hence the general materials are ideological. Consequently, Bacon focuses his outline upon the shifts in the presentation of ideas as found in the teachings of Jesus throughout the book. The result is an understanding of Matthean structure that deemphasizes the story of Jesus and that highlights the blocks of teaching found throughout the Gospel. Thus Bacon relegates the birth and infancy narratives (chaps. 1–2) and the passion and resurrection narratives (chaps. 26–28) to the subordinate status of "prologue" and "epilogue," and he divides the body of the Gospel (chaps. 3–25) into "five books," each of which begins with a narrative and culminates with (the truly important) body of teaching. Bacon sees a parallel between these "five books of Jesus" and the "five books of Moses" in the Pentateuch and draws the conclusion, at least in part on the basis of his structural analysis, that Matthew presents Jesus as a teacher, and especially as a new Moses, who delivers a new law to his church.

By way of contrast, some scholars implicitly assume that the general materials of Matthew are geographical; they judge that the major breaks come at 4:12, where Jesus positions himself

FIGURE 4

Main units identified through major shifts of emphasis

Major emphasis 1	Major emphasis 2	Major emphasis 3

| 1:1------------------------3:8 | 3:9------------------------------------10:20 | 11:1--------------------14:18 |

After identifying the main units on the basis of major shifts of emphasis (see fig. 4, which offers a hypothetical example), one should immediately examine each of these main units with a view toward identifying the major shifts of emphasis within each unit. The resulting divisions within the main units are the book's *subunits*.[10] Figure 5 illustrates (again, with a hypothetical example) the process of identifying subunits on the basis of shifts of emphasis within each main unit.

Thus far we have seen that one way to determine the main units and subunits of the book is to ascertain where the major shifts of emphasis occur. The

in Galilee; at 15:21, where he moves outside Galilee; at 19:1, where he begins his journey to Jerusalem; and at 21:1, where he arrives in Jerusalem. For them, Matthew presents Jesus primarily as the Christ, who fulfills his messianic destiny by traveling to Jerusalem, the heart of Judaism, where he will suffer at the hands of the Jews; they understand the First Gospel to be a Christian apologetic against Judaism. See Willoughby C. Allen and L. W. Grensted, *Introduction to the Books of the New Testament*, 3rd ed. (Edinburgh: T&T Clark, 1929), 23; cf. H. Conzelmann and A. Lindemann, *Arbeitsbuch zum Neuen Testament* (Tübingen: Mohr, 1975), 251.

But Jack Dean Kingsbury, *Matthew: Structure, Christology, Kingdom* (Philadelphia: Fortress, 1975), 1–39, judges that the general content of this Gospel focuses upon the person of Jesus, thus identifying biographical general materials, which leads him to divide the book according to shifts in the presentation of Jesus at 4:17 and 16:21; in his judgment, the three main units each culminate with the claim that Jesus is the Son of God. Thus Kingsbury understands Matthew's Gospel to present a Son of God Christology, which emphasizes the presence of God with his people through the person of God's Son, who through his life, ministry, and passion and resurrection is the agent of God's salvation for his people. See David R. Bauer, *The Structure of Matthew's Gospel: A Study in Literary Design*, JSOTSup 31, BLS 15 (Sheffield: Almond, 1988), 21–55.

10. The subunits deal with the division of *discrete portions* of the book and not the book-as-a-whole; therefore, these subunits will not necessarily correspond to the general materials of the book, as was the case with the identification of the main units.

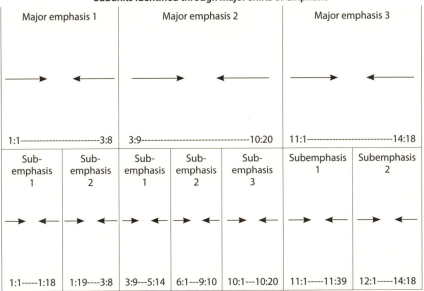

FIGURE 5
Subunits identified through major shifts of emphasis

second way to determine the main units is to note *implications from major structural relationships*. These relationships are described below, but at this point we need to note that some of the major relationships one identifies in the book may have direct bearing upon the book's breakdown. If, for example, a book is structured according to causation (i.e., the movement from cause to effect), it will have a major break between the presentation of the cause and the presentation of the effect. Or if the book is structured according to particularization (i.e., the movement from general to particular), one should expect a major break between the presentation of the general and the presentation of the particulars (see fig. 6).

These two means for identifying main units work together and in tandem to reinforce one another. Considering major shifts of emphasis will never result in one understanding of main units while considering implications from major structural relationships results in a different understanding. Rather, these two considerations will reinforce one another and lead to a common conclusion regarding the book's breakdown. In fact, sometimes one will identify the main units on the basis of major shifts in emphasis and then go ahead to ascertain what structural relationship may exist between the main units. At other times one will first identify the major structural relationships and then proceed to locate the main units on the basis of the major relationship(s) identified. Whether one first sees the major relationships and later locates main units or first identifies the main units and later

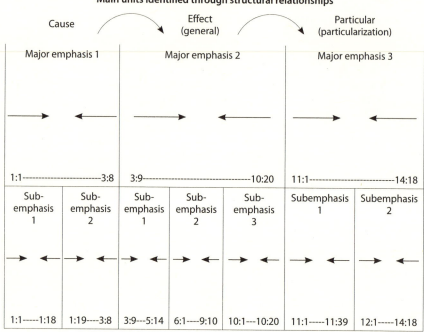

FIGURE 6

Main units identified through structural relationships

identifies major relationships between the main units depends on the student and perhaps even on the day.

Everything done in observation, including the tasks performed in the survey of the book, exists for the sake of interpretation and will thus be used intentionally when we reach the stage of interpretation. Identifying the main units and subunits of the book may aid interpretation in a number of ways.

First, identifying units and subunits aids in developing a sense of the flow or movement of the book. Writers frequently plan the relative placement of elements within their books in order to communicate meaning to the reader. Therefore what comes first is often important to note, in addition to what follows second and what the writer includes last of all. Thus a number of recent literary theorists describe the significance of "primacy" and "recency" in the reading process for construing the sense of the text.[11]

Incidentally, this goal of obtaining a sense of the flow or movement of the book suggests that it is helpful to present the book's breakdown into its main units and subunits in the form of a chart in which descriptive titles are given to each unit. Figure 7 gives an example from the book of Joel.

11. Meir Sternberg, *Expositional Modes and Temporal Ordering in Fiction* (Baltimore: Johns Hopkins University Press, 1978), 102–4. See also Iser, *Implied Reader*; idem, *Act of Reading*.

FIGURE 7

Main units and subunits in the book of Joel

General heading	I. The day of the Lord reflected in present historical events in Judah and Jerusalem 1:2--2:27				II. The day of the Lord as future cosmic judgment and salvation 2:28----------------------3:21	
	A. Devastation of Judah and Jerusalem (pointing to the day of the Lord), with consequent call to repentance 1:2-------------------------------------2:17			B. Deliverance of Judah and Jerusalem from devastation of locusts and drought	A. Deliverance and blessing for the righteous (repenting) remnant of Judah	B. Vindication of righteous Judah/ Jerusalem in the midst of judgment upon the wicked and exploitive nations
	1. Ruination of Judah and Jerusalem 1:2---------------------2:11		2. Consequent call to return to the Lord			
	a. Call to lamentation	b. Call to alarm				
1:1	1:2----1:20	2:1----2:11	2:12---2:17	2:18--------2:27	2:28--------2:32	3:1--------3:21

Identifying the breakdown of main units and subunits will also help us to locate the dominant themes or issues that control major blocks of material. In the example from the book of Joel, one will see that throughout the book Joel is concerned with the day of the Lord, but according to two major aspects: the day of the Lord reflected in present-historical events in Judah and Jerusalem, and the day of the Lord as future cosmic judgment and salvation. This consideration of what the writer has chosen to include is known as *qualitative selectivity*; it causes readers to ask themselves why a writer has selected these issues for discussion and development in the specific ways in which he has. For a fuller discussion of selectivity, see appendix C.

Furthermore, identifying the major divisions will help us to ascertain the relative amount of space given to various themes or issues. In the case of Joel, one notes that the book gives much more space (or we might say, more extended attention)[12] to the day of the Lord reflected in present-historical events in Judah and Jerusalem than it does to the day of the Lord as a future cosmic event. This consideration of the amount of space or attention given to one element over against others involves *quantitative selectivity* and can prompt readers to ask themselves why a writer has given more space or attention to one feature over against another.

12. We are aware of the recent and appropriate emphasis on the orality of ancient literature: ancient texts were typically read *aloud* in groups, and even individual reading was typically done orally (see, e.g., Acts 8:30). One could, therefore, substitute "amount of space" with "amount of time." But the importance of selectivity stands, whether one wishes to describe it in spatial or temporal terms.

Likewise, identifying the breakdown within a book will enable us to begin to discern where a given passage fits in the scheme of the book. Often *where* a passage is located within the movement of the book is significant for its interpretation. In the book of Joel, for example, one notes that the deliverance of Judah and Jerusalem from the devastation of locusts and drought (2:18–27) comes immediately after the call to return to the Lord (2:12–17), and immediately before Joel's description of the day of the Lord as future cosmic judgment and salvation (2:28–3:21). The very meaning of that passage is significantly informed by this positioning.

Finally, identifying units and subunits will enable us to note *turning points* in the book: passages that are often significant for discerning the message of the book. Frequently these most significant passages come at transition points where one main unit or even a significant subunit ends and the next begins. Again, to cite the example from Joel, chapter 2:12–17 (consequent call to return to the Lord) may well serve as a significant turning point because it marks the transition from the devastation of Judah and Jerusalem (1:2–2:17) to the deliverance of Judah and Jerusalem from the devastation of locusts and drought (2:18–27). Then 2:28–32 is possibly another significant turning point because it marks the transition from the first main unit (1:2–2:27) to the second main unit (2:28–3:21).

Identifying Major Structural Relationships

The second component of the structure of the book, in addition to the main units and subunits, involves the major structural relationships operative in the book-as-a-whole. Main units and subunits have to do with linear arrangement of material, the movement of the book according to major shifts of material emphasis. These structural relationships are *organizational systems* that pertain to the dynamic arrangement of various thoughts and themes throughout the book. As we shall see, the relationships about to be described are found in all cultures, all genres, all time periods, and all forms of art, not simply in literature. They are pervasive and foundational for communication. Communication seems to be impossible without these structural features; therefore a recognition of their presence and an analysis of their use is extremely helpful in accurate, specific, and penetrating interpretation. Again, readers should remember that in practice, separating form and material is ultimately impossible; the only way fully to understand the material that is presented is to examine seriously the form (i.e., structure) in which the material comes to us.

In book survey, students should identify only *major* relationships. Major relationships are comprehensive. They control all of the book or at least the bulk (more than half) of the book. The unfortunate tendency of becoming bogged down in details while doing book survey comes to expression not only in identifying units that are prematurely narrow but also in noting structural relationships that control only a small portion of the book and do not pertain to the macrostructure of the book-as-a-whole. For example, one of the structural relationships we will describe—namely, contrast—is found in Acts 4:32–5:11, where Luke emphasizes the difference between Barnabas on one hand, and Ananias and Sapphira on the other hand. The contrast here is real, yet it is not a *major* relationship but only a minor one because it controls only about eighteen verses in a book of twenty-eight chapters.

Structural relationships can be grouped according to three overarching categories: recurrence structures, semantic structures, and rhetorical structures.[13]

RECURRENCE

Recurrence is the repetition of the same or similar terms, phrases, or other elements,[14] which may involve motifs, concepts, persons, literary forms, or other structural relationships (see fig. 8 for a graphic representation). William Freedman insists that one of the major emphases of recent literary investigation is the attempt "to discern clusters or families of related words or phrases that, by virtue of their frequency and particular use, tell us something about the author's intentions, conscious or otherwise."[15]

FIGURE 8

Recurrence

ELEMENTS OF RECURRENCE

As a major structural relationship, recurrence involves three necessary elements. The first is *frequency*. The term *recurrence* means "reoccurrence," and central to this structural feature is frequency of occurrence. Although

---

13. The difference in function between these three types of relationships will be made clear in the discussion. In a sense, the specific designations "recurrence," "semantic," and "rhetorical" are somewhat arbitrary; other terms might be used to differentiate these types of structures. This terminology does reflect the language used by some practitioners of discourse analysis when describing these types of structural relationships. See esp. Joseph E. Grimes, *The Thread of Discourse*, Janua linguarum, series minor 207 (Berlin: Mouton, 1975), 207–10; Eugene A. Nida, *Exploring Semantic Structures*, International Library of General Linguistics 11 (Munich: Wilhelm Fink, 1975), 50–65; John Beekman, John Callow, and Michael Kopesec, *The Semantic Structure of Written Communication*, 5th ed. (Dallas: Summer Institute of Linguistics, 1981), 112–13.

14. William Freedman, "The Literary Motif: A Definition and Evaluation," *Novel* 4, no. 2 (1970–71): 123; James Muilenburg, "Form Criticism and Beyond," *JBL* 88 (1969): 16; Meyer Howard Abrams, *A Glossary of Literary Terms*, 4th ed. (New York: Holt, Rinehart & Winston, 1981), 111; R. Alan Culpepper, *Anatomy of the Fourth Gospel: A Study in Literary Design*, Foundations and Facets (Philadelphia: Fortress, 1983), 73, 87, 97, 128; Joanna Dewey, *Markan Public Debate: Literary Technique, Concentric Structure, and Theology in Mark 2:1–3:6*, SBLDS 48 (Chico, CA: Scholars Press, 1980), 32; Northrop Frye, *Anatomy of Criticism: Four Essays* (Princeton, NJ: Princeton University Press, 1957), 77; Sternberg, *Poetics of Biblical Narrative*, 92, 365–440.

15. Freedman, "Literary Motif," 123.

abundant frequency is normally involved in this structural relationship, a term or other element will not necessarily occur *many times* in order for recurrence to be present. Recurrence can occur as a major structural feature when a term or phrase is found only two or three times, if the second and third necessary elements (see below) are present.

The second element involved in recurrence as a major relationship is *distribution*. For example, a term may occur many times in one limited passage within a book but be absent outside of that passage. In such a case, the recurrence would lack sufficient distribution to qualify as a major relationship at the level of book structure. The phrase "by faith" occurs nineteen times in Hebrews 11 but does not appear in Hebrews outside of that chapter. Because it is not distributed throughout the bulk of the book (more than half of the book), it is not a major structural feature in the book-as-a-whole.

The third element that is necessary for recurrence to be present as a major structural relationship is *significance*. To take an extreme example, one finds a recurrence of the conjunction *and* within the book of Joshua, but it is a basic and weak conjunction used to link sentences and phrases and lacks significance in terms of bearing meaning along. It is not sufficiently important in terms of communicating sense to qualify as a major structural feature.[16]

MAJOR FUNCTIONS OF RECURRENCE

Recurrence has three major functions. First, it is usually employed to indicate emphasis. When an implied author makes use of recurrence, he is normally indicating that this term or concept is important and the reader should take pains to ascertain its meaning and significance. Second, recurrence allows a writer to develop a theme or concept throughout the book. Readers find a recurrence of the person of Nicodemus throughout the Gospel of John. The evangelist employs this recurrence to trace the development of the character of Nicodemus from a timid, frightened, and benighted inquirer (3:1–15), to a halting defender of Jesus in the council of the religious leaders (7:50–52), and finally to a courageous and daring disciple who buries the body of Jesus (19:38–42). Third, recurrence allows the writer to develop depth and richness of presentation, for it invites readers to interpret individual occurrences in light of the other occurrences and in light of the recurring pattern as a whole.

The book of Joshua is structured according to a recurrence of "rest,"[17] while 1 John is characterized by a recurrence of "abide/remain/dwell" language.[18] (All of the examples appearing in this discussion of structural relationships are

16. Freedman (ibid., 126–27) mentions four criteria for structurally significant recurrence: avoidability or unlikelihood in the content being communicated (not simply part of the "color"); significance of contexts; coherence between various references to the motif; and (in symbolic motifs) appropriate representation to the thing being symbolized.

17. See Josh. 1:13, 15; 11:23; 14:15; 21:44; 22:4; 23:1.

18. See 1 John 2:6, 10, 14, 17, 19, 24, 27; 3:6, 9, 14, 15, 17, 24; 4:12, 13, 15, 16.

plausible cases; we are not presenting them as absolutely definitive but simply as possibly present and therefore useful for illustrative purposes.)

Semantic Structures

Semantic structures are characterized by binary or twofold progression employed to indicate sense connection: movement from something to something.

Contrast

Contrast is the association of opposites or of things whose differences the writer wishes to stress. Key terms for contrast are *but* or *however*, although contrast is often present when no such connections explicitly appear. Nevertheless, the idea of *but* or *however* is central to the notion of contrast, which emphasizes difference.[19] An illustration of contrast is the description of the two ways in Psalm 1, where verses 1–3 discuss the way of the righteous while verses 4–6 discuss the way of the wicked (see fig. 9).[20]

Figure 9

Contrast in Psalm 1

Contrast

Way of righteousness (1:1–3) ◄——► Way of the wicked (1:4–6)

The psalmist has so structured this passage as to invite readers to consider the difference between the way of the righteous and the way of the wicked. The psalm fosters a view toward understanding more completely the meaning of each and committing to the way of righteousness while repudiating the way of the wicked.

Moreover, the Gospel of John has repeated or recurring contrast between belief/faith versus unbelief;[21] thus the Gospel of John is structured according to

---

19. Contrast might be used in books or passages in three ways. The first is *contradiction*, in which the contrasted elements are presented as mutually exclusive, as in the example from Ps. 1. The second is *complementarity*, in which the contrasted elements actually say the same thing but in differentiated ways, as in John 20:27: "Do not doubt but believe"; or James 1:5–6: "But ask in faith, never doubting." The third is *concession*, in which the validity of a statement is granted, though it is followed by an assertion that seems to contradict on one level the first statement (employing the notion of "although"), as Heb. 5:8 says, "Although he was a Son, he learned obedience through what he suffered"; or Ps. 23:4, "Even though I walk through the darkest valley, I fear no evil." The type of contrast encountered at the level of the book-as-a-whole is usually contradiction. While the complementary and concessive forms of contrast may be found at the book level, they are usually encountered in smaller units of material.

20. This example illustrates the principle, mentioned previously in the discussion of main units and subunits, that major structural relationships often have implications for the breakdown of the text. Here the contrast between vv. 1–3 and vv. 4–6 indicates that the major break in Ps. 1 occurs at v. 4.

21. John 1:11, 12, 46, 50; 2:23; 3:12, 15, 16, 18, 36; 4:21, 41–42, 48, 50, 53; 5:10–47; 6:29–30, 35–36, 40, 47, 60–67; 7:5, 31, 39, 48; 8:13–59; 9:13–10:6; 10:18–21, 24–39, 42; 11:26–27, 40, 42,

the recurrence of contrast. One will recognize the potential richness and depth that an analysis of this repeated description of differences between belief and unbelief offers to the student of the Gospel of John. This example illustrates that relationships can be combined: sometimes two relationships are so closely bound together in terms of the way they are employed in a given biblical book that readers cannot describe how one relationship functions within the book without also describing a second relationship. In such a circumstance, one may combine the two relationships into a *complex* one.[22]

COMPARISON

Comparison is the association of like things, or of things whose similarities are emphasized by the writer. The key terms, or ideas, involved in comparison are *like* or *as* or *so*. But again, we often encounter implicit comparison where these terms do not expressly appear.

Psalm 1 offers an example not only of contrast but also of comparison. The psalmist uses comparison to describe righteous persons when he declares, "They are like trees planted by streams of water" (v. 3). He uses comparison also to describe the wicked: "[The wicked] are like chaff that the wind drives away" (v. 4). Clearly the psalmist invites the reader to consider what are, from the perspective of the psalm itself, the major points of similarity between the righteous and trees on one hand, and the wicked and chaff on the other, and to reflect on ways in which these likenesses illumine the meaning of the life of righteousness and the life of wickedness.

Because this example involves the coordinated repeated use of comparison, we can say that Psalm 1 is structured according to the recurrence of comparison. We have seen that Psalm 1 involves both contrast and the recurrence of comparison; thus we note that a book or a psalm may be structured according to more than one relationship. Indeed, books and other units of various sizes will usually contain more than one major structural relationship, for biblical literature tends to be thick and somewhat complex, with the result that more than one structural organizational schema is involved.

The book of 1 Thessalonians presents an example of a recurring comparison between Paul (and Silvanus and Timothy) and the Thessalonians. Repeatedly Paul commends the Thessalonians for becoming like him, and he exhorts them to become even more like him.[23] Readers may carefully analyze what is involved in these repeated declarations of similarity between proclaimers of

---

45–57; 12:4, 9–19, 37, 42, 44, 46; 13:1–38; 14:1–12, 29; 16:9, 13; 17:8, 20–21; 18:1–30; 18:33–19:16; 19:22, 35; 20:8, 25, 27, 29, 31.

22. This example also illustrates the consideration previously mentioned under "Recurrence": recurrence can involve the repetition of another structural relationship.

23. See 1 Thess. 1:6; 3:6, 12; 4:1; cf. 2:1–12 with 1:2–10; 2:13–16; cf. 3:1–5 with 2:1–8; 5:4–10.

the gospel and recipients of the gospel's proclamation to understand fully and profoundly the message and formative impact of this letter.

The structural relationship of comparison at the paragraph level is found typically in parables: "The kingdom of heaven is like" or "The kingdom of heaven may be compared to." Although the composition of these parables would not normally involve book-level structure, it does illustrate nicely what is involved in the structural relationship of comparison.

CLIMAX

Climax is the movement from the lesser to the greater, toward a high point of culmination. The term *climax* derives from the Greek word for *ladder* or *staircase* and suggests the element of climbing. Although one often has a sense of gradual development throughout from the lesser to the greater to the greatest, this sense of gradual development is not essential for climax. It only needs movement toward a high point of culmination. Climax normally comes at or very near the end of the book (or unit) surveyed. Placing a climax toward the beginning or middle of a writing would result in a lengthy anticlimax, and effective writers try to avoid anticlimax.

FIGURE 10
Climax in the book of Acts

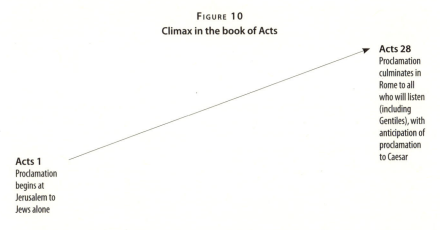

Acts 28
Proclamation culminates in Rome to all who will listen (including Gentiles), with anticipation of proclamation to Caesar

Acts 1
Proclamation begins at Jerusalem to Jews alone

The book of Acts offers an example of climax (see fig. 10). Acts is concerned with the geographical movement of the gospel from Jerusalem westward. The book reaches its climax with Paul at the farthest distance in the *narrative world* of Acts from Jerusalem, in Rome, the chief city of the civilized world and the capital of the Roman Empire. In this city, Paul is relatively unhindered in spreading the gospel as he is about to make his defense before Caesar, which (on the basis of Paul's defenses in chaps. 22–26) will involve Paul's preaching the gospel to Caesar himself. This climactic movement is clearly central to Luke's communication of his message through the story of the book of Acts. Readers are encouraged to ask how the material that leads up to the climax of chapter 28 illumines the climactic passage. Conversely, readers should study how the climactic development and the climax itself of chapter 28 illumine the story that precedes, and even illumine the meaning of certain individual passages and occurrences in the preceding chapters.

The book of Exodus also contains climax. Already in Exodus 3:12, when God addresses Moses on Sinai at the burning bush, God declares, "I will be with you; and this shall be the sign for you that it is I who sent you: when you have brought the people out of Egypt, you shall worship God on this mountain." The entire book involves the movement toward the high point of culmination when that promise of Israel's worship of God on Sinai is fully accomplished. This crest is illustrated at the end of the book: "Then the cloud covered the tent of meeting, and the glory of the LORD filled the tabernacle" (40:34).

PARTICULARIZATION

Particularization is the movement from general to particular and can take several forms. *Identificational particularization* involves a general heading that presents the essential character of the material that follows. According to this general heading, the reader is to understand how the particular material that follows is to be understood. Joel 1:1 is a general heading to the specific material that follows throughout the rest of the book: "The word of the LORD that came to Joel, the son of Pethuel." Here the writer indicates that the essential character of this book is that it is of the nature of "the word of the LORD." The rest of the book, and every passage within the book, is to be understood according to this statement. This observation may have various points of significance when one reaches the phase of interpretation. It may, for example, alert us to the fact that Joel was able to make the connection between catastrophic events of locusts and fire and God's judgment upon Judah's sin because of his unique experience of prophetic inspiration ("the word of the LORD that came to Joel"). This consideration may serve as a warning to those of us who do not share Joel's experience of prophetic inspiration—a warning that this book does not give us warrant to draw a definite and direct connection between catastrophic events in our own nation and the judgment of God upon the nation's sins.

Another example of identificational particularization comes from the Song of Solomon, which begins with the general heading, "The Song of Songs." The book is of the nature of a "song of songs," and an understanding and appreciation of the general heading may provide profound insights into the message of the book-as-a-whole as well as the meaning of passages throughout the book.

Ideological particularization involves a general statement that the writer spells out or unpacks or develops in the material that follows. Proverbs 1:7 forms something of a *thesis statement* that is specifically developed throughout the remainder of the book of Proverbs: "The fear of the LORD is the beginning of knowledge; fools despise wisdom and instruction." The book of Proverbs can be read in such a way as to understand how, in multifarious and rich ways, the individual proverbs throughout the book are developing various aspects of that thesis.

The book of Hebrews begins with what most scholars take to be a general statement regarding Christ (1:1–4). Indeed, we seem to have here seven claims regarding the Son:

1. The Son has been appointed the heir of all things by God.
2. The Son was the agent of creation of the worlds (or ages).
3. The Son reflects the glory of God and is the imprint of God's very being.
4. The Son sustains all things by his powerful word.
5. The Son has made purification for sins.
6. The Son has sat down at the right hand of the Majesty on high.
7. The Son has become superior to angels.

In the rest of the book of Hebrews, the writer spells out or develops these claims, especially numbers 1, 5, 6, and 7. The author gives these general claims specific content in his later christological exposition, and the specific exposition that follows is informed by the general claims that stand over it. For example, when one moves to the interpretation phase, one might note that the original Greek has only one main verb in verses 2b–4: "he sat down." This main verb, surrounded by participles and relative clauses, suggests that the exaltation of Christ may be central to the christological claims, not just of 1:2b–4, but also of the entire book of Hebrews, and these other claims may derive from the central affirmation of Christ's exaltation. Conversely, the way in which the writer of Hebrews weaves together Christ's superiority to the angels, his exaltation, and his high-priestly work of purification for sins in 1:5–2:18 gives specific understanding to the relationship between the general claims in 1:2b–4.

Historical particularization involves the movement from a general description of a historical event or period to a specific description of the details of that event or period. Thus John 1:14 declares, "The Word became flesh and lived among us, and we have seen his glory, the glory as of a father's only son, full of grace and truth." John goes on to present the specifics of this event in the narrative that begins in 1:19 and extends throughout the rest of the Gospel. The text invites readers to understand the narrative of Jesus in John's Gospel in light of the general description of the Christ event in 1:14 and, conversely, to allow the specific and extended story of Jesus throughout the Gospel to give specific content to the claim of 1:14.

Psalm 78 also provides an excellent example of historical particularization as one of the historical psalms, a psalm that narrates the history of Israel or a portion of that history. In verses 2–4 the psalm begins with a general description of the whole of Israel's history, presumably up to the point of the psalm's composition:

> I will open my mouth in a parable;
>   I will utter dark sayings from of old,
> Things that we have heard and known,
>   That our ancestors have told us.
> We will not hide them from their children;
>   We will tell to the coming generation
> The glorious deeds of the LORD, and his might
>   And the wonders that he has done.

The psalmist then proceeds to describe events throughout Israel's history in chronological sequence, thus placing the sequence as a whole and described individual events within the general description of Israel's history as set forth in verses 2–4.

Geographical particularization involves the movement from the presentation of a broader geographical area to the description of a specific location within that broader area. For example, the book of Genesis contains geographical particularization. Chapters 1–11 are concerned with the world (and even the cosmos) in general; then chapters 12–50 focus upon one place within this cosmos: the land of Canaan. This observation may prove critical for the later work of interpretation because this structure invites the reader to consider the role of *the land* of Canaan (a significant theological concept in Genesis and the rest of the Old Testament) in relation to God's plan and purposes for the cosmos he has created.

Biographical particularization involves the movement from the presentation of a group of persons to the specific description of a subgroup or even an individual person within the originally presented larger group. The book of Genesis offers an example of biographical particularization because it includes a correspondence between the geographical and biographical particularization. In chapters 1–11 the book begins with a concern with humanity in general and then proceeds to focus on one family: Abraham and his descendants (see fig. 11).

The book of Genesis thus places Abraham and his descendants within the context of humanity in general. In understanding the message of Genesis, it is critical to take seriously into account this movement from humanity in general to one specific family in order to construe properly this book's perspective on the relation of Israel to the nations, that is, to humanity as a whole.[24]

---

24. Of course, some passages throughout Gen. 12–50 are set outside of Canaan, especially in Egypt. But these are exceptions to the rule, and in each case what happens in Egypt seems to be significant because of God's plan for his people in the land of Canaan. Likewise, within Gen. 1–11 is a concern to describe certain individuals; but this does not undercut the claim that

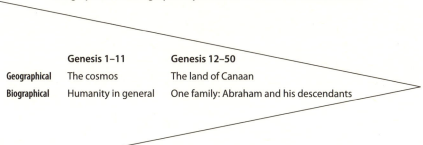

FIGURE 11
Geographical and biographical particularization in the book of Genesis

	Genesis 1–11	Genesis 12–50
Geographical	The cosmos	The land of Canaan
Biographical	Humanity in general	One family: Abraham and his descendants

A further example of biographical particularization is found in the Gospel of John, where 1:19–12:50 describes Jesus's public manifestation to all Israel, and then the focus narrows in 13:1–20:31, which describes Jesus's private manifestation to just his twelve disciples, one subgroup within the larger group of Israel. This narrowing of (biographical) focus may be significant in John's communication of his message.

GENERALIZATION

Generalization is the movement from particular to general. It involves the same two components as particularization but in reverse sequence. The five subcategories of particularization apply to generalization as well.

Identificational generalization involves a general description of the essential character of the material that precedes this general description. As such, identificational generalization at the book level typically involves the inclusion of this general description at or near the end of the book. The book of Hebrews concludes with such an identificational generalization. In 13:22 the writer urges, "Bear with my word of exhortation." The writer thus identifies the essential character of the book as a "word of exhortation." Scholars have long been occupied with the issue of the nature of Hebrews and the significance of understanding this nature or character for interpreting the book. They have recognized the importance of ascertaining the precise meaning of this general designation for construing the message, function, and purpose of the book of Hebrews both in the large and in specific passages within the book.

Ideological generalization involves setting forth something similar to a thesis statement at or near the end of the book, one that in a general way encapsulates the message of the book or a significant aspect of the book's

---

the primary concern in these chapters is upon the presentation of humanity as a whole, because these individuals are consistently presented in terms of their representation of, or relation to, humanity as a whole.

message. The book of Hosea concludes with ideological generalization at 14:9: "Those who are wise understand these things; those who are discerning know them. For the ways of the LORD are right, and the upright walk in them, but transgressors stumble in them." The book of Hosea emphasizes the themes of wisdom and knowledge and develops them according to a contrast between uprightness and transgression. In the space of a single verse, this statement at the end of the book thus sets forth at least some of the book's primary concerns; it invites the reader to understand the developed argument in light of this general conclusion and to construe this general declaration in light of its more or less full development throughout the book.

Historical generalization involves the movement from a relatively detailed description of an event or historical period to a general description of that event or historical period. Judges 21:25 is an example of historical generalization: "In those days there was no king in Israel; all the people did what was right in their own eyes." The writer has spent twenty-one chapters describing in some detail a society without a divinely ordained kingly authority, a society in which the decision regarding right and wrong was made by individuals on the basis of their private judgment. The last verse of the book of Judges, then, provides a general rubric according to which the individual accounts of the book are to be read; this rubric in turn is given specific content from these earlier individual accounts.

Geographical generalization involves the movement from the presentation of one geographical area to the presentation of the larger area of which this smaller area is a part. The book of Acts offers an example of geographical generalization. As noted above, many readers sense that Acts 1:8 serves as a virtual table of contents for the book of Acts: "You shall receive power when the Holy Spirit has come upon you; and you will be my witnesses in Jerusalem, in all Judea and Samaria, and to the ends of the earth." Luke presents the witness to Jerusalem mostly in chapters 2–7, the witness to all Judea and Samaria in chapters 8–12, and the witness to "the ends of the earth" in chapters 13–28. Yet he describes the witness to Jerusalem continuing even in chapters 8–12, where the emphasis is on Judea and Samaria. He indicates, too, that the witness to Jerusalem and to Judea and Samaria continues even in chapters 13–28, where the emphasis is on the witness spreading through the Mediterranean basin as far as Rome. Thus Luke does not move simply from one specific area to another specific area but presents an ever-widening geographical expansion of the gospel. Clearly Luke employs the story of this geographical expansion in order to communicate what he takes to be significant insights regarding the nature, meaning, and importance of the Christian mission.

Biographical generalization involves the movement from one person or subgroup to the presentation of a larger group of which the originally described person or subgroup is a part. The book of Acts provides an example (see fig. 12), for in Acts this biographical generalization corresponds to the geographical generalization just described. The witness to Jerusalem in chapters 2–7 is made only to Jews, while the witness to all Judea and Samaria in chapters 8–12 involves both the continuing witness to Jews and now also the witness to Samaritans and Gentile God-fearers. Samaritans were considered in a sense as half-Jews, in that they represented a mixture of Hebrew and Gentile blood, and had developed a faith that was regarded as a hybrid of Hebrew and pagan religions. God-fearers, such as Cornelius (chap. 10), were Gentiles who participated in synagogue worship and identified themselves as adherents to the Jewish faith but who had not fully converted to Judaism by submitting to circumcision and other rites that would represent full inclusion. Hence, the witness in Acts 8–12 involved evangelization of those who had some connection to Jews and Judaism. The witness to "the ends of the earth" in chapters 13–28 continues to be directed to Jews and God-fearers but now includes also Gentiles who had no association with Judaism. Again, this biographical expansion of the gospel (involving both ethnic and religious considerations) seems to be critical in Luke's attempt to communicate his message through the book of Acts. Luke also clearly wishes readers to construe specific passages throughout Acts in light of this broader program of biographical expansion.

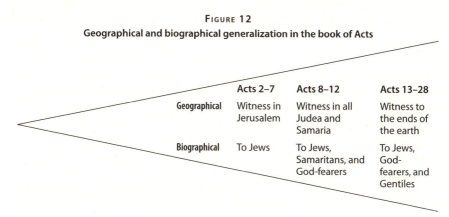

FIGURE 12

Geographical and biographical generalization in the book of Acts

	Acts 2–7	Acts 8–12	Acts 13–28
Geographical	Witness in Jerusalem	Witness in all Judea and Samaria	Witness to the ends of the earth
Biographical	To Jews	To Jews, Samaritans, and God-fearers	To Jews, God-fearers, and Gentiles

A further example of biographical generalization is found in the book of Ruth. The narrative of the book (1:1–4:17) describes one generation, involving Ruth and Boaz. But at the book's end the scope widens, with the inclusion of a genealogy that spans ten generations, from Perez (a son of Judah) through David, with Boaz being approximately in the center of the genealogy. Thus the story of Ruth and Boaz is placed within a broader family and possibly within a salvation-historical perspective.

CAUSATION

Causation is the movement from cause to effect. The key term here is *therefore*, although some uses of *so* or *then* also suggest causation. Once again, implicit causation can also be present, in which case the causal connection must be inferred from the material in the absence of an explicit connective such as *therefore*. Causation has three major forms.

Historical causation occurs when a historical event causes, or produces, another event. We can paraphrase it thus: "Because A happened, therefore B happened." The book of Amos is structured according to a repeated, hence recurring, causation between sin and judgment: "Because Israel has sinned, therefore God will judge Israel."[25]

Logical causation occurs when one statement logically causes, or leads to, another statement, when a writer draws an inference from what he has just said. Because A is so, therefore B also is so. In Hebrews 8:1 the writer draws a logical conclusion from what he has written in chapters 5–7. Throughout these chapters, the writer has argued for the high priesthood of Jesus. At 8:1 he draws his conclusion: "Now the main point in what we are saying is this: we have such a high priest, one who is seated at the right hand of the throne of the Majesty."[26] An example of logical causation at the segment level is found in Matthew 1:1–17, where verse 17 draws out the evangelist's inferences from the genealogical list of verses 2–16 (note "so" or *oun*).

Hortatory causation occurs when a writer moves from a statement in the indicative (i.e., a claim or statement of fact) to a command, or exhortation, in the imperative: because A is so, therefore you ought to do B. The book of Ephesians is structured according to hortatory causation. Paul sets forth the doctrinal argument in chapters 1–3, where he includes no exhortations at all; however, he gives one command or exhortation after another throughout chapters 4–6. Moreover, Paul links the doctrinal argument of chapters 1–3 to the exhortations of chapters 4–6 with the word *therefore* (*oun*) at 4:1: "I therefore, the prisoner in the Lord, beg you to lead a life worthy of the calling to which you have been called."[27] This observation may be important in interpreting the book of Ephesians because it suggests that the doctrine set forth in the first three chapters is to be embodied in life and behavior along the lines commanded in the final three chapters; it also implies that the Christian life as set forth in chapters 4–6 has as its necessary foundation the doctrinal considerations of chapters 1–3. It suggests, too, that even individual passages in the doctrinal section may be significantly illumined by the lifestyle that is meant to express the doctrine, and it suggests that specific exhortations in

---

25. This causal connection, sometimes termed the "judgment pattern," is found throughout the book of Amos. But note esp. 1:2–2:16; 3:2, 9–12; 4:1–3; 5:25–27; 8:4–10.

26. The writer of Hebrews develops this conclusion at least through 10:18.

27. The reference to leading a life "*worthy* of the calling to which you have been called" (a calling presumably described in Eph. 1–3) suggests that chaps. 1–3 relate to chaps. 4–6 not only in terms of causation, but also as comparison: Paul seems to be emphasizing the likeness, or commensurability, of the calling described in the first three chapters of this epistle to the kind of life he is exhorting throughout the final three chapters.

chapters 4–6 should be interpreted in light of certain doctrinal claims as set forth in chapters 1–3.

Substantiation

Substantiation involves the same two components as causation, but used in reverse sequence; substantiation is the movement from effect to cause. Thus the key terms in substantiation are *because* or *for*, and in explicit substantiation these connectives will be expressly present. The three types of substantiation parallel the three types of causation as previously described.

Historical substantiation occurs when the reason why an event took place, the cause, is given later in the book: the reason why *A* occurred is *B*. The book of Jonah offers an example of historical substantiation. Toward the end of the book, at 4:1–2, Jonah is engaged in angry disputation with God over God's decision to spare Nineveh in light of Nineveh's repentance (chap. 3). Here Jonah prays to God: "O Lord! Is not this what I said while I was still in my own country? That is why I fled to Tarshish at the beginning; for I knew that you are a gracious God and merciful, slow to anger, and abounding in steadfast love, and ready to relent from punishing." Here Jonah declares the reason why he fled from the presence of the Lord when the Lord originally called him to proclaim a message against Nineveh at the beginning of the book (1:1–2). If we did not have chapter 4, we might think that the reason Jonah disobeyed God's call in chapter 1 was that he was afraid the Ninevites would reject his message and destroy him. But 4:1–2 gives us the actual reason for Jonah's actions at the beginning of the book: Jonah was afraid that the Ninevites *would* accept his message (as they eventually did) and that God would not destroy them.

Hortatory substantiation occurs when the writer moves from an exhortation, or a passage characterized by exhortation, to the reason why (i.e., the cause) the exhortation should be obeyed: you ought to obey *A* because of *B*. The book of Revelation may be structured according to hortatory substantiation (see fig. 13). The letters to the seven churches, in chapters 2–3, are essentially exhortations to be or to remain righteous and faithful in difficult circumstances. The great apocalyptic vision of chapters 4–22 then substantiates or supports these exhortations by describing the flow of history, which is moving toward the judgment of God, when God will reward the righteous and faithful but will condemn the unrighteous and faithless (esp. chaps. 21–22).

Logical substantiation occurs when a writer moves from declaration(s) or claim(s) to the reasons why (i.e., the cause) the declaration or claim is true and ought to be accepted: the reason I say (and why you should believe) *A* is *B*. Paul seems to structure his great theological argument in Romans 1:16–11:36 according to logical substantiation. He presents the essential claim of the argument in 1:16–17: "For I am not ashamed of the gospel; it is the power of

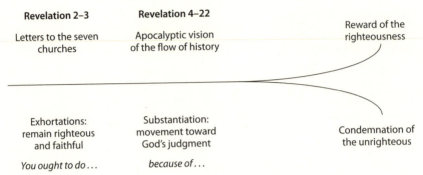

FIGURE 13
Hortatory substantiation in the book of Revelation

God for salvation to everyone who has faith, to the Jew first and also to the Greek. For in it the righteousness of God is revealed through faith for faith; as it is written, 'The one who is righteous will live by faith.'" One can understand the whole argument from 1:18–11:36 as giving the cause or reason or support for the essential claim of 1:16–17.

CRUCIALITY

Cruciality involves the device of the pivot. Elements on each side of the pivot differ from those on the other side because of the pivot. It involves a change of direction, a radical reversal, a total turning around of the material because of the pivot passage. In cruciality, the movement following the pivot virtually cancels out what preceded the pivot. It thus does not involve simply a change of emphasis but also an undoing of what preceded the pivot because of the pivot passage.

This relationship is found in 2 Samuel (see fig. 14). The presentation of David in chapters 1–10 is one of unmitigated blessing and prosperity, in terms of both family and reign. But David faces one disaster after another in chapters 13–20 and experiences decline in terms of family and reign. The reason for the radical reversal from growing prosperity to decline is apparently David's sin of adultery with Bathsheba and murder of Uriah, recounted in 2 Samuel 11–12, the pivot passage.

Recognizing this structural feature is significant for an accurate understanding of the message of the book-as-a-whole and for the interpretation of individual passages within the book, which should be construed in light of the role they play in this larger program of the book. For example, a rather famous sermon on 2 Samuel 13–20 argues that David's problems are due to the fact that he was an ineffective father, that he had not adequately mastered essential parenting skills. But the observation of this cruciality at the level of book structure suggests rather that David's problems in chapters 13–20 did not ultimately come from a poor relationship with his children

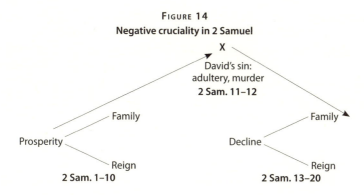

Figure 14
Negative cruciality in 2 Samuel

X

David's sin:
adultery, murder
2 Sam. 11–12

Family

Family

Prosperity

Decline

Reign
2 Sam. 1–10

Reign
2 Sam. 13–20

but were because of his relationship with God, or more precisely, because of God's continuing and vestigial judgment even of David's confessed sin (12:1–15).[28]

We might refer to this type of cruciality as *negative* since it begins well and, because of the pivot, turns unfavorably. Frequently in the Bible, though, *positive* cruciality occurs when the negative beginning is radically reversed toward the positive because of the pivot passage. In the book of Acts, the presentation of Saul of Tarsus (later Paul) begins negatively: He is the great opponent of the gospel and the chief persecutor of the church (7:58–8:3; 9:1–2), but because of the pivot of his conversion on the road to Damascus in 9:3–19a, Saul subsequently becomes the great proponent of the gospel and the persecuted one par excellence (see fig. 15).

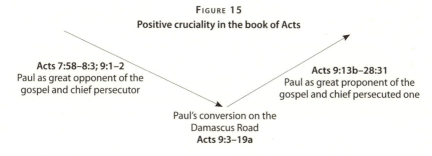

Figure 15
Positive cruciality in the book of Acts

Acts 7:58–8:3; 9:1–2
Paul as great opponent of the gospel and chief persecutor

Acts 9:13b–28:31
Paul as great proponent of the gospel and chief persecuted one

Paul's conversion on the
Damascus Road
Acts 9:3–19a

28. It is possible that the implied author of 2 Samuel is concerned also with issues of parenting. If one takes seriously the "thickness" or "density" of the biblical materials, one will be open to the possibility that a text has more than a single agenda. Nevertheless, the clear and dominant relationship of cruciality within this book may suggest that the primary and ultimate concern of the text is David's relationship with God. One should also observe that although David experiences decline in 2 Sam. 13–20, this decline is not total. David maintains his throne, and his family is not entirely lost or taken from him, which might involve God's gracious work in leading David to confession of his sin and God's consequent forgiveness of David's sin (12:13). In this case, the point might be that David and others continue to suffer to a great extent even for confessed and forgiven sin.

We note that this relationship (linking before and after) contains implicitly two other relationships: contrast (between what precedes the pivot and what follows it) and recurrence of causation. A causal movement often flows from the material that precedes the pivot to the pivot itself, and one will always find a causal movement from the pivot toward what follows it.

Thus, in the case of 2 Samuel, David's experience of blessing might itself have been a contributing (though not a sole and sufficient) cause for his sin in chapters 11–12. In other words, David's experience of unmitigated blessing from the hand of God might have lulled David into thinking that he was not accountable and that God would continue to bless him no matter what David did or did not do (what Walter Brueggemann describes as "moral autonomy").[29] This gracious blessing perhaps led also to David's indolence, which possibly occasioned his lust toward Bathsheba (see 11:1–2). The causal movement from the pivot of David's sin in chapters 11–12 to the judgment of decline in chapters 13–20 is quite evident. In the case of Acts, Saul's dangerous and threatening acts toward the church might be understood as causing the exalted Christ to accost Saul on the road to Damascus and bring him to a point of conversion. Certainly Saul's conversion led directly to the life and vocation of Paul as set forth in the remainder of Acts.

SUMMARIZATION

Summarization is an abridgment or compendium (summing up) either preceding or following a unit of material. Summarization is thus similar to the general component in generalization or particularization, especially ideological generalization or particularization. But a general statement is usually less precise, more vague, with fewer details, while summarization is a more deliberate attempt to bring into the statement, in abridged form, the various components of what is being summarized. Summarization is actually a point-by-point recapitulation (or if the summary statement precedes what is being summarized, it is a *precapitulation*) of what is being summarized.[30]

The interpretive significance of summarization is threefold. First, the *selectivity* of the summary statement indicates to the reader what is of prime

29. Walter Brueggemann, *First and Second Samuel*, IBC (Louisville: John Knox, 1990), 285.

30. The difference between a general statement and a summary statement may be illustrated by the distinction between a thesis statement for a sermon (a single sentence that tries to express the one overarching claim being made in the sermon), and a summary of the main points of the sermon (e.g., one might end a sermon by recapitulating the main points: "First we saw, . . . then second we saw, . . . and finally we argued that. . . .") Of course, in some instances in the Bible one might have difficulty determining whether the passage in question is a summary statement or a general statement. Some statements can go either way. In these cases, it is not necessary to judge between a summary and a general statement, yet passages that are clearly summaries do tend to function somewhat differently than passages that are clearly general statements. Hence the distinction is often helpful.

importance in the material being summarized. In a summary statement, the implied author must select, from a more or less extensive mass of material, what will be included, thus pointing to matters that he wishes to emphasize. Second, the *manner of description* of a summary statement points to the way in which the reader is to construe the main elements in the material being summarized. A writer of any summary statement could choose a variety of terms to employ in his summary and could structure his summary in several different ways. A reader should carefully note the manner of description, with regard to both terms and structure, to ascertain exactly how the writer wishes the reader to interpret the larger presentation. Third, the *immediate context* of a summary statement may be significant for fully realizing its interpretive function. Readers should note the emphases in the immediate setting of the summary statement as part of their quest to derive deep and penetrating insights into the meaning of the material that the summary statement recapitulates.

An example of a summary statement at the end of a book is Esther 9:24–28, where the writer recapitulates the story of Esther, which has required eight and a half chapters to tell in detail:

> Haman the son of Hammedatha the Agagite, the enemy of all the Jews, had plotted against the Jews to destroy them, and had cast Pur—that is "the lot"—to crush and destroy them; but when Esther came before the king, he gave orders in writing that the wicked plot that he had devised against the Jews should come upon his own head, and that he and his sons should be hanged on the gallows. Therefore these days are called Purim, from the word Pur. Thus because of all that was written in this letter, and of what they had faced in this matter, and of what had happened to them, the Jews established and accepted as a custom for themselves and their descendants and all who joined them, that without fail they would continue to observe these two days every year, as it was written and at the time appointed. These days should be remembered and kept throughout every generation, in every family, province, and city; and these days of Purim should never fall into disuse among the Jews, nor should the commemoration of these days cease among their descendants.

One notes here the selectivity employed in this summary, especially the prominence given to the casting of the lot (Pur). If one did not have the advantage of this summary statement, one could easily pass over the reference to the casting of the lot in the larger narrative; but this recapitulation directs the reader to the prime importance of this detail in the story of Esther (3:7).

Here one also notes the emphasis, within the summary statement itself and within the immediate context, upon the issue of writing. Reference is made to writing in 9:20, 23, 25, 26, 27, 29, and 32. In addition, the immediate context indicates a great concern for the continuing significance of this story of Esther, a perpetual significance to be embodied in the Feast of Purim, characterized by joyful and generous remembrance. The immediate context of this summary statement thus indicates that the story told in this book is not simply a pleasant and gratifying tale from the past but also a formative event in the ongoing life of the people of Israel.

Even as the book of Esther presents a summary statement that appears at the end of the material being summarized, so the book of Acts includes a summary statement that precedes what is being summarized. As previously mentioned, many have claimed that Acts 1:8 serves as a listing of the subject matter of the book of Acts: "You will receive power when the Holy Spirit has come upon you; and you will be my witnesses in Jerusalem, in all Judea and Samaria, and to the ends of the earth." As stated, the witness to Jerusalem is presented chiefly in chapters 2–7, the witness to all Judea and Samaria is narrated in chapters 8–12, and the witness to "the ends of the earth" is found in chapters 13–28.

When coming to interpretation, one will note how the structure of this summary statement itself illumines the narrative of the remainder of the book of Acts. The causal movement within 1:8 between the coming of the Spirit (cf. Acts 2) and the progressively expanding witness (cf. chaps. 3–28) alerts the reader that the powerful and remarkable witness of the church described in Acts 3–28 comes as a result of the reception of the Spirit, especially the coming of the Spirit at Pentecost in Acts 2. Moreover, at the stage of interpretation, one will recognize that insofar as the summary statement of 1:8 is in the form of a command from Christ, the church's toil to accomplish the geographical expansion of the gospel narrated throughout Acts is understood to be an extended and complex act of obedience to the word of Christ himself. And insofar as this summary statement is a promise from Christ at the point of his exaltation, the reader will understand that the geographical expansion of the gospel ultimately is not the result of the church's labors or the courage of its proclaimers or the genius of its leaders, but is finally due to the power of the exalted Christ.

In the interpretation stage, one will discover that the wording of this summary statement clearly reflects Isaiah 43:10, where Yahweh declares, regarding the eschatologically (i.e., end-time) reconstituted Israel when the people finally experience return from their exile, "'You are my witnesses,' says the LORD, 'and my servant whom I have chosen, so that you may know and believe me and understand that I am he.'" Hence the interpreter will recognize that the role God gave to Israel to make known the sovereign saving grace of Yahweh to the nations of the world is the same role God and the exalted Christ have given to the church. And the church will effectively fulfill Isaiah 43:10 and reveal God to the peoples of the world precisely by bearing witness to the saving power of the exalted Christ. Again, at the point of interpretation the reader will attend to the fact that the immediate context of this summary statement emphasizes the resurrection and parousia (second coming) of Christ, drawing the possible conclusion that the primary content of the "witness" to Christ is that he is the resurrected and returning Lord.

INTERROGATION

Interrogation is the employment of a question or a problem followed by its answer or solution. As such, interrogation is found in two forms:

1. The *question* raised (in the interrogative) followed by an answer. This form is the simpler and more straightforward of the two. Psalm 15 is structured around interrogation of the question-answer type. The psalm begins with questions: "O LORD, who may abide in your tent? Who may dwell on your holy hill?" (v. 1). Then follows the psalm's answer in verses 2–5: "Those who walk blamelessly, and do what is right, and speak the truth from their heart. . . . Those who do these things shall never be moved." A penetrating interpretation of the psalm-as-a-whole clearly requires a careful analysis of the question at the beginning of the psalm and the way the question is answered in the remainder of the psalm, and a full understanding of individual statements in the psalm requires the reader to take account of the ways in which these individual statements contribute to the larger question-answer framework.

2. The statement of a *problem* followed by the solution to the problem. This form has no explicit grammatical markers, such as question marks; the movement is subtle and implicit. The book of Genesis seems to be structured around interrogation of the problem-solution type (see fig. 16). The double problem of sin leading to curse (chaps. 1–11) is answered/solved by covenant leading to blessing (chaps. 12–50). The implied author of Genesis has employed this problem-solution structure to give readers guidance in understanding the movement of the book, to indicate to readers a major emphasis within the

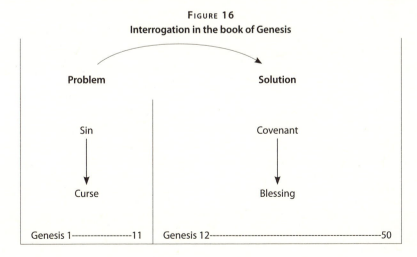

FIGURE 16
Interrogation in the book of Genesis

Problem   Solution

Sin   Covenant

Curse   Blessing

Genesis 1------------------11 | Genesis 12--50

book, and to encourage readers to understand individual passages in light of
their role in this problem-solution framework.

PREPARATION / REALIZATION

Preparation/realization, or introduction, is the inclusion of background
or setting for events or ideas. *Preparation* pertains to the background or introductory material itself, while *realization* is that for which the preparation
is made.

The book of Job provides an example of preparation/realization. Possibly the main concern of the book of Job is the issue of the suffering of the
righteous as developed in the dialogues between Job and his "comforters,"
and finally in the encounter between Job and God, in chapters 3–42. But the
book begins in chapters 1–2 by providing background or setting according
to which the reader is to understand the dialogues that follow; thus the essential function of Job 1–2 is to provide an introduction to the remainder of
the book. In these first two chapters we learn that Job had been blessed by
God in terms of family, wealth, and health. We learn that Satan, acting in his
capacity as a member of God's council and more specifically as the accuser
of persons before God, asserts that Job serves God out of selfish motives, in
order to experience for himself the good life, and that if Job should experience hardships, he would turn against God. Twice Satan convinces God to
test Job's righteousness by the imposition of woe; yet in spite of the loss of
property, family, and health, Job remains faithful to God. Even the characters
of the book of Job do not know many of these details, but the reader knows
them and is encouraged to interpret the dialogues that follow according to
this background knowledge.

A further example of preparation/realization is the Gospel of Mark. Mark
begins his Gospel with the account of the ministry of John the Baptist (1:2–11).
Yet Mark is not finally interested in the ministry of John as such but includes
this account only insofar as John's ministry provides background for the real
concern of the Gospel of Mark: the ministry of Jesus. The reader of this
Gospel, then, is to interpret Mark's narrative of Jesus's ministry according to
the background or setting of Mark's account of John's ministry.

A specific form of preparation/realization is the *prediction-fulfillment* pattern, in which a prediction made in the book comes to realization later in the
same book. The two books of Kings are structured according to a recurrence
of preparation/realization: twenty-five times throughout these books a prediction is made that is realized later in the narrative.[31] When one moves to inter-

---

31. Note the following: 1 Kings 11:11, 26–37 → (is mentioned as fulfilled in) 12:16–24.
1 Kings 13:2 → 2 Kings 23:15–20. 1 Kings 13:3 → 5. 1 Kings 13:22 → 26–32. 1 Kings 14:14 →
15:29. 1 Kings 16:7 → 12. 1 Kings 17:1 → 7. 1 Kings 17:14 → 16. 1 Kings 18:1 → 41–46. 1 Kings
20:13 → 19–21. 1 Kings 20:28 → 29–30. 1 Kings 20:42; 21:17–19; and 22:17 → 22:34–40. 1 Kings
21:23, 27–29 → 2 Kings 9–10. 2 Kings 3:16–19 → 20–27. 2 Kings 4:16 → 17. 2 Kings 4:43 → 44.

pretation, one recognizes the significance of this pattern of prediction ("the word of the LORD") and realization ("according to the word of the LORD") for grasping the theology of history and of the divine word as presented in the books of Kings.

INSTRUMENTATION

Instrumentation involves the movement from means to end:

$$\text{Means (by, through)} \longrightarrow \text{End (that, in order that)}$$

Instrumentation may take one of two forms: the statement of purpose and the description of means.

The first of these two forms, the *statement of purpose*, is an explicit declaration of purpose or end and includes the phrase *in order that* or its equivalent (e.g., often *so that* or *that* in English translations).[32] The Gospel of John may offer an example of instrumentation. In 20:31 John includes a statement of purpose that may pertain to the entire Gospel: "These [things] are written so that you may come to believe that Jesus is the Messiah, the Son of God, and that through believing you may have life in his name." "These [things]" are the means, referring probably to the entire Gospel of John. And John includes a twofold end: The immediate end is "that you may come to believe that Jesus is the Messiah, the Son of God," and the ultimate end is "that you may have life in his name." The significance of this statement of purpose for the interpretation of John's Gospel is obvious. John himself alerts the reader that the message of the entire book must be understood in light of this twofold purpose, and he invites readers to construe individual passages throughout the book in light of their role in fulfilling the purpose he sets forth in 20:31. In the interpretation of each passage, the reader should ask, How does the overall purpose of John's Gospel as presented in 20:31 illumine the meaning and function of this passage, and how does this passage serve to fulfill, in its own way, the twofold goal John has explicitly set forth?

The second form of instrumentation, the *description of means*, is the presentation of the means by which something is accomplished. The key ideas here are *by means of* or *through*, yet in contrast to the statement-of-purpose type of instrumentation, these terms are not necessarily explicitly stated. Even when these terms are absent from the text, the notion of means might be clearly present in the text.

---

2 Kings 6:9 → 10. 2 Kings 7:1 → 16–20. 2 Kings 8:10 → 15. 2 Kings 13:16–20 → 24–25. 2 Kings 19:32–34 → 35–37. 2 Kings 21:10–15 → 2 Kings 24–25. 2 Kings 22:18–20 → 23:28–30. 2 Kings 23:27 → 2 Kings 24–25.

32. Both Greek and Hebrew use various means to express purpose. One should consult original-language grammars for discussions. For an assessment of these grammars, see Bauer, *Annotated Guide to Biblical Resources*, 54–56, 191–95.

The book of Hebrews is structured according to the recurrence of instrumentation: repeatedly the book emphasizes that atonement comes by means of the sacrificial work of Christ. Indeed, Hebrews repeatedly contrasts the sacrificial work of Christ, which is the effective means of atonement, over against the sacrificial system of the Levitical priests, which is an ineffective means of atonement. Thus the book of Hebrews is structured according to recurrence of contrasting instrumentation. Another example is in the book of Joshua: The person of Joshua is the means that God employs to bring his people Israel into the land of Canaan and to give them the land as their possession.

RHETORICAL STRUCTURES

This category refers to structural relationships that involve the arrangement of material within the text. Semantic relationships, we remember, involve sense connection: they inherently communicate sense or meaning. For example, contrast involves the sense connection of *difference*, and instrumentation involves the sense connection of *purpose*. Rhetorical relationships, however, do not include within themselves a certain sense or meaning; rather, they pertain only to the ordering or placement of elements within the text. Because writers typically employ structural features to communicate meaning, they normally do not use rhetorical relationships by themselves but typically combine a rhetorical relationship with a semantic relationship in order to strengthen (and perhaps develop) that semantic relationship.[33]

INTERCHANGE

Interchange is the exchanging or alternation of certain elements in an a-b-a-b arrangement. The book of Micah is structured according to interchange used to strengthen contrast (see fig. 17). The book moves back and forth between

FIGURE 17
Interchange in the book of Micah

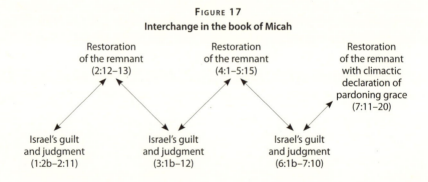

33. This statement is not intended to suggest that rhetorical relationships cannot stand alone or are never used by themselves. Nevertheless, they are typically combined with semantic relationships. Thus, when readers encounter a rhetorical relationship, they should ask themselves if this relationship is combined with a semantic one so as to strengthen or develop that semantic relationship.

declarations of guilt and judgment of Israel, and then promises of restoration of the righteous remnant of Israel.

The book of Hebrews seems to be structured according to an interchange between blocks of theological argument and blocks of exhortations (or commands; see fig. 18). Insofar as the theological argument is the cause, or basis, for the exhortations, which are the effect or result of the theological argument, this interchange in Hebrews strengthens the relationship of causation and substantiation. In other words, each block of exhortation is the effect of the theological arguments that precede and follow it.

FIGURE 18

Interchange in the book of Hebrews

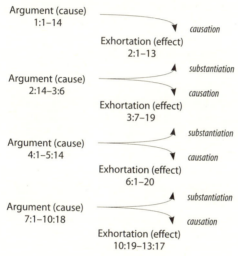

Argument (cause)
1:1–14

causation

Exhortation (effect)
2:1–13

substantiation

Argument (cause)
2:14–3:6

causation

Exhortation (effect)
3:7–19

substantiation

Argument (cause)
4:1–5:14

causation

Exhortation (effect)
6:1–20

substantiation

Argument (cause)
7:1–10:18

causation

Exhortation (effect)
10:19–13:17

INCLUSIO

Inclusio is the repetition of words or phrases at the beginning and end of a unit, thus creating a bracket effect (see fig. 19).[34] At the boundaries inclusio establishes the main thought of the book (or passage), pointing to the essential concern of the book (or passage). One should note the relationship between these bracketing statements and the intervening material in order to identify the semantic relationship with which an inclusio is used. An example of inclusio is found in Psalm 150 (see fig. 20), which begins and ends with the same statement: "Praise the LORD!" (vv. 1a, 6b). The intervening verses (1b–6a), which describe the specific ways in which the Lord is to be praised, relate to verse 1a in terms of particularization and to verse 6b in terms of generaliza-

---

34. See also David E. Aune, "Inclusio," in *The Westminster Dictionary of New Testament and Early Christian Literature and Rhetoric* (Louisville: Westminster John Knox, 2003), 229.

tion. Thus the bracketing statement is a general claim that is spelled out, or particularized, in the intervening material. Therefore Psalm 150 is structured according to particularization and generalization by inclusio.[35]

FIGURE 19

Inclusio

The Gospel of Matthew may also be structured according to inclusio. At almost the beginning of the book, 1:23 declares, "'And they shall name him Emmanuel,' which means 'God is *with us*'" (emphasis added). And at the very end of the Gospel, we have this strikingly similar statement: "And remember, I am *with you* always, to the end of the age" (28:20, emphasis added). Thus the beginning and end of the book have a reference to *with-ness*; indeed, the original Greek has a difference of only one letter between the "with us" of 1:23 and the "with you" of 28:20. The inclusio seems to be used in combination with the structural relationship of climax, for the book reaches its ultimate climax in the missionary commissioning of 28:18–20 and especially in the promise of continuing presence in 28:20. The whole period of the audience of Matthew's Gospel—the period of the post-Easter church, from the resurrection itself to the second coming of Christ—is characterized by the presence of Jesus Christ, the Son of God, in the midst of his church. But the inclusio with 1:23 indicates that God himself is present in his church in the person of his Son, who is "Emmanuel, God with us." The inclusio also reveals how important this notion of presence is for the message of Matthew's Gospel.

FIGURE 20

Inclusio in Psalm 150

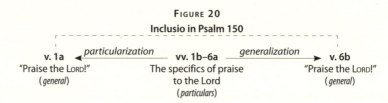

CHIASM

Chiasm is the repetition of elements in inverted order: a-b-b'-a'. Sometimes chiasm has a middle element, in which case the order would be a-b-c-b'-a'. The word *chiasm* comes from the Greek letter X (*chi*) because that letter presents a graphic representation of chiastic ordering (see fig. 21).

35. One might note that Ps. 150:2 provides the reason, or cause, to praise the Lord; thus v. 2 substantiates v. 1 and causes v. 6b. Therefore one could say that the psalm is structured according to particularization and substantiation, with generalization and causation by inclusion. One might observe also that within vv. 1b–6a is a climax, with the culminating call in v. 6a for everything to praise the Lord.

FIGURE 21

Chiasm

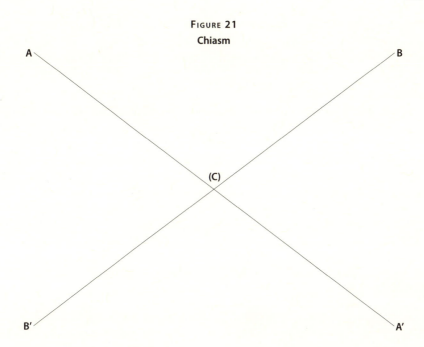

An example of chiasm in a book, or complete literary unit, is Psalm 67 (emphasis added):[36]

> A   May *God* be gracious to us and bless us,   v. 1
>   and make his face to shine upon us, *Selah*
>   that your way be known upon *earth*,   v. 2
>   your saving power among *all* nations.
>
> B   Let the *peoples* praise you, O God;   v. 3
>   let *all* the *peoples* praise you.
>
> C   Let the *nations* be glad and sing for joy,   v. 4
>   for you judge the *peoples* with equity
>   and guide the *nations* upon *earth*. *Selah*
>
> B′   Let the *peoples* praise you, O God;   v. 5
>   let *all* the *peoples* praise you.

---

36. See Nils W. Lund, *Chiasmus in the New Testament: A Study in the Form and Function of Chiastic Structures* (1942; repr., Peabody, MA: Hendrickson, 1992), 97–99, for a careful analysis of the chiastic arrangement of this psalm. Lund's book is an excellent study of chiasm in the Bible generally, although he, like many other scholars, tends to see chiasm in books and passages where its presence is somewhat dubious. See also Ian H. Thomson, *Chiasmus in the Pauline Letters* (Sheffield: Sheffield Academic Press, 1995); "Chiasmus," in Aune, *Westminster Dictionary*, 93–96.

A′   The *earth* has yielded its increase;   v. 6

        God, our *God*, has blessed us.

    May *God* continue to bless us;   v. 7

        let *all* the ends of the *earth* revere him.

This chiasm is combined with (and strengthens) the relationships of causation and substantiation. God's blessing upon his people (A, A′, vv. 1–2, 6–7) is the cause for the nations' knowing God's saving power and the nations' praise to God (B, B′, vv. 3, 5). The middle section, C (v. 4), stands at the center of the chiastic arrangement and may thereby suggest that the primary concern of the psalm is the joyful worship of God among the nations.

Although chiasm (or *chiasmus*) was frequently used in the Bible, its presence is not nearly as ubiquitous as most scholars have claimed; many scholars see chiasm almost everywhere and identify it even where the alleged coordinate members (e.g., A and A′) are not clearly parallel. Although chiasm is sometimes plausibly present in books-as-wholes, it is more often found in smaller units of material. An example of chiasm in a smaller unit is Isaiah 6:10:

A Make the *mind* of this people dull,
   B And stop their *ears*
      C And shut their *eyes*
      C′ So that they may not look with their *eyes*
   B′ And listen with their *ears*
A′ And comprehend with their *minds*. . . . (emphasis added)

Note the movement from mind to ears to eyes, and then from eyes to ears to mind. Here chiasm reinforces the relationship of instrumentation; "so that" indicates statement of purpose.

A final example of chiasm, this time in a very small unit, is Matthew 5:45b:

A He makes his sun rise on the *evil*
   B and on the good
   B′ and sends rain on the *righteous*
A′ and on the *unrighteous*. (emphasis added)

This movement goes from evil to good, and from righteous to unrighteous. The chiasm strengthens the relationship of comparison (and contrast): God bestows his blessings *alike* upon the good and the evil, in spite of, that is, *in contrast to*, the fact of their moral differences.

Chiasm carries a number of points of potential significance in interpretation. In chiasm the writer invites us to interpret the corresponding elements in light of one another. For example, in Matthew 5:45 we are encouraged to understand "good" in terms of "righteous" and "evil" in terms of "unrighteous." Moreover, chiasm invites us to consider seriously the relationship between the sets of coordinate elements (A/A′ to B/B′). Often at this point of the relationship between the sets of coordinate elements, we find the semantic relationship being combined with the chiasm, as in our examples from Psalm 67 and Matthew 5:45. In addition, chiasm normally involves an emphasis upon the first and last elements mentioned (A and A′). Thus in Matthew 5:45 it is perhaps not surprising that God would send the blessings of sun and rain upon the good and the righteous (B and B′), but it is remarkable, and therefore emphasized, that God likewise blesses the evil and unrighteous (A and A′). The emphasis in the chiasm of Isaiah 6:10 seems to be upon the mind (sometimes translated "heart"), with "ears" and "eyes" subordinate to this central feature of personality (indeed, the stopping of the ears and the shutting of the eyes may be the means by which the mind becomes dull and unable to comprehend). Finally, sometimes when a passage has a middle element (e.g., C), the chiasm suggests that this middle element is the primary concern around which the other features of the chiasm (A and B) revolve. This phenomenon is sometimes called "ring" or "concentric" structure. As we saw, Psalm 67 seems to have this type of chiasm, where the C element points to the primary emphasis of the entire passage.

INTERCALATION

Intercalation is the insertion of one literary unit in the midst of another literary unit. It usually means a *splitting apart* of a narrative in order to interpose another narrative within it, causing the reader to pause and to ponder the relationship between the intercalated material and the material that surrounds it. Although, as this description suggests, we normally find intercalation in narrative material, we can encounter it in other types of material; for example, some Pauline digressions might be considered a form of intercalation (e.g., 2 Cor. 6:14–7:1).

FIGURE 22
Intercalation in Mark's Gospel

A	B	A
11:12–14	11:15–19	11:20–24

Mark uses intercalation throughout his Gospel (see fig. 22). For example, Mark intercalates the story of the healing of the woman with a hemorrhage (5:25–34) into the story of the raising of Jairus's daughter (5:21–24, 35–43). He intercalates the story of the beheading of John the Baptist (6:14–29) into the story of the sending of the Twelve on their mission and their return to Jesus (6:7–13, 30–31). And he intercalates the cleansing of the temple (11:15–19) into the story of the cursing and withering of the fig tree (11:12–14, 20–24). In all these cases, Mark employs intercalation to strengthen the relationship of comparison. For instance, by intercalating the story of the beheading of John the Baptist at the hands of Herod into the story of the sending out of the Twelve on their mission, Mark is perhaps indicating that even as the ministry of John led to his rejection unto death, so also the disciples can eventually expect the same kind of dangerous negative reaction in their ministries. The insertion of the cleansing of the temple into the account of the cursing and withering of the fig tree might suggest that even as the fig tree was fruitless and thus good for nothing but to be cursed and die, so also the temple had ceased to function as God intended it and is therefore to be destroyed. The Gospel of Mark, then, is characterized by a recurring comparison by intercalation.

One also finds intercalation in the extended story of Joseph in the book of Genesis. Joseph is introduced along with his brothers in chapter 37, and his story continues in chapters 39–50. But chapter 38 seems to be an interruption. This chapter contains the story of Tamar and Judah. Specifically, it narrates the refusal of Judah's son Onan, and eventually Judah himself, to raise up children to Onan's deceased brother Er, by "going in to" Er's widow, Tamar. Finally Tamar tricks Judah into raising up descendants on behalf of his deceased son by assuming the trappings of a prostitute, with whom Judah has a dalliance. This account stands in contrast to the presentation of Joseph, who remains sexually pure in spite of the seductions of Potiphar's wife (chap. 39) and who works to preserve the family of Jacob, the covenant people of Israel, into the future. Thus chapter 38 involves an intercalation that reinforces the contrast between Joseph and his brothers.[37]

Significant Features of Structural Relationships

A number of significant features pertaining to structural relationships are worthy of note. First, although this list of structural relationships has been incorporated into the discussion of surveying the book, these relationships are present on all levels of literature. They are found not only on the book level but also on the level of the division, the section, the segment, the paragraph, and even the sentence. We will examine the significance of structural analysis when we move to the observation of these smaller units.

Second, a distinction can be made between general and specific relationships. By their nature some relationships are more general, less precise, or less specific than others, that is, they are found implicitly in other more specific relation-

---

37. For a detailed examination of this intercalation in Gen. 38, see Robert Alter, *The Art of Biblical Narrative* (New York: Basic Books, 1981), 3–10.

ships. Preparation/realization, for example, is a rather general relationship in that it often shades off into other more specific relationships in which it is implicit. For example, causation (the movement from cause to effect) includes implicit preparation/realization: the cause in causation always prepares for the effect that follows. And particularization (the movement from general to particular) always involves implicit preparation/realization since the general statement prepares for the particulars that follow. And we saw previously that cruciality contains implicit recurrence of causation and contrast. But when we encounter a radical reversal caused by a pivot passage, the more specific and precise identification is cruciality, and when we observe the movement from general to particular, the more precise label is particularization. The principle is that one should try to identify the structural relationship involved in the most precise way, for precision in observation will lead to precision, depth, and accuracy in interpretation.

A third point worth noting is that a structural relationship may be either explicit or implicit. An explicit relationship is marked by an expressly stated connection. The word *but*, for example, indicates contrast, and the word *therefore* indicates causation. However, contrast can be present without an explicit *but*, and causation is often found when the word *therefore* is absent. In such cases, we say that the relationship is implicit and that it must be inferred from the sense of the text. An explicit relationship is not necessarily more important or emphasized than an implicit one. An implied author might employ an explicit marker for a number of reasons or choose to omit it. The reader should be aware that a relationship may be present either implicitly or explicitly.

Students should also note that relationships may be simple or complex. A *simple* relationship is one relationship, such as causation. A *complex* relationship is more than one relationship used in combination. For example, *recurrence of comparative causation* involves three relationships so closely bound up with one another in the way they function within the book (or passage being observed) that a reader cannot describe how one is used without at the same time talking about the other(s). In such a case, the reader should combine these relationships so as to form a complex one. The statement just made actually describes the criterion for combining relationships: *If one cannot describe the function of a relationship in a book or passage without at the same time talking about another one(s), the relationships should be combined. If, however, one can describe the functioning of a relationship without bringing in other structural relationships, one should keep the relationships separate.* Given the complexity and depth of the dynamics of literary communication in books and passages, there will almost always be more than one major structural relationship identified in survey. Sometimes these relationships will function essentially independently of one another, in which case students should describe them separately as simple relationships.

But sometimes two or more of these relationships will be bound up with one another in their functioning within a book or passage. In such cases students should combine them into complex relationships.

The examples given in the discussion of structural relationships contain some instances of complex relationships. We saw that the book of Proverbs is structured according to a recurrence of contrast between wisdom and foolishness. Clearly one cannot describe this recurrence without at the same time mentioning the contrast, and vice versa. We mentioned, too, that Hebrews is structured according to a recurrence of contrasting instrumentation in that the writer repeatedly (recurrence) contrasts Christ as the effective means (instrumentation) of atonement over against the Levitical priesthood, which was not effective as the means of atonement. In addition, we mentioned that rhetorical relationships typically are not used by themselves but are normally employed in combination with semantic relationships in order to strengthen the semantic relationship.

Another significant point worth noting in regard to structural relationships is that readers often make a distinction between conscious and subconscious relationships. In regard to the writer, sometimes the relationship is employed consciously, sometimes subconsciously. Some students have expressed concern that they might be reading these structural relationships into the text because one cannot be certain that the writer actually intended to employ, say, the recurrence of contrast in a given book or passage. But this separation of conscious from subconscious use of relationships on the part of a writer is in many ways a distinction without a difference. For one thing, any serious intentional communication involves some attention to the form in which the communication will be cast. For example, the writer of 1 Samuel probably did not say to himself, "I think I will use recurrence of contrast here in my book." Nevertheless, we have every reason to believe that he considered how best to communicate his message and in the process chose to do so by repeatedly developing the differences between David and Saul.

In addition, the structural relationships described here are necessarily involved in the thinking process itself and indeed are generally present in all forms of art, not just literature. They are represented in all language groups, all cultures, all time periods, and all genres of literature. John Ruskin, who organized a list of some of these structural relationships in an essay that was influential in the inductive Bible study movement, claimed that they represent the structures found in nature itself.[38] Remembering, however, the necessity of processing our sense perceptions through the grids of our minds, it is perhaps better to understand these structural relationships as part of the human cogni-

---

38. Ruskin's classic essay on the laws of relationships appears in Kuist, *These Words upon Thy Heart*, 161–81. It is also available at www.inductivebiblicalstudy.com.

tive and communication processes. At any rate, specialists in linguistics and in the analysis of discourse have observed that humans appear to think and communicate by using a limited number of relationships (especially semantic relationships), somewhere between ten and twenty (depending on how one joins them or subdivides them).[39]

The point is that one cannot communicate without utilizing these relationships. Usually we employ them as we speak (or write) or as we read without being consciously aware that they are present, much as in the same way we make use of grammatical forms and syntactical devices without being aware of them. But a precise, specific, and penetrating understanding of serious literature, such as the Bible, is greatly advanced by careful consideration and intentional analysis of the structural relationships that are the building blocks of communication. The reader should remember the principle that pure material content does not exist; all material content is mediated to us through form, especially that dimension of form that we have described as literary structure. Everything being equal, therefore, the better we understand the form, or structure, in which a book or passage comes to us, the better we will understand its material content. In other words, *we can best understand what is said as we carefully analyze how it is said.*

In addition, we should remember that the goal of interpretation is to understand what the *implied author* is communicating in the text, for the implied author is the only author we actually have. Often, determining what was in the consciousness of a historical author is impossible, and at any rate our target is not, precisely speaking, the reconstruction of the consciousness of the flesh-and-blood author. Instead, we seek to grasp the sense of the text (the intention of the implied author, which is essentially coterminous with the sense of the text). As such, we need only *justify the plausibility that a structural relationship is present within the text.* If a structural relationship is present, it is part of the communication of the text itself, whether or not (or to whatever degree and in whatever sense) it might have been consciously intended by the flesh-and-blood author.

The purpose of identifying these major structural relationships is to begin to identify the main themes or issues of the book, the ways in which the (implied) author develops these main themes throughout the book, and the manner in which the writer relates these main themes to one another. In other words, we identify major structural relationships in order to begin

39. We are indebted to our colleague Dr. Joseph Dongell for a review of research from linguists and discourse analysts. See esp. Grimes, *Thread of Discourse*, 207–10; Nida, *Exploring Semantic Structures*, 50–65; Beekman, Callow, and Kopesec, *Semantic Structure of Written Communication*, 112–13; Robert E. Longacre, *The Grammar of Discourse* (New York: Plenum, 1983), 77–149; Mildred L. Larson, *Meaning-Based Translation: A Guide to Cross-Language Equivalence*, 2nd ed. (Lanham, MD: University Press of America, 1998), 205–351; Cotterell and Turner, *Linguistics and Biblical Interpretation*, 188–229.

to explore the dynamics of the movement, arrangement, and thought of the book.[40]

Raising Interpretive Questions

Having identified a major structural relationship, readers may raise questions directed toward that relationship. These questions serve as the bridge between observation and interpretation. They arise from observations made (in this case, from structural observations pertaining to the book-as-a-whole), and they form the basis for interpretation. In fact, as we shall see, interpretation is the answering of questions raised in the observation stage. This principle of making use of questions raised in observation as the basis for interpretation is extremely critical. Often eisegesis (reading our own ideas into passages) occurs because interpreters (at least implicitly) direct improper questions to the text, questions that the text does not invite the reader to pursue and that the text is not prepared to answer. In other words, interpretation that involves the answering of questions extraneous to the text and dissonant with the agenda of the text will likely be skewed.

If time permitted, it would be helpful to raise questions of all observations made in book survey. But given the limitation of time and the goal of making the most efficient use of time, we would best restrict questions to observations regarding major structural relationships. The answering of questions pertaining to structural relationships is normally more fruitful for interpretation than questions pertaining to other types of observations made in book survey.[41]

The three *primary* types of questions correspond (as we shall see) to the three major phases of interpretation:

- The *definitive* or *explanatory* question: what does this mean?
- The *rational* question: why is this included, and why here?
- The *implicational* question: what does this imply?

There are also four *auxiliary* questions:

- The *identificational* question: who or what is involved?
- The *modal* question: how is this accomplished?
- The *temporal* question: when is this accomplished?
- The *local* question: where is this accomplished?

40. For a detailed presentation of the main units/subunits and major structural relationships applied to a biblical book, see Bauer, *Structure of Matthew's Gospel*.

41. In the process of making use of various kinds of observations from survey (e.g., the main units and subunits) in interpretation, one at least implicitly directs questions to these observations in order to draw out their interpretive significance.

The auxiliary questions are actually specific forms of the definitive or explanatory question. Below is a list of the structural relationships described earlier in this chapter, along with key terms for some and sample interpretive questions for each of them. In some cases, the more general relationships that are implicit in more specific structural relationships are also noted (so, for example, particularization implicitly involves preparation/realization).

Recurrence

Recurrence: repetition of the same or similar terms, phrases, or other elements

Questions: What is the primary meaning of this recurring element (specify what recurs)? How do the individual occurrences relate to and illumine one another? Why this recurrence? What are the implications?

Semantic Structures

Contrast: association of things whose differences are stressed by the writer

Key terms: *but, however*

Questions: What major differences are here emphasized by the writer? What is the precise and specific meaning of each of these differences, and why did he deal with them as he did? What are the implications?

Comparison: association of things whose similarities (likeness) are stressed by the writer

Key terms: *like, as*

Questions: What are the major points of similarity here? What is the precise and specific meaning of each? Why did the writer stress these similarities, and why did he deal with them as he did? What are the implications?

Climax: movement from lesser to greater, toward a high point of culmination and intensity (implicitly involves an element of contrast, and usually of causation)

Questions: How does this unit reach its climax in (specify the climactic passage)? How does this climactic development illumine the climactic passage and the material leading to it? Why did the writer include this climax? What are the implications?

Particularization: movement from the general to the particular (implicitly involves preparation/realization)

Questions: What is the meaning of this general statement? How is the general statement particularized in the material that follows? How do the particulars illumine the general statement? Why did the writer include this movement from general to particular? What are the implications?

Generalization: movement from the particular to the general (implicitly involves preparation/realization)

Questions: What is the meaning of the particular statement? How is the particular statement generalized in the material that follows? How does the general statement illumine the particulars? Why did the writer include this movement from particular to general? What are the implications?

Causation: movement from cause to effect (implicitly involves preparation/ realization)

Key terms: *therefore, consequently*

Questions: How does this cause produce this effect? What are the major elements involved in this movement from cause to effect, and what is the meaning of each? Why did the writer include this causation? What are the implications?

Substantiation: movement from effect to cause (implicitly involves preparation/realization)

Key terms: *for, because, since*

Questions: How does the substantiatory passage cause (that is, support or give reason for) the preceding passage? What are the major elements involved in this movement from effect to cause, and what is the meaning of each? Why did the writer include this substantiation? What are the implications?

Cruciality: device of the pivot to produce a radical reversal or complete change of direction (implicitly involves recurrence of causation and contrast)

Questions: How does this cruciality illumine the material on both sides of the pivot? Why did the writer include this cruciality? What are the implications?

Summarization: an abridgment (summing up) either preceding or following a unit of material (sometimes similar to a general statement, but contains more specifics than a general statement)

Questions: How does this passage summarize the material that precedes (or follows)? How does the preceding material illumine this summarization? Why did the writer include this summarization? What are the implications?

Interrogation: a problem or question, followed by its solution or answer (implicitly involves preparation/realization, and often causation; problem/solution type involves contrast)

Questions pertaining to problem/solution type: What is the meaning of the problem presented here? How is this problem solved? What are the major elements involved in the movement from problem to solution, and what is the meaning of each? Why did the writer include this interrogation? What are the implications?

Questions pertaining to question/answer type: What is the meaning of this question? How does the answer address this question, and what is the full and precise meaning of this answer? Why did this writer include this interrogation? What are the implications?

Preparation/realization: background or setting of the events or ideas

Questions: What is the meaning of this background material? How does it prepare for what follows? Why did the writer prepare for what follows? Why did the writer prepare for what follows in this way? What are the implications?

Instrumentation: movement from means to end (implicitly involves causation), which takes the forms of either statement of purpose or description of means

Key terms: *in order that*, *so that* (statement of purpose); *by*, *through* (description of means)

Questions pertaining to statement of purpose: What is the meaning of the purpose statement itself? How does it illumine the means? How does it illumine the end? How does the means cause or produce the end? Why did the writer include this purpose statement? What are the implications?

Questions pertaining to description of means: How does the writer describe this means or agency, and what is the meaning of this description? What is the meaning of the ways in which this means produces the end? Why did the writer thus present this means in such a way as to produce this end? What are the implications?

Rhetorical Structures

Interchange: exchanging or alternation of blocks of material (a-b-a'-b')

Questions pertaining to contrast by interchange: What are the major differences presented here, and what is the meaning of each? How does this interchange strengthen this contrast, and how does it illumine the major differences? Why did the writer emphasize these differences? Why did he thus support or strengthen the contrast by this use of interchange? What are the implications?

Inclusio: repetition of the same word(s) or phrase at the beginning and end of a unit, thus producing a bracket effect

Questions pertaining to comparison by inclusio: What are the major similarities presented here, and what is the meaning of each? How does this inclusio strengthen the comparison, and how does it illumine the major points of similarity? Why did the writer emphasize these similarities? Why did he thus support or strengthen the comparison by this use of inclusio? What are the implications?

Chiasm: repetition of elements in inverted order (a-b-{c}-b'-a')

Questions pertaining to contrast by chiasm: What are the major differences presented here, and what is the meaning of each? How does this chiasm strengthen this contrast, and how does it illumine the major differences? Why did the writer emphasize these differences? Why did he thus support or strengthen the contrast by use of chiasm? What are the implications?

Intercalation: insertion of one literary unit in the midst of another literary unit

Questions pertaining to comparison by intercalation: What are the major similarities presented here, and what is the meaning of each? How does this intercalation strengthen this comparison, and how does it illumine the major points of similarity? Why did the writer emphasize these similarities? Why did he thus support or strengthen the comparison by use of intercalation? What are the implications?

The reader will note that the sample questions above are asked in the following order: definitive/explanatory, rational, and implicational. This order is important because the rational question(s) builds upon the definitive/explanatory question(s), and the implicational question seeks the implications of the answers to the definitive/explanatory and rational question(s). In our examination of the interpretation phase, we will see that normally one must attend to the definitive/explanatory question(s) before one can adequately address the rational question(s), and one must always answer the definitive/ explanatory and rational questions before addressing the implications of the answers to these questions.

The reader will note, too, that these sample questions are general and indeed generic. However, one always ought to tailor the question to the way in which the relationship is employed in a given book over against asking general or rote questions. In other words, one should try to ask specific, penetrating, probing questions; these kinds of questions will be the most helpful when we reach the interpretation phase.

When crafting questions, describe specifically the way in which the structural relationship functions in the book (over against simply identifying a relationship as present), and immediately raise interpretive questions directed toward this description of how the structural relationship functions.

When recording questions, move toward using terms that address the *significance* of the relationship rather than simply employing the *name* of the relationship itself. For example, when asking questions about contrast, ask about the *differences* rather than about *contrast*. Thus one might ask, much more specifically than in the sample questions above, Exactly what are the major differences here, and what is the specific and precise meaning of each of these differences? rather than asking, What is the meaning of the contrast? When raising questions about particularization, one might ask, How is the statement in 1:1 spelled out, or expanded, throughout 1:2–3:21? rather than asking, What is the meaning of this particularization?

Remember, too, that the value of interpretive questions is in their function of directing the process of interpretation. As such, use imagination to discern the kinds of questions that will be most helpful in drawing out the interpretive significance of the structural relationship. In other words, one should imagine oneself at the interpretation phase and consider what questions one might direct at the structural relationship in order to massage that relationship for all of its interpretive worth.

We should point out, however, that while the student should specifically tailor definitive/explanatory and rational questions to the way in which the relationship functions in a particular book, the same cannot be said of the implicational question. The implicational question should be kept general and always asked in the same way: What are the implications? If one were to ask the implicational question in a more specific way, one would begin answering the question in the process of asking it, for one would assume that the answers to the definitive/explanatory and rational questions had implications for a specific area or topic. But one should not prejudge the kinds of implications that might emerge from the answers to the definitive/explanatory and rational questions.[42]

At the point of observation, which includes book survey, we simply raise these questions; at this juncture we do not try to answer them. As mentioned previously, the answering of questions belongs to the interpretation phase of study and in-

---

42. The fact that the articulation of the implicational question is always the same may raise doubts about the usefulness of regularly asking it. But it should always be asked, for it will remind the interpreter that the meaning of passages involves what is implicit as well as what is explicit and that sometimes the key to interpretation is found in the intentional pursuit of answering the implicational question.

deed serves as the basis for interpretation. Part 3 (on interpretation) will include a discussion of the process of answering these various kinds of questions.

Because all three types of questions—definitive/explanatory, rational, and implicational—address the interpretation of the book or passage, these questions are closely related and sometimes overlap. For example, in answering the definitive/explanatory question, we often find that we are moving into answering the rational question. But the distinctions are helpful to identify the primary targets of interpretation.[43] At this juncture, we would do well to develop briefly the character and function of each of these types of questions.

The *definitive/explanatory question* is the most basic one. It asks after the meaning, or sense, of the passage. In other words, it seeks to determine the basic communicative content that the implied author is conveying to the implied reader. To answer a definitive/explanatory question concerning the structural relationship of contrast in a given passage would involve identifying the specific dimensions or aspects of the differences set forth in the passage, analyzing the ways in which these differences are developed, and ascertaining the essential message that the implied author is thereby sending to the implied reader.

The *rational question* can take two forms. One form is directed to the *logic of the text*. This form asks why, according to the text's logic, certain things that are reported in the text happened or were said, or why they are true. For example, in observing the contrast between Jesus and the religious authorities in the Gospel of Mark, one might ask why, according to the logic of the narrative of Mark's Gospel, these differences between Jesus and the religious leaders existed, and why they developed and manifested themselves as they did.[44] Or in noticing in the book of Amos the repeated causation between Israel's sin (cause) and God's consequent judgment (effect), one might ask why, according to the book's logic, God thus responded to Israel's sin with this kind of judgment.

The other form of the rational question may be directed to the *purpose of the writer*. In other words, we may ask why the writer wished to include this feature, or why he wished to employ a certain structural device (e.g.,

43. To these three categories of questions one might add the observational question. An observational question is one that is raised regarding the legitimacy of an observation made. For example, having observed the possible (but debatable) presence of particularization in a book, one might ask, Is particularization actually present here? This kind of question is always implicit because later stages of study (esp. interpretation) will either confirm or correct observations made.

44. Since the focus of interpretation is upon the text, one does not direct the question to the conflict between the historical Jesus and the actual historical religious authorities in the days of Jesus's earthly ministry; rather, one directs the question to the reason for these differences (conflict) as set forth in the narrative of Mark's Gospel. As we see below, probing issues in the life of the historical Jesus is a legitimate, if somewhat speculative, inquiry. But one should not confuse the interpretation of the text with the interpretation of historical events; for the text involves the creation of its own world, which is necessarily distinct from the "real" world of historical events, no matter how reliable and historically accurate a biblical narrative is. On the other hand, any historical reconstruction of narrated events should begin with the interpretation of the text.

contrast) to communicate his message. By these questions we do not intend to reconstruct, in a way characteristic of interpretation during the Romantic period (as in Schleiermacher), the psychology of the flesh-and-blood author or to imitate more recent attempts to identify deep and largely hidden motives in the flesh-and-blood author.[45] Instead, one directs these questions to the implied author, meaning the author as he presents himself and can be inferred from the text. One asks, What kinds of communicative effects did the implied author wish (or intend) to accomplish, and why was it important for him to accomplish these effects and to accomplish them in this way?[46]

The rational question is characterized by the interrogative *why*. It can be expressed in other ways, too, but the term *why* best conveys its inherent meaning. One should ask the *why* question even if the reasons and motives for biblical statements are not explicit, for they are always present when intelligent communication is at work. If they are not expressed, they may be implied, and one should seek them out because they are of supreme importance in understanding the text.

The *implicational question* is actually an expansion of the rational question, and its answer begins forming the bridge between interpretation and application. First comes observation, answering the question, What is here? Then follows the definitive/explanatory question: What does it mean? This question is succeeded by the question of reason: Why is this particular thing here? Finally comes the implicational question: What are the full implications of this particular thing with this particular meaning having been placed here for these particular reasons?

The importance of the implicational question stems from the recognition that the meaning of books or passages often transcends what is overtly or expressly stated in the book or passage. In other words, the authors we encounter in texts often communicate implicitly. Thus the nature of communication requires that we ask after implications.

There are two types of implications. The first involves *presuppositions*: what lies behind or beneath a statement. This discovery process involves exploring what a writer must accept as a prior belief in order to communicate what he does in a book or passage. We might illustrate presuppositions by noting these implications from Genesis 1:1: "In the beginning when God created the heavens and the earth. . . ."[47]

45. For a helpful word of caution pertaining to the problematic of psychological reconstruction of writers' motives, see Fowl, "Role of Authorial Intention," 74. In some instances, however, almost no distinction exists between the motives/intentions/purposes of the implied author and those of the flesh-and-blood author, such as with the Pauline Epistles, where the text explicitly connects the implied author with the historical Paul (see, e.g., Rom. 1).

46. Here is an especially clear example of the close relationship between the definitive/explanatory and rational questions.

47. Although Gen. 1:1 is obviously a statement rather than a structural relationship, this passage may effectively illustrate what is meant by implications as such.

- God exists (note that no argument is made here for God's existence; it is simply assumed).
- God is distinct from creation.
- God is free.
- God is preexistent to creation.
- God is powerful.
- God is intelligent.
- God is purposeful.
- God is active.

The second type of implication involves *natural outgrowths*: For the writer to communicate this truth or teaching, he must also believe the claim that flows naturally and logically from the truth or teaching. These implications are notions that are logically necessary conclusions from the truth or teaching. Again, examples from Genesis 1:1 include the following:

- God is expected to be concerned for the well-being of his creation.
- God has absolute prerogative over this creation, including the prerogative to destroy or judge it.
- God has authority to make demands upon his creation.
- God has power to sustain his creation.
- God has power to control the destiny of creation or the universe that he has made.
- God has power to repair or redeem creation, should such repair or redemption become necessary.

Students should raise interpretive questions about each major structural relationship in book survey, for these questions participate in the interpretation phase in the following ways: First, at the conclusion of the interpretation of all passages in the entire book (or at least a number of significant passages within the book), these questions are answered to synthesize the book's message. Second, in shorter books the reader can move immediately from survey to the interpretation of the book-as-a-whole by answering these questions raised in survey. In such cases these questions can serve as the means to interpret the book.[48] Moreover, the very asking of specific and penetrating questions often clarifies the structural relationship and points to significant dimensions of the relationship that might otherwise be missed, a principle that educational theorists call "metacognition."

---

48. Using questions in this manner is quite possible with shorter books (normally those that contain fewer than five chapters) but is more difficult to manage with longer books.

Locating Key Passages

Having identified the major structural relationships of a book, one should look at each of these major relationships and ask, What one or two brief passages best represent this major structural relationship? The answer to that question involves the selection of key verses or strategic areas that represent major structural relationships and thus provide insight into the book-as-a-whole. Every reader at least implicitly identifies certain passages as key or strategic. In an inductive approach, readers need to allow the dynamics of the text itself to determine, at least in the first instance, the passages that are especially prominent in the book.

Some structural relationships point directly to strategic areas. In summarization, for example, clearly the summary passage itself would typically be the strategic area that best represents that relationship; in climax, the climactic passage; in cruciality, the pivot passage; and in the statement-of-purpose form of instrumentation, the statement of purpose itself. But other structural relationships do not so clearly and directly point to a specific passage that best represents the relationship. In such cases, the reader will need to consider more fully which passage best represents the relationship. For example, in the case of recurrence, the key passage would be the one occurrence that best represents the recurrence.

Identifying strategic areas serves a number of purposes. First, they provide insights into the book-as-a-whole, insights that otherwise might be missed. The interpretation of key passages, in other words, is especially significant for understanding the message of the entire book. Readers will often gain greater understanding of the message of the book-as-a-whole as they reflect seriously on the meaning of key passages and the special role these passages play in the program of the book.

Additionally, strategic areas provide help for ministry by assisting us to identify the most important sections of the book. One will want at least to be aware of the most significant passages in the book, with a view toward possibly giving priority to these portions in teaching or preaching. Indeed, one person described his experience of teaching a series of Bible studies at a local church when he was asked to speak for an hour on successive Wednesday evenings on each book of the Bible. Already in the first week, he was confronted with the book of Genesis, which has fifty chapters. He chose to develop the message of Genesis by focusing on one or two key passages in the book, which thus served as a kind of entrée into the message of the book-as-a-whole. Then he continued this practice of focusing on key verses of each book throughout the remainder of his series.

Finally, the identification of strategic areas gives direction as to where to place stress in study, especially when time is limited. By focusing study on key passages, one is placing stress on the parts of the book that are most significant according to the structure of the book itself.

Identifying Higher-Critical Data

In addition to identifying general materials and structure, students may wish to locate higher-critical data. Higher-critical data are data within the book itself that bear upon such higher-critical issues as the author, the recipients, the place and date of writing, and the occasion of writing, which need to be identified. As one reads through the book in survey, one should keep questions pertaining to these issues in the back of one's mind, such as, What does this text suggest regarding the person of the author? What clues does the book itself give as to the recipients? Some books yield much more of these kinds of data than do others, but these questions should always be posed. The identification of these data is limited to the book itself. At the point of book survey, naturally, the reader needs to be tentative about the conclusions that one begins to draw regarding author, audience, or occasion.

At this point one should not typically go to other biblical books or to secondary sources. Considering other biblical books so soon may involve the naive acceptance of a number of historical and literary assumptions (some of which may prove to be invalid). Consulting secondary sources at this time may prejudice the reader and therefore may prevent one from seeing possibilities regarding higher-critical issues that actually exist, or, conversely, may lead one to accept conclusions that are problematic in terms of the data of the text itself.

By looking for these data within the book itself, readers will be prepared to read scholarly discussions regarding these historical matters in an informed, discriminating, and helpful way. They will also learn a great deal about historical background, some of which might not be covered in even the more significant scholarly discussions.

Noting Other Major Impressions

Other major impressions is a catchall category involving any significant observation relative to the book-as-a-whole that did not fit into any of the previously mentioned phases. As such, this category has a number of possibilities. For example, one might want to identify subtle elements in the book, such as tone or atmosphere. Every book or passage has a certain tone or *feel*, the affective or emotional sense that one gathers from reading the book or passage. One might identify the tone of Galatians as one of frustration, or one might recognize the feel of the anger from personal hurt in 2 Corinthians. One might catch the tone or atmosphere of calm contentment in Philippians or the tone of affirmation in 1 Timothy or the tone of resignation in 2 Timothy. We discuss the role of tone or atmosphere in interpretation in part 3 (below). In addition, one might use the category of other major impressions to identify literary or theological peculiarities of the book with a view toward (eventually) understanding their nature and meaning. Thus one might observe that in the Gospel of Mark, Jesus repeatedly refers to himself as the "Son of Man," and yet no one else in Mark's narrative ever calls Jesus "Son of Man" or addresses him in this way. Or one might want to use this category to identify the nature and quality of the literature, such as the fast-paced character of Mark's Gospel or Luke's artistic manner and expressive vocabulary.

Implementation of Book Survey (2 Timothy)

As previously mentioned, 2 Timothy 3:16–17 will serve throughout as a continuous example of the process of method. The following is a sample book survey of 2 Timothy.

General Materials: Ideological

Main Units and Subunits

Introduction	I. Thanksgiving and general exhortation: "Rekindle the gift"	II. Particular exhortations developing the command to rekindle the gift, applied to specific circumstances and challenges 1:8--4:8			
		A. Exhortations concerning the challenge of suffering for the truth of the gospel	B. Exhortations concerning the challenge of disputes and quarrels within the church	C. Exhortations concerning the challenge of (future) apostasy	Conclusion
1:1–2	1:3-------------------7	1:8------------------2:7	2:8----------------2:26	3:1-----------------4:8	4:9--------4:22

Major Structural Relationships and Interpretive Questions

A. PREPARATION AND REALIZATION

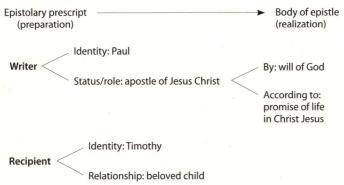

Epistolary prescript (preparation) ————————————→ Body of epistle (realization)

Writer < Identity: Paul / Status/role: apostle of Jesus Christ < By: will of God / According to: promise of life in Christ Jesus

Recipient < Identity: Timothy / Relationship: beloved child

Questions

1. What are the major elements in this description of Paul and Timothy, and in the blessing, and what is the meaning of each? How does each illumine the body of the epistle that follows, both in the large and in individual passages? How does the body of the epistle illumine main features within 1:1–2?
2. Why did Paul, the implied author, introduce the book in precisely this way?
3. What are the implications?

B. Particularization

General exhortation	Particular exhortations
"Rekindle the gift of God that is within you through the laying on of my hands" (1:6).	Paul develops the command to re-kindle the gift, as applied to *specific* circumstances (1:8–4:8).

Questions

1. What is the meaning of the general exhortation of 1:6, and how precisely is it developed in 1:8–4:8 through the various exhortations in the remainder of the book? How do these particular exhortations addressing specific circumstances and challenges illumine 1:6, and how does 1:6 illumine these particular exhortations found throughout the remainder of the book?
2. Why did Paul frame the general hortatory concern of the book as he has in 1:6, and why did he develop this general concern as he has throughout the rest of the book?
3. What are the implications?

C. Recurrence of causation and substantiation (hortatory pattern) by contrast

Repeated exhortations are preceded and followed by reasons (causes) why the exhortations should be obeyed. There is a twofold contrast.

1. In terms of *exhortations*:

Positive exhortations	vs.	Negative exhortations
What Timothy *ought* to do		What Timothy *ought not* to do
	(complementary contrast)	

2. In terms of *reasons/causes*:

Positive examples	vs.	Negative examples
Paul (1:3, 8, 11–14; 2:1, 8–10, 11–13; 3:10–13; 4:6–8, 16–18) Onesiphorus (1:16–18) Lois and Eunice (1:5) Luke (4:11)		Phygelus and Hermogenes (1:15) Hymenaeus and Philetus (2:17) Jannes and Jambres (3:8) Demas (4:10) Crescens and Titus (4:10) Alexander (4:14–15)

(contradictory contrast)

Questions

1. What is the meaning of each of the exhortations in this book, and how are the individual exhortations related to and illumined by one another? Is there development in the exhortations as they appear throughout the book? If so, what is the meaning of this development, and how does it illumine the vision of the Christian life and ministry as set forth here? How does the complementarity between positive and negative exhortations illumine Paul's instruction in this book? What are the major elements in Paul's support for the exhortation throughout the book, and how does an analysis of these warrants for the exhortations illumine the vision of Christian life and ministry? How does Paul's use of positive and negative models contribute to and illumine the bases for Christian life and ministry as presented here?

2. Why did Paul include each of these exhortations, and why did he relate these individual exhortations to one another as he has? Why did Paul thus move between positive and negative exhortations in this complementary fashion? Why did Paul support these exhortations as he has, especially by his use of both positive and negative personal models?

3. What are the implications?

D. Climax

Final testimony of Paul's faithfulness throughout his Christian life; declaration of confidence of reward as he faces his imminent death and eschatological judgment (4:6–8)

Repeated autobiographical references to Paul's patient endurance in suffering for the truth of the gospel (1:3–7; esp. 1:8–2:13; 3:1–14)

Questions

1. Specifically and precisely, how does Paul's final testimony in 4:6–8 bring to a climax his repeated autobiographical references throughout the book? How does this culminative progression toward Paul's final testimony in 4:6–8 illumine these earlier references, and indeed point to the meaning of the book's message as a whole? How does this movement toward culmination illumine 4:6–8?

2. Why did the author develop these autobiographical references toward this point of culmination as he did? Why did he thus conclude the body of the book with this culminative final testimony?

3. What are the implications?

Key Verses/Strategic Areas

1:1–2—Represents preparation and realization

1:3–7—Represents particularization

1:8–18; 4:6–8—Represents recurrence of causation and substantiation (hortatory pattern) with contrast, as well as climax

Higher-Critical Data

A. The author
   1. Identifies himself as Paul, an apostle (1:1), and a preacher and teacher (1:11)
   2. Is suffering in prison in Rome for the sake of Christ, and especially because of the preaching of the gospel (1:8, 12, 16, 17; 2:3, 9); has apparently made his way to Rome by way of Corinth and Miletus (4:20), and perhaps also Ephesus (1:18)
   3. Has been bereft of many friends and erstwhile supporters, including Phygelus and Hermogenes (1:15), Demas, Crescens, Titus (4:10), Alexander the coppersmith (4:14–15), and also Erastus and Trophimus (4:20), but is being assisted by Onesiphorus (1:16) and Luke (4:11)
   4. Believes he is about to be executed (4:6)
   5. Speaks of his "first defense" made before Gentiles at some point in the past, when he was rescued "from the lion's mouth," suggesting that he is now engaged in, or has already conducted, a second defense (4:16–17)
B. The recipient
   1. Identified as Timothy, Paul's "beloved child" (1:2)
   2. Has been a long-standing and intimate acquaintance of Paul's (1:3, 15, 18); received divine giftedness (perhaps for ministry) from the laying on of Paul's hands (1:6) and was carefully instructed by Paul

(1:13; 2:1); was with Paul at Antioch, Iconium, and Lystra (3:11), and possibly also at Ephesus (1:18)

3. Has in the past felt sorrow and/or is now experiencing sorrow (1:4); is being called upon now to endure shame and suffering for the sake of the gospel (1:8; 2:3)

4. Has a heritage of godliness and instruction in "the sacred writings" from his childhood (3:15) from his grandmother Lois and mother, Eunice (1:5)

5. Is young (2:22)

6. Is engaged in pastoral ministry characterized by reminder (2:8, 14), instruction (2:1–2; 4:2), and evangelism (4:5)

7. Is located in the same vicinity as Mark (4:11), Prisca and Aquila, and the household of Onesiphorus (4:19); and Paul assumes Timothy will come to him via Troas (4:13)

8. Is known by many at Rome, particularly Eubulus, Pudens, Linus, and Claudia (4:21)

C. The occasion (and purpose)

1. Paul was unable to visit Timothy and writes to urge Timothy to visit him soon, indeed before winter (4:21; cf. 1:3–7).

2. Timothy is enduring hardship (1:8; 2:1–7), and Paul thus writes out of a concern to encourage him. Possibly, too, Timothy is experiencing problems among his congregation(s), including vain disputes (2:16, 23) and false teaching linked to lawless behavior (3:1–9; 4:3–4), especially the teaching promoted by Hymenaeus and Philetus that the resurrection has already occurred (2:18).

Other Major Impressions

The tone of this book is characterized especially by resignation; Paul knows he is about to be executed, yet throughout he exudes a peaceful resignation that stems from confidence in the Lord to judge him according to his faithfulness (4:6–8, 18).

Exercise: Book Survey

1. Read through the book of Jonah as many times as possible in one sitting. Following the suggestions presented in chapters 1–7 above, survey the book.

a. Identify the general materials of the book.

b. Locate the major units and subunits in the book and identify the major structural relationships operative throughout the majority of the book.

    c. Ask a few interpretive questions based on each major structural relationship observed.

    d. Identify the key verses or strategic areas that provide insight into the book-as-a-whole.

    e. Note other major impressions pertaining to the book-as-a-whole.

2. Follow the same process with the Gospel of Mark.

12

Survey of Parts-as-Wholes
(Divisions, Sections, Segments)

We mentioned at the end of chapter 10 the three levels in observation: the book-as-a-whole, parts-as-wholes, and focused observation. The second level, the survey of parts-as-wholes, now occupies our attention. This process involves the survey of more or less extended units within the book: the division, the section, and the segment. In general, we can say that the main units of the book are the *divisions*, the main units within divisions are the *sections*, and the book's sections are themselves broken down or divided into *segments*. Thus proceeding from more broad to more detailed, the progression is from the book to the division, from the division to the section, and from the section to the segment.[1]

But a further word of clarification about segments is necessary. As the term is used in the present volume, a *segment* is defined by its length. A segment is a unit of material, about the length of an average chapter (though not always corresponding to a chapter), bound together by a common theme or structure. Keeping in mind this definition of a segment according to the length of the passage, a major division of a book could also be a segment. Thus in the Gospel of John, the first major division of the book may be the prologue (1:1–18), but given the fact that the prologue is "a unit of material, about the length of

---

1. When sections are sufficiently large, we might add the additional category of subsection between sections and segments.

an average chapter, bound together by a common theme or structure," this first major division of John's Gospel is also a segment.

For the sake of simplicity in our present discussion, we assume that we are talking about the survey of segments, but what is said here regarding the survey of segments pertains for the most part to the survey of divisions or sections.

Phases of the Survey of Parts-as-Wholes

Four phases are involved in the survey of segments, and these phases correspond generally to the phases followed in the survey of the book.

Describing the Segment's Structure

As in book survey, this process involves two components: the identification of main units and subunits, and the identification of major structural relationships operative throughout the segment. The main units and subunits should be as broad as the material allows and should be based on (1) shifts of emphasis within the segment and (2) implications from the major structural relationships identified. One should identify only the *major* structural relationships, those that control the bulk (more than half) of the segment. The fact that parts-as-wholes (e.g., segments) tend to be shorter in length than entire books does not mean that they will necessarily contain fewer major structural relationships. Sometimes relatively short segments contain more major structural relationships than even long books.

Raising Interpretive Questions

Immediately after identifying and describing a major structural relationship, one should raise questions about the structural relationship. The questions should be asked in this order: definitive/explanatory, rational, and implicational; with the exception of the implicational question, they should be tailored to the way the structural relationship functions in the segment. The questions raised in segment survey share the same characteristics as those described under book survey (see chap. 11).

Locating Key Passages/Strategic Areas in the Segment

As in book survey, one should examine each major structural relationship identified in order to determine the one or two brief passages that best represent that relationship. These passages should be as brief as possible if they are truly to function as strategic passages. The purposes of identifying key passages or strategic areas in segment survey parallel the purposes for identifying these passages in book survey.

Identifying Literary Form(s) Employed

At this point we make a distinction between book survey and segment survey. As we saw, in book survey we identify the higher-critical data in the book-as-a-whole. Because this process has been accomplished in book survey, it does not need to be repeated in the survey of individual units throughout the book. However, identifying the literary forms, or genres, employed in the segment is helpful. A more complete discussion of the role of literary forms comes below, in the presentation on interpretation. At this point we note that a number of levels of literary forms exist, from general and broad categories to progressively more narrow and specific ones, for each of the most general literary forms can be subdivided into more specific ones. These in turn can be subdivided into yet more specific ones.[2]

At this stage readers should identify only the most general literary forms, for to move to more specific ones often involves an interpretive judgment: it would assume some interpretive work on the passage itself.[3] The process of identifying more specific forms now would also tend to be somewhat speculative because scholars disagree about the existence of some of these forms and about their recognition and use in the cultures and subcultures represented by the biblical writers.

The literary forms discussed below are some of the most commonly and easily identified genres in the biblical literature.[4]

PROSE NARRATIVE

Prose narrative is the literary form of story or of historical reportage. Examples include Matthew 3:1–17 and Genesis 31:1–55. The default assumption in prose narrative is that the language is literal rather than figurative. Figurative language sometimes does appear in prose narrative, but in such cases either the figurative character of the language will be obvious from the sense of the text, or literary clues will indicate that, in a particular instance, figurative language is being employed. In the absence of these indications, the reader will normally be safe in assuming the literal use of language.

Readers of prose narrative also assume that the material moves according to chronological sequence—for example, that what is described in verse 13 takes place in time after what was described in verse 12. Chronological sequence can have two exceptions. The first exception is *flashback* (*analepsis*), which

---

2. This phenomenon is manifested even in the short list of "general" literary forms described immediately following, for parable and apocalyptic texts can be viewed as more specific forms of prose narrative.

3. Much of this is taken up in form criticism, a critical approach that is discussed under "History of the Tradition" in chap. 14.

4. The literary forms described here are also *midlevel*: they belong especially to segment-length or section-length units. Some of the more specific literary forms address book-level genre (e.g., ancient biography), or paragraph-level genre (e.g., *chreia*, or "pronouncement story").

involves an interruption of chronological sequence in order to describe an event that occurred before the point in time at which it occurs in the movement of the story. An example is 1 Samuel 9:14–18:

> So [Saul and his servant] went up to the town. As they were entering the town, they saw Samuel coming out toward them on his way up to the shrine.
>
> Now the day before Saul came, the LORD had revealed to Samuel: "Tomorrow about this time I will send to you a man from the land of Benjamin, and you shall anoint him to be ruler over my people Israel. He shall save my people from the hand of the Philistines; for I have seen the suffering of my people, because their outcry has come to me."
>
> When Samuel saw Saul, the LORD told him, "Here is the man of whom I spoke to you. He it is who shall rule over my people." Then Saul approached Samuel inside the gate.

Note that the writer has interrupted his account of the day of Saul's arrival with a reference to the Lord's revelation to Samuel the day before.

The second exception to chronological sequence is *foreshadowing* (*prolepsis*), which involves an interruption in order to describe an event that will occur, in time, after the point at which it is placed in the movement of the story. An example of foreshadowing is John 2:18–23:

> The Jews then said to him, "What sign can you show us for doing this [driving the money changers out of the temple]?" Jesus answered them, "Destroy this temple, and in three days I will raise it up." The Jews then said, "This temple has been under construction for forty-six years, and will you raise it up in three days?" But he was speaking of the temple of his body. After he was raised from the dead, his disciples remembered that he had said this; and they believed the scripture and the word that Jesus had spoken.
>
> When he was in Jerusalem during the Passover festival, many believed in his name because they saw the signs that he was doing.

Typically, when a writer employs foreshadowing or flashback in prose narrative, he is inviting the reader to pause so as to consider what is the relationship between the event that he has presented out of chronological sequence and the surrounding narrative, and to explore why the writer would have interrupted chronological sequence to describe *this* event *here*.[5]

Prose narrative normally emphasizes the relationship of events to one another—that is, plot—and characters (their description, development, and

---

5. For fuller and more technical discussions of flashback and foreshadowing, see Seymour Chatman, *Story and Discourse: Narrative Structure in Fiction and Film* (Ithaca, NY: Cornell University Press, 1978), 62–79; Gerard Genette, "Time and Narrative," in *Aspects of Narrative*, ed. J. Hillis Miller (New York: Columbia University Press, 1970), 93–118; idem, *Narrative Discourse: An Essay in Method* (Ithaca, NY: Cornell University Press, 1980), 32–76.

relation to one another) or characterization. Exploring these issues can be highly significant for interpretation. The critical discipline that has arisen around prose narrative is *narrative criticism*. Readers interested in exploring narrative criticism should consult especially the work of Robert Alter for Old Testament narrative criticism and the works of Mark Allan Powell and James L. Resseguie for New Testament narrative criticism.[6]

POETRY

Poetry is a form of literature characterized by the use of emotive and associative figurative language, by meter, and by parallelism between lines or strophes. Poetic literature may contain literal language; but the default assumption in poetry is that the language will be figurative unless the sense of the passage requires a literal construal or literary clues exist to indicate that the language is to be construed literally. And the figurative language tends to be highly affective, addressing the emotions rather than simply the rational-cognitive faculties. Moreover, the figurative language in poetry is usually associative in that it is intended to bring to mind a whole cluster of ideas or thoughts. As such, poetic language tends to be relatively indeterminate; it conveys a rather broad (though still limited) range of possible construals.

The poetic literary form makes no assumption that the material will move along according to chronological sequence, as is the case with prose narrative. The assumption, rather, is that it is concerned for the total effect that the passage will have upon the mind and emotions of the reader. Sometimes poetic passages will develop chronologically, yet readers should not assume a chronological sequence is present unless there are literary indications.

Poetry includes rhythm or meter. It has a certain cadence. When trying to identify the points of emphasis in the passage or when exploring the relationships between specific details in the passage, attending to the rhythm or meter of the poetry should be helpful. But although scholars are aware of meter in poetic literature, they still do not fully understand the nature and function of biblical poetic meter; thus the recognition of meter at present offers only minimal interpretive assistance.

Biblical poetry is characterized also by the presence of *parallelism*, which has three primary (though not exclusive) types. The first is *synonymous parallelism* (a → a') in which the second line or strophe says essentially the same thing as the first, only in different words or phraseology. A second type is *antithetic parallelism*, in which the second line or strophe stands in contrast with the first (a → but b). Finally, *synthetic parallelism* has the second line

---

6. Alter, *Art of Biblical Narrative*; James L. Resseguie, *Narrative Criticism of the New Testament: An Introduction* (Grand Rapids: Baker Academic, 2005); Powell, *What Is Narrative Criticism?*

or strophe say the same (or essentially the same) as the first and adds to it (a → a' + b).

Readers who want to identify poetic passages in the Bible should observe the format employed in modern English translations; they indicate the presence of poetry by means of constant indentation (see modern translations of the Psalms). For a number of passages in the Bible, scholars disagree as to whether they are in the form of poetry or not. At times the decision must ultimately await the interpretation phase, and for some passages a final determination is impossible and judgment must remain suspended. By far the majority of biblical examples of poetic literary form are in the Old Testament, but the New Testament also has some instances, especially when a New Testament writer is quoting an Old Testament passage or quotes a hymn that was in use in the early church.

Readers who want more specifically to explore the nature and interpretive significance of poetry should consult especially the works of Robert Alter, David Petersen, and Kent Harold Richards.[7]

PARABLES

A parable is a fictitious story, usually drawn from everyday life, that points to a spiritual truth. As such, the parabolic form employs the principle of analogy. This emphasis on analogy is suggested by the derivation of the word *parable*, which is a combination of the Greek terms *para* and *ballō*, meaning literally, "that which is cast alongside." This expression indicates that a parable is a story that is cast alongside the spiritual truth to which it points by way of analogy. Therefore a parable consists of two components: the spiritual truth that is being communicated, and the narrative that is placed beside it for the purpose of communicating the spiritual truth.

But one should remember the adage that "no analogy walks on all fours." In other words, an analogy always has points of discontinuity as well as continuity between its components, in this case between the story of the parable and the spiritual truth to which it points. Readers, once they come to the point of interpretation, must consider exactly how the parable story relates to the spiritual truth. Indeed, the history of parable interpretation is essentially a history of attempts to understand the precise relationship between story and the spiritual truth to which the parable points. Our present discussion is too limited to chart the history of parable interpretation and to describe the major considerations that should be kept in mind as one interprets passages of this genre. Students who wish to pursue these issues should consult the many fine books on parables.[8] When one thinks of biblical parables, the parables

7. Robert Alter, *The Art of Biblical Poetry* (New York: Basic Books, 1985); David L. Petersen and Kent Harold Richards, *Interpreting Biblical Poetry*, GBS (Minneapolis: Fortress, 1992).

8. For a list of books on parables, with some annotation, see Bauer, *Annotated Guide to Biblical Resources*, 227–31. For a clear and helpful description of the history of parable inter-

of Jesus immediately come to mind, such as in Matthew 13, Mark 4, or Luke 15. But the Old Testament also has parables, such as the parable that Nathan delivered to David in 2 Samuel 12.

APOCALYPTIC TEXTS

Apocalyptic literature is found in several portions of the Bible, but as a literary form it has largely passed from the current scene. In fact, apocalypticism was a socioreligious movement in Judaism and early Christianity from about 200 BC until AD 200. It was a movement of people largely on the margins, who felt alienated both socially and religiously. From their perspective, the sovereign action of God in the world was not obvious, nor were they sure, on the basis of empirical evidence, that God's good purposes for his people would ever be realized in the here and now. But the apocalyptists had confidence that God was indeed active, albeit in hidden ways, and that God would achieve his purposes in his great cataclysmic eschatological action in the future. The apocalyptic literature reflects such a conviction and seeks to uncover God's presently hidden and future action.[9]

Apocalyptic literature is characterized by the use of figurative language. As in poetry, the default assumption is that the language is figurative unless the plain sense of the passage or literary clues indicate that in a given apocalyptic passage the language is to be understood literally. But unlike the figurative language of poetry, the figurative language of apocalyptic literature tends to be esoteric (at least in the minds of many modern readers), strange, and bizarre. This language is an attempt to appeal to the eye of the imagination, to challenge readers to understand reality differently than do the powerful and oppressive elites who surround them; this language is visual and pictorial, designed to make real what is hidden. Indeed, we see some consistency in the figures used: Animals and numbers tend to be used repeatedly in various apocalyptic works, and they frequently point to the same literal realities.

Like poetry, apocalyptic material does not necessarily move according to chronological sequence. It actually tends to move topically rather than chronologically: the linear movement is frequently driven by topical concerns. Therefore one cannot assume that what is described in, say, chapter 10 of an apocalypse is necessarily presented as occurring temporally after what has been described in chapter 9.[10]

---

pretation, see Craig L. Blomberg, *Interpreting the Parables* (Downers Grove, IL: InterVarsity, 1990), 13–167; John W. Sider, "Rediscovering the Parables of Jesus: The Logic of the Jeremias Tradition," *JBL* 102 (1983): 61–83.

9. The word *apokalypsis* means "uncovering."

10. A large literature dealing with the apocalyptic movement and the apocalyptic literary form has emerged. For major contributions, see Bauer, *Annotated Guide to Biblical Resources*, 176–78. The most helpful treatments include D. S. Russell, *The Method and Message of Jewish Apocalyptic, 200 BC–AD 100*, OTL (Philadelphia: Westminster, 1964); John J. Collins, *The*

One can find apocalyptic literary form in some portions of the Old Testament, notably the book of Daniel. The most extended example of apocalyptic in the Bible, though, is the book of Revelation, especially chapters 4–22.

Discursive Texts

Logical argument, such as one finds in all of the New Testament Epistles, is a discursive literary form that can also be found elsewhere throughout the Bible, including the Sermon on the Mount (Matt. 5–7) and the Sermon on the Plain (Luke 6), and some of the sermons of Jeremiah (e.g., 18:1–12; 19:1–13; 23:23–40). Legal material may be considered a more specific form of the discursive genre (e.g., Deut. 28).

The assumption of discursive literary form is that the language will be literal rather than figurative. But this is only a general assumption, and in the end the sense of the individual passage must determine whether figurative or literal language is being employed. Still, one typically expects to find literal language in discursive literary form.

A further assumption is that discursive passages move according to logical sequence over against chronological progression. We are not suggesting that readers should never consider the possibility of temporal sequence, but one cannot assume that what is presented in, for example, verse 16 of a chapter is intended to be understood as occurring in time after what has been described in verse 14. In discursive literary form, the emphasis is upon the flow of the argument. Moreover, in contrast to poetic literary form, discursive passages tend to be relatively determinate in terms of range of meaning. In other words, while poetic passages will often contain language that is designed to be associative, causing the reader to consider a host of related ideas and images, discursive passages usually aim at cognitive precision, inviting the reader to consider what seems most specifically to be communicated in the passage. Furthermore, the assumption in discursive literary form is that the importance falls upon the development of the flow of the argument and that logical connectives, such as *therefore*, *so*, and *because*, carry special weight and deserve particular interpretive attention.

Finally, discursive literary form assumes the importance of concepts, the development of concepts, and the relationship between concepts. Thus passages bearing the mark of discursive genre stand in contrast to prose narrative, which, as we saw, emphasizes the relation between events (plot), the development of characters, and the relationship between characters.

Although *rhetorical criticism* deals with the communicative force and power of all speech, including literature of whatever form, the discipline of rhetori-

---

Apocalyptic Imagination: An Introduction to Jewish Apocalyptic Literature, 2nd ed., Biblical Resources Series (Grand Rapids: Eerdmans, 1998); Paul D. Hanson, *Old Testament Apocalyptic*, IBT (Nashville: Abingdon, 1987); Paul S. Minear, *New Testament Apocalyptic*, IBT (Nashville: Abingdon, 1981).

cal criticism has focused especially upon devices and techniques employed in discursive speech. As in all of these critical disciplines, a vast literature is developing. But one can point especially to the work of George A. Kennedy, particularly his book *New Testament Interpretation through Rhetorical Criticism*, as representative.[11]

DRAMATIC TEXTS

Drama and dramatic prose involve the personification and vivid description of ideas for the sake of their moving effect. Dramatic texts present ideas through a dramatic description of persons or events that are not intended to be taken literally but rather symbolically. Dramatic prose is closely related to the poetic expression of truth. In view of these considerations, one must determine whether a writer is speaking in terms of actual history or whether he is using the dramatic approach to make the truth that he is conveying more striking. For example, one should realize that in Isaiah 2:1–4 the prophet may be utilizing drama in his description of the future place and destiny of Jerusalem and that one would not be safe in assuming that what the prophet declares there is intended to be literally factual. Ezekiel's famous vision of dry bones (Ezek. 37) is an example of dramatic prose.

One must beware of classifying all or most of the literature of the Old Testament in the category of drama. One should study the literature itself to ascertain its own claim as to its literary form, and one should avoid superimposing the dramatic approach onto actual history. At the same time, the observer must recognize that the dramatic method is a legitimate form of literary communication and that its presence needs to be taken into account in the process of interpretation.

Readers who wish to pursue these and other literary forms should explore the relevant articles in standard Bible dictionaries. They may wish also to consult such works as James L. Bailey and Lyle D. Vander Broek's *Literary Forms in the New Testament: A Handbook*.[12]

11. George A. Kennedy, *New Testament Interpretation through Rhetorical Criticism* (Chapel Hill: University of North Carolina Press, 1984); also see Burton Mack, *Rhetoric and the New Testament*, GBS (Minneapolis: Fortress, 1990); Carl Joachim Classen, *Rhetorical Criticism of the New Testament* (Leiden: Brill, 2002). For an example of rhetorical criticism directed toward a literary form other than discursive, in this case prose narrative, see Phyllis Trible, *Rhetorical Criticism: Context, Method, and the Book of Jonah*, GBS (Minneapolis: Fortress, 1994); cf. also "Rhetorical Criticism" in Aune, *Westminster Dictionary*, 416–18.

12. James L. Bailey and Lyle D. Vander Broek, *Literary Forms in the New Testament: A Handbook* (Louisville: Westminster John Knox, 1992). For major Bible dictionaries, see esp. Bromiley, *International Standard Bible Encyclopedia*, rev. ed.; David Noel Freedman, ed., *The Anchor Bible Dictionary*, 6 vols. (New York: Doubleday, 1992); Katharine Doob Sakenfeld, ed., *The New Interpreter's Dictionary of the Bible*, 5 vols. (Nashville: Abingdon, 2006–2009); cf. also Bauer, *Annotated Guide to Biblical Resources*, 26–28.

Example of Segment Survey (2 Timothy 3:1–4:8)

Observational surveys are by nature preliminary and tentative. They are subject to correction and completion as the study progresses. Likewise, at times one may decide that more than one possibility may be noted, as illustrated in figures 23 and 24.

Students should note that the more they develop survey skills, the more they will discover in the survey stage of the inductive process. Therefore students should not be discouraged if they do not duplicate what is included in the following illustration. Rather, they should be encouraged to develop the

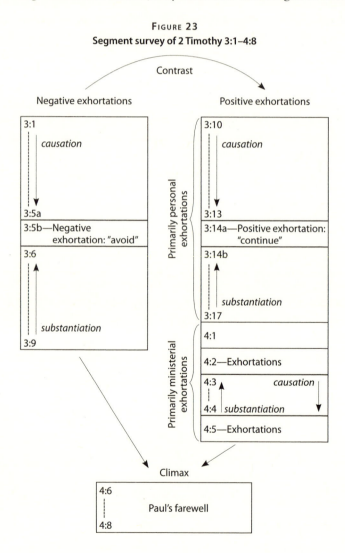

FIGURE 23

Segment survey of 2 Timothy 3:1–4:8

survey skills that are so important in beginning to observe the contextual data necessary for understanding individual statements within the segment.

Recurrence of Causation and Substantiation

A hortatory pattern is comprised of exhortations preceded and/or followed by their causes or the reasons they ought to be heeded. Several such patterns are discernible in 2 Timothy 3:1–4:8, as shown in the schema that follows.

Causes/Reasons for Exhortation/Causation (3:1–5a)

Exhortation/effect = "Avoid them!" (3:5b)

Further reasons/causes for this exhortation/substantiation = ultimate exposure (3:6–9)

Causes/reasons for further exhortation/causation (3:10–13) = Note contrast in 3:13: "But wicked people and imposters" = Progressive deception of others and of self-deception = reiterates the emphasis in 3:1–9

Exhortation/effect = "But as for you, continue in what you have learned and firmly believed" (3:14a)

Further reasons/causes to follow this exhortation/causation (3:14b–17)

Causes/reasons for heeding further exhortations/causation (4:1)

Additional exhortation/effects = "Proclaim the message; be persistent whether the time is favorable or unfavorable; convince, rebuke, and encourage, with the utmost patience in teaching." (4:2)

Further causes/substantiation for previous exhortations in 4:2, and causes/causation (4:3–4) for exhortations in 4:5

Effects/exhortations = "As for you" versus "people" described in 4:3–4 = "Always be sober, endure suffering, do the work of an evangelist, carry out your ministry fully." (4:5)

Further cause/substantiation = "As for me" = example of Paul (suggests comparison in terms of emulation) = returns to autobiographical emphasis made in 3:10–11 = includes ultimate destiny: "crown of righteousness" (4:6–8)

Interpretive Questions: What is the meaning of each exhortation? What do they indicate regarding the implied writer's concerns and Timothy's needs? How are the exhortations related to each other, and what is the significance of these relationships? How do the reasons support the exhortations? How are they related to each other, and what is the import of these relationships? How do the reasons given illuminate and support the "distressing" nature of the coming "last days"? Why is each exhortation given? Why are they all given? Why does the writer have these concerns? What reasons are stated for each exhortation, and what does each mean? Why are these particular reasons given? What are the major thrusts of the reasons given? What are the implications?

Recurrence of Contrast

1. Between negative exhortations (3:1–9) versus positive (3:10–4:8): "avoid" versus "continue"/"embrace," and so forth
2. Between persons: "wicked people and imposters" versus the "godly" (3:12), namely, Timothy, Paul, those from whom Timothy learned, and all believers
   a. Primarily character/being: vice list versus virtue list (3:2–5a vs. 3:10–11)
   b. Primarily conduct/doing (3:6–9, 13; 4:3–4 vs. 3:15–17)
3. Between attitudes toward truth: those who themselves "oppose the truth" (3:8) and who influence others accordingly (3:6–7; 4:3–4) versus those who are concerned about the truth (3:10, 15–17; 4:2)
4. Between destinies: ultimate exposure (3:9) and progressive worsening (3:13) versus receiving the crown of righteousness (4:8)

Interpretive Questions: What are the negative and positive exhortations, and what are the differences between them? Why do these differences exist? Why are these contrasting exhortations made?

What differences are indicated between the persons to be avoided and those to be emulated, both as to character and as to conduct? What does each mean? Why is each suggested? How are these related to each other? What is the relationship between being and doing? Why does the implied writer point out this relationship? What are the implications?

Recurrence of Positive Exhortations (especially in 3:10–4:8)

1. Primarily personal (3:10–17) and primarily ministerial or pastoral (4:1–8)
2. Persecution/suffering motif (3:3–4, 8, 11–12; 4:5, 6)
3. Autobiographical and biographical emphases (3:10–11; 3:14b; 4:6–8)

Interpretive Questions: What are the personal exhortations, and what does each mean? Why is each made, especially in view of the negative exhortation in 3:5b and the reasons given for it? What ministerial or pastoral exhortations are given, and what is the meaning of each? How are they related to each other and to the personal exhortation, and what is the meaning of the relationship(s) discovered? Why is this relationship(s) suggested, and why is it important? Who will persecute Timothy and other Christian believers and leaders? How? Why? How is the implied writer's emphasis on suffering related to the "last days" as "distressing times" (3:1)? Why is it so important to alert Timothy and others to such persecution? What are the implications?

Climax as Epitome and Culmination (4:6–8)

The climax (4:6–8) epitomizes and brings to a culmination the following:

1. Paul's example (3:10–11), in terms of both personal life and ministerial life, which are the two concerns of the positive exhortations (4:6–7)
2. The urgent need to be prepared to face persecution and suffering, stressed in regard to Paul's experience and in relation to others, including Timothy (3:11–12; 4:5, 6a)
3. The exalted destiny of Paul and of those who follow his example (4:8), in contrast to ungodly, wicked imposters (3:9, 13)
4. The imminent execution of Timothy's personal and pastoral exemplar

Interpretive Questions: What is included in this climactic statement? What is the meaning of its various emphases? How may its emphases serve as a culmination of the writer's positive exhortations and of the reasons cited for them? How do they highlight Paul's instructions/directives in regard to Paul's example? In regard to Paul's and Timothy's personal and ministerial life? In regard to facing persecution and suffering? And in regard to his eschatological destiny? Why use this kind of climax? What are the implications?

Strategic Areas in 2 Timothy 3:1–4:8

3:1	General, preparatory statement that relates to the segment-as-a-whole
3:5b, 14a	Key negative and positive exhortations regarding Timothy's personal life, which is one of Paul's main concerns
4:5d	Encapsulates recurring emphasis on ministerial life
3:15–17	Emphasizes both personal and ministerial elements in connection with Scripture as the primary source for truth versus myths (4:4), which along with Paul's teaching (3:10a) form the basis for the injunctions to "proclaim the message" (4:2a)
4:6–8	The climax of the passage

Literary Form

This passage employs the discursive literary form.

Other Major Impressions

1. There seems to be a great sense of urgency in Paul's warnings and injunctions, both as to the serious and worsening problems that Timothy will be facing in the "last days" as a faithful believer and a pastor and especially in view of the imminent execution of the implied writer, who had a key role in the recipient's life.
2. The proportioning of the material seems to indicate a greater emphasis on the positive than on the negative.
3. There may be another possibility regarding the structure of this unit over against what was presented above, one that involves the relationship between 3:1 and the rest of the segment: 3:1 may be the preparation or introduction stated in general terms that sets the stage for the remainder of the passage and thus illuminates the whole. If so, one might add the relationship of preparation and realization with particularization. Figure 24 shows an alternative breakdown, and the following considerations would support this possibility:
   - The use of the imperative (*ginōske*) along with the mild adversative (*de*) may suggest that the statement in 3:1 approaches the level of an exhortation in its own right, though not of the same order as the other exhortations in the segment. It seems to introduce an element of urgency, especially in light of the imminent death of Paul, Timothy's personal and pastoral exemplar (3:10–11; 4:6–8).
   - The emphasis is on what is to be known: the time (the coming "last days") and the nature of the time ("distressing").
   - Perhaps 3:2 begins with a "for" (*gar*) to indicate that the following statements through 3:5a may play a dual role, that is, to substantiate 3:1 and provide reasons for the exhortation in 3:5b, along with those stated in 3:6–9.
   - The focus in 3:2–9 is on the "people" who will occupy/inhabit the "last days" rather than on the time itself or on its nature.
   - The "people" can be avoided, though the times and their nature cannot be avoided (3:5b). Thus, though 3:2–9 is related to 3:1, there seems to be a distinction between them that may set 3:1 apart from what follows.
   - An echo of the motif of 3:1 seems to be in 4:3–4, suggesting that 3:1 sets the stage for the entire segment.

If the structural observation illustrated in figure 24 seems valid, it should be added to those previously described.

FIGURE 24

Seeing 2 Timothy 3:1 as preparation for 3:2–4:8

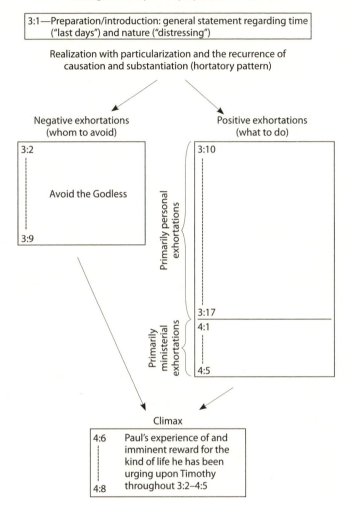

3:1—Preparation/introduction: general statement regarding time ("last days") and nature ("distressing")

Realization with particularization and the recurrence of causation and substantiation (hortatory pattern)

Negative exhortations (whom to avoid)

Positive exhortations (what to do)

3:2

Avoid the Godless

3:9

Primarily personal exhortations

3:10

3:17

Primarily ministerial exhortations

4:1

4:5

Climax

4:6   Paul's experience of and
       imminent reward for the
       kind of life he has been
       urging upon Timothy
4:8   throughout 3:2–4:5

Interpretive Questions: What is meant by the coming "last days"? When does the writer expect the "last days" to occur? How are they related, if they are, to "his appearing" (4:8)? In what sense will they be "distressing times"? Who will experience this distress? How? Why does the writer consider it important to call attention to these times and to their nature at the outset of this passage?

How does this general introductory statement set the stage for and illuminate the rest of the passage, including both the exhortations and the reasons cited for heeding them? In turn, how do the particulars in the remainder of the segment illuminate 3:1? Having set the stage in 3:1, why does the writer proceed as he does in 3:2–9?

What are the implications of the answers to all of these questions?[13]

Exercise: Survey of the Segment

1. Read through the segment Jonah 4:1–11. Following the suggestions in this chapter, survey the segment.
    a. Locate the main units and subunits within this segment and the major structural relationships operative throughout the majority of the segment.
    b. Ask a few interpretive questions based on each major structural relationship observed.
    c. Identify the key verses or strategic areas that provide insight into the segment-as-a-whole.
    d. Identify the literary form(s) employed in the segment.
2. Follow the same process with Mark 4:1–34 and Mark 15:1–47.

---

13. This discussion illustrates that "other major impressions" may include additional reflections on structural matters in the segment.

13

Focused Observation

While observation of the book-as-a-whole and of parts-as-wholes has to do with the more or less extended units of material and thus involves survey, focused observation of the details of individual passages has to do with the observation of smaller passages, and thus it involves analysis. It is a matter of turning the microscope onto paragraphs or even sentences. If one chooses to move from the survey of the book and the survey of the segment to focused observation, one will come to focused observation with a sense of the broader context in which the individual passage is set. At this point of focused observation, students with facility in Greek or Hebrew will find the employment of the original language especially helpful.

The Bible consists of large units such as books or divisions. In addition, books consist of individual sentences and phrases. Thus an inductive approach gives space to the examination of details within smaller passages. This examination may take one of two forms: detailed observation or detailed analysis.

Detailed Observation

For detailed observation, one makes specific and descriptive observations about every significant detail in a (brief) passage.[1] Then one raises interpretive questions of each observation made. The same types of questions previously

1. It may be well to begin by making observations about the passage-as-a-whole, then to move through the passage verse by verse. As one approaches the verse, one will make observations about the verse-as-a-whole. At this point it is helpful to move through the verse clause by clause,

discussed under "Raising Interpretive Questions" in chapter 11 are relevant here: definitive/explanatory, rational, and implicational. As we mentioned, these questions should be asked in this order because the rational question builds on the definitive/explanatory question, and the implicational question asks after the implications of the answers to the definitive/explanatory and rational questions.

Types of Observation

Several types of observation are especially pertinent for this phase of study.

Termal observations have to do with, as the name suggests, terms. This category involves all observations relating to individual words in a passage, including such things as the root of the word (its basic dictionary or lexical form), its inflection (changes in the form of the word that indicate case, gender, number, tense, person, mood, voice), and type of term (whether the term is literal or figurative). The term *he sang*, for example, comes from the root *to sing*, and in terms of inflection is third-person singular simple past (or preterite past). An example from Greek is the term *ēlthomen*, the first-person plural aorist active (deponent) indicative from the root *erchomai*. An example from Hebrew is the term *lammēd*, the Piel infinitive (construct) of *lāmad*.

Grammatical observations pertain to the grammatical function, or syntax, of words or phrases within the sentence, for example, as a subject, predicate, or prepositional phrase. This kind of observation can be quite significant when we come to interpretation. Someone has famously remarked that "the gospel is in the prepositions." Moreover, the grammatical structure of some passages points to what is the *main issue or point* of the passage and what are the *subordinate issues or concerns.*

Students with facility in Greek or Hebrew will be well versed in the syntax of those languages, but many students who are able to work only with a vernacular translation are less aware of the intricacies of the syntax of their mother languages. This unfortunate situation is especially the case with Americans. Such readers may therefore benefit from reviewing at least the major parts of speech of their own language.[2]

Structural observations involve the literary structural relationships (e.g., contrast, substantiation, climax) that were discussed under "Major Structural Relationships" in chapter 11. As mentioned previously, these relationships

---

making observations about each clause-as-a-whole (if one can make relevant observations about the clause in its entirety), then finally about each phrase and word within the clause.

2. English-speaking students will find especially helpful Francis Braun, *English Grammar for Language Students: Basic Grammatical Terminology Defined and Alphabetically Arranged* (Ann Arbor, MI: Ulrich's Books, 1947); John C. Hodges and Mary E. Whitten, with Suzanne S. Webb, *Harbrace College Handbook*, 10th ed. (San Diego: Harcourt Brace Jovanovich, 1986).

are present in all levels of literature, including the paragraph, sentence, and even clause.

Logical observations involve the logical function of a term or statement: the *type of meaning* expressed by the term or statement or the *issue* that it addresses. There is no limit to the number of types of meaning or of issues that might be addressed; thus one should establish the habit of choosing just the right labels to indicate the issues one encounters as one reads through a passage. Some of the more common labels include *scope* (e.g., "all people" is inclusive in scope; "some people" is partial in scope; and "no one" is exclusive in scope), *extent* (e.g., "a great multitude of people" points to numerical extent), *action, location, number, actor, situation, attitude*, and *negative* or *positive*. This category includes also *relational dynamics* of the text that might point toward social realities, roles, and expectations, such as *priority* or *honor* or *power*. Having a thesaurus at hand enables readers to identify the most precise label.

Note some of the possible logical observations in Matthew 28:16–17: "Now the eleven disciples went to Galilee, to the mountain to which Jesus had directed them. When they saw him, they worshiped him; but some doubted." "Eleven" indicates *number*; "disciples" points to *actors* or *status* or *role* or *relationship*; "went" indicates *action*; "to Galilee, to the mountain to which Jesus had directed them" refers to *destination*; "Galilee" has to do with *regional destination*; "the mountain" refers to *topographical destination*; "to which Jesus had directed them" involves *imperatival destination*, and it points also to *motivation* and to their *recognition of Jesus's authority*. "And when they saw him" describes *occasion*; "they worshiped him, but some doubted" points to *reaction*. One finds a *dual reaction* here. The *positive reaction* is found in the first description: "They worshiped him." The *negative reaction* is found in the second description: "but some doubted." "Some" refers to *partial scope*; they did not all doubt (that would be *inclusive scope*), nor does the text say that none doubted (that would be *exclusive scope*). The consideration that the text moves from describing positive reaction to describing negative reaction involves *order* or *sequence*.

Identifying these logical issues can be extremely helpful in enabling readers to locate the various concerns of a passage, with a view toward pursuing the specific meaning and interrelationship of these concerns when readers come to interpretation.

Contextual observations have to do with identifying points of connection between details observed in the passage under examination and elements in the surrounding context. We advise students to limit contextual observations to the immediate context, to the verses that directly precede and follow the passage under study.[3] The reason for this suggestion is twofold. First, in the

---

3. One normally will want to stay within the limits of the segment when making contextual observations in detailed observation. But if the passage being observed stands at the beginning

attempt to be consistent, one would not be able to identify every contextual connection among elements in the passage being observed *and* every other passage in the book-as-a-whole, especially in longer books. Second, in interpretation one will find that considering the immediate context is often critical. In the observational phase, students need to make room to examine particularly connections between the passage being observed and its immediate context.

Literary observations form a broad category pertaining to any features of the passage that may strike the reader as potentially significant in the communication of the sense of the passage. This category includes *literary techniques*, such as irony or figures of speech. It includes also *selectivity*, the recognition that the implied author has chosen to express his thoughts in the way that he has over against other possible ways. Readers should always ask themselves, "Why has the writer selected this expression over against others that would be available to him?" For example, we note that in Psalm 23 the writer declares, "*The* LORD is my shepherd," over against using another name for the Deity, such as "God." And the writer declares that "the LORD is *my* shepherd," rather than saying that the Lord is "our" shepherd or "the" shepherd or "a" shepherd." He also asserts that "the LORD is my *shepherd*," over against "my fortress" or "my shield" or "my king" or "my friend." And he declares that "the LORD *is* my shepherd," versus "was," or "has been," or "will be." Literary observations may involve noting what is *unstated*, gaps in the flow of the passage that the reader must fill in, or clear (but unarticulated) assumptions or implications arising from the text. This category involves also *what is problematic*, elements in a passage that lead to confusion or uncertainty or ambiguity in the mind of the reader. Certain passages, for example, may suggest a kind of contradiction, as when Jonah confesses in 1:9 that he worships "the LORD, the God of heaven, who made the sea and the dry land," even as he is trying to flee "from the presence of the LORD" (1:3, 10): How can Jonah think that he could flee from the presence of the Lord, who is the sovereign creator of the cosmos?[4]

We do not suggest that this list of types of observations is exhaustive. One can find many other kinds of observations. The student, for example, may wish to consult two or three translations and to observe significant differences in the way the various translations render certain terms or phrases. Or the student may observe potentially significant variant readings in the manuscript tradition; these are often listed in the margins or at the bottom of the pages in modern English translations and are presented in the textual apparatus of critical editions of the Hebrew Bible and the Greek New Testament.[5]

---

or end of the segment, one may want to make connections with the immediately adjoining verses that stand just outside the segment.

4. We are indebted to our colleague Dr. Joseph Dongell for some of the nomenclature adopted here, especially the terms "unstated" and "problematic."

5. See "History of the Text" in chap. 14 for the potential interpretive significance of textual variants.

Guidelines for Detailed Observation

As students pursue detailed observation, they will benefit from the following guidelines:

1. Students should be careful not to engage in premature interpretation at this point. To do so would have the psychological effect of constructing parameters around their construal of the passage, making it difficult to break out of these interpretive boundaries so as to consider other interpretive possibilities once they reach the interpretation stage. As a general principle, observations should include only the things that are incapable of being challenged by any reasonable person. This principle does not suggest that one's detailed observations should be obvious, superficial, or pedestrian. They should be penetrating observations. But this principle does indicate that *once it is pointed out*, the observation should be incapable of being challenged. To strike the balance between observations that are penetrating and original on one hand, and uncontestable on the other, students may state some observations in tentative terms, using expressions such as "may" or "might" or "can."

2. Students should aim at specific and descriptive observations, over against simply quoting or paraphrasing the text. A quote or paraphrase does not constitute an observation. One needs to say something about the passage or elements within the passage.

3. Students should always be clear and explicit in making observations. They should err on the side of specificity and explicitness so as to leave nothing to the imagination regarding what they mean by their observations. If students make unclear or ambiguous observations, they will find that when they later come back to their detailed observation and try to use it, they will often wonder what they themselves meant by the observations they recorded.

4. Students will find making a distinction between routine and nonroutine observations helpful. A routine observation pertains to elements in the text that are typically found in all passages and seem to be relatively insignificant in communicating the message of the passage. Usually basic conjunctions such as *and* or articles (both definite *the* and indefinite *a* or *an*) or the copula (a form of the verb *to be*) fall into this category. Granted, it is somewhat risky to make judgments at this time about what may or may not turn out to be significant for interpretation, and indeed sometimes employing this distinction will cause a student to omit observations on features that might be much more important than initial impressions would suggest. Nevertheless, such a distinction is beneficial because it will result in the student (1) focusing on elements in passages that are more significant and (2) investing time more efficiently.

Nonroutine observations fall into three classes: (1) those that are difficult to understand; (2) the crucial features of a passage, and those that, though not crucial, are nevertheless significant for understanding the statements of a passage; and (3) those that otherwise express profound or theologically significant ideas. These three classes pertain to objective criteria: considerations from the passage itself. But one might add also a fourth class, which pertains to subjective considerations: things of personal interest. Sometimes students approach a passage with a particular concern, or the passage contains a component that is especially relevant to them even though it might not be of crucial significance to the communication of the main idea. Their natural instinct is to make observations about these features, and these observations are appropriate so long as students recognize that the importance of the observations is found not so much in the dynamics of the passage as in their own personal situation or background.

This distinction between routine and nonroutine features is not intended to discourage careful and thorough observation; rather, it is meant to develop discretion. The more one's discretionary powers are developed, the more one will see the elements that deserve special consideration. Thus it will eventuate in more incisive and therefore more thorough observation.

Purposes for Detailed Observation

We have three major purposes for pursuing detailed observation. First, these observations may be significant in producing specific evidence that will be used as we interpret the passage. Indeed, the discussion of interpretation in part 3 will make clear that evidence from the immediate context is normally critical for the interpretation of passages, and this evidence comes largely from the detailed observation. Second, the process of detailed observation will typically enable students to identify the primary overarching concern of the passage and the precise ways in which that major concern or issue is developed. Third, these observations serve as the basis for developing questions; answering them constitutes interpretation.[6]

Example of Detailed Observation (2 Timothy 3:16–17)

[16]*pasa graphē theopneustos kai ōphelimos pros didaskalian, pros elegmon, pros epanorthōsin, pros paideian tēn en dikaiosynē,*

[17]*hina artios ē ho tou theou anthrōpos, pros pan ergon agathon exērtismenos.*

[16]All scripture is inspired by God and is useful for teaching, for reproof, for correction, and for training in righteousness,

[17]so that everyone who belongs to God may be proficient, equipped for every good work.

---

6. We previously mentioned that questions raised in book or segment survey can play a "metacognitive" role: the very asking of specific and penetrating questions may clarify our understanding of the observation about which the question is asked. The same possibility exists for questions raised in detailed observation. Quite often at this stage, the very process of asking penetrating questions of the observations can inform the observation itself and assist us in more effectively describing the observation.

1. *Structural observations of 3:16–17-as-a-whole*: There may be a paratactical (implicit) *causal* relationship between the statement regarding the divine inspiration of scripture (v. 16a) and its usefulness (vv. 16b–17).

2. *Recurrence of instrumentation with particularization*: God-inspired scripture (*means*) to achieve certain intermediate *purposes*: "for teaching, for reproof, for correction, and for training in righteousness" (3:16b). These in turn become the *means* for achieving the ultimate *purpose*: "so that . . . everyone who belongs to God may be proficient, equipped for every good work" (3:17; *recurrence of instrumentation*). Note that *pros*, "for," is used five times in this short statement, along with *hina* in a purpose clause. The precise relationship(s) of the instrumental statements in 3:16–17 to the goal of salvation mentioned in 3:15 need to be explored.

Following are observations of 3:16–17 that go into greater detail, along with interpretive questions:

Observations	Questions
1. "All scripture is inspired by God" (3:16a) a. "Scripture" in the singular is used here whereas the plural "sacred writings" is used in 3:15, although both come from the same root, *to write*. The form is anarthrous (lacking the definite article). "Scripture" is used instead of other possible expressions, such as "the law and the prophets" or "the message" (4:2). The writer seems to emphasize "scripture" in 3:15–17 in relation to what the reader has "learned and firmly believed" and "knows" as the basis for the exhortation to continue" (3:14). If the "scripture" to which Paul alludes is identical with the "sacred writings" of 3:15, it would have been accessible to Timothy "from childhood" (3:15). It would also suggest a *recurring* use of the theme of "scripture." There is a possible relationship between the scripture motif and Paul's teaching (3:10).	What is the "scripture" to which 3:16 alludes? What are the "sacred writings" mentioned in 3:15? How are they related to each other? If they are identical, why does the implicit writer use one designation in 3:15 and another in 3:16? Why not use other expressions? If identical, why the recurring use of the motif of "scripture"? If identical, what were the "sacred writings" and "scripture" that were extant and therefore accessible to Timothy from childhood? Why does Paul use the plural in 3:15 and the singular in 3:16? What is entailed in the anarthrous form in 3:16? Why is it used? How is "scripture" related to Paul's teaching mentioned in 3:10? Why does the writer call attention to "scripture" in this context?" What are the implications of the answers to these questions? (Add similar standard questions.)
b. "All scripture": The term *pasa* may be used collectively ("all") or distributively ("every"). In either case the concept seems to be inclusive.	What would be meant by the collective or the distributive use here? How does one determine which is used? What difference, if any, would it make if the use is collective or distributive? Why does the writer use whichever is here? If in either case the term is inclusive, why does the writer indicate inclusiveness? What are the implications?

Observations	Questions
c. The sentence is elliptical since it lacks a verb and requires the insertion of a copula. Both the placement and the tense of the implied copula "is" are significant.	What is involved in the use of an ellipsis? Why is it used? What would be the meaning of each of the two possible placements of the copula? What difference does this placement make, particularly with regard to whether the statement is restrictive or nonrestrictive? Which is used and why? What are the implications?
As to the placement, there are two possibilities: First, the copula could be inserted after "inspired of God," as in ASV: "Every scripture inspired of God [is]," in which case the phrase "inspired of God" might be viewed as essentially attributive and perhaps restrictive. This option is also suggested in the footnotes in the NRSV. The second option, followed by the NASB and the NRSV, is to place a copula between "all scripture" and "God-inspired" rather than after "God-inspired." Thus the text would read: "All scripture *is* inspired by God." This translation is nonrestrictive, and "God-inspired" amounts to a predicate adjective. Both possibilities would exist whether *pasa* is translated as "all" or "every."	As to tense, the present copula is used in the NRSV and other versions instead of the past "was" or the future "will be."
	What is the meaning of the use of the present tense instead of the past or the future tense? What does it suggest, if anything, regarding the nature of the "scripture" to which the writer is alluding? What difference does the use of the present rather than the past or future tense make? Which tense is proper here and why? What would the inferred use of the present tense indicate, if anything, regarding the origin of scripture? Why? What are the implications?
d. "Inspired by God" is the translation of *theopneustos*, which is a compound consisting of *theos* (God) and a derivative from the verb *pneō* (blow, breathe), from which the word *pneuma* (spirit) comes. It serves either as a predicate or an attributive adjective and immediately follows *graphē* in the original text. It seems to parallel the word "sacred" in 3:15 and may indicate the reason why the "writings" alluded to are considered "sacred." The twofold description of "scripture" in 3:16 follows the call to Timothy to "continue" in what he has "learned and firmly believed . . . from childhood" (3:14–15; 1:5). It may thus serve as *substantiation* for the call for him to continue, as well as the implied appeal to imitate Paul, especially with regard to Paul's teaching (3:10). Note also the *contrast* between what Timothy is asked to continue and the actions of the "wicked people and imposters" mentioned in 3:13 and in 3:7–9.	What is meant by "God-inspired"? What is the meaning of "sacred"? How is "God-inspired" in 3:16 related to "sacred" in 3:15? How may the relation to "sacred" illumine the meaning of "God-inspired"? If related, why does the text use two distinct expressions: "sacred writings" and "scripture"? Why the emphasis on "God-inspired" and "sacred"? How are the "sacred writings" and "scripture" related to Paul's history, especially his teaching? How are they related to the deceitfulness of evil persons and imposters (3:13)? What is meant by these relationships? Who taught Timothy what he had learned and firmly believed? Why does Paul point this out? What is meant by "from childhood"? How did Timothy come to know the "sacred writings" from childhood? Why is this temporal element indicated? How may the answers to these questions illumine both the identity of the "sacred writings" and of "scripture"

Observations	Questions
This *contrast* serves also as a further reason (*causation*) why Timothy should follow Paul's example and continue in what he has learned and firmly believed, in view of the challenge that these persons would present to him.	and the meaning of their divine inspiration? What are the differences among the "sacred writings" and "scripture," the teachings and life of Paul, and the teachings and life of "wicked people and imposters"? How are these differences important? Why are they important? What are the implications?
2. "and is useful for teaching, for reproof, for correction, and for training in righteousness" (3:16b) a. *"and* is useful": as indicated previously, the translation of *kai* depends on the placement of the inferred copula "is." If the copula is placed after "scripture" ("all" or "every" God-inspired scripture "*is*"), *kai* would need to be translated "also." The NRSV inserts "is" after "God-inspired" and another "is" after *kai*, so *kai* is translated "and." The NRSV translation indicates a double predicate adjective, thus emphasizing two aspects of scripture, namely, that it is both "God-inspired" and "useful." Note also that the supplied copula after "and" (*kai*) in the NRSV is again in the present tense rather than in the past tense or future tense: "is," not "was" or "will be." The implied writer could have expressed the copula in the past tense with regard to scripture's being "God-inspired" and in the present tense in relation to its being "useful." That the writer omits the copula might suggest that the copula in the present tense should be supplied in relation to both of the traits of the "scripture" to which the implied writer and the reader have access. There may be a twofold parallel between 3:16 and 3:15: the "God-inspired" in 3:16 may be *causally* related to "sacred" in 3:15, and the emphasis on "scripture" as "useful" (3:16) may relate to the concept of the potential of the "sacred writings," what they are "able" to do (3:15). There may also be a *causal* relationship between the divine inspiration of scripture and its usefulness (3:16).	What is the meaning of "useful"? Are the two traits of "scripture," its being "God-inspired" and "useful" in certain ways, causally related to each other, and if so, how? If the two are causally related, what is involved in this relationship? Why would this relationship be important in view of the context? What is the importance of the implied use of the copula in the present tense rather than in the past or future tense with regard to both of the traits of "scripture"? Why did not the writer explicitly use the past tense with regard to the scripture's being "God-inspired" and the present tense with regard to its being "useful"? What reasons are there, if any, for holding that, according to the intent of the implied writer, "scripture" had a "God-inspired" origin but was not still "God-inspired" at the time of the writing of the epistle? What are the implications?
b. There is a fourfold use of prepositional phrases, each beginning with "for" (*pros*): "*for* teaching," "*for* reproof," "*for* correc-	What is the meaning of "for" in these phrases? Why the recurring use of this preposition? What is meant by "teaching,"

Observations	Questions

tion," and "*for* training in righteousness." This *recurring* use of "for" may suggest both the areas in relation to which "scripture" is "useful" and the various purposes for its usefulness, that is, "useful" with respect to each and for the purpose of accomplishing each (*recurrence of instrumentation*). The exact relationship between the four is unclear. Note that the word for "teaching" (*didaskalia*) represents a recurrence of the word that Paul uses in 3:10 with regard to his "teaching."

"reproof," "correction," and "training in righteousness"? Why does Paul use the same word for "teaching" here as he does in 3:10? How are these various areas and purposes related to each other, and what do these relationships mean? Why is each mentioned, and why are all four mentioned? Why are they mentioned in this order? How are they important in view of the implied recipient's life and ministry in relation to the various matters highlighted in this segment and in the epistle? How are these related to Paul's example, including his teaching? What is meant by this relationship? Why does it exist? How are these areas and purposes related to the contrasting description of the opposition in 3:13 and in 3:1–5a and 6–9, especially 3:8–9? What is involved in these relationships, and how are they important? How is the "scripture" "useful" in each of the various areas mentioned? If "for" includes *instrumentation*, how can "scripture" be used by the recipient to realize each of these purposes? Who needs the "teaching," "reproof," "correction," and "training in righteousness" made possible by "scripture"? What are the implications?

3. "so that everyone who belongs to God may be proficient" (3:17a)
a. 3:17 contains a *purpose* clause (with *hina*) that flows from the statement of 3:16. If the recurring use of "for" (*pros*) in 3:16 suggests purpose, the writer may be indicating the intermediate purposes of "scripture" in 3:16, and a more ultimate purpose in 3:17 (*recurrence of instrumentation*). The NRSV translates what is literally "the man of God" with the gender-free expression "everyone who belongs to God." This translation does not indicate the definite article found in the Greek. Rather, it makes an all-inclusive statement: "everyone." Here the word for "man" is *anthrōpos* (human being) rather than *anēr* (male person). This word along with the definite article might be translated "the person" and still be gender-free. The NRSV also translates the genitive "of God" as possessive rather than relational: "belongs to God" rather than "one who trusts and serves God."

If 3:17 indicates the ultimate purpose of the "scripture," whose intermediate purposes are stated in 3:16b, how is this ultimate purpose realized through the realization of the intermediate purposes of "scripture"? What is meant by "the man of God"? What might be the reasons for and against translating "the man" using the gender-free term "everyone"? What is involved in the writer's use of *anthrōpos* rather than *anēr*? Why not translate "the man" as "the person"? What is the significance of the use of the definite article in the Greek? Why is it valid, if it is, to make the statement all-inclusive by using "everyone," which in effect means "every person"? What does "of God" mean here? What reasons are there for translating the phrase in the possessive sense rather than in a relational sense? Are there other possibilities, and if so, what would they be and why? What are the implications?

Observations	Questions
b. The goal of "scripture" and one's use of "scripture" seem to be expressed by the word "proficient." The verb "may be" is in the subjunctive mood and is singular in number. Such "proficiency" might be viewed in terms of *interrogation*, that is, the solution to the challenges and demands set forth by way of *contrast* in 3:1–9, 12–13 and 4:3–4 that relate both to Timothy's personal life and to his ministerial life. In 3:7 there is an indication of changing instruction or teaching that can never arrive at the truth, and in 3:8 the writer likens these teachers to Jannes and Jambres, who opposed Moses and the truth (*comparison with contrast*). In 3:13 the writer describes the same people as deceiving others and themselves. In 4:3–4 he indicates that the time is coming (perhaps returning to the theme of 3:1 regarding the "last days") when "people will not put up with sound doctrine, but . . . will accumulate for themselves teachers to suit their own desires, and will turn away from listening to the truth and wander away to myths." In contrast, the writer refers to his own teaching in 3:10, which apparently had not changed in step with what people wanted to hear. He also urges that the recipient "continue" in what he has learned and firmly believed, on the basis of what he has known from childhood, and knowing from whom he has learned it (3:14–15a), especially in view of the "sacred writings" that were the basis for the recipient's long-standing learning and faith. The writer also indicates the potential of the sacred writings, which have been central in the recipient's experience, to instruct one for salvation through faith in Jesus Christ (3:15b).	What is involved in being "proficient?" What are the criteria for being "proficient"? How does "the person of God" become "proficient" through the "teaching," "reproof," "correction," and "training in righteousness" that can be realized through "scripture"? When does such a person become "proficient"? Why should "the person of God" become "proficient"? What are the demands and challenges confronting Timothy in view of 3:1–9, 12–13 and 4:3–4? How does such proficiency help Timothy meet both the personal and ministerial challenges and demands that will confront him? Why? How are the "sacred writings/scripture" different from the teachings referred to in 3:8–9, 13 and 4:3–4? Why is it needed to meet these demands and challenges? Why are these differences emphasized by the implied writer? Why are they important? What are the implications?
4. "Equipped for every good work" (3:17b) a. "Equipped" (*exērtismenos*) translates a participial form of the verb *exartizō*. The tense of the participle is perfect, and its voice is passive; thus it could be translated "having been equipped." In a sense it may be viewed in apposition to "proficient," along with the prepositional phrase that follows; hence it may suggest that "the person	If the relationship between the phrase "for every good work" and "equipped" is *instrumentation*, what is its meaning? Why is it used? Does this phrase in turn illuminate the nature of, and the reason for, the proficiency previously mentioned, and if so, how? Why does the writer use these relationships? How is this purpose accomplished through scripture? Why is this

Observations	Questions
of God" who is "proficient" is one who is or has been "equipped for every good work." Thus this phrase may be viewed as a *particularization* of "equipped"; or it may indicate the action upon "the person of God" by means of "scripture" that results in one's becoming "proficient" (instrumental participle and participle of result: *instrumentation* with *causation*).	purpose important in light of the segmental and book context? How may this instrumental phrase be related to the previous purposes indicated in 3:16–17 and to the purpose clause in 3:15? In view of the recurrence of instrumentation in these verses, what is involved in closing this series with "equipped for every good work"? Why close the series in this way? What are the implications?
b. The participle is followed by the prepositional phrase "for every good work," which may further indicate the purpose of equipping the person of God by means of scripture, which in turn results in one's becoming "proficient," and thus may help to define both the nature of and the reason or cause for the proficiency mentioned (*instrumentation with substantiation*). This is the fifth use of "for" in 3:16–17 to indicate the various purposes of scripture (*recurrence of instrumentation*). If the "sacred writings" of 3:15 are identical with the "scripture" mentioned in 3:16, this recurring use of instrumentation in relation to scripture begins with the phrase "for salvation" in 3:15, though the Greek preposition in 3:15 is *eis* rather than *pros*. The relation between the purpose statements in 3:16–17 and the one in 3:15 needs to be explored.	
c. The use of "every" suggests inclusiveness in scope in relation to "good work." The singular "every good work" is used rather than the plural "all good works." So 3:16–17 begins and ends with a form of the all-inclusive *pas*: "all/every scripture . . . every good work."	What is a "good work"? Why the emphasis on "good work"? Why the use of "every good work" rather than the plural "all good works"? How does "scripture" enable "the person of God" to be "equipped for every good work"? Why does "the person of God" need to be "equipped for every good work"? What is the connection, if any, between beginning and ending 3:16–17 with a form of *pas*: "*all/every* scripture . . . *every* good work"? If there is a connection, what would be its meaning? In light of the context, how are the various statements in 3:16–17 relevant to the recipient of the epistle? Why is such relevance significant? What are the implications?

Further observations: The realization of the purposes and usefulness of the sacred writings/scripture stated in 3:15–17 would make possible the fulfillment of the exhortations stated in 4:1–5, which will in turn counteract the challenges faced by the recipient in the coming times. Timothy will be able to *proclaim the message* (4:2; cf. 3:15–17); to have the qualities of character that will be required in both favorable and unfavorable times (4:2, 5); to convince, rebuke (cf. 3:16; 4:3), encourage, and have the utmost patience in teaching (4:2; cf. 3:16; 4:30); to do the work of an evangelist, and to carry out his ministry fully (4:5). The reason for realizing the scriptural potential is that he will need to cope with people who eschew *sound doctrine*, who desire to accumulate for themselves *teachers* to suit their own desires, and who turn away from the *truth* and wander into *myths* (4:3–4).

Detailed Analysis

We have mentioned above the two forms of focused observation, which focus on the details of individual passages. The first, detailed observation, has just been described. The second possibility for focused observation, detailed analysis, is otherwise known as thought-flow, tracing the thought of a passage.

Detailed analysis is essentially an *outline* of the passage that emphasizes structural relationships and contextual connections.[7] Detailed analysis is distinct from detailed observation in a number of ways. For one thing, detailed analysis tends to be more selective in the observations made. As we have just mentioned, detailed analysis focuses on the *structural features* of the passage, including breakdown into increasingly smaller units and structural relationships, such as contrast or generalization, and on *contextual connections* between details within the passage itself and between details in the passage and elements present in the verses that immediately precede and follow the passage. In detailed analysis, readers may make additional types of observations (e.g., the inflection of a verb or the syntax of a phrase), but normally one would note such observations much less frequently in detailed analysis than in detailed observation; in other words, the threshold of significance for these kinds of observations is much higher in detailed analysis than it is in detailed observation.

Also, detailed analysis is well fitted for longer passages, while detailed observation is most helpful in smaller passages. Given the relatively complete range of observations made in detailed observation, it is more difficult to perform this process on passages that are longer than three or four verses. In such circumstances, detailed observation simply takes too much time. But when one considers the more selective character of detailed analysis, one will recognize that a detailed analysis of a longer passage may be quite manageable.

7. Note that the outline character of detailed analysis should not be confused with the more formal outlines that we discuss below (see "Interpretive Integration" in chap. 15 and appendix F) in our treatment of logical outlines and topical outlines.

Finally, although one will find detailed analysis helpful in observing passages of all literary forms, one will discover that detailed analysis is particularly effective for passages in the form of *logical argumentation*, as in epistolary passages. In such passages, tracing the thought is especially critical in capturing the communicative intent of the text.

Process for Detailed Analysis

We have found the following process for conducting detailed analysis to be helpful:

1. Begin by making observations regarding the relationship of the passage-as-a-whole to its immediate context. These observations will often involve structural relationships. For example, one might observe that a certain passage relates to the immediately preceding verses in terms of comparison.

2. Note the general structure of the passage: its main units and subunits and the major structural relationships operative in the passage-as-a-whole.

3. Examine the first main unit identified. Locate its main divisions and subdivisions, and break each subdivision down into increasingly smaller and more specific units. In the process, assign appropriate labels descriptive of those units, identify structural relationships, and note contextual connections. Follow the same process with each of the other main units identified.

4. From the detailed analysis, extrapolate the major unifying theme of the passage, as well as the subthemes, and observe how the subthemes contribute to, expand, or support the main theme. Thereby try to identify the *structure of the thought* of the passage.

5. Note very selectively the major interpretive questions that come to mind as the result of the detailed analysis.

Suggestions for Detailed Analysis

Following are a few general suggestions for carrying out detailed analysis:

1. Move from broader units to progressively smaller ones. Where appropriate use the units and subunits identified in segment survey as a framework for detailed analysis.

2. Note especially the following in detailed analysis:

   a. Structural relationships
   b. Contextual connections
   c. Logical categories (i.e., the type of meaning expressed by the word or statement or the issue involved). Be careful to label these logical categories as accurately, specifically, and precisely as possible.
   d. Unusual or unexpected statements, words, or other features

e. Difficulties, things hard to understand, or things whose basic meaning is unclear at least on the surface

3. Realize that a detailed analysis can be as specific (detailed) or as general as you wish to make it. Personal preference, need, or time limitations will determine the degree of specificity or thoroughness of your detailed analysis.

Reasons for Detailed Analysis

The following are the major reasons for pursuing detailed analysis:

1. Detailed analysis allows one to observe the significant details of a longer passage (over against detailed observation, which is normally performed on shorter passages) and to relate these details to one another.

2. Detailed analysis allows one to focus attention on the flow of the passage and the movement of thought. It is therefore especially helpful in discursive literary form (but is applicable in all literary forms).

3. It allows one to identify the main emphasis in a passage and the precise ways in which other concerns or elements within the passage relate to this main emphasis. It thus aids in the interpretation of the passage by providing specific contextual insights.

4. The detailed analysis serves as a basis for asking interpretive questions. (The number of questions depends upon both the passage and the student.) Here are some helpful questions (generically stated):

- What is the main issue of emphasis in the passage? How are the more specific concerns related to this main emphasis? How do they illumine this main emphasis? Why did the author emphasize this issue, and why did he develop it in the ways he has?

- What are the major problems or difficulties in this passage, and how can an examination of these major difficulties help me understand the message of the passage?

- What are the subissues or specific details here that especially interest me, and how does their relation to the main theme and to other details help me understand their meaning?

Detailed analysis can also generate more-specific questions. Detailed analysis helps both in raising questions and later, in the interpretation phase, in answering them.

Example of Detailed Analysis (Psalm 8)

Figure 25 is an example of detailed analysis from Psalm 8. It reveals how one might combine a survey of a segment-length unit with a detailed analysis.

FIGURE 25

Detailed analysis of Psalm 8

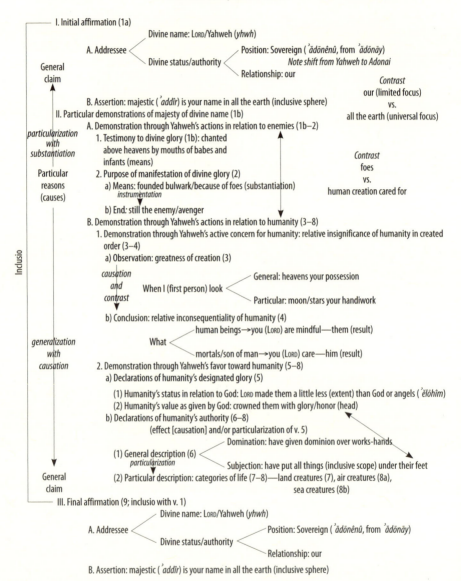

One might begin by identifying two major structural relationships operative in the psalm-as-a-whole. The first relationship pertains to verses 1 and 9: we see that verse 1 and verse 9 form an inclusio around the psalm. Between these statements the psalmist has included the specifics of the majesty of the name of the Lord (hence vv. 2–8 particularize v. 1 and are generalized in v. 9) and the reasons for, or causes of, Yahweh's name as majestic in all the earth (hence vv. 2–8 substantiate v. 1 and cause v. 9).[8] One might also note a major contrast between the insignificance of humanity relative to creation in verses 3–4 over against humanity's designated glory in verses 5–8. These structural observations provide a general framework for the detailed analysis of the psalm.

Readers will note that we have graphically identified the structural relationships operative in the entire psalm (e.g., the inclusio between v. 1 and v. 9 and the movement from the general claim of v. 1 to the particular reasons for the claim in vv. 2–8 [particularization with substantiation]), as well as the structural relationships in smaller units (e.g., the contrast between the greatness of creation and the relative inconsequentiality of humanity in vv. 3–4). Readers will note too the descriptive labels that express logical categories or types of issues (e.g., "testimony" and "purpose" in vv. 1b–2), and they will note that we made contextual connections (e.g., between "head" and "feet" in vv. 5–6).

It is important to recognize how the outline character of this detailed analysis clearly reveals the flow of the passage. Furthermore, in comparing this detailed analysis with the detailed observation on 2 Timothy 3:16–17, readers will see certain types of observations made in detailed observation that may not typically be found in detailed analysis. For example, detailed analysis does not include much in the way of termal observations, such as the root or inflection of terms. While there are some similarities between the two processes, each offers a unique way of studying and understanding the various facets of a text.

Exercise: Detailed Observation

Following the suggestions in this chapter, do a detailed observation of Mark 15:33–39.

Exercise: Detailed Analysis

Following the suggestions in this chapter, do a detailed analysis of Jonah 4:1–11 and Mark 4:10–20.

---

8. Thus the psalm is structured according to particularization and substantiation, with generalization and causation by inclusio.

Part 3

Answering or Interpreting

We title this part "Answering or Interpreting" because students interpret the text by answering questions they have raised in the observation phase. Interpretation involves precisely and specifically ascertaining the sense of the text by identifying, on the basis of evidence within and surrounding the text itself, the communicative intent of the implied author toward the implied reader, that is, the reader that the text itself assumes. The interpretive process thus depends on the guidance that the text gives to the reader in the construal of meaning. This determinative role of textual guidance in interpretation requires that students understand interpretation as the answering of questions raised in the observation phase.

When students link interpretation to answering questions that arise out of observations of the text itself, they adopt a procedure that allows the data and dynamics of the text to determine the agenda of the text's interpretation. The history of interpretation bears witness to the fact that much eisegesis has resulted from interpreters' practice of addressing to the text questions that the text is not prepared to answer, questions alien to the agenda of the text itself. An inductive approach, which seeks to hear the text on its own terms, will try to ensure that interpretation stems from observation of the text. And students will connect observation and interpretation when they conceive of interpretation as the answering of questions they have raised under observation.

Some ask why interpretation is necessary at all. Is it not enough, they ask, simply to *read* the text? This suspicion toward interpretation is often linked with the cheery assertion that "the Bible says what it means and means what it says." True, the essential meaning of most texts can be obtained through the process of careful reading. Indeed, all such reading is a basic form of interpretation. As such, much of what we have described previously under observation and much of what we discuss under interpretation involves practices that most competent readers adopt in a general and virtually unconscious way. In some sense, careful attention to observation and interpretation involves becoming more competent readers, practicing in a more effective way what competent readers already typically do.

But a distinction does exist between reading and interpretation, a distinction that Ben F. Meyer describes well: "Interpretation is a methodically mounted effort to read a text that does not yield its sense immediately."[1] The biblical text arose out of cultures that have a profound strangeness to most modern readers, and the text possesses a depth and thickness of meaning. Hence, biblical passages consistently refuse to yield their full sense immediately; therefore "a methodically mounted effort" of interpretation is necessary.

---

1. Meyer, *Reality and Illusion*, 90.

14

Selecting Questions
and Formulating Premises

Selecting Questions to Answer

Criteria for Selection

The discussion of observation, presented in part 2, makes clear that as one moves through the observation process and asks questions of observations, one generates so many questions that answering them all would be impossible. Although in some ways the ideal would be to answer all the questions raised in the observation process, such a task is not realizable.[1] Therefore students may choose to select the questions to answer according to four criteria.

Importance. Which questions seem to be most important for ascertaining and exploring the central concern(s) of the passage? The focused observation (either detailed observation or detailed analysis) may point toward the main issue of the passage by helping to identify the structure of thought of the passage. Considerations of grammatical/syntactical structure, literary structure, or context might also assist in judging the relative importance of questions to answer.

---

1. The phrase "in some ways" is important. The goal of absolute completeness is valid, and some questions that on the surface seem not to have much interpretive potential can be highly significant for ascertaining the message of passages. Both of these considerations point to the ideal of answering all questions raised. But some questions raised in observation not only *appear* not to have much interpretive potential but also do not *actually* have much interpretive potential. Answering such questions would be distracting and enervating.

Difficulty. While avoiding difficult tasks and situations is natural, the process of exploring and addressing the difficulties of a passage is a principle of interpretation and often critical to understanding the meaning of a passage. Therefore we ought to ask ourselves, Where are the problems here? What are the questions that pertain specifically to the major problems? Some questions practically answer themselves, and we can safely pass them over in interpretation.

Interrelatedness. Often answering one question will necessarily involve addressing other questions raised. For example, often one cannot answer a rational question unless one has first answered the definitive/explanatory question because the rational question presupposes the definitive/explanatory question. Also, answering a more general question often necessarily entails answering certain of the more specific questions one raised in detailed observation.

Interest. Quite often students come to a passage with a particular concern in mind, either a personal or professional interest in an aspect of a passage, and these interests may be different from those that dominate the passage itself. This individual interest or purpose with which students come to a passage may naturally and legitimately lead them to answer questions related to that interest or purpose.

Time Frame for Selection

Students have two possibilities regarding when in the process they select questions to answer. They might select the questions to be answered during the observation process itself. As they raise a question immediately, they may be struck by the apparent importance of that question, either for the message of the passage itself or for their own personal or professional purposes. In such a case, they may wish to mark the question for possible answering immediately upon asking the question. On the other hand, students might wish to wait until they have completed the observation process and have asked all the questions so as to examine all of the questions with a view toward identifying the one or two that seem to have the most promise for interpretation. Moreover, sometimes at the end of observation, additional significant questions may come to mind.

Answering Selected Questions and Formulating Premises

Answering the question involves two broad elements: (1) identifying relevant types of evidence as the basis for formulating premises; and (2) drawing proper inferences from the evidential premises, which are possible answers to the question raised, and adjudicating among the possible answers to determine which has the best and weightiest evidence in its favor. All the while, students must be careful to avoid various interpretive, or exegetical, fallacies.

A number of *types of evidence* might have a bearing upon answering the interpretive question selected. A relatively complete list of these types of evidence follows, but almost never will all of them be relevant or at least significantly helpful in answering a given interpretive question. Therefore, on the basis of the question raised, the interpreter should consider which of the following types of evidence or *interpretive determinants* will be most useful in answering the question selected:

- Preliminary definition
- Literary context
- Word usage
- Scriptural testimony
- Kinds of terms
- Inflections and syntax (grammatical structure)
- Literary forms
- Psychological factor
- Tone or atmosphere
- Author's purpose and viewpoint
- Historical background
- History of terms
- History of the text
- History of the tradition
- Interpretation by others

Because premises are based on the citation of various kinds of evidence, students should become acquainted with the range of possible types of evidence that may be employed in formulating premises. A description of the major types of evidence follows.

Preliminary Definition

When the question pertains to the meaning of a term, a preliminary definition is usually helpful. Preliminary definition involves looking up the word in a standard Hebrew lexicon (for Old Testament passages) or Greek lexicon (for New Testament passages). Original-language resources are needed because students are interested in the meaning of the term that the biblical writer has employed. This process will pose no difficulty for students who have facility in Greek and Hebrew, but readers who do not know these languages can nevertheless make use of these resources. Such readers should consult appendix D, "The Use of Original-Language Resources."

We wish to make two suggestions pertaining to preliminary definition. First, at this stage we recommend that students use only standard lexicons rather than theological wordbooks or theological dictionaries.[2] The latter are useful for exploring the "history of the term," which is an interpretive determinant that will be discussed later. But at this point we wish to obtain only a basic definition, and the theological wordbooks or theological dictionaries go into great detail regarding the history and use of the term in various contexts, often including the passage that students are interpreting.

Second, because students now need to encounter only the basic definition, they may wish to note only the basic meaning of the term, which is usually given at the top of the entry. In other words, they may do well to refrain from reading down very far into the entry or reading the entire entry. Indeed, often the lexicographer will discuss the meaning of the term in the very passage that students are interpreting, at which point the lexicon functions essentially as a commentary. As a general principle we recommend that students examine commentaries last of all as part of the final type of evidence considered. Once they come to examine the interpretation of others in the form of commentaries, they might then come back to the lexicon and note the lexicographer's comments on their passage. But at the point of preliminary definition, the aim is to gain a basic sense of the term's meaning. This basic sense serves as a kind of *beginning point* for their own work on the passage.[3]

2. For example, G. Johannes Botterweck, Helmer Ringgren, and Heinz-Josef Fabry, eds., *Theological Dictionary of the Old Testament*, trans. J. T. Willis et al., 15 vols. (Grand Rapids: Eerdmans, 1974–2006); Willem A. VanGemeren, ed., *New International Dictionary of Old Testament Theology and Exegesis*, 5 vols. (Grand Rapids: Zondervan, 1997); Colin Brown, ed., *New International Dictionary of New Testament Theology*, 4 vols. (Grand Rapids: Zondervan, 1975–79); Gerhard Kittel and Gerhard Friedrich, eds., *Theological Dictionary of the New Testament*, trans. Geoffrey W. Bromiley, 10 vols. (Grand Rapids: Eerdmans, 1975–76). Additional resources can be found in Bauer, *Annotated Guide to Biblical Resources*, 58–59, 198–200.

3. The following are among the most popular Hebrew lexicons: Francis Brown, S. R. Driver, and Charles A. Briggs, *A Hebrew and English Lexicon of the Old Testament* (1907; repr., Peabody, MA: Hendrickson, 1979, 1996, with *Strong's* numbering); Benjamin Davidson, *The Analytical Hebrew and Chaldee Concordance*, 2nd ed. (Peabody, MA: Hendrickson, 1990); William L. Holladay, *A Concise Hebrew and Aramaic Lexicon of the Old Testament* (Grand Rapids: Eerdmans, 1971); Ludwig Köhler and Walter Baumgartner, *The Hebrew and Aramaic Lexicon of the Old Testament*, rev. Walter Baumgartner and Johann Jakob Stamm, 3rd ed., 5 vols. (Leiden: Brill, 1994–2000). For a fuller list and for annotations on these lexicons, see Bauer, *Annotated Guide to Biblical Resources*, 56–58.

The most widely used Greek lexicons include the following: W. Bauer, F. W. Danker, W. F. Arndt, and F. W. Gingrich, *A Greek-English Lexicon of the New Testament and Other Early Christian Literature*, 3rd ed. (Chicago: University of Chicago Press, 2000), based on the 6th ed. of Walter Bauer's *Griechisch-deutsches Wörterbuch zu den Schriften des Neuen Testaments und der frühchristlichen Literatur*; Wesley J. Perschbacher, ed., *The New Analytical Greek Lexicon* (Peabody, MA: Hendrickson, 1990); Joseph Henry Thayer, *Greek-English Lexicon of*

Literary Context

Literary context is generally the most significant type of evidence for interpretation, and it is always to be considered a relevant type of evidence no matter what passage one is studying. Because the basic literary unit of the Bible is the biblical book, the literary context involves all evidence found within the book in which the passage is located. As such, contextual evidence has three levels.

The first level of contextual evidence is *immediate context*: evidence from the verses that immediately precede and follow the passage. Typically, through the step of observation students will have already completed either a detailed observation or a detailed analysis in which they have made a number of contextual observations. Therefore, they will want to begin their examination of immediate context by noting observations they have made in detailed observation or detailed analysis, asking themselves if they have made any observations in those stages that they can turn into evidence for answering the interpretive question that they have raised. If so, they may present those elements here as evidence with a view toward drawing inferences that will form possible answers to the question raised. However, they should not stop with consulting their detailed observation but should look again at the immediate context with their interpretive question specifically in mind, to discover any other evidence from the verses that immediately precede and follow that might have a bearing upon answering their interpretive question.

The second level of contextual evidence is *segment context*. Again, students may have already produced a segment survey during the observation stage, and if so they might begin this examination of evidence from segment context by noting any observations they made in their segment survey that might help them answer the question raised. They will present such observations as evidence so that they can draw inferences from them. But students will not want to stop there; rather, they will examine the segment again, keeping in mind the interpretive question with a view toward identifying any other elements in the segment that might be employed now as evidence for interpretation.

The third level of contextual evidence is *book context*. Assuming that students have completed a survey of the book during the observation stage, they might begin by identifying observations made there that they may use as evidence for the interpretation of their passage. But they will also want to consider any other features in the book that they might employ as evidence for their interpretation.

---

the *New Testament: Coded with the Numbering System from Strong's Exhaustive Concordance of the Bible* (Peabody, MA: Hendrickson, 1996); Barclay Newman, *A Concise Greek-English Dictionary of the New Testament* (Stuttgart: United Bible Societies, 1993). For a fuller list and for annotations on these lexicons, see Bauer, *Annotated Guide to Biblical Resources,* 195–98. For both Hebrew and Greek, the student might use basic definitions given, e.g., via BibleWorks software.

We previously suggested that because contextual evidence comprises all evidence of any kind within the book itself, it might take a variety of specific forms. Two kinds of contextual evidence are particularly relevant, and interpreters should be careful always to consider them.

The first of these particularly relevant forms of contextual evidence is *literary structure*. We have emphasized the role of structural analysis in the observation stage because we are persuaded of the great importance of literary structure for interpretation. Indeed, when one considers that one can fully grasp *what* is communicated only by attending to *how* it is communicated, one recognizes the central role of structural features for interpretation. Thus interpreters will wish to take seriously the ways in which literary structure informs the meaning of passages. We believe that one ought always to ask oneself, How does the structure of the sentence, of the paragraph, of the segment, and of the book illumine the meaning of this passage that I am interpreting? Clearly literary structure will play a more significant role in the interpretation of some passages than it will in others. But almost always it will affect the meaning of passages.

The second of these particularly relevant forms of contextual evidence is the *employment of the term elsewhere in the book*. The interpreter might well ask, Where else in this biblical book do we find this term that appears in the passage I am interpreting? And how does its occurrence elsewhere in the book illumine its meaning here in my passage? The term in question will always be the word employed by the implied author himself and is thus a Hebrew (Old Testament) or Greek (New Testament) word, whose occurrences elsewhere within the book can be located by the use of an original-language concordance. Therefore the interpreter begins to use the concordance as contextual evidence.

The use of original-language concordances is no problem for those who know Greek or Hebrew. But even those who do not know the original languages need to make use of Greek or Hebrew concordances for the most accurate and thorough interpretation of a term. Appendix D, "The Use of Original-Language Resources," will alert such persons to processes that will enable them to identify passages where a given Greek or Hebrew term appears. All interpreters should own either standard Greek and Hebrew concordances or a Bible software program that has extensive and accurate word-search capabilities. Such Bible software programs actually create a concordance whenever a search is executed.[4]

---

4. For a list with some annotations of Hebrew and Greek concordances, see Bauer, *Annotated Guide to Biblical Resources*, 60–61, 200–202. The most significant Hebrew concordances are these: Abraham Even-Shoshan, *A New Concordance of the Old Testament* (Jerusalem: Kiryat Sepher, 1977–80; Grand Rapids: Baker Academic, 1984); John R. Kohlenberger III, *The Hebrew-English Concordance to the Old Testament: With the New International Version* (Grand Rapids: Zondervan, 1998); George V. Wigram, *The Englishman's Hebrew Concordance of the*

Nevertheless an implied author may use even the same Greek or Hebrew term within a single book in different ways. One should not simply assume that the writer is employing the word in exactly the same sense in other passages within the book. Yet in writing a book, an implied author is creating a *world*, and this *world of the text* implicitly invites the reader to understand one occurrence of a term within the book in light of other occurrences of that word within the same book. The writer's assumption, then, is that the reader will relate the occurrences of the same term within the book to one another.

To elucidate, we offer a brief illustration of how contextual relations are significant for interpreting the individual statements of Romans 12:1–15:13. The first part affords an example of the importance of the more immediate contextual relations, whereas the latter part concerns the significance of more remote relations.

One notes that the connection between Romans 12:1–2 and 12:3–15:13 is what we have previously described as logical particularization, which involves the movement from a general statement to the specifics. The general statement contains several major parts: first, an exhortation to the Romans to present their bodies as a living sacrifice; second, the indication that such a sacrifice constitutes spiritual worship; third, an exhortation involving the contrast between the conformed and the transformed life; and fourth, the means and purpose of such a life: through a renewed intelligence to discern God's good and acceptable and perfect will.

When a reader applies the relationship of particularization and tries to discover wherein these general ideals are explicated by the particulars of 12:3–15:13, one finds that for Paul the living sacrifice of the body involves the proper evaluation of one's own gifts, such as avoiding conceit, loving others genuinely, hating evil, showing hospitality, blessing those who curse one, and living in empathy with one's fellow Christians. These are concrete expressions of the sacrificial life. As a matter of fact, these and other practices found in 12:3–15:13 constitute God's "good and acceptable and perfect" will (12:2), which the Romans are enabled to discern if they surrender themselves to God. These are the elements involved in the transformed life rather than the life that is molded according to the world.

The people of this world persecute those who persecute them and repay evil for evil. If the Roman Christians are like the world, they will do the same. But if through dedication to God, their mental outlooks are changed, then

---

Old Testament (Peabody, MA: Hendrickson, 1996). The most significant concordances for the Greek NT are the following: Kurt Aland, ed., *Vollständige Konkordanz zum griechischen Neuen Testament*, 2 vols. (Berlin: de Gruyter, 1975–83); H. Bachmann and W. A. Slaby, collaborating eds., *Computer Concordance to the Novum Testamentum Graece*, edited by the Institute for New Testament Textual Research and the Computer Center of Münster University (Berlin: de Gruyter, 1985); W. F. Moulton and A. S. Geden, *A Concordance to the Greek Testament*, ed. I. Howard Marshall, 6th ed. (New York: Continuum, 2002).

if their enemies hunger, they will feed them; if their enemies thirst, they will give them something to drink. They will overcome evil with good. This kind of surrender to God and his will is spiritual worship, the liturgy that engages the very heart of the Christian. Paul is saying in effect to the Romans: "Do you want to worship with the spirit and therefore truly? Then bless those who persecute you instead of cursing them. Give your enemy food and drink. These actions constitutes true worship. Without them worship is empty. Only the transformed life is the life of spiritual worship!" By examining the significance and outworkings of particularization, one is thus able to arrive at the deeper meaning of Paul's statements in Romans 12:1–15:13.

But the exposition of Romans 12:1–15:13 holds so much more. For one thing, note that the first verse contains a "therefore," indicating that this passage presents the effects of the preceding causes. In other words, the law of hortatory causation is operative in the overall arrangement of the letter. It throws the interpreter into the more remote contextual relations of this passage. Consequently, if one is to ascertain the full impact of the exhortations of Romans 12:1–15:13, one must find in the first eleven chapters the grounds that make possible and imperative the reader's obedience to these exhortations. This examination would involve the study of all the relations and interrelations of chapters 1–11. Such a study cannot be made at this point, but the reader will be able to see some of the potentialities inherent in the utilization of all these structural relations. It also gives further evidence of the complexity of connections and interconnections that must often be taken into consideration in the interpretation of a passage.

Word Usage

This interpretive determinant involves examining how a word that appears in the passage and is under interpretive consideration is employed outside of that biblical book. One should remember that all evidence of whatever kind within the biblical book, including the occurrences of the word itself within the book, falls under *context*. As such, word usage involves only the occurrence of the word outside of the book. Word usage has two broad categories: biblical and extrabiblical.

BIBLICAL WORD USAGE

Biblical word usage pertains to the use of the word elsewhere in the Bible. Because word usage concerns the word employed by the implied author of our text, word usage tracks the term via occurrences of the Hebrew word (for the Old Testament) and Greek word (for the New Testament).[5] Therefore, as we mentioned previously under "Literary Context," the interpreter would do

5. See bibliographic information on significant Hebrew and Greek concordances in note 3 above.

best to make use of original-language concordances. Again, readers who are not proficient in Greek or Hebrew should consult appendix D. Those who do possess knowledge of Hebrew or Greek should consult a standard Hebrew or Greek concordance or make use of a Bible software program with original-language search capabilities.

Biblical word usage itself may be divided into three types. First of all, word usage occurs within the *corpus*. The word *corpus* refers here to a body of literature and specifically to a body or collection of books written by the same author. Everything else being equal, interpreters may assume that the way in which the same author uses a word in another book he has written is more significant for its employment in a passage than the way in which other authors have used it. The same individual is likely to use the same word in the same (or similar) ways in the various things he has written. Accordingly, interpreters may wish to give priority to word usage within the corpus. When interpreting the meaning of a word from a passage in Romans, for example, one may begin the study of word usage by examining how Paul employs that word in his other epistles. This suggestion is not meant to indicate that one should examine only how Paul uses the term but that one should begin with Paul's use of the term before examining how the term is employed elsewhere in the Bible, outside of the Pauline corpus.[6]

Most biblical books are not part of an authorial corpus but were written by persons who contributed only a single book to the biblical canon. In such cases, one may move directly to the second type of biblical word usage: checking how the word is used within the *Testament*.

The third type of biblical word usage, appearances in the *other Testament*, applies only to the study of New Testament passages and to the occurrences of the Greek term from an Old Testament passage in the Septuagint,[7] which was the primary Greek translation of the Old Testament available in the

---

6. Another example of the employment of word usage within a corpus would be the interpretation of a passage from the Deuteronomic history, Joshua through 2 Kings, assuming that the whole of this material in its final form bears the marks of a single redactor or editor. This view has been accepted by the vast majority of scholars since the groundbreaking work of Martin Noth, *The Deuteronomistic History*. But this example from the Deuteronomic history illustrates a potential complication when talking about authorial corpora because sometimes it is not entirely clear whether a given book is part of a particular corpus. Note the scholarly debate surrounding the extent of the corpus of the Chronicler in OT studies, or the debate regarding the question as to whether the Minor Prophets constitute simply a canonical collection (i.e., a group of books joined within the organization of the canon) or bear the marks of a common final redaction (as allegedly is the case with the Deuteronomic history). On the question of the Chronicler's history, see Joseph Blenkinsopp, *Ezra-Nehemiah: A Commentary*, OTL (Louisville: Westminster John Knox, 1988); and on the question of the Minor Prophets, see Paul R. House, *The Unity of the Twelve*, JSOTSup 97 (Sheffield: Almond, 1990).

7. The Septuagint is sometimes represented by the Roman numeral for seventy, LXX, because of the tradition that it was originally produced by seventy scholars (or seventy-two, according to *Letter of Aristeas* 35–40).

first-century Greco-Roman world. Virtually all the New Testament writers were familiar with the Septuagint, and most of them used the Septuagint exclusively when quoting or alluding to Old Testament passages. But the Old Testament authors obviously wrote in Hebrew; thus the Greek terminology of the New Testament would not qualify as word usage for passages written by the authors of the Old Testament. In contrast, the New Testament writers and their audiences were acquainted with the Greek Old Testament, and they would be inclined to employ especially theological language in ways that were informed by their vernacular Scripture in the same way modern Christians conceptualize theological terms and categories according to their function in our English translations. Old Testament writers and audiences did not know Greek and certainly did not know the Greek New Testament, which these Old Testament persons predated by centuries.

Students who have facility in Greek should make use of Old Testament (Septuagint) word usage when interpreting New Testament passages. They can do so by utilizing a concordance to the Septuagint. The standard concordance continues to be *A Concordance to the Septuagint and Other Greek Versions of the Old Testament*, by Edwin Hatch and Henry A. Redpath.[8] Bible software programs that have Septuagintal search capabilities can also be utilized, often even by students who do not know Greek.

The purpose of word usage is to provide *linguistic background* for the passages under consideration. Word usage seeks to answer the question "How did the implied author use this term?" The more precise question is, "How did the implied author of this passage expect the implied readers of the passage to understand the term here?" As we mentioned previously, literary context normally provides great help in answering this question, but often context alone is not fully adequate. Authors typically assume that their readers will bring to the passage linguistic background, knowledge about the ways in which the term was employed in that culture or subculture. Modern people, coming from a different linguistic culture, do not have that background; therefore, in order to arrive at a competent reading of the text, they need as much as possible to acquaint themselves with the original linguistic background. Modern readers acquire this linguistic competency by means of a critical examination of the employment of the word elsewhere in the culture and subculture, especially in the subculture of the religious community. This acquisition involves the understanding of the word within the community of Israel as represented in the books of the Old Testament for Old Testament word usage; and an understanding of the word within the community of the church as represented

8. Edwin Hatch and Henry A. Redpath, *A Concordance to the Septuagint and Other Greek Versions of the Old Testament*, 2 vols. (Oxford: Clarendon, 1897–1906). For discussion of major resources for the study of the Septuagint, see Bauer, *Annotated Guide to Biblical Resources*, 62–65.

above all in the books of the New Testament and in the Septuagint for New Testament word usage.

When readers acknowledge that the purpose of word usage is to acquire a sense of the linguistic background of the passage, they will understand the importance of critical interaction between the word as used in the passage they are interpreting and the word as used in other biblical passages. One cannot assume that the way an author wished his readers to construe the word in his passage is completely identical with the way in which the word is used in other passages in the Bible. Authors are free to use words in ways that are at least somewhat different from the ways other authors use them.

In the process of examining word usage, therefore, students ought always to ask themselves whether the use of the word in their passage stands in essential continuity or discontinuity with the use of the word in another passage in a different biblical book. If the word seems to be used in essentially the same way, it has essential continuity or complementarity, and so students employ the *background principle*. They ask themselves how the use of the term in the other biblical passage provides richness, depth, and clarity for the way the term is used in their passage.

However, the word appearing in the passage they are interpreting may be employed differently than in another biblical passage. Such a case involves essential discontinuity or peculiarity, and students employ the *foil principle*.[9] They should ask themselves how the use of the word in the other biblical passage serves as a foil, how that other use differs from its use in the passage they are interpreting, and how this very differentness illumines the specific concerns of the author in the passage they are now interpreting.

This commitment to critical conversation between the employment of the word in the passage being interpreted and its employment in other biblical passages will protect students from the exegetical fallacy, or interpretive mistake, of *illegitimate totality transfer*.[10] This exegetical fallacy is the practice of reading the connotations of every other occurrence of the word into the passage being interpreted. This uncritical dumping in of suggested meanings from other occurrences fails to acknowledge the hermeneutical principle that every occurrence of a word has some significant individuality, which is determined by its context. Linguistically, students cannot assume that when Jude, for instance, employed a given term, he had in mind every connotation that the word carried in every other occurrence of the word in the Bible.

9. If the use of the same word in the other passage stands in essential contrast to the way the word is used in the passage being interpreted, then the contrast itself can illumine the meaning of the word in the passage we are interpreting. For example, *justify* (*dikaioō*) is used in an essentially different way in Luke 10:29, which describes the lawyer who asked Jesus a question, wishing to justify himself in the sense of validating the posing of his question, than it is in Romans 6, where Paul employs the same term to refer to right relationship or right standing with God.

10. James Barr, *The Semantics of Biblical Language* (London: SCM, 1983), 218, 222.

For example, some have suggested that Luther, in spite of his great acumen as a biblical interpreter, tended to read all biblical books, and especially the New Testament, in light of Paul. Thus, when Luther encountered the term *law* (*nomos*) in Matthew, some have claimed that he tended to interpret it in accordance with Paul's use of the same word and may have insufficiently appreciated the differences between Matthew's use of *nomos* and Paul's use of the word. Consequently, Luther may not have been fully able to hear Matthew's specific and somewhat unique witness to the function of the law in the Christian life.

The necessity of critical interaction between the employment of a term in a given passage and its use elsewhere points to two issues of process. The first is *sequence*, and particularly the importance of dealing with evidence from context before moving on to examine evidence from word usage. Critical interaction between a passage being interpreted and the use of the word in other passages assumes that the student has already conducted a thorough investigation of the immediate and broader-book context of the passage being interpreted.

The necessity of this critical interaction points, second, to the *specific procedure* for the examination of other occurrences of the word in the Bible. One will wish to note the immediate context of each of the passages where the word occurs in order to make at least basic and tentative judgments about the meaning and significance of the word in each of these passages. Such an investigation of the significance of an occurrence in its immediate context is obviously required for the kind of critical interaction we have been describing.

EXTRABIBLICAL WORD USAGE

The same principle of critical conversation between the use of the term in a passage being interpreted and its employment in other passages applies also to extrabiblical word usage. Extrabiblical word usage pertains especially to New Testament materials because we have almost no witness to ancient Hebrew outside of the Old Testament itself.

Two types of extrabiblical word usage relate to the New Testament: classical Greek usage and Koine Greek (i.e., common, everyday spoken Greek in the Hellenistic and Roman periods). Searching for extrabiblical Greek usage typically requires a knowledge of Greek. Students who wish to pursue classical Greek usage should consult especially *A Greek-English Lexicon* by Liddell and Scott;[11] and those who wish to pursue Koine Greek usage should consult

---

11. Henry George Liddell and Robert Scott, *A Greek-English Lexicon*, rev. and augm. Henry Stuart Jones and Roderick McKenzie (Oxford: Clarendon, 1940). As a lexicon, it references many if not most of the occurrences of the words in Greek literature; thus it is not restricted to classical Greek but also includes Koine Greek, with occurrences in the Septuagint and the Greek NT.

The Vocabulary of the Greek Testament Illustrated from the Papyri and Other Non-Literary Sources, by Moulton and Milligan.[12]

Scriptural Testimony

Scriptural testimony involves all evidence, of whatever kind, in the whole Bible, outside of evidence from the book context and evidence from word usage in the passages where the term itself explicitly appears. As we discussed previously, the various biblical books exhibit differences from one another, but the biblical materials have a core unity. In fact, with some qualification one can speak of a world within the biblical canon. This unity within the Bible is due in part to the fact that later writings were largely adaptations and new applications of earlier material within the Bible.[13] In addition, over a long period of time the community of faith came to recognize a kind of theological coherence among the books that the community finally accepted as canonical. Thus, while refusing to uncritically read one biblical passage into another, but being careful to allow each passage to speak on its own terms, students are justified in constantly examining how biblical passages throughout the canon may illumine the communicative content of an individual passage.

On the basis of this definition of scriptural testimony, it is clearly a broad determinant. In fact, we find at least three major forms.

The first form is *conceptual scriptural testimony*, which involves examining the scriptural treatment of a concept that appears in the passage being interpreted. For example, Romans 1:18 says, "For the wrath of God is revealed from heaven against all ungodliness and wickedness." As students interpret this passage, they might well begin by examining the occurrences of the word *wrath* (*orgē*) in the book of Romans; that study would involve *context* because all evidence of whatever kind within the book itself falls under context. They might move next to examine the occurrences of this Greek word within the Pauline corpus, the New Testament, and the Septuagint. That study would involve *word usage*. But they might then proceed to examine the *idea* or *concept* of God's anger or judgment within biblical passages where the word itself does not occur. Such a study would involve *scriptural testimony*. Thus in scriptural testimony we ask, How is this concept, found in this passage, treated in the rest of the Bible, and how may its treatment elsewhere illumine its meaning here?

The question is how students can identify all of the passages where a concept is treated. Few can claim for themselves what was said of Luther, that he

---

12. James Hope Moulton and George Milligan, *The Vocabulary of the Greek Testament Illustrated from the Papyri and Other Non-Literary Sources* (Grand Rapids: Eerdmans, 1930).

13. The constant readaptation of earlier material within the Bible has frequently been noted, especially by the prominent OT scholar Gerhard von Rad; see his *Old Testament Theology*, 2 vols. (New York: Harper & Row, 1962–65).

had essentially memorized the Bible from cover to cover. Most students need assistance, and that assistance comes in the form of *topical concordances*, sometimes called *topical Bibles*. This type of resource lists concepts that are prominent in the Bible and cites biblical passages where these concepts are found. In our judgment, the most effective topical concordance is *Zondervan NIV Nave's Topical Bible* by John R. Kohlenberger III.[14]

In the above discussion about word usage, we made a point of insisting that interpreters should avoid uncritically reading other occurrences of the word into the passage under consideration and should engage in a critical conversation between the meaning and significance of the word in the other biblical passage and its employment in the passage being interpreted. The same principle holds true for the examination of concepts presented in other passages throughout the Bible. Students should observe points of both continuity and discontinuity between the concept as presented in the passage being interpreted and in the other biblical passages where the concept appears. In cases with essential continuity, interpreters might employ the background principle, assessing how the use of the concept in the other biblical passage provides richness, depth, and precision to its meaning. In cases with essential discontinuity, interpreters might employ the foil principle, considering how the difference between the presentation of the concept in the other biblical passages and the passage being interpreted can illumine the specific and peculiar concerns of the passage being interpreted.[15]

The second major form is *textual scriptural testimony*. It involves the examination of the ways in which the passage under interpretive scrutiny makes use of other biblical passages that are either quoted or alluded to in the passage being interpreted. Luke 17:26–27 is one example: "Just as it was in the days of Noah, so too it will be in the days of the Son of Man. They were eating and drinking, and marrying and being given in marriage, until the day Noah entered the ark, and the flood came and destroyed all of them." Luke alludes to the story of the flood in Genesis 6–9. Students might examine the Genesis account in its original wording and context to ascertain exactly how Luke wishes the reader to relate the story of Noah in Genesis to the meaning of Jesus's declarations in Luke 17. Again, readers of the Gospel should not assume that Luke necessarily wishes them to bring into Luke 17 everything that is narrated in Genesis regarding Noah and his times. Students need to engage in a critical conversation between the context of Luke 17 and the material in the referenced passage, Genesis 6–9.

14. John R. Kohlenberger III, *Zondervan NIV Nave's Topical Bible* (Grand Rapids: Zondervan, 1992). See Bauer, *Annotated Guide to Biblical Resources*, 25–26, for additional titles.

15. A possible example of conceptual discontinuity may be the apparently different perspectives and assessment of the violent overthrow of the wicked as reflected in the presentations of Jehu's coup against the house of Ahab in 2 Kings 9–10 and in Hosea 1:4–5. Second Kings presents Jehu's actions as zealous obedience to God's commands, but Hosea presents Jehu's behavior as vicious cruelty that has brought divine judgment.

Jonah 1:1 provides a second example: "Now the word of the LORD came to Jonah the son of Amittai." The implied author of Jonah alludes to a man by the name of "Jonah the son of Amittai." This name is an apparent allusion to 2 Kings 14:25–27, which describes the prophet Jonah, who ministered to the northern kingdom of Israel during the reign of Jeroboam II. The implied author of Jonah, then, may be inviting the reader to construe the presentation of Jonah in the book of Jonah in light of what was said regarding Jonah in 2 Kings. Because 2 Kings 14:25–27 describes Jonah as the prophet who announced undeserved blessing to sinful Israel, that passage contributes to the irony of the presentation of Jonah within the book of Jonah. The irony is that Jonah, possibly representing Israel, gladly accepts God's gracious forgiveness toward himself but resents God's similar forgiveness toward the Ninevites.

These examples represent allusions to other biblical passages, but often we encounter quotations of other biblical passages. For example, Matthew 2:15 states, "This was to fulfill what had been spoken by the Lord through the prophet, 'Out of Egypt I have called my son.'" Matthew quotes Hosea 11:1, a passage that in its original context is not presented as a messianic prophecy but is rather a description of God's act of delivering Israel from Egyptian bondage at the time of the exodus.[16] Some have objected that Matthew has ripped this passage out of its original context and made it say something quite foreign to anything the prophet Hosea had in mind. But a close reading of Matthew 2 shows how Matthew repeatedly makes the point that Jesus brings to eschatological fulfillment various persons and events in Old Testament history.[17] As such, Matthew clearly wishes the reader to consider the original context of Hosea 11 and thereby to think of the exodus with a view toward the reader's understanding that the ultimate significance of the exodus event is found not in the political liberation of a people from Egyptian slavery but in the Christ event as presented in this passage. In other words, Jesus gives final meaning and significance to the exodus, which anticipated the deliverance that Jesus Christ would experience and finally mediate.

Another example of the inclusion of a biblical quotation is Matthew 2:5–6: "They told him, '[The Christ is to be born] in Bethlehem of Judea; for so it has been written by the prophet: "And you, Bethlehem, in the land of Judah, are by no means least among the rulers of Judah; for from you shall come a ruler who is to shepherd my people Israel."'" This quotation is drawn from two Old Testament passages: Micah 5:2 and 2 Samuel 5:2. The consideration that Matthew has brought together two originally separate passages and united them indicates a change introduced by the evangelist. The very combination of two

16. As such, Hosea 11:1 itself forms an example of a biblical passage that alludes to an earlier passage: the exodus account in the book of Exodus (esp. 4:22–23).

17. See R. T. France, "The Formula-Quotations of Matthew 2 and the Problem of Communication," *NTS* 27 (1980–81): 233–51.

distinct quotations has the result of creating a new passage that transcends the meaning of either one understood on its own terms. In addition, remarkably, the evangelist has apparently introduced a radical change of wording in his quotation from Micah 5:2. The Micah passage, in both the Hebrew and the Septuagint, reads, "But you, O Bethlehem Ephrathah, who are least among the clans/rulers of Judah" (authors' translation). Matthew has inserted the word *oudamōs* ("by no means") into the quotation, thus changing its meaning completely.[18] Here is a case of apparent discontinuity between the original wording of a passage cited and the quotation of that passage itself. Possibly the implied author of Matthew's Gospel is drawing the attention of the reader to the original construction of Micah 5:2,[19] with the intention that the reader consider how that text is brought to eschatological fulfillment precisely through the opposite of the way the Micah text originally read.[20]

The third major form, which involves the examination of parallel passages, is *parallel scriptural testimony*. It includes passages in other biblical books that record the same event or the same saying as a passage in the book being studied. Clearly this kind of scriptural testimony pertains especially to the Gospels, where to a great extent the same events and sayings of Jesus are found in two or more of our Gospels. But this type of scriptural testimony is not limited to the Gospels. It is also relevant for the study of the two great narratives of Israel's history in the Old Testament: the Deuteronomic history (Joshua–2 Kings) and the Chronicler's history. These two great historical works deal with many of the same events. Indeed, parallels can be found in other

18. Another possibility is that Matthew was familiar with a variant of the text that contained this reading, though there is no extant textual evidence to support this possibility.

19. The implied reader of Matthew's Gospel knows the OT and is expected to construe the Matthean text in light of allusions and quotations from the OT. See Robert H. Gundry, *The Use of the Old Testament in St. Matthew's Gospel with Special Reference to the Messianic Hope*, Novum Testamentum Supplements 18 (Leiden: Brill, 1967), 205–15; C. H. Dodd, *According to the Scriptures: The Sub-Structure of New Testament Theology* (London: Nisbet, 1952).

20. Over the years, scholars have been engaged in intense discussion regarding the use of the OT by NT writers. Specifically, debate concerns whether, and if so, to what extent, NT writers intend to draw the attention of the reader to the original contexts of OT passages they quote or to which they allude. It is our judgment that, methodologically, students must make a decision on the basis of an examination of each passage. We conclude, materially, that by far the majority of the quotations or allusions made by NT writers to OT passages do take into account the original context of the OT passage, with the intention of drawing the reader's attention to certain features in that original context. This practice on the part of NT writers of implicitly referencing the context of OT passages cited or alluded to is termed *metalepsis*. For discussions of *metalepsis*, see Richard Hays, *Echoes of Scripture in the Letters of Paul* (New Haven: Yale University Press, 1989), esp. 29–33; idem, "The Conversion of the Imagination: Scripture and Eschatology in 1 Corinthians," *NTS* 45 (July 1999): 391–412; Mark Allan Powell, "Expected and Unexpected Readings in Matthew: What the Reader Knows," *Asbury Theological Journal* 48, no. 2 (1993): 31–52; Dodd, *According to the Scriptures*. For works dealing with the broader issue of the use of OT passages by NT writers, see Bauer, *Annotated Guide to Biblical Resources*, 218–20.

parts of the biblical canon. Examples include possible parallels between the Pauline teachings in Ephesians and Colossians, or between the teachings of Jude and the very similar, and perhaps parallel, teachings of 2 Peter 2.

The primary resource for the study of parallel passages in the Gospels is a "Gospel harmony" or "Gospel synopsis." These works will typically print the parallels in columns across the page so that readers can easily compare and contrast what is presented in the parallel passages.[21] Harmonies or synopses are also available to study parallels between the Deuteronomic and Chronicler's histories.[22]

As with other forms of scriptural testimony, a possibility of continuity and discontinuity exists between the passage being interpreted and related scriptural passages. Students can expect to find either essential continuity or discontinuity. Thus they may wish to engage in a critical conversation between the passage being interpreted and its parallel(s).

Essential continuity exists between the studied passage and its parallel(s) when the parallel passage(s) expresses knowledge or perspective that the writer of the passage under interpretive scrutiny assumed his readers had and would bring to bear on their construal of his passage. Students may make this judgment based on the literary context of their passage and upon historical probability. Such essential continuity indicates complementarity between a passage and its parallel(s), and the background principle goes into effect. Students can use the parallel passage to obtain the kind of knowledge that the implied author of their passage assumed the implied readers would have and would use.

Essential discontinuity between the studied passage and its parallel(s) exists when the parallel passage(s) does not contain information or perspective that the implied author of the text assumed his readers would have or would bring to bear on the interpretation of the passage in question. When such essential discontinuity exists, the passage has a peculiarity over against its parallel(s), and the foil principle goes into effect. In such a case, a student might ask, How

---

21. The most helpful Gospel harmony based on the English text is probably Burton H. Throckmorton, *Gospel Parallels: A Comparison of the Synoptic Gospels*, 5th ed. (Nashville: Nelson, 1992). The most authoritative Gospel harmonies based on the Greek text are Kurt Aland, ed., *Synopsis of the Four Gospels: Completely Revised on the Basis of the Greek Text of Nestle-Aland, 26th Edition, and the Greek New Testament, 3rd Edition* (New York: United Bible Societies, 1985); Albert Huck, *A Synopsis of the First Three Gospels with the Addition of the Johannine Parallels*, rev. Heinrich Greeven, 13th ed. (Grand Rapids: Eerdmans, 1982). For further comment on these resources and additional titles, see Bauer, *Annotated Guide to Biblical Resources*, 236–37.

22. See esp. Abba Bendavid, *Maqbilôt ba-Miqra* [Parallels in the Bible] (Jerusalem: Carta, 1972); John C. Endres, William R. Millar, and John Barclay Burns, eds., *Chronicles and Its Synoptic Parallels in Samuel, Kings, and Related Biblical Texts* (Collegeville, MN: Liturgical Press, 1998); Primus Vannutelli, *Libri synoptici veteris testamenti seu librorum regum et chronicorum loci paralleli* (Rome: Pontifical Biblical Institute Press, 1931–34). For additional comments and titles, see Bauer, *Annotated Guide to Biblical Resources*, 91–94.

do the very differences in information or perspective between the passage at hand and its parallel(s) illumine the specific and peculiar concerns that the implied author of my passage is communicating?

An example of essential continuity is the relation between Matthew 27:1–2 and John 18:31. Matthew 27:1–2 describes the act of the religious authorities, who in the Sanhedrin had just condemned Jesus to death, handing Jesus over to the Roman governor, Pilate: "When morning came, all the chief priests and the elders of the people conferred together against Jesus in order to bring about his death. They bound him, led him away, and handed him over to Pilate the governor." The passage itself, in its immediate context, raises a question that it does not answer: Why do the religious authorities who have condemned Jesus to death hand him over to Pilate rather than simply putting him to death themselves? The passage raises this question in the mind of the reader but does not try to answer it; this consideration suggests that the implied author assumes the implied reader knows why the Sanhedrin handed Jesus over to the Roman governor rather than killing him. But modern readers do not have this kind of background information; in this case, they can find it in the Johannine parallel. John explicitly gives the answer to this question in his own parallel account; thus John 18:31 tells us, "Pilate said to them, 'Take him yourselves and judge him according to your law.' The Jews replied, 'We are not permitted to put anyone to death.'" This consultation of the parallel passage, then, helps the reader of Matthew's Gospel to understand the narrative of Matthew 27. The implied author of Matthew's Gospel is not assuming that the implied reader would know the Gospel of John; rather, the implied author of Matthew's Gospel assumes that the implied reader would know information or have a perspective that happens to be expressed in the Johannine parallel.

An example of essential discontinuity is the relation between Jesus's statement recorded in Matthew 13:11 and its parallel in Mark 4:11. Matthew 13:11 reads, "To you it has been given to know the secrets of the kingdom of heaven, but to them it has not been given." But the Markan parallel reads, "To you has been given the secret of the kingdom of God, but for those outside, everything comes in parables." The reader recognizes immediately the difference between the inflection of the noun "secret" in the two passages. In Matthew it is plural, "secrets," while Mark employs the singular. The question that occupies us at this point is not what the historical Jesus said; our focus is upon the interpretation of the text and the significance for interpreting Matthew 13 and Mark 4 that arises from the difference between these parallel passages. The interpreter may conclude that the "secrets" of Matthew 13 refer to the characteristics and principles of the kingdom that Jesus sets forth in the surrounding parables. The interpreter may also ascertain that the "secret" of Mark 4 refers to the mystery hidden from human understanding, as so much emphasized throughout the Gospel of Mark: the amazing reality that God has chosen to usher in his end-time rule precisely through the shameful death upon the cross of God's own Son.[23] The critical comparison, then, between the parallel passages illumines the unique or peculiar concern of both the Matthean and the Markan passages.[24]

The question is always, What kind of background knowledge does the implied author of this passage assume that his implied readers would have? In response, students must avoid uncritically reading into a given passage material from parallel passages in such a way as to collapse the two passages together. We can recall hearing a sermon on Matthew 26:6–13, the anointing of Jesus's head at the home of Simon in Bethany, in which the preacher immediately turned to the parallel account in Mark 14:3–9 and used elements in the Markan account that were absent in the Matthean one to fill in the gaps. The result was that the preacher actually created a new text, a composite one, and it did not correspond either to the Matthean or Markan account. Now students may find an appropriate time to pursue a study of the New Testament presentation of this event in the attempt to bring together the concerns of each of the accounts. Such a study is entirely warranted. But it will have hermeneutical integrity only if one conducts it in such a way as to allow the unique features and concerns of each of the evangelists to be heard and to stand in conversation with each other.[25]

At this point we must discuss the relationship between evidence from context and evidence from word usage and scriptural testimony. Evidence from context is generally the most significant kind because it involves authorial direction. Through the immediate and broader-book context of the biblical book, which is the basic literary unit in the Bible, the author gives direction as to how the reader should understand the meaning of passages within the book. When writers compose books, they necessarily create a kind of alternative world, a world of the text. Context then pertains to the world of the text. This "world"

23. This mystery, emphasized strikingly in Mark, is known as the "messianic secret." See esp. Christopher Tuckett, ed., *The Messianic Secret*, Issues in Religion and Theology 1 (Philadelphia: Fortress, 1983); Kingsbury, *Christology of Mark's Gospel*, 1–22; cf. William Wrede, *The Messianic Secret*, trans. J. C. G. Greig, Library of Theological Translations (Cambridge, UK: James Clarke, 1971), originally published as *Das Messiasgeheimnis in den Evangelien* (1901).

24. At times the operative difference between parallel passages involves not the wording of the passages but their contexts. Thus the parable of the lost sheep is presented in almost identical terms in Matt. 18 and Luke 15. But the context of Luke 15 indicates that the point of the Lukan parable is that one should not be offended that God seeks the lost, even the religiously and socially unacceptable. The context of Matt. 18 indicates that the point of the Matthean parable is that disciples should be careful to avoid offending (causing to stumble and fall away from the faith) other disciples in the church through an insistence on their own rights in God's eschatological kingdom, without concern for the ways in which this insistence might negatively and even destructively affect the spiritual lives of their fellow Christians.

25. Coalescing the teaching of parallel accounts actually belongs to the process of *correlation*, which is discussed below in part 5.

is a more or less self-contained system that exists for the explication of the meaning of individual passages as well as the meaning of the entire book. But the phrase *more or less* is highly noteworthy because every book assumes a great deal of background information from "the real world": linguistic, conceptual, and historical knowledge that the implied author assumes the reader, as envisaged by the text (i.e., the implied reader), possesses. A major purpose of both word usage and scriptural testimony (and historical background; see below, in this chapter) is to provide the kind of background information that the text assumes the reader has and will bring to bear on the interpretation of the passage. Thus, one needs to conduct a critical interaction between the context and other biblical passages encountered in word usage and scriptural testimony. This critical interaction affirms the employment and importance of word usage and scriptural testimony as well as recognizes the limitations that attend word usage and scriptural testimony. Figure 26 illustrates this combination of affirmation and limitation.

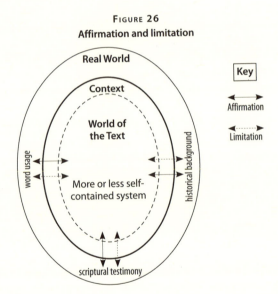

FIGURE 26
Affirmation and limitation

Accurate interpretation involves possessing and appropriating the kind of background knowledge from the *real world* that the implied author expects the implied reader will bring to the passage. Underinterpretation occurs when readers lack, or fail to make use of, such background information. Overinterpretation occurs when readers construe passages according to information that the implied author does not expect the implied reader to possess or to employ in the interpretation of a passage. Overinterpretation also occurs when readers use background information in ways contrary to what the implied author expects of readers of his text.

Kinds of Terms

This type of evidence involves deciding whether a given term is employed in a literal or figurative sense and, if figurative, determining the meaning of the figurative language and its significance for interpreting the passage. Much of the language of the Bible is figurative or metaphorical. Almost all expressions pertaining to God—for example, *El Shaddai* or *Abba*—come from specific spheres of human life and are applied to the Deity in an attempt to explicate certain aspects of God and of God's relation to persons or the world. As Grant Osborne says, "In fact, most theological concepts in Scripture are metaphorical. This is because eternal truths cannot be expressed in human temporal language with exactness."[26] Yet we typically do not recognize the various divine names as metaphorical because with time and use their metaphorical character has become muted, and they have become part of the concept of the Deity himself.

While being aware of the (at least originally) metaphorical character of much of the Bible's language, it is very important to note figurative terminology especially in passages where writers draw attention to their metaphorical practice. We refer to passages that emphasize the use of metaphor and in which metaphor is central to communicating the sense of the passage.

Metaphorical language employs the principle of analogy, which involves comparison.[27] One adopts metaphorical language to draw an analogy between the figure, or metaphor, that is used (*signifier*) and the reality to which the figure is compared (*signified*). But remember the saying that we mentioned earlier: "No analogy walks on all fours." In other words, both continuity and discontinuity exist between the figure employed and the reality to which it refers. Continuity is present insofar as the figure is like the reality to which it refers. But because analogous elements are not identical, there will necessarily be differences or discontinuity between the figure/metaphor and the reality to which it refers. We may express the combination of continuity and discontinuity by the image of two partially overlapping spheres (see fig. 27).

The interpreter has the responsibility of identifying the points of continuity and discontinuity so as to ascertain the purpose of the metaphor. G. B. Caird has provided a helpful example of the importance of clearly recognizing the meaning of metaphorical language within a biblical passage. He refers to Psalm 133:1–2: "How very good and pleasant it is when kindred live together

26. Grant R. Osborne, *The Hermeneutical Spiral: A Comprehensive Introduction to Biblical Interpretation*, 2nd ed. (Downers Grove, IL: InterVarsity, 2006), 387.

27. Janet Martin Soskice defines metaphorical language as "speaking about one thing in terms which are seen to be suggestive of another" (*Metaphor and Religious Language* [Oxford: Clarendon, 1985], 49). Specifically, "simile" involves a linguistic analogy or comparison using the terms "like" or "as," while "metaphor" is a linguistic analogy or comparison that occurs without the use of such terms. "Metaphorical language" refers to both metaphor and simile.

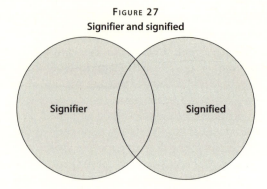

FIGURE 27
Signifier and signified

in unity! It is like the precious oil on the head, running down upon the beard, on the beard of Aaron, running down over the collar of his robes." Caird says, "When the psalmist tells us that a unified family is like oil dripping down Aaron's beard onto the skirts of his robe, he is not trying to persuade us that family unity is messy, greasy, or volatile; he is thinking of the all-pervasive fragrance that has so deeply impressed itself on his memory at the anointing of the high priest (Ps. 133:2)."[28]

Ascertaining the significance of figurative language may involve the use of other types of evidence, such as context, word usage, and scriptural testimony. In fact, the various types of evidence are not rigidly separable in their use; in practice, they often overlap.

While metaphorical language involves the principle of analogy, it cannot be reduced to analogy or to analogical propositions. Thus interpreters should not think that they have fully captured the meaning of a metaphor by saying something like, "This metaphor teaches us six things about the concept that it describes, and we can state these six truths in the form of simple declarative propositions." This kind of analogical reductionism reflects the *substitution theory* of metaphor associated especially with Aristotle. The substitution theory posits that metaphors are merely aesthetically motivated substitutes for literal descriptive statements and thus can be fully translated into such literal descriptive statements.

More recently many scholars have argued against the substitution theory in favor of the theory of semantic opposition or semantic interaction.[29] According to this view, the very combination of similarities and differences between signifier and signified provides a tension between the two, and this *tensive* character of metaphorical language is precisely what gives the metaphoric signifier its power to clarify or describe the signified. Thus metaphorical language dynamically transforms readers' understanding of both elements in the

28. Caird, *Language and Imagery of the Bible*, 145.
29. Osborne, *Hermeneutical Spiral*, 388.

metaphorical construction: signifier and signified.[30] Metaphorical language appeals to the imagination. Students can imagine in new ways how the juxtaposition of signified and signifier opens up previously unexplored meanings of each as well as otherwise hidden dimensions of their relationship. As David deSilva states, "A metaphor does not merely 'stand for' or 'represent' the reality it replaces; it also interprets that reality, bringing to it a new perspective gained from setting it in the light of some other known reality."[31]

But this appeal to the imagination is not an encouragement of unrestrained or freewheeling use of imagination. Instead, it involves a *disciplined* use of imagination, directed by the context of the passage in which the metaphorical language is employed.[32] Thus the interpreter has the critically important job of exploring the specific meaning of the figurative language, but with a recognition that one cannot reduce metaphorical language to literal propositions.

Inflections and Syntax

INFLECTIONS

In the discussion on inflections, presented under "Detailed Observation" (in chap. 13), we described inflections as changes in the form of words, indicating their grammatical sense and significance. Inflections involve such things as person, number, case, tense, mood, and voice.[33] The identification of

---

· 30. One continuing popular tendency is to understand metaphorical language as purely decorative. But the work of metaphorical theorists over the past thirty years clearly indicates that such a view cannot be justified. These theorists have demonstrated conclusively that metaphor is much more than decorative and aesthetically pleasing language. Instead, it is cognitively active, creating something new, possessing a "cognitive punch." Here one should consult the work done in cognitive linguistic science. See George Lakoff and Mark Johnson, *Metaphors We Live By* (Chicago: University of Chicago Press, 1980); George Lakoff and Mark Turner, *More Than Cool Reason: A Field Guide to Poetic Metaphor* (Chicago: University of Chicago Press, 1989); Raymond Gibbs, *The Poetics of Mind: Figurative Thought, Language, and Understanding* (Cambridge: Cambridge University Press, 1994); Lynne Cameron and Graham Low, eds., *Researching and Applying Metaphor*, Cambridge Applied Linguistics (Cambridge: Cambridge University Press, 1999); Gerard Steen, *Understanding Metaphor in Literature: An Empirical Approach* (London: Longman, 1994). See also Paul B. Armstrong, *Conflicting Readings: Variety and Validity in Interpretation* (Chapel Hill: University of North Carolina Press, 1990); John Darr, *On Character Building: The Reader and the Rhetoric of Characterization in Luke-Acts*, LCBI (Louisville: Westminster John Knox, 1992), 85–126; Caird, *Language and Imagery of the Bible*, 144–59; Max Black, "Metaphor," in *Philosophical Perspectives on Metaphor*, ed. Mark Johnson (Minneapolis: University of Minnesota Press, 1981), 63–82.

31. David deSilva, *Perseverance in Gratitude: A Socio-Rhetorical Commentary on the Epistle "to the Hebrews"* (Grand Rapids: Eerdmans, 2000), 426.

32. Ps. 23 offers an excellent example of the importance of context for clarifying the meaning of metaphorical language. The notion of the Lord as a "shepherd" in v. 1 is carefully controlled by the description found in the remainder of the psalm.

33. See "Types of Observation" in chap. 13 for a discussion of observations pertaining to inflections.

inflection belongs to observation, but the exploration of the specific meaning and import of inflection belongs to the interpretive phase. In some cases, the interpretive significance of an inflection will be quite apparent and will not require specific research into scholarly discussions. Thus one can consider the interpretive import of the future tenses of Isaiah 11:1 ("A shoot *shall come out* from the stump of Jesse, and a branch *shall grow out* of his roots") as describing events that have not yet transpired at the time of this prophecy from Isaiah; rather, they refer to certain things that will transpire in the future (from Isaiah's perspective). But often specific and intentional research is helpful in order to capture more precisely the nuanced elements of the sense that is being communicated through the inflection. In cases such as these, knowledge of the original language is especially helpful. For both inflection and syntax, discussed below, the essential resources that assist in original-language analysis are grammars or grammatical studies.[34]

But the possibility of developing the significance of inflections is available in many instances even to students who have no facility in Hebrew or Greek and are thus dependent upon the vernacular translation. The reader of the English Bible should note the plural in Matthew 2:20: "*Those* who were seeking the child's life are dead." The use of the plural here is arresting, for up to this point in the narrative, only King Herod has been presented as intent upon the murder of the infant Jesus. Is Matthew suggesting, by use of the plural, that "the chief priests and scribes" to whom Herod posed the question of the birthplace of the Christ (2:4) were complicit in Herod's attempt to kill Jesus and have subsequently died? Or is Matthew suggesting that not

---

34. Original-language grammars come in two classes: *Intermediate* grammars provide essential and accessible discussions of the major types of inflections and syntactical structures one encounters in the Bible and are thus designed for handy reference as one moves through the reading or analysis of passages. *Comprehensive* grammars provide fuller and more complete information on virtually all aspects of the language. Intermediate grammars for Hebrew include Bill T. Arnold and John H. Choi, *A Guide to Biblical Hebrew Syntax* (Cambridge: Cambridge University Press, 2003); Bruce K. Waltke and M. O'Connor, *An Introduction to Biblical Hebrew Syntax* (Winona Lake, IN: Eisenbrauns, 1990). Comprehensive Hebrew grammars include Paul Joüon and T. Muraoka, *A Grammar of Biblical Hebrew*, 2 vols., Subsidia biblica 14.1–2 (Rome: Biblical Institute Press, 1991); E. Kautzsch, ed., *Gesenius' Hebrew Grammar*, 2nd ed., revised in accord with the 28th German ed. by A. E. Cowley (Oxford: Clarendon, 1909). Intermediate Greek grammars include Daniel B. Wallace, *Greek Grammar beyond the Basics: An Exegetical Syntax of the New Testament* (Grand Rapids: Zondervan, 1996); H. E. Dana and Julius R. Mantey, *A Manual Grammar of the Greek New Testament* (New York: Macmillan, 1927); James A. Brooks and Carlton L. Winbery, *Syntax of New Testament Greek* (Lanham, MD: University Press of America, 1979); David Alan Black, *It's Still Greek to Me: An Easy-to-Understand Guide to Intermediate Greek* (Grand Rapids: Baker Academic, 1998). Comprehensive Greek grammars include A. T. Robertson, *A Grammar of the Greek New Testament in Light of Historical Research* (Nashville: Broadman, 1934); F. Blass and A. Debrunner, *A Greek Grammar of the New Testament and Other Early Christian Literature*, trans. and ed. Robert W. Funk (Chicago: University of Chicago Press, 1961). See Bauer, *Annotated Guide to Biblical Resources*, 54–56, 191–95.

only Herod but also all of the soldiers whom Herod sent to Jerusalem to kill Jesus (2:16) had died? What is the significance of the plural number here? Perhaps Matthew is drawing the reader's attention to Exodus 4:19, where the same phrase occurs. There God commands Moses to return to Egypt "for all those who were seeking your life are dead." If so, the use of the plural refers the reader to the Moses narrative and, in accord with the Matthean emphasis throughout the chapter, suggests that the experience of the infant Jesus at the hands of Herod was anticipated in Moses's experience and that Jesus brings Moses's experience to its eschatological fulfillment. Again, the alert reader will consider what might be the full significance of the use of the singular number of the noun in John 1:29, "Here is the Lamb of God, who takes away the *sin* [not sins] of the world." And the reader of 1 John might consider the use of the present tense in 2:17 rather than the future: "And the world and its desire *are passing* away."

The potential significance of original-language inflectional analysis may yield great insight in the interpretive analysis of inflections in both verbs and nouns. In terms of verbs, students of New Testament Greek know that grammarians discuss various possible functions of the aorist tense. The *constative aorist*, for example, describes an action occurring as such, without reference to the duration or lack of duration of the action described by the verb. In contrast, the *culminative aorist* describes the completion of an action, and the *ingressive aorist* describes action at its beginning. The imperfect tense in Greek also has various functions. For example, the *voluntative imperfect* describes an action that is attempted but not actualized. Many scholars take the imperfect tense of Matthew 27:48 to be voluntative. Most translations render this verse as the NRSV has done: "At once one of them ran and got a sponge, filled it with sour wine, put it on a stick, and gave it to him to drink." But the verb translated "gave to drink" is in the imperfect tense (*epotizen*), and thus, if it is the voluntative imperfect, one should understand it as "*tried* to give him to drink," suggesting that Jesus did not actually take it.

Most grammarians insist that Hebrew does not have tenses but does have *aspects*, which function much as tenses. One function of the imperfect aspect in Hebrew is to indicate frequentative or habitual action. An example is found in Genesis 43:32: "They served [Joseph] by himself, and [Joseph's brothers] by themselves, and the Egyptians who ate with him by themselves, because the Egyptians could not eat with the Hebrews, for that is an abomination to the Egyptians." In this verse, the imperfect aspect of the verb "could not" (*yûklûn*) indicates that such an impossibility was the case not simply for that particular meal or at that particular moment in time, but that it was constantly or habitually the case during the period of the patriarchs.[35]

---

35. In this case the repeated or habitual character of the verbal action is confirmed and clarified by the next statement: "for that is an abomination to the Egyptians" (Gen. 43:32).

In terms of nouns, readers with facility in Greek will recall that every case has a range of possible functions, and each function contains potential interpretive significance. There are, for example, various types of genitives, including the *genitive of source*. In the genitive of source, the noun in the genitive is the origin or cause of the noun that it modifies. Thus 1 Thessalonians 1:3 has a series of genitives (work *of faith*, labor *of love*, steadfastness *of hope*) that are almost certainly genitives of source: "remembering before our God and Father your work of faith and labor of love and steadfastness of hope in our Lord Jesus Christ." One should therefore understand them as meaning, "your work, which is the expression or result of your faith; and labor, which is the expression or result of your love; and steadfastness, which comes from your hope in Jesus Christ."

One of the most debated passages in the New Testament is controversial because of the genitive that Paul employs in Galatians 2:16, which reads, "We know that a person is justified not by the works of the law but through faith in Jesus Christ." The word "in" does not appear in the original. The Greek actually contains a genitive construction and might be rendered literally as "through the faith of Jesus Christ" (*dia pisteōs Iēsou Christou*).[36] The NRSV translators have thus assumed that the genitive in question is an *objective genitive*, which indicates that the name and title in the genitive, "Jesus Christ," is the object of faith: "faith *in* Jesus Christ." But many scholars have recently argued that evidence from immediate and book context and from Paul's other epistles (word usage and scriptural testimony) suggests that Paul is employing here the *subjective genitive*. According to this understanding, the name and title in the genitive, "Jesus Christ," is the subject of "faith." Thus, one could read it as "we are justified by the kind of faith [in God], or faithful obedience [to God], that Jesus Christ had."[37] The very sense of the passage, then, depends upon how one takes the genitive. And indeed, the interpretive judgment regarding this genitive may in significant ways inform our understanding of Paul's doctrine of justification by faith.

Recognizing the possible uses of the Hebrew genitive can also be invaluable for interpretation. When one reads in Deuteronomy 10:17 that the "Lord your God is God of gods" (*'Ĕlōhê hā'ĕlōhîm*), one should remember that one of the functions of the genitive in Hebrew is to indicate the superlative; thus this genitive expression may signify that the Lord is the supreme God and in no way suggests the existence of other deities.

Syntax

While inflections focus upon changes in the form of a word that point to the grammatical sense of the word itself (e.g., tense, person, mood, case),

---

36. As indicated in the margin of the NRSV and as already in the KJV.

37. See esp. Richard B. Hays, *The Faith of Jesus Christ: An Investigation of the Narrative Substructure of Galatians 3:1–4:11*, SBLDS 56 (Chico, CA: Scholars Press, 1983).

syntax pertains to the grammatical structure of a sentence.[38] Like inflections, grammatical structure or syntax (e.g., subject, predicate, adverbial modifier, independent and dependent clauses) is noted in the observation stage; but at the point of interpretation, we probe its significance for the passage's meaning. Moreover, like inflections, grammatical structure can be profitably pursued to some extent on the basis of the English translation. Yet a certain level of clarity, depth, and reliability in interpretation is possible only when one is dealing with the analysis of the original languages. Therefore, here in the process of dealing with inflections and grammatical analysis, a working knowledge of the original languages is especially helpful. And those with facility in Hebrew and Greek should make full use of all the linguistic competencies they possess.[39]

Examples of the interpretive significance of New Testament syntax abound.[40] Even on the basis of the English text, one may see that the grammatical structure of Matthew 28:19–20a involves one main verb, "make disciples" (*mathēteusate*), followed by two coordinate participles, "baptizing" (*baptizontes*) and "teaching" (*didaskontes*), thereby indicating that the main concern in this sentence is making disciples, and that the references to baptizing and teaching are secondary to that main concern and are subordinate (in parallel ways) to it.[41]

Moreover, students with proficiency in Greek will recall the two ways of expressing prohibition in that language. Biblical writers normally employ *mē* with the aorist subjunctive to express prohibitive action that may be contemplated but is not yet being done ("Don't even begin to . . ."), as in Matthew 3:9 ("Do not presume"), for example. But they use *mē* with the present imperative to express prohibitive action that is already in progress ("Stop doing . . ."). When the Lord commands Paul in Acts 18:9, "Do not be afraid," he uses *mē* with the present imperative. Consequently, we recognize that this Greek construction

---

38. Scholars often use "syntax" to refer both to inflections and to the grammatical structure of sentences, but we find making a distinction between the study of inflections and grammatical structures somewhat helpful, while recognizing the close relationship between them.

39. We recommend that students make use of the original languages to the extent that they have competency in these languages. But students should identify the limits of their knowledge of the original languages and avoid trying to work with the original languages in ways that transcend their competencies, keeping in mind the expression, "Some people know just enough Greek or Hebrew to be dangerous."

40. The grammatical diagramming of sentences is often beneficial for noting syntactical relationships. For a helpful discussion of diagramming, with examples of various diagramming models, see Osborne, *Hermeneutical Spiral*, 45–50.

41. Even here, though, knowledge of Greek is helpful; for students who know Greek will recognize that the main verb *mathēteusate* is not only followed by two participles in the present tense but also preceded by an aorist participle, *poreuthentes*, which most English versions translate with *mathēteusate* as a compound main verb. Moreover, students with Greek proficiency will recognize a number of ways in which Greek participles may relate to a main verb; they will be able to identify the most likely grammatical relationship between the participles and the main verb and draw out the interpretive significance of this relationship.

may suggest that Paul is indeed afraid and that the Lord is commanding him to cast aside the fear he is already experiencing.

A further example of the interpretive significance of syntax is seen when Satan tempts Jesus in the wilderness: "If you are the Son of God, command this stone to become a loaf of bread" (Luke 4:3; cf. 3:9). One might note that in the original Satan does not use the third-class conditional statement (*ean* with the subjunctive) but instead uses the first-class conditional statement (*ei* with the indicative). The first-class conditional statement assumes the reality of the condition as fact. One might thus take this statement to mean, "Since you are the Son of God . . . " Accordingly, Satan is not asking Jesus whether he is the Son of God, as if Satan wishes Jesus to *prove* his divine sonship by turning the stone into bread, but Satan is tempting Jesus thereby to *express* his divine sonship.

Evidence from syntax may at times have great theological significance. John 1:1c is a predicate nominative construction: "and the Word was God." In Greek the subject of a predicate nominative construction has the definite article, whereas the predicate nominative is anarthrous (lacking the definite article). Here "Word" (*ho logos*) has the article and therefore is the subject; "God" (*theos*) is anarthrous and is the predicate nominative. Consequently, this statement is not, strictly speaking, an assertion about God; rather, the fact that the subject is "the Word" indicates that the declaration is an assertion about the Word. John is not saying that "God is the Word." If that had been the case, John would have been making "God" and "the Word" interchangeable, as if God equals the Word in the sense that God is reducible to the Word without remainder, that God is nothing more than the Word. Rather, when John declares that the Word is God, he is indicating that there may be more to God than the Word. The Word is fully God, but God is not limited to the Word. As C. K. Barrett says, "θεός [*theos*, God], being without the article, is predicative and describes the nature of the Word. The absence of the article indicates that the Word is God, but is not the only being of whom this is true; if ὁ θεός [*ho theos*, with the definite article] had been written it would have implied that no divine being existed outside the second person of the Trinity."[42] In other words, it would have denied the reality of God the Father as in some ways distinct from God the Son. And the grammarian A. T. Robertson insists that if the article had appeared not just before "Word" (*logos*) but also before "God" (*theos*), the grammatical structure would have suggested that these terms were completely interchangeable and would have supported Sabellianism (i.e., modalism) over against the trinitarian theology that we actually find expressed in the passage, both in the grammatical structure of this sentence and in the context of the rest of the prologue and the remainder of the Gospel of John.[43]

42. Barrett, *Gospel according to St. John*, 156.

43. Robertson, *Grammar of the Greek New Testament*, 767–68. See also George R. Beasley-Murray, *John*, WBC 36 (Waco: Word, 1987), 11, who insists that this construction "denotes [the

The Old Testament also offers ample and rich examples of the interpretive significance of syntax. Here are just a few examples from the first chapter of Joshua. Joshua 1:1 has a *waw*-consecutive grammatical construction (literally, "and it happened after the death of Moses"), possibly indicating that Joshua 1:1 is a continuation of a preceding narrative, almost certainly the book of Deuteronomy. This construction, then, emphasizes that the first chapter of Joshua should be taken in some sense as a continuation of the narrative of Deuteronomy.[44]

Joshua 1:7 reads, "Only be strong and very courageous." The sentence begins with the adverb "only" (*raq*), which in both English and Hebrew is a mild adversative, expressing a slight contrast with the preceding. This adverbial construction indicates that the promise of divine presence in verse 6 is not absolute or completely adequate in itself to realize victory but must be supplemented by the human response/action of strength and courage. Divine presence or divine help is the necessary but not the sole and sufficient cause or basis for success in conquest.

But this verse also contains, in the English translation, a participial construction: "being careful to act in accordance with all the law that Moses my servant commanded you." Students with competency in Hebrew will note that the construction is actually *lamed* (ל) with the infinitive construct, which usually, or at least very often, indicates purpose. It might thus be rendered, "in order that you might be careful to do according to all the law."[45] This syntactical construction, in other words, raises the possibility that somehow being strong and courageous has as its purpose the fulfillment of the whole Mosaic law; and this possibility, in turn, suggests a number of implications of the relationship between strength, courage, and obedience to the law of Moses in its comprehensiveness.

Finally, one might observe that Joshua's speech to the Transjordanian tribes in 1:14 contains the adverb "before" (Hebrew: *liphnê*): "All the warriors among you shall cross over armed before your kindred and shall help them." Although

---

Word as] *God in his nature*, as truly God as he with whom he 'was,' yet without exhausting the being of God."

44. Thus Kautzsch, *Gesenius' Hebrew Grammar*, 133, says, "This name [*waw consecutive*] best expresses the prevailing syntactical relation, for by *waw consecutive* an action is always represented as the direct, or at least temporal consequence of a preceding action. . . . The fact that whole books (Lev., Num., Josh., Judges, [1 and 2] Sam., 2 Kings, Ezek., Ruth, Esth., Neh., 2 Chron.) begin with imperfect *consecutive* . . . is taken as a sign of their close connexion with the historical books that now or originally preceded them."

45. See, e.g., Arnold and Choi, *Guide to Biblical Hebrew Syntax*, 71, 111; Kautzsch, *Gesenius' Hebrew Grammar*, 348–51, points out that the construction normally indicates purpose but allows that it can sometimes be used more "loosely," including "attendant circumstances," which is reflected in the rendering of the NRSV. But even if one takes it as indicating attendant circumstances, one should reflect upon the ways in which this construction illumines the meaning of the relationship between these clauses and hence the interpretation of the entire verse.

this adverb may be used temporally (i.e., before in time), here it is clearly used spatially (i.e., before in space, in front of). It indicates that the men from the Transjordanian tribes, who had already received their inheritance east of the Jordan and had nothing personally to gain from the conquest of Canaan, were to be on the front lines of the campaigns to win territory for their fellow Israelites. They were not to go in after their kindred and only engage in the relatively safe mopping-up operations. On the contrary, Joshua commanded them to assume the most dangerous and risky positions. Such was the sacrificial commitment that they were ordered to bear for their fellow Israelites.

Literary Forms

We described general literary forms at some length while discussing the "Survey of Parts-as-Wholes" (chap. 12). There we mentioned that one can understand literary forms, or genres, in very general terms, according to broad categories whose presence in literary texts is quite obvious. These broad categories include prose narrative, poetry, drama or dramatic prose, parable, apocalyptic, and discursive. These general categories pertain to passages of midlevel size, meaning segments or sections rather than macro-units such as the book-as-a-whole, or pertain to mini-units such as paragraphs or sentences. The more specific literary forms or genres that are subcategories of the general ones tend to be found either at the macrolevel of the book-as-a-whole or at the microlevel of individual sentences or paragraphs.[46] Readers should consult the "Survey of Parts-as-Wholes" (chap. 12) for the characteristics of each of these general literary forms and for indications regarding the interpretive significance of these forms.

A literary form or genre represents a sociolinguistic agreement between the writer and readers. Every culture and subculture has certain recognized genres, each manifesting its own characteristic combination of material content and structure. Implied writers assume that their implied readers will recognize the genre and will read the text according to the *rules* of the genre. Genre thus involves an implicit encoding. Competent readers, for their part, will recognize the genre employed and will construe the text accordingly. Thus Wittgenstein speaks of genre as "the rules of the language game."[47] And James L. Bailey describes genres as "the conventional and repeated patterns of oral and written speech, which facilitate interaction among people in specific social situations."[48]

46. One could cite some exceptions to this statement. For example, parables are frequently paragraph length.

47. Ludwig Wittgenstein, *Philosophical Investigations*, trans. G. E. M. Anscombe (New York: Macmillan, 1953), 108, quoted in Osborne, *Hermeneutical Spiral*, 26. Cf. Eco, *Role of the Reader*, 17–18.

48. James L. Bailey, "Genre Analysis," in Green, *Hearing the New Testament*, 200.

Once students arrive at the point of interpretation, they will often find it helpful to explore the interpretive significance of the general literary forms of a passage (e.g., prose narrative). Moreover, at the interpretive phase, students may even want to identify the more specific literary forms found in the passage. For example, genealogy is a more specific subcategory of prose narrative, and *household code* (*Haustafel*) is a more specific subcategory of discursive texts.[49] Students may wish to consider how an understanding of this more specific literary form might illumine the meaning of the passage. Then, too, as part of the interpretation phase, students may wish to identify the more specific literary form that pertains to the book-as-a-whole, whether gospel, biography, history, or saga—with a view toward pursuing the interpretive significance of the literary form in which the entire book is cast.

The following principles should be kept in mind as one considers the interpretive potential of genre analysis.

First, genres work from the *principle of selectivity*. When a writer employs a genre, he implicitly decides to include certain features that belong to that genre and exclude other elements that would be foreign to that genre. The writer's selection of genre, then, communicates to the reader the kinds of elements that the writer wishes to emphasize and the way he wants to employ them. A writer can present certain elements in certain ways through a parable, for example, that would be impossible to do if he were to employ the literary form of genealogy.

Genres also tend to *reflect certain social situations or settings*. For example, a song of thanksgiving such as Exodus 15 suggests a quite different social setting than a funeral dirge such as Habakkuk 2, which itself assumes a social setting distinct from that of a proverb. The example of the funeral dirge from Habakkuk 2 indicates that in a literary document the actual social situation related to a particular literary form may be very much in the background because this passage does not describe an actual funeral but employs the language of the funeral for the sake of rhetorical effect. Any specific genre or literary form typically assumes a particular social setting. That social setting may stand at the origin of the communicative event, as in the psalms of thanksgiving, which presumably arose as liturgical expressions of thanksgiving in temple worship. Or the writer may simply intend to bring the social setting to the consciousness of readers, who will construe the passage with the aid of their own experience of the social situation suggested by the passage, as in the case of the example from Habakkuk.[50]

49. The NT examples of the *household code* include Eph. 5:21–6:9; Col. 3:18–4:1; and 1 Pet. 2:13–3:6.

50. These considerations suggest some overlap between this literary form and historical background, discussed later. More specifically, literary form relates to social history, which makes use of social-scientific categories. The examination of literary forms also pertains to the history of the tradition and particularly to form criticism. See "History of the Tradition" in this chapter.

Finally, the use of genre involves the *principle of flexibility or malleability*. A literary form must typically have some consistent features; otherwise, readers would be unable to identify discrete literary forms or even to talk about literary forms. But every individual occurrence has unique qualities and characteristics. In other words, one will almost never find a perfect example of a genre; rather, one will encounter passages that seem to belong more to one genre than to others. Indeed, often individual passages manifest a mixture or combination of genres, where one genre tends to bleed into another. Thus scholars have often disagreed about the genre of books such as Hebrews or James. They seem to belong to the genre of epistle, but Hebrews also bears the marks of a sermon.[51] James has been described as combining epistolary elements with other generic features, including those that belong to Hellenistic paraenesis[52] (exhortation) or to "protreptic discourse."[53] Therefore interpreters should note points of continuity and discontinuity between standard features of a genre and the specific features of the particular manifestation of the genre in the passage being interpreted. Students will construe standard features of the genre that are found in the passage on the basis of genre expectations. But points of departure from genre expectations may invite the reader to note especially these modifications as being significant for the communication of meaning in a passage.

The most helpful resource for examining both general and more specific genres is the Bible dictionary. Numerous books have been written on specific literary genres, concentrating, for example, on ancient epistles[54] or biographies.[55] For a list of specific genres in the New Testament and examples of the practice of genre analysis on New Testament texts, methodologically applicable also to Old Testament texts, see the essay on "genre analysis" by James L. Bailey.[56]

Psychological Factor

This type of evidence involves exploring the state of mind of the writer or of characters described within a passage to ascertain how such psychological

---

51. See, e.g., William L. Lane, *Hebrews*, 2 vols., WBC 47A–B (Dallas: Word, 1991).

52. See Martin Dibelius, *A Commentary on the Epistle of James*, rev. Heinrich Greeven, Hermeneia (Philadelphia: Fortress, 1975).

53. This means "an exhortation to follow a particular profession." See Luke Timothy Johnson, *James*, AB (New York: Doubleday, 1995), 16–25.

54. See, e.g., Stanley K. Stowers, *Letter Writing in Greco-Roman Antiquity*, LEC (Philadelphia: Westminster, 1986).

55. See, e.g., Philip L. Shuler, *A Genre for the Gospels: The Biographical Character of Matthew* (Philadelphia: Fortress, 1982); Richard A. Burridge, *What Are the Gospels? A Comparison with Graeco-Roman Biography* (Cambridge: Cambridge University Press, 1992).

56. Bailey, "Genre Analysis," 203–21. Additional significant resources on genre analysis include Gary Saul Morson and Caryl Emerson, *Mikhail Bakhtin: Creation of a Prosaics* (Palo Alto, CA: Stanford University Press, 1990); Osborne, *Hermeneutical Spiral*, 181–322; David E. Aune, *The New Testament in Its Literary Environment*, LEC (Philadelphia: Westminster, 1987).

considerations might inform the interpretation. At times the emotional or psychological condition of an author, as he presents himself within the text, is critical for ascertaining the meaning of the passage. One might wish to probe the psychological and emotional factors in Paul as he presents himself in 2 Timothy. Here Paul clearly states that he is suffering in prison (1:8, 11–12), having experienced the desertion of many of his friends (1:15; 4:9–18), and that he is anticipating his execution (4:6–8). The text itself leads the interpreter to ask, How do the emotional and psychological effects on the author of this kind of situation illumine the meaning of the various passages in 2 Timothy?[57]

But the psychological factor may apply also to characters presented within a text. Thus, for example, the person of Job, who functions really as a character within the book that bears his name, is portrayed as a man who has suffered repeated trauma and is consequently under severe stress. Certainly the reader is obliged to consider these factors in interpreting Job's actions and speech throughout the book. A similar example would be the character of Jeremiah: the book of Jeremiah presents him as a prophet who suffers excruciating emotional stress under the burden of the prophetic word, during the greatest crisis in Judah's history. Again, the psychological factor is pertinent in the accounts of the death of Jesus in the Gospels; the interpreter might consider the emotional and psychological impact of crucifixion in the construal of Jesus's cry of dereliction: "My God, my God, why have you forsaken me?" (Matt. 27:46; Mark 15:34).[58]

Scholars often warn against the "psychological fallacy" or the "psychologizing fallacy," meaning the tendency to pursue psychological analysis of the biblical writers or characters within a biblical text when the text itself does not invite such analysis. This counsel against improper introduction of psychological or emotional considerations is sound: it reminds us that the locus of our interpretation is the text itself. Thus students need to allow the indications of the text to direct its interpretation.[59] The operative questions, then, are these: Does the description emphasize the emotional or psychological elements or otherwise point to a frame of mind? Does the text employ emotive, attitudinal, or affective language?

57. The designated author of this epistle, Paul (2 Tim. 1:1), is the implied author. We are aware that many contemporary critical scholars assign 2 Timothy to an unnamed disciple (or disciples) of Paul who allegedly composed the document after Paul's death. If such is the case, then Paul would effectively be a fictive author. The same kind of psychological or emotional considerations would be pertinent, whether Paul was the actual or fictive author, since the reader is urged to construe these words placed into Paul's mouth according to the kind of situation the book describes Paul as enduring.

58. One should recall that the evangelists emphasize the humanity every bit as much as the deity of Jesus.

59. Moreover, moving behind the text to reconstruct a psychological or emotional condition of the person as a historical figure often involves a high degree of speculation because most of the biblical characters are not described in extrabiblical materials.

Keeping these questions in mind, students might judge that they should consider, for example, certain emotional aspects of the experiences of Joseph as they interpret the Joseph narrative in Genesis. The writer himself, at critical points in that narrative, draws the reader's attention to Joseph's emotions (e.g., 42:21; 43:30–31; 45:1–3). In contrast, the book of Joshua presents the wars in which the Canaanites are destroyed from the land with an almost studied distance and objectivity, which draws the reader away from identifying with, or even considering, the suffering and distress of the Canaanites.

Tone or Atmosphere

The discussion of the psychological factor should remind students that textual communication involves more than the conveying of cognitive content. There is often a concern for the total impact of the text upon the reader. Indeed, cognitive meaning is often affected, and at points even determined, by the tone or atmosphere. These are metaphorical terms—*tone* drawn from the realm of sound; *atmosphere* from the realm of space—to refer to the emotional or visceral *feel* of the passage, to the *feeling-impact* of the text upon the reader. Yet readers come to passages from their own background and situations; thus various readers may experience different feelings as they read the same passage. Indeed, individuals reading the same passage may have a somewhat different feeling-impact each time they read it, depending upon their mood or situation at that particular moment. But as a category of evidence, tone or atmosphere involves the consideration of elements within the text that may prompt the kind of feeling-impact that the implied author invites the reader to experience.

Tone or atmosphere may affect one's work with a passage in two ways. We believe, first, that it should have an impact on the way in which one communicates the message of a passage. Specifically, it may determine how one preaches or teaches a passage. Students could interpret a passage with technical accuracy, to gain a precisely correct sense of the terms employed and to articulate the essential claims of the passage on the basis of immediate and broader-book context; yet they might employ in preaching or teaching a tone that is dissonant with the tone of the passage itself. In so doing, at deep levels of communication and reception, they would convey a feeling that contradicts what the passage itself expresses. The result would be to leave hearers with an experience that is inconsistent with what the implied author intended.[60] In such a situation, from a passage that conveys a tone of encouragement and affirmation (e.g., Phil. 4:14–20), one might preach a sermon that is censorious or critical in its feel. Obviously the full impact upon the hearers would

---

60. Donald G. Miller, *The Way to Biblical Preaching: How to Communicate the Gospel in Depth* (Nashville: Abingdon, 1957), 142–53.

be quite different from the impact that Paul intended his words to have upon the Philippians.

But tone or atmosphere can be significant, second, for grasping the substantive meaning of the passage itself. Sometimes the same statement—the same set of words—can be understood either positively (to be accepted) or negatively (to be rejected), depending upon the tone or atmosphere. An excellent example of the importance of tone or atmosphere for the sense of a passage would be an author's use of the tone of sarcasm. Often sarcasm involves the use of facetious or ironic speech; thus the sentiment is actually the opposite of the essential meaning of the statement's wording. In Amos 4:4–5, the prophet urges:

> Come to Bethel—and transgress;
> to Gilgal—and multiply transgression;
> bring your sacrifices every morning,
> your tithes every three days;
> bring a thank-offering of leavened bread,
> and proclaim freewill offerings, publish them;
> for so you love to do, O people of Israel!

Amos is not actually intending to suggest that his audience should offer sacrifices at Gilgal and Bethel. On the contrary, he is exhorting them to examine their behavior and to bring their behavior into line with God's demands of justice before pursuing their sacrificial rituals. Indeed, Amos suggests that if they refuse to fulfill God's moral demands, they should not engage in those rituals at all. In 1 Corinthians 4:8, Paul tells the Corinthians, "Already you have all you want! Already you have become rich! Quite apart from us you have become kings!" Here Paul is claiming that although they may think they are filled, they are actually empty. And although they believe that they have become rich and that they reign, in reality nothing could be further from the truth.

Author's Purpose and Viewpoint

This category of evidence involves considering the ways in which the perspective of other persons or voices presented within a book relates to the writer's perspective, and it probes the writer's purpose for including these other perspectives.[61] The perspective of another person or voice may completely agree,

---

61. Several fine studies have been published dealing with an author's point of view. Among the most extensive and helpful are Boris Uspensky, *A Poetics of Composition: The Structure of the Artistic Text and Typology of a Compositional Form* (Berkeley: University of California Press, 1973); Susan Sniader Lanser, *The Narrative Act: Point of View in Prose Fiction* (Princeton, NJ: Princeton University Press, 1981). For application of point of view to the biblical materials, see, e.g., Danna Nolan Fewell and David M. Gunn, *Compromising Redemption: Relating Characters*

partly agree, or completely disagree with that of the implied author. When, for example, students read that the man born blind declares in John 9:31, "We know that God does not listen to sinners," students might explore whether, and to what extent, this sentiment agrees with the viewpoint of the implied author of John's Gospel. In addition, they might ascertain whether the implied author intends that the reader should accept this statement entirely or whether it represents a perspective that the implied author wishes to critique.

Sometimes writers will present characters as entirely reliable, as persons whose point of view agrees completely with that of the implied author. Such is manifestly the case with the presentation of Jesus in all of the Gospels. Everything Jesus says and does accords with the perspective of the evangelists, and they intend that the audience should accept all that Jesus says and does as completely true and valid. Most scholars believe that in the book of 1 Samuel, the implied author presents Samuel's viewpoint as reliable. Thus a question is raised when Walter Brueggemann argues that in the Saul narrative the writer presents Samuel the prophet as speaking cunningly so as to entrap Saul, in order to further Samuel's own self-centered agenda. One might conclude that Brueggemann's attempt to purge the moral character of Saul at the expense of Samuel's character contradicts the viewpoint of the implied author, which is really the viewpoint of the text.[62]

But the case may be somewhat different in Luke's portrayal of Gamaliel in Acts 5. Luke records that Gamaliel urges the Sanhedrin to abandon their abuse of the apostles in favor of waiting to see what will happen to the emerging Christian movement. Gamaliel bases his appeal on the principle that the movement's continuation as a unified group of followers after the death of the leader would indicate that the movement is of God. We judge that Luke may only partially agree with the viewpoint of Gamaliel. Luke certainly presents his own convictions through the mouth of Gamaliel when he records that Gamaliel urges openness to the theological and christological claims of the apostles; and further, Luke accepts Gamaliel's view that the claims of the leader (in this case, Jesus) are validated through the miraculous unity of his followers

---

in the Book of Ruth, LCBI (Louisville: Westminster John Knox, 1990); Lyle M. Eslinger, "Viewpoints and Point of View in 1 Samuel 8–12," *JSOT* 26 (1983): 61–76; Richard D. Nelson, "The Anatomy of the Book of Kings," *JSOT* 40 (1988): 39–48; David J. A. Clines, "The Arguments of Job's Three Friends," in *Art and Meaning: Rhetoric in Biblical Literature,* ed. David J. A. Clines, David M. Gunn, and Alan J. Hauser (Sheffield: JSOT Press, 1982), 199–214; Mark Allan Powell, "Characterization on the Phraseological Plane in the Gospel of Matthew," in *Treasures New and Old: Contributions to Matthean Studies,* ed. David R. Bauer and Mark Allan Powell (Atlanta: Scholars Press, 1996), 161–77; Robert L. Brawley, *Centering on God: Method and Message in Luke-Acts,* LCBI (Louisville: Westminster John Knox, 1990); James L. Resseguie, *Narrative Criticism of the New Testament,* 167–96; idem, *The Strange Gospel: Narrative Design and Point of View in John* (Leiden: Brill, 2001); Gary Yamasaki, *Watching a Biblical Narrative: Point of View in Biblical Exegesis* (New York: T&T Clark, 2007).

62. Brueggemann, *First and Second Samuel,* 97–118.

in the wake of the leader's removal. But as far as Luke is concerned, to wait any longer to make this positive assessment about the Christian movement is not necessary or proper. Up to this point in Acts 5, the story as reported in Luke-Acts has provided abundant evidence of the legitimacy of the Christian claims regarding Jesus. What is called for, then, is not to "wait and see" but to "repent . . . and turn to God" (Acts 3:19).

The book of Job offers an interesting case study in viewpoint. Many sermons preached on statements from Job's friends assume that these statements are true and valid and that all should accept them completely. But in spite of their superficial orthodoxy and their pious expressions, these statements from Job's friends may be, from the perspective of the implied author of the book of Job, at best half-truths and at worst flatly wrong. The implied author wishes the reader to critique these views rather than simply to accept them at face value.[63]

Historical Background

Historical background as a type of evidence takes two forms. First, it may pertain to the *background of the writing itself*. It thus addresses the interpretive significance of issues of critical introduction, such as the person of the writer, the place of writing, the date of writing, the occasion of writing, the recipients, and the historical connection with other biblical writings. To be sure, often the ability to identify this background is limited, and scholarly attempts to explore these issues sometimes devolve into speculation. Nevertheless, historical background is part of the existence of the text, and interpreters are therefore obliged to make use of this background information insofar as it can be discerned and does not wander off into speculation. The most helpful and reliable background information is normally what readers can infer from the text itself. But articles in Bible dictionaries frequently offer useful discussions devoted to the specific biblical books. Moreover, commentaries typically include introductions that discuss background information. The primary repositories for such information are Old Testament or New Testament introductions—for example, *An Introduction to the Old Testament* by Raymond Dillard and Tremper Longman or *New Testament Introduction*

---

63. These examples indicate that point of view tends to be especially significant in narrative material. But the relationship between the point of view of the author and that of other persons or voices may be significant even in discursive material. The rhetorical device of *diatribe*, frequently employed in the NT Epistles, involves an argument against an *imaginary interlocutor*, whose point of view the epistolary writer sets forth in order to challenge and correct it. See "Diatribe" in Aune, *Westminster Dictionary*, 127–28. Moreover, the epistolary writer may include the point of view of his opponents, as Paul presents the perspective of the Judaizers in Galatians (cf. J. Louis Martyn, *Galatians*, AB [New York: Doubleday, 1997]), of other Christian leaders with whom he disagrees (as in Gal. 1–2), or even that of his readers (as in 2 Corinthians).

by Donald Guthrie.[64] These critical introductions usually present extended discussions of all relevant background issues.[65]

Second, this category pertains also to *the historical background of persons or things that are mentioned or alluded to within the book.* Every writer assumes a certain amount of background information on the part of the readers. Students would do well to acquire as much as possible of this background information in order to become competent readers of the biblical text. When Mark mentions the Pharisees for the first time in his Gospel (2:16), for example, he does not pause to describe this sect to the reader, for he assumes that his readers know who these people are and how they function in Palestinian Jewish society. But modern readers are not acquainted with the sect of the Pharisees; therefore they need to acquaint themselves with pertinent information so as to understand what is being communicated through the text. The parables offer an excellent example of the necessity for relevant background information. As we mentioned above in chapter 12, parables are stories usually taken from everyday life that point to a spiritual truth, but they reflect everyday life in first-century Palestine; those who are far removed in time and space from that culture can woefully underinterpret or misinterpret the parables if they fail to attend to the relevant historical background.

Bible dictionaries or encyclopedias are the most natural and accessible resource for this type of background information.[66] Moreover, one may profitably consult volumes that focus particularly on historical background, such as *The Oxford History of the Biblical World* (for the entire Bible), Roland de Vaux's *Ancient Israel: Its Life and Institutions* (for the Old Testament), and Everett Ferguson's *Backgrounds of Early Christianity* (for the New Testament).[67] In addition, one specific form of commentary deals exclusively with historical

---

64. Raymond B. Dillard and Tremper Longman III, *An Introduction to the Old Testament* (Grand Rapids: Zondervan, 1994); Donald Guthrie, *New Testament Introduction*, 4th ed. (Downers Grove, IL: InterVarsity, 1990). For additional major works in this category, see Bauer, *Annotated Guide to Biblical Resources*, 69–72, 208–12.

65. Many Christians have a tendency to accept early traditions regarding the background of a biblical book as practically infallible, especially traditions from the church fathers. Early traditions may reflect reliable information that was available to those who lived much closer than do we to the production of the biblical books and should thus be taken seriously. But these traditions should not simply be accepted at face value. A serious study of the fathers reveals that often the claims they make regarding the authorship, readership, or occasion of the various biblical books involve making informed guesses on the basis of data within the books themselves, or repeating (and sometimes misunderstanding) earlier testimony. One of the values of OT and NT introductions is the inclusion of careful discussions of the reliability of traditional claims.

66. For a discussion of the most significant Bible dictionaries, see Bauer, *Annotated Guide to Biblical Resources*, 26–27. A Bible dictionary that deals specifically with matters of historical background for the NT is Craig A. Evans and Stanley E. Porter, eds., *Dictionary of New Testament Background* (Downers Grove, IL: InterVarsity, 2000).

67. Michael D. Coogan, ed., *The Oxford History of the Biblical World* (New York: Oxford University Press, 1998); Roland de Vaux, *Ancient Israel: Its Life and Institutions*, 2 vols. (New

background. Notable among these works are *Social World of Ancient Israel, 1250–587 B.C.E.* by Victor Matthews and Don Benjamin and *The IVP Bible Background Commentary: New Testament* by Craig Keener.[68] Bible atlases[69] and the work of biblical archaeology are also indispensable for historical background.[70] A promising area of historical background that pertains especially to New Testament interpretation includes studies of discussion regarding rhetoric (i.e., devices of persuasive communication) by ancient Greco-Roman writers.[71]

Interpreters who make use of historical background must be careful to ascertain as accurately as possible the level and type of background information the implied author assumes his readers have and will bring to bear on the interpretation of the passage. One should make use of this background information and *only* this background information when interpreting the passage. In other words, interpreters should consider how the text itself, read in its literary and historical contexts, indicates the kind of historical background that is appropriate for the interpretation of the passage.

Carefulness at this point will help the interpreter avoid two errors. The first error is *underinterpretation*, which occurs when the interpreter fails to make use of all appropriate background information. The second error is *overinterpretation*, which results when the interpreter brings in background information that goes beyond what the implied author assumed his readers would know and would utilize in their construal of the text. Interpreters can collect all sorts of background information on the Pharisees and uncritically introduce all of that information into their interpretation of a Markan passage

York: McGraw-Hill, 1965); Everett Ferguson, *Backgrounds of Early Christianity*, 2nd ed. (Grand Rapids: Eerdmans, 1993).

68. Victor H. Matthews and Don C. Benjamin, *Social World of Ancient Israel, 1250–587 B.C.E.* (Peabody, MA: Hendrickson, 1993); Craig S. Keener, *The IVP Bible Background Commentary: New Testament* (Downers Grove, IL: InterVarsity, 1994); see also John H. Walton, Victor H. Matthews, and Mark Chavalas, *The IVP Bible Background Commentary: Old Testament* (Downers Grove, IL: InterVarsity, 2000). For discussions and a relatively complete list of the major works on the historical background of allusions within the text, see Bauer, *Annotated Guide to Biblical Resources*, 48–51, 185–90.

69. Note especially the following two recent, thorough, and highly reliable atlases: Anson F. Rainey and R. Steven Notley, eds., *The Sacred Bridge: Carta's Atlas of the Biblical World* (Jerusalem: Carta, 2006); Siegfried Mittmann and Götz Schmitt, eds., *Tübinger Bibelatlas* (Stuttgart: Deutsche Bibelgesellschaft, 2001). Additional significant Bible atlases are listed and described in Bauer, *Annotated Guide to Biblical Resources*, 18–20.

70. For works on biblical archaeology (including journals in the area of archaeology), see Bauer, *Annotated Guide to Biblical Resources*, 20–24.

71. For study of Graeco-Roman rhetoric, see Kennedy, *New Testament Interpretation through Rhetorical Criticism*; Stanley E. Porter, *Handbook of Classical Rhetoric in the Hellenistic Period (330 B.C.–A.D. 400)* (Leiden: Brill, 1977); Ben Witherington III, *New Testament Rhetoric: An Introductory Guide to the Art of Persuasion in and of the New Testament* (Eugene, OR: Cascade, 2009); Duane Frederick Watson, *The Rhetoric of the New Testament: A Bibliographic Survey*, Tools for Biblical Study 8 (Blandford Forum, UK: Deo, 2006).

that mentions the Pharisees. In such a case, they can conceivably introduce certain information that Mark himself did not have, or that he did not assume his readers would have, or at least that he did not assume his readers would bring to bear in the interpretation of that passage in his Gospel.[72] Such a practice would lead readers to impose ideas onto the text that go beyond what the implied author wishes to communicate. We believe that readers need to target the level of background knowledge that the passage assumes and to identify and use that background knowledge and only that background knowledge in the construal of the text.[73]

A specific form of historical background involves sociological or cultural/anthropological considerations. The distinction between sociological and cultural/anthropological study is somewhat ambiguous, but essentially sociological study focuses upon specific social relationships and institutions among a people, while cultural/anthropological study examines the broad structures and dynamics of an entire society. David deSilva helpfully defines *culture* as "those values, ways of relating and ways of looking at the world that its members share and that provide the framework for all communication."[74] Although to some extent these considerations have been employed in the study of the Bible for over a century,[75] they have become a major focus of attention, especially since 1970.

72. The potential problem we address here is that of uncritically introducing into the interpretation of a passage some background material that the text does not invite us to consider. However, all historical information pertaining to the biblical world is at least indirectly helpful for understanding the text. One should not take the cautions here to be a warrant to engage in a restrictive, selective, or superficial study of the history of the biblical world.

73. This concern to gauge the use of historical background on the basis of the examination of the passage itself understood in its context exemplifies the importance of the principle of sequence, and particularly the importance of working seriously with context before moving on to focus upon historical background. One might object that sometimes the interpreter cannot with certainty identify the level of background knowledge assumed on the part of the implied author. This claim is quite true and underscores the point we made previously: according to an inductive framework, required by the nature of the Bible, the interpreter must operate on the principle of probability rather than absolute certainty. The operative question, then, is this: On the basis of the evidence from the text itself in its context and from historical considerations, what is most likely the background information that the implied author assumes the reader of this text to have and to employ in the construal of this passage?

74. David A. deSilva, *Honor, Patronage, Kinship and Purity: Unlocking New Testament Culture* (Downers Grove, IL: InterVarsity, 2000).

75. Sociological study of the Bible is often traced to the influence of Max Weber, and particularly a series of articles by Weber that were published posthumously as a collection in *Ancient Judaism*, trans. Hans H. Gerth and Don Martindale (Glencoe, IL: Free Press, 1952), originally published as *Antike Judentum* (1920). Early forays into the social history of the Bible include, from the side of the OT, W. Robertson Smith, *Lectures on the Religion of the Semites* (London: Black, 1889); and from the side of the NT, Adolf Deissmann, *Light from the Ancient East*, trans. Lionel R. M. Strachan (New York: Doran, 1927), originally published as *Licht vom Osten* (1908); Shirley Jackson Case, *The Social Origins of Christianity* (Chicago: University

Sociological or cultural/anthropological exegesis has essentially two levels: (1) social/cultural description, which examines the sociological or cultural realities and dynamics suggested by, or reflected in, biblical passages; and (2) social/cultural analysis, which employs sociological or cultural/anthropological theories or models to explain the meaning and significance of sociological or cultural realities and dynamics reflected in the biblical passages.[76]

The difficulty with the first level, that of social/cultural description, involves limits of evidence. Sometimes the presence of sociological or cultural data—even with the aid of comparison with other ancient Near Eastern cultures in the case of the Old Testament, or with the first-century Greco-Roman world in the case of the New Testament—is too sparse to yield very satisfying or helpful insights into the meaning of the text. Some scholars have tried to address this difficulty by moving to the second level and employing broad sociological or anthropological theories that are intended to illumine the significance of the sociological and cultural realities expressed in the Bible. But this process introduces the potential of creating a grid that functions as a kind of Procrustean bed into which the data of the biblical text may be forced.[77]

---

of Chicago Press, 1923). For a history of the development of sociological exegesis in biblical studies, see Cyril S. Rodd, "Sociology and Social Anthropology," in *A Dictionary of Biblical Interpretation*, ed. R. J. Coggins and J. L. Houldon (London: SCM, 1990), 635–39; for the OT, see Charles E. Carter, "Opening Windows onto Biblical Worlds: Applying the Social Sciences to Hebrew Scripture," in *The Face of Old Testament Studies: A Survey of Contemporary Approaches*, ed. David W. Baker and Bill T. Arnold (Grand Rapids: Baker Academic, 1999), 421–51; A. D. H. Mayes, *The Old Testament in Sociological Perspective* (London: Pickering, 1989); Robert R. Wilson, *Sociological Approaches to the Old Testament*, GBS (Philadelphia: Fortress, 1984), 10–29; and for the NT, see Howard Clark Kee, *Knowing the Truth: A Sociological Approach to New Testament Interpretation* (Minneapolis: Fortress, 1989).

76. Note, e.g., the attempt by Norman Gottwald to interpret Israel's history by applying anthropological and sociological models (informed by Marxist ideology). See esp. Norman K. Gottwald, "Domain Assumptions and Societal Models in the Study of Pre-Monarchic Israel," in *Community, Identity, and Ideology: Social Science Approaches to the Hebrew Bible*, ed. Charles E. Carter and Carol L. Meyers, Sources for Biblical and Theological Study 6 (Winona Lake, IN: Eisenbrauns, 1996), 170–81; idem, *The Tribes of Israel: A Sociology of the Religion of Liberated Israel* (Maryknoll, NY: Orbis Books, 1979). See also Bruce Malina, *The New Testament World: Insights from Cultural Anthropology*, 3rd ed. (Louisville: Westminster John Knox, 2001); especially Malina's adoption of Mary Douglas's anthropological model in his *Christian Origins and Cultural Anthropology: Practical Models for Biblical Interpretation* (Atlanta: John Knox, 1986); cf. Louise Joy Lawrence, *An Ethnography of the Gospel of Matthew: A Critical Assessment of the Use of the Honour and Shame Model in New Testament Studies*, Wissenschaftliche Untersuchungen zum Neuen Testament, 2nd ser., 165 (Tübingen: Mohr Siebeck, 2003). Note also the very influential work of George H. Mendenhall, *Law and Covenant in Israel and in the Ancient Near East* (Pittsburgh: The Biblical Colloquium, 1955).

77. One should note that the interpretation of the text according to broad grids or models may have a heuristic effect at times by yielding some significant insights into the meaning of passages, even if the grid is in general rejected as an alien imposition onto the data of the text.

These considerations indicate limitations and potential dangers within sociological or cultural/anthropological exegesis, and they warrant an appropriately high level of care and caution in employing these exegetical methods.[78] But the presence of these limits and dangers in no way undercuts the essential legitimacy and value of this study. The Bible does claim to bear witness to the transcendent God; therefore one cannot assume that the realities of the Bible are reducible to social structures and cultural expectations. Yet the Bible, in both the Old and New Testaments, also presents an incarnational theology in which transcendent realities are embedded within the cultural and sociological matrix of human life. Professor M. Robert Mulholland describes this principle well, and what he says regarding the New Testament applies equally to the Old Testament:

> The revelation of God takes place within the particularities of historical human existence. In Jesus, God became enfleshed in a Jewish man whose life was set within the social, political, economic, religious, and cultural contexts of the Judaisms of first-century Palestine. . . . For God, in Jesus, to communicate with those in whose midst the incarnation took place, the communication necessitated using the varied matrices of the sociological world in which Jesus lived.[79]

Interpreters of the Bible might, therefore, explore how the universe of social and symbolic relationships within the cultures of the Bible and the cultural and sociological assumptions that are reflected in the text illumine the meaning of biblical passages. Readers cannot accurately and fully understand passages that speak of clean and unclean or of honor and shame without engaging in this kind of exploration. Paul's instructions regarding life within Christian communities are not fully understandable without attending to the social dynamics that were operative within those communities. And grasping the full meaning of prophecy in Israel is impossible without attending to the social and cultural expectations that belonged to this and similar phenomena not only in Israel but also among neighboring peoples in the ancient Near East. The meaning of Old Testament dietary regulations may not be known without

---

78. Helpful presentations on the methodological issues surrounding sociological and cultural interpretation can be found in Naomi Steinberg, "Social-Scientific Criticism," in *Dictionary of Biblical Interpretation*, ed. John H. Hayes (Nashville: Abingdon, 1999), 2:478–81; John F. Priest, "Sociology and Hebrew Bible Studies," in Hayes, *Dictionary of Biblical Interpretation*, 2:483–87; Thomas Schmeller, "Sociology and New Testament Studies," in Hayes, *Dictionary of Biblical Interpretation*, 2:487–92; Thomas W. Overholt, *Cultural Anthropology and the Old Testament*, GBS (Minneapolis: Fortress, 1996); John H. Elliott, *What Is Social-Scientific Criticism?* GBS (Minneapolis: Fortress, 1993); Bengt Holmberg, *Sociology and the New Testament: An Appraisal* (Minneapolis: Fortress, 1990); Richard L. Rohrbaugh, ed., *The Social Sciences and New Testament Interpretation* (Peabody, MA: Hendrickson, 1996); David G. Horrell, *Social-Scientific Approaches to New Testament Interpretation* (Edinburgh: T&T Clark, 1999).

79. M. Robert Mulholland, "Sociological Criticism," in Black and Dockery, *Interpreting the New Testament*, 170.

an appreciation of the broad significance of food within ancient Near Eastern culture in general and within ancient Israelite society in particular. And Jesus's statements regarding family relationships or Proverbs' instructions to fathers and children may not be understood in depth without an appreciation for the social dynamics of the household.

Most readers of the Bible are not expert in sociological/cultural background or exegesis; therefore they will be dependent upon scholarly discussions. The more recent Bible dictionaries contain helpful information on sociological and cultural background. Moreover, increasingly large numbers of volumes deal specifically with these sociological and cultural dynamics. Indeed, whole commentaries have been written from the sociological or cultural/anthropological perspective.[80]

History of Terms

History of terms as a category of evidence pertains to what is typically labeled *etymology*, which includes three specific aspects.[81] The first aspect of etymology is the history of the formation of the word, its *morphology*. At one time scholars generally assumed that the way in which a word was originally formed determined its essential meaning. For example, because the Greek word for *church*, *ekklēsia*, is formed by a combination of the prefix *ek*, meaning "out of," with the root *kaleō*, meaning "to call," many thought that the word always carried the meaning "called-out ones."

The second aspect of etymology is the relation of the word to *similar words in cognate languages*, ones that have a common origin and are thus related. Hebrew is a Semitic language; it has a family relationship with and is cognate to all other Semitic languages, such as Akkadian or Ugaritic. Greek is an Indo-European language and is thus cognate to languages within its

---

80. Here one notes commentaries such as deSilva, *Perseverance in Gratitude*; Bruce J. Malina and Richard L. Rohrbaugh, *Social-Science Commentary on the Synoptic Gospels* (Minneapolis: Fortress, 2003); Bruce J. Malina and John J. Pilch, *Social-Science Commentary on the Letters of Paul* (Minneapolis: Fortress, 2006); John van Seters, *The Pentateuch: A Social-Science Commentary* (London: T&T Clark, 2004); Thomas C. Romer, *The Deuteronomistic History: A Social-Science Commentary* (New York: Continuum, 2000); Lowell K. Handy, *Jonah's World: Social Science and the Reading of Prophetic Story* (Oakville, CT: Equinox, 2007). Some commentaries that are not expressly identified as social-scientific studies nevertheless emphasize cultural or sociological aspects, such as Jerome H. Neyrey, *2 Peter, Jude*, AB (New York: Doubleday, 1993); John H. Elliott, *1 Peter*, AB (New York: Doubleday, 2000).

81. Here we are adopting the generally accepted understanding that etymology is a broad category including within it the history of the morphological development of the word, the relationship to parallel words in cognate languages, and the history of the word's use. One finds this typical understanding, e.g., in Richard N. Soulen and R. Kendall Soulen, *Handbook of Biblical Criticism*, 3rd ed. (Louisville: Westminster John Knox, 2001). For a slightly different categorization, see Moisés Silva, *Biblical Words and Their Meaning: An Introduction to Lexical Semantics* (Grand Rapids: Zondervan, 1983), 38–44.

family group, such as Latin and Sanskrit. Especially for Hebrew, its words can be illumined by closely related words in cognate languages. The massive Anchor Bible commentary on the Psalms by Mitchell Dahood offers repeated examples of the use of parallel words in languages cognate to Hebrew, especially Ugaritic, to inform our understanding of the meaning of a Hebrew word or phrase.[82]

The third aspect of etymology is the *history of the use of the word*. Students can trace the development of the word's meaning throughout the history of the language, with a view toward ascertaining how its use in earlier times, or even in later times, may illumine its meaning in a biblical passage. Students may choose to trace the development of the meaning of a Hebrew word throughout its use in the long history of the Hebrew Bible, with a view toward situating its employment in a given Old Testament passage within that history; or students may wish to study the development of a Greek word throughout the history of the Greek language.[83] This examination will cause them to understand more clearly, on the basis of both earlier and later history of the word's use, the meaning of that word in the passage under consideration.

A specific form of this third aspect of etymology involves the *semantic field* of the word under investigation. The notion of semantic field emerges from the consideration that a single concept might be expressed through several individual words. Thus every concept has a semantic field in which individual words find residence. Therefore students will find it helpful to explore the relationship of a word to other words that belong to the same semantic field, in order to probe points of overlap or commonality as well as points of distinctiveness.[84] In previous generations this kind of examination was presented in books that dealt with biblical "synonyms."[85] But the more recent studies of semantic fields make use of critical insights from the emerging discipline of linguistics and so avoid some of the semantic errors that characterized earlier studies. Students can find insights from the linguistic study of semantic fields

82. Mitchell Dahood, *Psalms*, 3 vols., AB (Garden City, NY: Doubleday, 1965–70).

83. This aspect of etymology is closely related to "Word Usage," as discussed earlier in this chapter. The distinction, insofar as one exists, is that the category of word usage typically involves the student's direct examination and analysis of passages, both biblical and extrabiblical, in which the word occurs; and etymology involves the student's making use of secondary sources that discuss the history of the term's use.

84. This critical combination of connection and distinction pertains to the logical notion of *per genus et differentiam* (through genus and a difference). See S. Morris Engel, *With Good Reason: An Introduction to Informal Fallacies*, 2nd ed. (New York: St. Martin's Press, 1982), 44: "A definition *per genus et differentiam* is one whose defining expression refers the item to its generic class and then distinguishes it from all other kinds of items in that class."

85. The best examples are Robert B. Girdlestone, *Synonyms of the Old Testament: Their Bearing on Christian Doctrine* (1897; repr., Grand Rapids: Eerdmans, 1976); Richard C. Trench, *Synonyms of the New Testament: Studies in the Greek New Testament* (1880; repr., Grand Rapids: Eerdmans, 1953).

in most recent original-language lexicons and theological wordbooks, but the most complete presentation is the *Greek-English Lexicon of the New Testament Based on Semantic Domains*, by Louw and Nida.[86]

Clearly all three aspects of etymology can at times illumine the meaning of a word within a biblical passage, but etymology cannot in itself *determine* the meaning of a word. Words convey meaning on the basis of the linguistic and literary contexts in which they are employed and not on the basis of a once-for-all meaning established long ago. *Linguistic context* refers to the use and understanding of a word in a specific geographical area and at a specific time. One cannot assume, for example, that people in the days of Homer (ninth century BC) used and understood a Greek word in the same way as those who wrote the New Testament. Languages are dynamic; therefore the meanings of terms tend to shift over time.[87] As we mentioned earlier in this chapter (see "Literary Context"), *literary context* refers to the verses that immediately precede and follow the passage in the text (immediate context), and indeed refers also to the entire biblical book in which the passage is found (broader-book context). In general, literary context is the principal indicator of the meaning of terms. It is therefore problematic to base understanding of a word in an Old Testament passage primarily upon the meaning of a possible Ugaritic cognate, or upon inferences from the way in which the word was originally formed morphologically, or upon the meaning of the term as it was used centuries before the passage was written. To depend upon etymology for the ultimate determination of a term's meaning is to commit a serious exegetical mistake, what James Barr calls "the root fallacy."[88]

Another mistake is simply to neglect etymology altogether. It can function as a heuristic device that may illumine or clarify the meaning of terms as used in their linguistic and literary contexts. It can thus be of service if it is subservient to the primary determination of context.[89] Although the etymology—and, more precisely, the morphology—of *ekklēsia* (called-out ones) had been largely forgotten by the first century and apparently played no significant role in the

---

86. Johannes P. Louw and Eugene A. Nida, eds., *Greek-English Lexicon of the New Testament Based on Semantic Domains*, 2nd ed., 2 vols. (New York: United Bible Societies, 1989); cf. Johannes P. Louw, *Semantics of New Testament Greek* (Philadelphia: Fortress, 1982). Sponsored by the United Bible Societies, the Semantic Dictionary of Biblical Hebrew project (edited by Reinier de Blois with the assistance of Enio R. Mueller) is producing the "Hebrew-English Lexicon of the Old Testament Based on Semantic Domains." This work is still in process, but the material is appearing incrementally and is accessible at http://www.sdbh.org.

87. This phenomenon is illustrated many times over in the English language. Readers of the KJV are often confused when they read "conversation," for the word was used in seventeenth-century Britain to refer to what we today would call "lifestyle" and had nothing to do at that time specifically with dialogue between persons.

88. Barr, *Semantics of Biblical Language*, 100–116.

89. Silva, *Biblical Words and Their Meaning*, 47–51.

meaning of the term as employed in the New Testament,[90] the etymology of the word translated "gospel," *euangelion* (from *eu*, "good" + *angelion*, "news/tidings") does accord with, and thus to some extent illumines, the meaning of the word in its New Testament contexts.

The primary resource for examining etymology is a theological dictionary of biblical terms, which discusses in detail the origins, cognates, and history of the use of the word. The most complete and authoritative are the *Theological Dictionary of the Old Testament* and its corollary, the *Theological Dictionary of the New Testament*.[91] However, a number of other fine works belong to this category.[92]

Obviously, in dealing with the etymology of biblical words, one is working with the original Greek or Hebrew words.[93] Using the etymology of a word that appears in an English translation as the basis for making any claims regarding the meaning of a term employed by the biblical writer would be an egregious form of eisegesis.

History of the Text

Before the invention of the printing press in the fifteenth century, the transmission of the text of the Bible was accomplished by scribal copying; consequently, such copying made the biblical text vulnerable to errors that inevitably crept into the manuscript tradition.

These various kinds of errors fall broadly into two types: unintentional and deliberate. Unintentional errors involve those of eye or ear. In terms of errors of the eye, a scribe may, for example, accidentally repeat a word or a line (dittography) or omit a word or phrase (haplography). Moreover, scribal copying often involved the text being read aloud by one person, likely a monk, and recorded by a number of other persons in the room. This procedure introduced the possibility of errors of the ear. The reader may have mispronounced or misread a word, or a scribe might have incorrectly perceived what was read aloud.

Although an apparent contradiction in terms, some errors are deliberate. Scribes did not intentionally introduce what they knew to be errors into the

90. This is not to say that the notion of being "called out" plays no role in NT ecclesiology. But when certain NT writers on occasion emphasize the "called-out" status of the church, they do so through contextual indicators and not on the basis of the original morphological development of the word *ekklēsia*. The text gives no indication that NT writers typically chose to speak of the church by the use of *ekklēsia* because of its etymology; its choice was chiefly because the LXX uses *ekklēsia* for *qāhāl* ("congregation, meeting"), from *qāhal* ("to call together, assemble").

91. *TDOT*; *TDNT*.

92. See Bauer, *Annotated Guide to Biblical Resources*, 58–59, 198–200. In addition, standard Hebrew or Greek lexicons will often at least mention etymology.

93. Or Aramaic, in the few OT passages where Aramaic is employed.

text; rather, some errors arose from scribes' attempts to "correct" the texts they were copying. For example, a scribe might think, "Jesus would not have made a certain statement. He must have said this instead." Thus the scribe would change a word or perhaps the inflection of a word, or a scribe might introduce a brief explanation (a gloss) to ensure that readers did not misunderstand the sense of the text. Such glosses often eventually found their way into biblical texts themselves. Or a scribe might try to bring the wording of a passage in Chronicles into line with its parallel in 1 Kings, or to bring the wording of a passage in Mark into line with its parallel in Matthew.

Consequently, a major discipline called "textual criticism"[94] has developed within biblical scholarship; its principal purpose is to identify scribal errors with a view toward establishing the original wording of the text.[95] Scholars

94. Textual criticism is sometimes labeled "lower criticism" in order to differentiate it from a "higher criticism," which deals with the history of the tradition, including reconstruction of earlier sources. See "History of the Tradition" below.

95. The "original wording of the text" refers to the text as it came from the principal writer, such as the Second Evangelist in the case of the Gospel of Mark. Although the situation is generally straightforward with the NT, the case is complicated in the OT: the text of the OT was quite fluid in the sense that a number of competing textual traditions existed at least until the first century AD (as indicated, e.g., in the various recensions of the Septuagint, the Hebrew text as represented in the Dead Sea Scrolls, and the proto-Masoretic tradition). At the end of the first century AD, and associated with official canonization of the Hebrew Scriptures in the Jewish community, a significant textual stabilization occurred, coalescing around the tradition that found eventual expression in the Masoretic Text. Scholars differ, therefore, regarding the goal of OT textual criticism. Some argue that the goal is to establish the text as it came from the writers themselves. But the fluidity of the early history of the text along with the frequent difficulty of differentiating between the literary development of certain OT books (in which a number of hands over a long period of time were involved in the writing of the book) and the process of scribal transmission complicate one's ability to discern exactly what one means by the form of the text as it came from the principal writer. Thus other scholars abandon the hope of establishing an original text and instead contend that the goal of OT textual criticism is simply to catalog and assess the earliest textual readings and traditions to which we have access. But this goal may be too modest, for it fails to establish a text having the kind of reliability and coherence that is necessary to serve as the theological basis for the community of faith. Consequently, scholars such as Childs, *Introduction to the Old Testament as Scripture*, 84–106, argue on historical, pragmatic, and theological grounds that the goal of OT textual criticism should be to establish the text as it was at the time it stabilized as the canonical text, around the end of the first century AD; the Masoretic Text would be the "vehicle" for this text, and the earlier textual traditions would be indispensable for our understanding and assessment of this stabilized canonical text. For a description of these three perspectives and a history of OT textual criticism, see Emanuel Tov, *Textual Criticism of the Hebrew Bible*, 2nd ed. (Minneapolis: Fortress, 2001), 14–20, 155–97, 287–91; Al Wolters, "The Text of the Old Testament," in Baker and Arnold, *Face of Old Testament Studies*, 19–37. The principles and procedures of textual criticism will generally be the same, whichever stage of the text one identifies as the target for OT textual criticism. We are inclined to agree with the third position, finding Childs's arguments to be generally compelling. But students should become acquainted with the arguments pertaining to the goal of OT textual criticism and decide on the basis of evidence which stage of the tradition ought to be targeted.

have isolated a number of signs, or indications, of scribal errors and have correspondingly developed principles that enable them to locate, from among the readings of all the ancient texts in the manuscript tradition, what is most likely the original wording of a passage.[96] Students will presumably wish to interpret passages as they were originally written and so attend to identifying the right, or at least the best, reading of the text. For example, in interpreting the Gospel of Mark, they may recognize that 16:9–20, the longer ending of Mark, is almost certainly a later scribal addition intended to round out Mark's Gospel, which a scribe believed ended all too abruptly at 16:8. Or in interpreting Luke 22:39–46, readers might note that the text most probably lacked the statement "and his sweat became like great drops of blood falling down upon the ground."

The text of some passages is so corrupt that recovering the original wording is impossible, as in 1 Samuel 13:1.[97] Yet for the vast majority of textual variants, we can arrive at a high degree of probability, often approaching virtual certainty, regarding the original wording. In any case, the inability to operate with absolute certainty regarding the wording of every single biblical statement is no reason to doubt the reliability of the biblical text or its functional usefulness in serving as the basis for the Christian faith or the Christian church, as some have recently suggested.[98] As often noted, no major doctrine of the Christian faith is affected by significant textual variants.

Although the primary purpose of textual criticism is to establish the original wording of the text, another function belongs to this study of the history of the text: Deliberate errors—meaning attempts to correct the text—can serve

96. Text critics employ both *internal* and *external* evidence to determine the authenticity of a textual variant. Internal evidence involves features in the variant reading that suggest either scribal error or originality. External evidence has to do with the age and reliability of the manuscripts in which the variant appears. The specific method for assessing the variant readings was clarified and given classic expression in Brooke Foss Westcott and Fenton John Anthony Hort, introduction to *The New Testament in the Original Greek*, vol. 1, *The Text Revised . . .* , followed by vol. 2, *Introduction and Appendix* (New York: Harper & Brothers, 1881–82). For brief discussions of the method of textual criticism, see Paul D. Wegner, *A Student's Guide to Textual Criticism of the Bible* (Downers Grove, IL: InterVarsity, 2006); J. Harold Greenlee, *Introduction to New Testament Textual Criticism*, rev. ed. (Peabody, MA: Hendrickson, 1995); P. Kyle McCarter, *Textual Criticism: Recovering the Text of the Hebrew Bible*, GBS (Philadelphia: Fortress, 1986). For fuller treatments, see Bruce M. Metzger and Bart D. Ehrman, *The Text of the New Testament: Its Transmission, Corruption, and Restoration*, 4th ed. (Oxford: Oxford University Press, 2005); Kurt Aland and Barbara Aland, *The Text of the New Testament: An Introduction to the Critical Editions and to the Theory and Practice of Modern Textual Criticism*, trans. Erroll F. Rhodes, 2nd ed. (Grand Rapids: Eerdmans, 1989); Ernst Würthwein, *The Text of the Old Testament: An Introduction to the Biblia Hebraica*, trans. Erroll F. Rhodes, rev. ed. (Grand Rapids: Eerdmans, 1995).

97. *Corrupt* is a technical term that designates passages in which the textual variants in the manuscript tradition make discerning the original wording practically impossible.

98. Bart D. Ehrman, *Misquoting Jesus: The Story behind Who Changed the Bible and Why* (San Francisco: HarperSanFrancisco, 2005).

as a heuristic device to bring to our attention interpretive or theological issues that believers, and more specifically scribes, at a certain time in the past found in the passage and that they tried to address or clarify by their textual emendations.[99] The limits of our own time and circumstances may blind us to these interpretive and theological issues that are present in the passage and that were serious matters to these Christians who lived centuries earlier. Their attempts to clarify, through textual alteration, can help students identify these issues and can reveal at least certain ways of understanding and resolving the issues. For example, almost certainly the phrase "without cause" was added by a scribe to Jesus's statement in Matthew 5:22: "if you are angry with a brother or sister [without cause], you will be liable to judgment" (NRSV and margin). When the scribe read the statement, "if you are angry with a brother or sister, you will be liable to judgment," it raised a question in his mind: Is Jesus's admonition an absolute command that allows no exceptions (i.e., anger is always wrong), or is it a general principle that carries the possibility of exceptions, say for anger at oppression or injustice (i.e., righteous indignation)? After all, elsewhere in Matthew's Gospel, Jesus seems to express anger (see 21:12–13; 23:13–36). This textual variant, then, alerts readers to these interpretive possibilities and suggests certain ways forward.[100]

Most students will never become expert in the practice of textual criticism. But they should acquaint themselves with the major issues and principles of textual criticism so as to be able to understand discussions of textual variants as found, for example, in commentaries. They will then be able with basic confidence to identify what is the most probable original wording of a passage; they will be able to employ the history of the text as an occasion for discovering and exploring significant interpretive and theological issues that otherwise might be missed. Students can gain a basic understanding of both Old Testament and New Testament textual criticism through some of the many books devoted to this area.[101]

99. See, e.g., Gordon D. Fee, "Textual Criticism of the New Testament," in *Studies in the Theory and Method of New Testament Textual Criticism*, ed. Eldon J. Epp and Gordon D. Fee, Studies and Documents 45 (Grand Rapids: Eerdmans, 1993), 3–16; and for a fuller and highly suggestive discussion, see Barbara Aland, "Welche Rolle spielen Textkritik und Textgeschichte für das Verständnis des Neuen Testaments? Frühe Leserperspektiven," *NTS* 52 (2006): 303–18.

100. This heuristic function of textual criticism is actually a part of the history of interpretation, or the interpretation by others, both of which are discussed later in this chapter.

101. See Bauer, *Annotated Guide to Biblical Resources*, 61–62, 202–4. For examples of textual criticism as applied to specific biblical passages, see Ellis R. Brotzman, *Old Testament Textual Criticism: An Introduction* (Grand Rapids: Baker Academic, 1994), 135–66; Michael W. Holmes, "Textual Criticism," in Black and Dockery, *Interpreting the New Testament*, 46–73. For a discussion of each of the major textual variants in the NT and the process employed to judge between the different readings in each case, see Bruce M. Metzger, ed., *A Textual Commentary on the Greek New Testament*, 2nd ed. (Stuttgart: United Bible Societies, 1994).

History of the Tradition

A more or less extended process of growth and development lies behind the final form of the text of many biblical books and passages. The text itself often bears witness to this historical development of traditions that lie behind the text.[102] Therefore this history of the tradition progressing toward its culmination in the final form is part of the broad existence of the biblical text and should be considered in the interpretation of passages where such matters are relevant. This study of the tradition's history involves making use of *critical methods*. Students should remember that inductive biblical study attends to all significant aspects of the existence of the Bible, including the prehistory of the text, as it bears upon the sense of the final form of the text. Therefore the employment of these critical methods is part of a comprehensive inductive approach.

The history of the tradition has four possible levels.

1. When passages relate historical events or speeches/teachings delivered in the past, they invite us to consider the original historical event or speech-event to which these passages bear witness. The process of reconstructing the historical event or speech in its original temporal context falls under the purview of *historical criticism*.[103] Examples include the various histories of Israel that discuss the precise nature and context of original events reported by the Old Testament[104] or various studies in the life and teachings of the historical Jesus.[105]

2. Scholars generally agree that in the period immediately following the events themselves, reports of these events and of the original speeches/teachings circulated orally, often in the service of preaching or teaching. The reconstruction of this oral stage of the tradition involves *tradition criticism*, which is commonly labeled *form criticism*[106] because the oral report of these events and

---

102. At times this witness is explicit, as when a writer names earlier sources employed (e.g., the books of Kings mention "the Book of Acts of Solomon" in 1 Kings 11:41; the "Annals of the Kings of Israel" in 1 Kings 14:19; 15:31; 16:5, 14, 20, 27; 22:39; 2 Kings 1:18; 10:34; 13:8, 12; 14:15, 28; 15:11, 15, 21, 26, 31; and "the Annals of the Kings of Judah" in 1 Kings 14:29; 15:7, 23; 22:45; 2 Kings 8:23; 12:19; 14:18; 15:6, 36; 16:19; 20:20; 21:17, 25; 23:28; 24:5). In many other passages, the text bears implicit witness to traditions that lie behind the final text, such as in the apparent dependence of the Chronicler's history upon the Deuteronomic history.

103. J. Maxwell Miller, *The Old Testament and the Historian*, GBS (Philadelphia: Fortress, 1976); Edgar Krentz, *The Historical-Critical Method*, GBS (Philadelphia: Fortress, 1975).

104. E.g., John Bright, *A History of Israel*, 4th ed. (Louisville: Westminster John Knox, 2000). For bibliography, see Bauer, *Annotated Guide to Biblical Resources*, 48–51.

105. For a survey of recent studies into the life and teachings of the historical Jesus, see Mark Allan Powell, *Jesus as a Figure in History: How Modern Historians View the Man from Galilee* (Louisville: Westminster John Knox, 1998); Ben Witherington III, *The Jesus Quest: The Third Search for the Jew of Nazareth* (Downers Grove, IL: InterVarsity, 1995). For bibliography and brief discussion of major works, see Bauer, *Annotated Guide to Biblical Resources*, 231–37.

106. Gene M. Tucker, *Form Criticism of the Old Testament*, GBS (Philadelphia: Fortress, 1971); John H. Hayes, ed., *Old Testament Form Criticism* (San Antonio: Trinity University Press, 1974); idem, *An Introduction to Old Testament Study* (Nashville: Abingdon, 1979); Klaus Koch,

speeches/teachings often assumed stereotypical forms. For example, healing stories tend to exhibit common content and arrangement. But form criticism can pertain not only to the oral phase of the retelling of historical events or speech but also to the *original formulation* of speech-acts as these were conditioned by certain formal assumptions or expectations that were part of the culture and reflected the demands of the original setting (*Sitz im Leben*) of the speech-act.[107] Thus, in the ancient Near East, wisdom sayings tended to be shaped according to various accepted and understood forms, reflecting the settings in which wisdom instruction took place.[108] The same was true for prophetic speech; therefore prophetic oracles generally fall into one or another commonly accepted prophetic speech form.[109] The psalms offer an excellent example of this phenomenon. From the days of Gunkel, scholars have recognized that the psalms can be categorized according to their various forms, such as psalms of thanksgiving or psalms of lament, which reflect largely the setting in which the psalm originally emerged.[110]

3. Over time the oral tradition tended to be reduced to writing, and so written documents emerged and served as sources for biblical passages and books. The reconstruction of these written sources belongs to *source criticism*. For example, the *documentary hypothesis* (usually dubbed JEDP, where the letters stand for

The Growth of the Biblical Tradition: The Form-Critical Method (New York: Scribner, 1969); Edgar V. McKnight, *What Is Form Criticism?* GBS (Philadelphia: Fortress, 1969); Martin Dibelius, *From Tradition to Gospel*, trans. Bertram Lee Woolf (Cambridge, UK: James Clarke, 1971), originally published as *Die Formgeschichte des Evangeliums* (1919); Vincent Taylor, *The Formation of the Gospel Tradition* (London: Macmillan, 1960). Note especially the OT commentary series written from a form-critical perspective: The Forms of the Old Testament Literature (FOTL), ed. Rolf P. Knieram, Gene M. Tucker, and Marvin A. Sweeney (Grand Rapids: Eerdmans, 1981–). Walter E. Rast, *Tradition History and the Old Testament*, GBS (Philadelphia: Fortress, 1972), makes a distinction between tradition criticism and form criticism, taking form criticism to be a subcategory of tradition criticism. Scholars often have some fluidity of nomenclature in their descriptions of these various critical methods.

107. This type of form criticism corresponds to the genre analysis discussed under "Literary Forms" earlier in this chapter.

108. See, e.g., Roland E. Murphy, *Wisdom Literature: Job, Proverbs, Ruth, Canticles, Ecclesiastes, and Esther*, FOTL 13 (Grand Rapids: Eerdmans, 1981); Claus Westermann, *Roots of Wisdom: The Oldest Proverbs of Israel and Other Peoples* (Louisville: Westminster John Knox, 1994).

109. Claus Westermann, *Basic Forms of Prophetic Speech* (Louisville: Westminster John Knox, 1991); Gene M. Tucker, "Prophetic Speech," in *Interpreting the Prophets*, ed. James Luther Mays and Paul J. Achtemeier (Philadelphia: Fortress, 1987), 27–40.

110. Hermann Gunkel, *The Psalms: A Form-Critical Introduction*, trans. Thomas M. Horner, Facet Books Biblical Series 19 (Philadelphia: Fortress, 1967), originally published as *Die Religion in Geschichte und Gegenwart* (2nd ed., 1930); idem, *Introduction to Psalms: The Genres of the Religious Lyric of Israel*, completed by Joachim Begrich, trans. James D. Nogalski, Mercer Library of Biblical Studies (Macon, GA: Mercer University Press, 1998), originally published as *Einleitung in die Psalmen* (1933); cf. Sigmund Mowinckel, *The Psalms in Israel's Worship*, trans. D. R. Ap-Thomas, 2 vols. (Nashville: Abingdon, 1963), originally published as *Offersang og sangoffer* (1951).

Jehovistic [=Yahwistic], Elohistic, Deuteronomic, and Priestly) involves the
identification of discrete earlier written sources within the Pentateuch,[111] while
the *synoptic problem*, which is the issue of the literary relationship between the
first three Gospels, leads to the attempt to locate written sources behind the Synoptic Gospels.[112] Sometimes scholars try to reconstruct earlier hymns or creeds
that possibly lie behind certain passages in the New Testament Epistles.[113]

4. The writers of our biblical books edited these written (and also oral)
sources so as to produce documents that were intended to fulfill the writers'
proclamatory (*kerygmatic*) or pastoral purposes. The reconstruction of this
editorial process or the study of the final edited documents involves *redaction
criticism*.[114] The term *redaction* has to do with editorship or editing. Redaction critics examine the changes, additions, omissions, and rearrangements
that the authors introduced to their sources. They do so in order to discern
something of the author's pastoral or proclamatory purpose, the ideological
and theological intention of the author, and the situation (*Sitz im Leben*) out
of which these books were written or into which they were addressed.[115]

One should recognize that each of these critical methods has arisen to
address a genuine aspect of the text; consequently, each of these methods
is legitimate, at least in principle. Conservative Christians, including some
evangelicals, have at times expressed resistance, if not fear, toward these
higher-critical approaches, but students have no reason to resist or fear these
approaches[116] if they keep in mind the warnings discussed below regarding

111. Julius Wellhausen, *Prolegomena to the History of Israel: With a Reprint of the Article
"Israel" from the Encyclopaedia Britannica* (Edinburgh: A. & C. Black, 1885); Ernest Nicholson,
The Pentateuch in the Twentieth Century: The Legacy of Julius Wellhausen (Oxford: Clarendon,
1998); Blenkinsopp, *Pentateuch*. For a different understanding of the source development of the
Pentateuch, see Rolf Rendtorff, *The Old Testament: An Introduction* (Philadelphia: Fortress,
1986); idem, *Das überlieferungsgeschichtliche Problem des Pentateuch*, Beihefte zur Zeitschrift
für die alttestamentliche Wissenschaft (Berlin: de Gruyter, 1992); Thomas B. Dozeman and
Konrad Schmid, eds., *A Farewell to the Yahwist? The Composition of the Pentateuch in Recent
European Interpretation* (Atlanta: Society of Biblical Literature, 2006); cf. K. A. Kitchen, *Ancient
Orient and Old Testament* (Chicago: InterVarsity, 1966).

112. See, e.g., Robert H. Stein, *The Synoptic Problem: An Introduction* (Grand Rapids:
Baker Academic, 1987).

113. E.g., Rom. 1:1–4; Phil. 2:5–11; Col 1:15–20. If such hymns or creeds were taken to be
written documents, this reconstruction falls under source criticism. If, however, the hymn or
creed involves oral transmission, its reconstruction would belong to form criticism.

114. Norman Perrin, *What Is Redaction Criticism?* GBS (Philadelphia: Fortress, 1969); Mark
Edward Biddle, "Redaction Criticism, Hebrew Bible," in Hayes, *Dictionary of Biblical Interpretation*, 2:373–76.

115. One of the major purposes of redaction criticism is to explore how the writer's editing of his sources to fulfill his pastoral purposes toward his audience illumines the historical
situation of the community to which he is writing. Insights from redaction criticism can thus
contribute to historical background.

116. Carl E. Armerding, *The Old Testament and Criticism* (Grand Rapids: Eerdmans, 1983);
John Goldingay, *Models for Interpretation of Scripture* (Grand Rapids: Eerdmans, 1995). Note

their limitations and possible abuses. In fact, conservative evangelicals are among the practitioners of each of these methods, and the conclusions of some critical scholars are in accord with the convictions of most conservative Christians. At any rate, an inductive approach does not operate on the basis of fear of possible conclusions or of the way in which certain persons may respond to these conclusions. Instead, inductive biblical study is open to all possible conclusions that represent sound inferences from relevant evidence.

In the actual practice of these critical methods, however, interpreters at times have a tendency to combine them with certain philosophical or theological presuppositions, which has resulted in skewed conclusions. This tendency stems from a deductive orientation and leads to an abuse of these methods. For example, often scholars have pursued historical criticism from the perspective of antisupernaturalism, where a commitment to the view of a closed universe in which anything that cannot be explained by the consistent pattern of empirically verifiable causation, such as miracles, is dismissed as impossible. When historical critics link their investigations to this kind of philosophical commitment, they conclude in advance that such events as the resurrection of Jesus are entirely outside the realm of possibility and must be unhistorical.

Moreover, practitioners of these methods have sometimes tended to claim more for these methods than the methods could reasonably achieve. Hence in the history of interpretation one repeatedly finds that when a particular critical method began to dominate the exegetical landscape, its advocates were inclined to believe that it provided an ultimate or at least comprehensive possibility for unlocking the meaning of the biblical text. But each of these methods eventually proved unable to deliver on this hope. As a result, throughout the nineteenth and twentieth centuries, a succession of new methods appeared, each of them enjoying its period of dominance only to be followed by a period in which the next emerging method predominated (see appendix E for fuller discussion of these critical approaches and their significance for inductive biblical study).[117]

In sum, students should try to take full advantage of the significant potential that these critical methods offer but should also be aware of the methods' limitations and possible abuse. As is the case with textual criticism, most students will

---

also, from a Roman Catholic perspective, Raymond E. Brown, *The Critical Meaning of the Bible* (New York: Paulist Press, 1981).

117. Scholars generally agree that source criticism dominated from around 1880 until 1920, that form criticism dominated from around 1920 until 1945, and that redaction criticism dominated from around 1945 until approximately 1980. Subsequently, literary and reader-response approaches, and to some extent sociological/anthropological approaches, have tended to dominate. To be sure, the values of each of these methods continue to be appreciated, and for the most part the methods have continued to be practiced after their period of predominance. Some of these methods were practiced before they emerged as dominant; thus some scholars were doing what later came to be called redaction criticism before redaction criticism emerged as a recognized method in its own right, and certainly before the period when redaction criticism was dominant.

not become expert practitioners of these methods, but they should be sufficiently aware of their purposes and functions to understand scholarly discussions as found, for example, in commentaries; then they should make informed use of their insights and conclusions for the interpretation of the text.[118]

Interpretation by Others

The interpretation of others as a type of evidence involves the examination of scholarly discussions on the interpretation of the passage or book under investigation. It is relevant to the study of any passage because interpretation has a necessary communal aspect[119] that requires the reader to participate in conversation with the history of interpretation. Students should never consider their work of interpretation complete until they have entered into dialogue with the interpretation of others. One may encounter the scholarly interpretation of passages in a variety of sources, including journal articles, books that discuss biblical themes or individual passages, or chapters within books.[120] But the most natural and common source for the interpretation of others is the biblical commentary.[121] We recommend consulting at least three or four commentaries in the interpretation of a passage.

118. For discussions of these critical methods, see Barton, *Reading the Old Testament*; Baker and Arnold, *Face of Old Testament Studies*; Douglas A. Knight and Gene M. Tucker, eds., *The Hebrew Bible and Its Modern Interpreters* (Chico, CA: Scholars Press, 1985); Eldon Jay Epp and George W. MacRae, eds., *The New Testament and Its Modern Interpreters* (Philadelphia: Fortress, 1989); Werner Georg Kümmel, *The New Testament: The History of the Investigation of Its Problems* (Nashville: Abingdon, 1972); Stephen Neill and Tom Wright, *The Interpretation of the New Testament, 1861–1986*, 2nd ed. (New York: Oxford University Press, 1988). For a presentation of these methods from an evangelical perspective, along with actual examples of the application of these methods to the text of the NT, see Richard J. Erickson, *A Beginner's Guide to New Testament Exegesis: Taking the Fear out of Critical Method* (Downers Grove, IL: InterVarsity, 2005); Marshall, *New Testament Interpretation*; Black and Dockery, *Interpreting the New Testament*.

119. See "Nature and Importance of Communal Study" in chap. 7.

120. Students of the Bible who have access to a theological library will find current and comprehensive bibliographic citations of scholarly discussions of each biblical passage in *Elenchus of Biblica*, published by the Biblical Institute Press of Rome; *Religion Index One: Periodicals*, published by the American Theological Library Association (also available by online subscription to individuals: http://www.atla.com/products/catalogs.html); *Old Testament Abstracts*, published by the Catholic Biblical Association; *New Testament Abstracts*, published by Weston Jesuit School of Theology in Cambridge, MA.; Watson E. Mills, ed., *Bibliographies for Biblical Research*, New Testament Series, 21 vols. (Lewiston, NY: Mellen Biblical Press, 1993–2002); Günter Wagner, ed., *An Exegetical Bibliography of the New Testament* (Macon, GA: Mercer University Press, 1983–). See Bauer, *Annotated Guide to Biblical Resources*, 3–8, 44–46, 179–81. Commentaries often list books and articles written on individual passages; see especially the helpful lists presented at the beginning of the discussion of each passage in the Word Biblical Commentary, published by Word (and more recently by Thomas Nelson).

121. The interpretation of others may be broadened to include the history of the reception or the history of the influence of the text, as found not only in commentaries or scholarly discus-

The selection of interpretive studies/commentaries is critical. We believe students should consult *exegetical* commentaries. Exegetical commentaries are those whose purpose is the actual interpretation of the passage, over against homiletic commentaries,[122] whose primary purpose is the presentation of preaching ideas or sermon resources and perhaps even sermon outlines. Exegetical commentaries also differ from devotional commentaries, whose primary purpose is the development of insights pertaining to spiritual formation.[123] Although homiletic and devotional commentaries carry value in their own right, they typically do not directly address the exegetical issues that are central to the interpretation process.

In addition, students should consult studies/commentaries that represent a range of theological traditions. Everyone naturally has a tendency to make use of studies/commentaries written by scholars within one's own theological tradition, and certainly one should consult such works. But the meaning of passages is larger than any one theological tradition, and those from other traditions will frequently offer perspectives and insights that students might otherwise miss because their reading is restricted by their theological preunderstandings and the limits of their own theological situation. Indeed, consulting scholars who advocate interpretations with which the students have disagreement will help the students to become acquainted with the evidence and arguments for those alternative readings and possibly change their minds if the evidence requires that.

Moreover, we believe that students should select studies/commentaries that represent different periods in the history of the church. Not only do people

---

sions but also in art, literature, liturgy, and hymnody. *Wirkungsgeschichte* is often the label given to the exploration of a passage's influence in these venues, using the history of its reception as a heuristic device to identify aspects of meaning in the text that we might otherwise miss. This German term means "history of influence" or "history of effects." See "Nature and Importance of Communal Study" in chap. 7.

122. Examples include the recently published Word Communicators Commentary and older works such as the *Pulpit Commentary*. Some homiletic commentaries do present serious exegetical insights and are, therefore, helpful for interpretation. Such is sometimes the case also with volumes containing expository sermons, such as the many expository sermons/studies of G. Campbell Morgan, and the classic expositions on the Psalms from Charles Spurgeon. See Charles H. Spurgeon, *The Treasury of David*, 3 vols. (New York: Marshall, 1869; repr., Grand Rapids: Zondervan, 1966). In fact, most of the "commentaries" from the church fathers were actually sermons. These kinds of homiletic works can clearly contribute to an exegetical understanding of the passage, and students might profitably consult them under "interpretation of others," but students should supplement them with exegetical commentaries, strictly speaking.

123. A classic example of a devotional commentary, and one that remains among the best, is Matthew Henry, *Commentary on the Whole Bible*, 6 vols. (1706; repr., New York: Revell, [1983?]). The popular Daily Study Bible (NT), by William Barclay, moves strongly in the direction of a devotional commentary. On the other hand, the Daily Study Bible (OT), which was written by a number of scholars, is essentially an exegetical commentary. In spite of its brevity, it is a helpful resource for the interpretation of others.

tend to read the Bible within the parameters of their theological traditions; they also tend to read the Bible within the parameters of their own time. The meaning of the text has dimensions that were much clearer to those who lived centuries ago than they are to people today. One of the most welcome developments over the past twenty years has been a renewed appreciation for interpretations from those who lived in the premodern periods, especially the church fathers.[124] Students will therefore find it helpful to select studies/commentaries from the fathers, from the postpatristic period (e.g., the Venerable Bede or Thomas Aquinas), from the Reformation period,[125] and also from the modern period.[126] This principle of employing studies/commentaries from a variety of periods reflects a commitment to hearing interpretive voices from other cultural contexts. It therefore suggests the importance also of consulting studies/commentaries written by persons from other cultures in current times. Such exposure to other cultural perspectives could assist students in identifying their own otherwise hidden assumptions and opening them to the possibility of more accurate interpretations of the text. As Markus Bockmuehl states, "Seeing things through other cultural eyes may offer excellent assistance in the notoriously difficult task of changing our mind."[127] For many this exercise would include African-American insights and voices from the developing world.[128]

Overall, the most helpful commentaries are those that cite all of the most relevant evidence for the meaning of the passage's central concerns and show clearly how the interpretive conclusions follow from this evidence. Some commentaries, however, focus on issues that are secondary or tertiary in the passage

124. See the multivolume series the *Ante-Nicene Fathers* and the *Nicene and Post-Nicene Fathers*, edited by Philip Schaff, A. Cleveland Coxe, and Henry Wace, reprinted by Hendrickson Publishers. These contain scriptural indexes. A more accessible (though limited) resource is the Ancient Christian Commentary on Scripture series, edited by Thomas C. Oden et al., published by InterVarsity Press. This series includes brief and selected patristic commentary on each passage of the Bible. A similar series, with volumes just now appearing, is The Church's Bible, edited by Robert Louis Wilken and published by Eerdmans.

125. Especially the commentaries of Calvin and the commentaries and other works of Luther.

126. Since the interpretive tradition develops over time and later works build on earlier ones, it is appropriate to give at least slightly more emphasis to the more recent studies.

127. Bockmuehl, *Seeing the Word*, 124.

128. See, e.g., Tokunboh Adeyemo, ed., *Africa Bible Commentary: A One-Volume Commentary Written by Seventy African Scholars* (Grand Rapids: Zondervan, 2006). Of course, some commentaries are written in such a way as to impose the ideological (e.g., feminist) or cultural (e.g., African-American) perspectives of the commentator upon the text. This is ideological interpretation, and it could hardly be called exegesis, let alone inductive biblical study. We believe that students should make use of commentaries written by persons of various cultural backgrounds whose purpose is the exposition of the text, with the recognition that the background out of which they write may at points cause them to understand certain aspects of the text better than do we, even as our particular background might cause us to see certain truths in the texts that they may miss.

and leave untouched the issues that seem to be central as indicated by the passage's structure, context, and historical setting. Certain commentators focus on earlier stages of the tradition and thus do not really comment on the text itself. And some present massive amounts of data that are not clearly relevant for the interpretation of the passage. Some commentaries are satisfied merely to cite background information and never address the actual theological meaning of these texts, which have as their primary purpose theological proclamation. Other commentaries are so laconic that they give only a brief interpretation and make no attempt to cite evidence or to discuss alternative possible interpretations. Such commentaries can offer some help, but they are of limited value as dialogue partners in interpretation. Over time, students might wish to become acquainted with the most authoritative and helpful commentaries; such acquaintance will come through consulting bibliographies, especially annotated ones, and through the trial-and-error process of using various commentaries in the ongoing work of biblical interpretation.[129]

Dealing with the interpretation of others does not involve simply accepting the meaning of the passage set forth by the scholar. The exegetical category of others' interpretation includes a process of critical interaction with the scholar/commentator. The student should probe the scholarly presentation by pursuing several key questions: What evidence does the scholar/commentator cite? Does the scholar/commentator cite all relevant evidence, or is the scholar/commentator selective in the citation of significant evidence? Does the scholar/commentator properly weigh the evidence, recognizing, for example, that evidence from context is typically more significant than evidence from word usage? Does the scholar/commentator draw sound, logical conclusions from the evidence cited? Does the scholar/commentator note alternative plausible interpretations and indicate why this interpretation has been chosen over against these other plausible possibilities, and is the rationale for this adjudication compelling?

Students will find that the interpretation of others results in one of four outcomes. Sometimes the interpretation of others will *confirm* what students have found from their own study of the text on the basis of the other determinants. This confirmation is encouraging, for it alerts students that their interpretation may not be implausible or idiosyncratic because others have seen the same kinds of meaning in the passage. But confirmation does not usually mean that the student's interpretation corresponds completely with that of commentaries. Students who have engaged in a relatively thorough study of passages, employing several of the types of evidence previously listed, will normally find that their interpretations contain insights and perspectives

---

129. See, e.g., Tremper Longman III, *Old Testament Commentary Survey*, 4th ed. (Grand Rapids: Baker Academic, 2007); D. A. Carson, *New Testament Commentary Survey*, 6th ed. (Grand Rapids: Baker Academic, 2007); Bauer, *Annotated Guide to Biblical Resources.*

that go beyond what the commentators describe. Essential confirmation means that the thrust of the student's interpretation agrees with the thrust of the commentator's interpretation. But independent study of the text that precedes the examination of scholarly discussions or commentaries will almost always provide a depth and breadth of understanding that transcends at points what one encounters in a commentary or scholarly discussion.

Then too, students will occasionally find that the interpretation of others *corrects* their initial interpretive conclusions. The commentaries may present evidence to which students had no access. Or in the commentaries students may encounter compelling new inferences from evidence with which they were already acquainted. Finally, sometimes the interpretation of others will *clarify* or *expand* students' initial interpretive conclusions.

We believe that, generally speaking, students should deal with the interpretation of others last of all. The reason for normally postponing the examination of scholarly discussions to the end of the interpretive process is twofold.[130] First, as we warned in chapter 5, consulting commentaries at the beginning of the interpretive process tends to prejudice students' work with the text so they have difficulty identifying interpretive possibilities that are not mentioned or advocated by the commentaries. Moreover, the purpose of consulting others' interpretation is not to find the answer. It is rather to engage in critical interaction with scholarly discussions in order to arrive at a fuller and more confident interpretation on the basis of that interaction. And students can participate in this process of interaction and dialogue only if they come to these discussions armed with knowledge of relevant evidence and a sense of the significance of this evidence for the meaning of the passage.

This suggestion to consult the interpretation of others at the end of the interpretation process does not mean that the examination of the text itself should be completely exhausted before one resorts to commentaries. Rather, it stresses the fact that independent study ought to be the initial step. When students have devoted a reasonable amount of time to the determinants that involve the direct study of the text, then they should investigate secondary sources. And after they have pursued a partial investigation of secondary sources, they should return to firsthand observation and interpretation, after which may follow a further examination of exegetical opinion. The student

130. The terms *generally speaking* and *normally* suggest that this principle of dealing with the interpretation of others last of all may be qualified. Indeed, it should be qualified in two ways. First, while consulting commentaries at the end of the interpretation process is ideal, in practice students may at times find themselves so befuddled about the basic sense of a biblical passage that they are unsure even how to begin to interpret the passage. In these rare instances, they may need to gain some sense as to what is broadly involved in the passage in order to begin to work through the interpretive process. Second, the inductive procedure is *spiracular* (see the introduction to this book): it requires that one often revisit earlier steps in the process. Thus the interpretation of others may force students back to examine again kinds of evidence that they have already considered.

thus becomes engaged in a recurring cycle that need never cease, especially from the standpoint of firsthand investigation. Firsthand study serves as the initial step of observation and interpretation as well as that to which the student constantly returns.

Conclusion

Several considerations should be kept in mind regarding these interpretive determinants or types of evidence. First, they are all interrelated, some more than others. For example, the *author's purpose and viewpoint* is largely dependent upon an examination of *context* and is practically a specific form of contextual evidence; and we have seen an overlap between *word usage* and the *history of the term*. In spite of this fact, an effort was made to distinguish between them because of the value of such an analysis in making one conscious of the specific factors that influence interpretation.

Second, this discussion of exegetical determinants is of necessity merely suggestive. In addition to the works indicated in texts and footnotes in the course of our presentation on each of these types of evidence, readers are urged to examine one or more of the books that give fuller treatment to the various exegetical determinants.[131] Moreover, we could identify other interpretive determinants beyond those noted here, such as the significance of figures of speech, which would include an examination of the interpretive ramifications of irony, synecdoche, and metonymy, among others.[132]

Third, these diverse interpretive determinants, or types of evidence, have varying degrees of significance, depending upon the nature and dynamics of the passage being studied. As mentioned previously, almost never will all of them be relevant for interpreting a given passage. The student should begin by probing how the interpretive demands of the passage under consideration indicate which of these types of evidence will be most useful in answering the interpretive question(s) selected; yet one important point, as mentioned earlier, is that context and the interpretation of others will always be relevant types of evidence.

Finally, the listing of these types of evidence does not imply a rigid sequence for interpretation. Seasoned interpreters are not expected to probe each type of

131. See, e.g., Osborne, *Hermeneutical Spiral*; Walter C. Kaiser Jr., *Toward an Exegetical Theology: Biblical Exegesis for Preaching and Teaching* (Grand Rapids: Baker Academic, 1981); Walter C. Kaiser Jr. and Moisés Silva, *An Introduction to Biblical Hermeneutics: The Search for Meaning*, rev. ed. (Grand Rapids: Zondervan, 2007); and William W. Klein, Craig L. Blomberg, and Robert L. Hubbard Jr., *Introduction to Biblical Interpretation*, 2nd ed. (Nashville: Nelson, 2004).

132. These issues are treated in Aune, *Westminster Dictionary*; Coggins and Houlden, *Dictionary of Biblical Interpretation*; and Milton S. Terry, *Biblical Hermeneutics*, rev. ed. (New York: Methodist Book Concern, 1911).

evidence in turn every time they want to study a passage. Rather, the purpose of laying out the sequence is to enable readers to develop interpretive instincts. True, beginning students may consciously want to apply these types of evidence one by one for a time, in order to gain a sense as to how each one functions in the overall interpretive process and how each one relates to the others. But the ultimate purpose for this initial emphasis on sequence is that working with these interpretive determinants may become second nature.

15

Drawing Inferences from the Premises

Role of Inductive Inferential Reasoning

Having identified the relevant types of evidence, one may describe each piece of evidence selected and incorporate this evidence into premises for drawing possible conclusions or inferences that bear on the answer to the interpretive question raised. This process involves the use of inferential logic in which the student probes what each piece of evidence implies regarding the answer to the question raised. Students should review the rather extensive discussion in chapter 1 on inductive inferential reasoning in order to appreciate the critical importance of this phase in the interpretive process, and to identify the primary components of inferential reasoning.

Possible Interpretive Models

Students may follow various specific procedures as they interpret passages. By no means should students feel bound to a particular way of laying out their interpretive work. Nevertheless, we will note two broad possible models: the analytical model and the synthetic model.

Analytical Model

Beginning students may wish to employ single pieces of evidence that represent distinct types of evidence as premises for interpretive inferences.[1] Students would generate simple premises dealing with each type of evidence in turn. Thereby students would develop an understanding of the character and function of each type of evidence, such as context, word usage, or scriptural testimony. This model may involve the following specific procedure:

1. When answering questions that involve the meaning of terms, begin with evidential premises having to do with preliminary definition. This jumping-off point is intended to obtain a general consideration of the basic lexical sense of key terms.
2. Move next to literary contextual evidence. Begin with evidential premises from immediate context (the verses immediately preceding and following the passage), then to the context of the segment, and finally to the broader context of the whole book.[2]
3. Move next to evidential premises from word usage, if relevant.[3]
4. Move next to evidential premises from scriptural testimony, if relevant.[4]
5. Then cite evidential premises that will require some use of secondary sources, such as Bible dictionaries (for historical background) or grammars (for inflection and syntax).
6. Last, cite evidence from the interpretation of others. Normally consult commentaries or scholarly studies for interpretation of the passage last of all. These sources actually present discussion and conclusions regarding the meaning of passages, and students can enter into critical conversation with these discussions only after they have worked through the same kinds of evidence that the commentaries or scholarly discussions consider.
7. At the end of the process of answering a specific question, summarize the main possible answers that have emerged in the inferences. If more

1. The choice of model may depend not only on the developmental stage of the student but also on the interpretive demands of the passage. The interpretation of some passages may be adequately or even most effectively pursued through the analytical model; whereas the interpretation of other passages may be significantly enhanced by the synthetic model.

2. Contextual evidence is examined early because it tends to be the most significant type of evidence. It is foundational and therefore presupposed for the use of other interpretive determinants. For example, the significance of word usage in other biblical passages is assessed by continuity or discontinuity between the employment of the word in those other passages and the context of the passage being studied.

3. After context, word usage tends to be the most significant determinant.

4. Evidence from context, word usage, and scriptural testimony involves direct, firsthand study of the text; therefore these are typically examined before types of evidence that involve use of secondary sources.

than one possibility exists, list the various interpretive possibilities and the evidence supporting each possibility.

8. Weigh the evidence supporting each possible answer to determine which has the preponderance of evidence in its favor. Two criteria are employed here. The first is the *significance* of evidence. Some evidence is more significant and weightier than other types of evidence. For example, evidence from context is normally weightier than evidence from word usage, for a given biblical writer may choose to employ a word somewhat differently from the way in which other biblical writers use it. The second criterion in deciding between alternative interpretive possibilities is the *amount* of evidence. One should ask which possible answer has the most evidence in its favor. Both of these criteria should be considered. But the significance of evidence will usually take precedence over the amount of evidence.

An example of how one might lay out the interpretation according to the analytical model is given below, with specific suggestions offered throughout in italic.

QUESTION: What is the meaning of . . . ?
   Begin by writing the selected question at the top of the first page.

RELEVANT TYPES OF DETERMINANTS: e.g., preliminary definition, context, word usage, scriptural testimony, inflections, historical background, interpretation of others

Evidential premises	Inferences
A. Preliminary definition (when the question involves the meaning of terms) *Use basic definition in original-language lexicon.*	→ This evidence implies that the basic meanings of the key terms involved in this question are . . . *Inferences from evidence other than preliminary definition should be possible answers to the question that appears at the top of the page.*[a]
B. Context *Begin with immediate context—the verses that immediately precede and follow the passage—then move progressively outward, to the context of the segment, then to the context of the book.*[b]	
1. First piece of contextual evidence *Cite the contextual passage, then make a brief, tentative statement about the meaning of the passage itself.*	→ This evidence implies that the answer to the question raised is *a.*[c]

Evidential premises		Inferences
2. Second piece of contextual evidence	→	This evidence implies that the answer to the question raised is *b*.
Cite the contextual passage, then make a brief, tentative statement about the meaning of the passage itself.		
3. Third piece of contextual evidence	→	This evidence implies that the answer to the question raised is *a*.
Cite the contextual passage, then make a brief, tentative statement about the meaning of the passage itself.		
4. Fourth piece of contextual evidence[d]	→	This evidence implies that the answer to the question raised is *a*. On the other hand, this evidence also implies that the answer to the question raised is *b*.
Cite the contextual passage, then make a brief, tentative statement about the meaning of the passage itself.		
		The same piece of evidence might point to two or more possible inferences.
		Summary of context: Evidence from context generally points toward *a* as the answer to the question raised, although some contextual evidence points toward *b* as the answer.

C. Word usage

New Testament word usage

1. First occurrence	→	This implies that the answer to the question is *a*.
Cite NT passage and briefly describe the way the term is used (its meaning) in that passage.		
2. Second occurrence	→	This implies that the answer to the question is *a*.
Cite NT passage and briefly describe the way the term is used (its meaning) in that passage.		
3. Third occurrence	→	This implies that the answer to the question is *a*.
Cite NT passage, and briefly describe the way the term is used (its meaning) in that passage.		

Old Testament Word Usage

1. First occurrence	→	This implies that the answer to the question is *a*.
Cite OT passage and briefly describe the way the term is used (its meaning) in that passage.		
2. Second occurrence	→	This implies that the answer to the question is *a*.
Cite OT passage and briefly describe the way the term is used (its meaning) in that passage.		

Evidential premises	Inferences
Extrabiblical Word Usage	
1. Classical Greek *Note the way the term is used (its meaning) in Classical Greek.*	→ This implies that the answer to the question is *a*.
2. Koine Greek *Note the way the term is used (its meaning) in Koine Greek.*	→ This implies that the answer to the question is *a*.
	Summary of word usage: Evidence from word usage points toward *a* as the answer to the question raised.
D. Scriptural testimony	
1. First piece of evidence from scriptural testimony *Make a brief, tentative statement about the meaning of the passage itself.*	→ This implies that the answer to the question is *b*.
2. Second piece of evidence from scriptural testimony *Make a brief, tentative statement about the meaning of the passage itself.*	→ This implies that the answer to the question is *b*.
	Summary of scriptural testimony: Evidence from scriptural testimony points toward *b* as the answer to the question raised.
E. Other determinants *Go through the same process with the other relevant types of determinants, e.g., inflections, historical background, interpretation of others.*	
	General summary of findings: Our study has shown that there are two possible answers to the question raised: *a* and *b*. *Weigh the evidence for each possibility, then decide which possible answer has the weightiest and most evidence in its favor. That will be the answer to the question selected.*

[a] Because inferences from preliminary definitions are more foundational in terms of providing a sense of the lexical meaning of terms, they tend not to generate specific answers to interpretive questions, as do inferences drawn from other types of evidential premises.

ᵇ It is critical that students discuss the meaning of biblical passages employed as evidence (whether under context, word usage, or scriptural testimony) over against simply identifying or quoting or even paraphrasing a passage. A simple quotation or paraphrase cannot function as evidence; rather, the result will normally be that either the inference is so general as to be of little assistance or the inference will not be sufficiently grounded in the evidence mentioned and will thus go beyond it. In citing a biblical passage as evidence, then, it is important that students state briefly and tentatively what they consider to be the meaning of each passage listed as evidence, giving reasons for their sense of the meaning of the passage cited as evidence. Only then can the passage cited under evidence serve as the basis for drawing inferences toward answering the question raised. This process involves what scholars refer to as the "hermeneutical circle": interpreting passages on the basis of our understanding of other passages. Such a circular process is not ideal, but it is inevitable—it cannot be avoided. This hermeneutical circle reminds us that all interpretive conclusions are more or less tentative; we must be open to the possibility of changing our minds regarding what we take to be the meaning of passages cited as evidence, and thus entertain the possibility of changing our minds regarding our answers to all of our interpretive questions.

ᶜ The letters *a* and *b* are used throughout this example to represent possible answers to the question raised.

ᵈ One should remember that sometimes a single piece of evidence can point to more than one inference. One must draw *all* legitimate inferences from each piece of evidence.

The example below demonstrates some evidential premises and inferences according to the analytical model from a portion of the interpretation of Joel 3:14: "Multitudes, multitudes, in the valley of decision! For the day of the LORD is near in the valley of decision."

QUESTION: What is the meaning of the phrase "for the day of the LORD is near"?

RELEVANT DETERMINANTS: Preliminary definition, context, word usage, scriptural testimony, historical background, history of interpretation

Evidential premises	Inferences
A. Preliminary definitions (see BDB; Holladay, *Concise Hebrew and Aramaic Lexicon of the* Old Testament)	
1. *Day* (*yôm*)—day, daylight, period of time	→ This implies that "day of the Lord" may designate a single day, or it may refer to a period of time, more or less extended.
2. *Near* (*qārôb*)—near (space or time)	→ This implies that the day of the Lord may be near temporally, i.e., soon, or be near spatially, i.e., close to the environs of the multitudes, writer, and/or readers.

Evidential premises	Inferences
B. Context	
The context indicates that the valley of decision here seems to be synonymous with the "valley of Jehoshaphat," mentioned several times in the immediate context. Yahweh will gather "all the nations" (3:2; or the "nations all around," 3:11–12) and bring them "down to the valley of Jehoshaphat" (3:2); Yahweh "will sit to judge" (*'ēšēb lišpōṭ*, 3:12)—a play on the name "Jehoshaphat," which means "Yahweh will judge"—the nations in the valley of Jehoshaphat (3:2). Yahweh thus incites the nations to come to the place of their own judgment—apparently an incitement that is ultimately determinative of their coming and yet is hidden from them. They believe they are coming on their own initiative to wage war against and conquer Jerusalem (3:9–12), but at a deeper level Yahweh is employing their own lust for war and conquest to bring them to the place of their own judgment.	→ This implies that Yahweh himself is active in his sovereign power to effect the events of the day of the Lord. It further implies that this day is the day *of the Lord* in the sense that he is active in ways and in extent that has not been the case generally in history, especially in working through the very evil impulse of the nations to bring them to the place of their own judgment. The day of the Lord thus involves the manifestation of Yahweh's sovereignty over the evil impulses and intentions of his adversaries: the day of Yahweh is a time when Yahweh uses the intentions of his adversaries to fulfill his own judgmental agenda.

Note: This is a highly selective example of evidential premises and inferences from Joel 3:14. We could have included many additional evidential premises from context and other types of evidence.

Synthetic Model

Students may wish to incorporate multiple pieces of various types of evidence into premises that serve as the basis for interpretive inferences. In the synthetic model, students employ an analytical process perhaps similar to the example just presented in order to identify the major interpretive possibilities of the passage. Students then combine pieces of various types of evidence into premises that form lines of reasoning leading to the major possible interpretive conclusions. The synthetic model might follow a pattern like the following:

PREMISE 1	Whereas B (piece of contextual evidence) and F (piece of evidence from word usage),
PREMISE 2	and whereas J (piece of evidence from scriptural testimony) and W (piece of evidence from historical background) and U (piece of evidence from syntax),
INTERPRETIVE INFERENCE	therefore all these considerations taken together lead to the conclusion that I_1 may be the answer to the question. . . .

But on the other hand,

PREMISE 1	Whereas M (piece of contextual evidence) and O (piece of evidence from scriptural testimony),
PREMISE 2	and whereas N (piece of evidence from history of the tradition) and Q (piece of evidence from history of the text),
INTERPRETIVE INFERENCE	therefore all these considerations taken together lead to the conclusion that I_2 may be the answer to the question. . . .

When the evidence for I_1 and I_2 are weighed, I_2 seems to be the most likely answer to the question.

The synthetic model acknowledges that pieces of evidence of different types may relate to each other and inform one another. Therefore they may be combined to form a strong argument for certain interpretive inferences. The interpretive example from 2 Timothy 3:16 that appears later in this chapter represents the synthetic model. That example includes explicit identification of the various types of evidence employed so that students can discern something of the analytical process behind the synthetic one.

Interpretive Integration

Whether students employ only the analytical process or pursue also the synthetic process, they will typically wish to integrate the answers to the various interpretive questions in order to determine the meaning of whole paragraphs and segments and the book-as-a-whole. After students answer the interpretive questions raised in connection with a particular unit, they have the task of integrating the various answers so as to arrive at the main message of the segment or division or book-as-a-whole. Sometimes students at least partially accomplish this task as they answer the questions themselves because some of the questions may be integrative in nature. Nevertheless, at some point integration must occur. Various possible techniques are available to students to integrate and summarize the exegesis of a paragraph, section, division, or entire book, several of which are noted below.

First, one may use the answering of survey questions to synthesize the meaning of larger units, including whole books. One of the purposes of raising interpretive questions directed at structural relationships in survey (book, division, section, or segment) is to answer those questions on the basis of the specific interpretation of particular passages throughout the unit in order to synthesize the teaching of the unit.

One can also *list the main truths* that have been found in a unit of Scripture. In so doing one may distinguish between the main, or primary, truth(s) and those that are subordinate. One must be prepared to develop these main and subordinate truths and to describe them in a synthetic and integrative manner. In other words, showing how these truths relate to each other within the grand thought scheme of the passage is helpful.

In addition, one may state the major theme of a passage by using a *descriptive title* or *proposition*. For example, the interpretation of Isaiah 5 may be summarized by the title "God's Best and Israel's Worst." Or the primary idea of Joshua may be stated in the proposition "The Conquest of Canaan Was Accomplished by Dependence upon the Indispensable and Dependable Yahweh." But one must do more than state these propositions in general terms; one must be able to spell out the specific meaning of the main terms of the major theme and the particular ways in which the major theme is amplified in the passage. For instance, in the example from Joshua, the critical point is that Joshua and Israel express their dependence upon Yahweh, manifested especially in obedience to the Mosaic law, even when such obedience seems risky and dangerous.

Preparing an *outline* is frequently helpful in integrating and summarizing a passage of Scripture. The outline may be either topical or logical, depending upon the nature of the passage. Generally speaking, a *topical outline* should not be used to summarize logical passages such as those found in the Pauline Epistles, for a topical outline cannot do justice to logical movement. The means used in summarization should be suited to the nature of the unit being considered. Again, this type of integrative project is not a substitute for thorough, detailed work. The student who employs a topical or a logical outline should be able to develop the points and subpoints from the specific answering of particular questions in the interpretation process.

The *logical outline* is different from the topical outline in that the former involves *successive* and *interdependent* steps while the latter concerns various parallel aspects of one topic. For example, if a topical outline were being formulated on the subject of New York City, some of its main divisions might be "Its Largeness," "Its Centrality," and "Its Cosmopolitanism." Now these phases are truly related to each other, but they are distinct enough so that they may be treated as separate features. In contrast, the logical outline involves, as we have already noted, successive and interdependent steps, each of which is grounded on what precedes it. Such an outline is *argumentative* in nature: it tries to prove something. It denotes logical development. It does not merely describe a topic: it supports a conclusion (see appendix F for an example of a logical outline).

Another technique for integrating one's interpretive findings might include using a *paraphrase* or *chart* as a means of integrating the main and subordinate truths of a passage. One may also use the *essay form* in this regard. Certain basic integrative questions may serve as guides, including the following: How does the structure of the passage reveal its main purpose and message? What are the major contributions of a passage to the larger structural unit of which it is a part?

General Suggestions regarding Interpretive Process

We recommend that students separate evidence from inferences. Mixing to-gether evidence and inferences makes showing the process of inferential rea-soning from evidence/premises to conclusions/inferences more difficult. Such mixing would also provide opportunity for assumptions and presuppositions to intrude surreptitiously into the process.

Each inference should follow from the evidence cited with clear and direct logic. Students will wish to avoid two dangers in drawing inferences from evidence. The first is reluctance or timidity in drawing out all relevant infer-ences from evidence cited. This situation will result in underinterpretation. Constructive reflection on the inferential possibilities and the employment of interpretive imagination will address the problem of underinterpretation. The second danger is that of drawing inferences that go beyond the evidence cited or that do not follow from the evidence presented. This will result in overinterpretation. We recommend that students engage in critical reflection on each inference they draw, probing to see if they can discover any deficiency in the logic between their evidence and the inference.

Students should keep in mind that the easiest explanation, the one that grows out of all the facts most naturally and without coercion or significant complexity, is usually the most accurate explanation/interpretation. The tricki-est interpretation is not necessarily the soundest.

And finally, students may wish to write a brief but specific concluding paragraph that puts forward the answer to the question raised. This conclud-ing paragraph clearly reflects the inferences drawn from evidence in the whole process.

16

Implementing Interpretation

Interpretive Fallacies

In order to elucidate what is involved in accurate exegesis, we will enumerate and discuss briefly some of the fallacious interpretive approaches that have surfaced in the history of interpretation. Students will note that many of these erroneous practices contain some truth or are motivated by at least a partially legitimate consideration. The fact that some of these practices involve certain elements of truth serves as a reminder that fallacious exegesis is often the result of an overemphasis on a valid but one-sided dimension of interpretation.

In fact, a vast number of possible exegetical errors exist. The following is a selective list. More extensive treatments can be found in works that focus on interpretive mistakes, such as *Exegetical Fallacies*, by D. A. Carson.[1]

Scholars tend to denote erroneous processes of interpretation in terms of "fallacies," a term that comes from logic. This language accords with the inductive approach, which emphasizes a process of inductive inferential logic from evidential premises to possible conclusions. We consequently use "fallacy" to speak of these erroneous interpretations, and we categorize these fallacies broadly according to the three dimensions of inductive inferential reasoning: fallacies of premises, fallacies of inferences, and fallacies of orientation. By *fallacies of orientation*, we mean errors that result from a deductive rather than an inductive perspective during the interpretation process. There is some overlap among the three categories. For example, some fallacies that involve

---

1. D. A. Carson, *Exegetical Fallacies*, 2nd ed. (Grand Rapids: Baker Academic, 1996).

premises pertain also to the operation of drawing inferences and so could fall under fallacies of inferences as well.

Fallacies of Premises

Some fallacies involve illegitimate citation or discussion of evidence. Because evidence functions as the basis for premises in the process of inductive inferential reasoning, we may refer to the errors of evidence as fallacies of premises.

FALLACY OF INVALID PREMISE

The most basic error in the interpretive process pertains to the citation of evidence that is factually incorrect. Even established scholars are vulnerable to such mistakes. A rather humorous story involves a scholar who spent thirty minutes reading a paper at a meeting of a major biblical society in which he probed the interpretive significance of the use of the Niphal rather than the Hiphil stem of a certain Hebrew verb in one of the psalms. In the discussion that immediately followed his presentation, a member of the group pointed out to him that the psalm actually did employ the Hiphil stem of the verb. The entire paper represented a basic mistake in the scholar's reading of the Hebrew text.

Another example comes from the pen of a New Testament scholar of an earlier generation, A. H. McNeile. In his interpretation of Matthew 5:48, "Be perfect, therefore, as your heavenly Father is perfect," he insisted that the Old Testament passage that lies behind this Matthean text, Leviticus 19:2, describes perfection in terms of negative prohibitions, while the context of Matthew 5:48 presents perfection in terms of "positive and spiritual fulfillment."[2] But the context of Leviticus 19:2 includes a number of positive commands, meaning commands for actions to be undertaken rather than behavior to be avoided, while the context of Matthew 5:48 contains several negative prohibitions. In this case, McNeile was simply wrong in his characterization of the biblical data.

FALLACY OF AMBIGUOUS PREMISE

Because words are flexible and fluid, the terms that students employ in their discussion of evidential premises must be as precise, or precisely developed, as possible. Students should avoid ambiguous or vague terms, and if students need to use such terms, they should clarify and specify the meaning of those terms. This problem occurs, for example, when students simply quote a biblical passage that they cite as evidence rather than saying something about what they take to be the specific meaning of the key terms in the passage cited. Words that are precise by virtue of their function within their literary context

2. Alan Hugh McNeile, *The Gospel according to Matthew* (London: Macmillan, 1938), 73.

become vague and may take on other meanings when they are abstracted from their context and simply repeated as a piece of evidence. A further instance of imprecise premises is found in the following line of argument:

Jesus was God (e.g., John 20:28; Heb. 1:8).

God cannot be tempted (James 1:13).

Therefore, Jesus could not be tempted and was not really tempted in Matthew 4:1–10 and Luke 4:1–13.

The problem with this syllogism lies in the ambiguity of the phrase "Jesus was God" in the first premise. One should make clear that these passages (and others) present Jesus as God *the Son*, who is consistently distinguished in the New Testament from God *the Father*, and God the Father is referenced in James 1:13. Although many things that pertain to the Father are also true of the Son, the same is not the case with everything. God the Father cannot be tempted, but such a claim does not necessarily mean that the same holds true for God the Son, at least during his earthly existence.

FALLACY OF LEXICAL REDUCTIONISM

Sometimes students limit their understanding of interpretation to the lexical definition of key terms in a passage. This limitation may involve students believing that if they simply identify the basic definition of each term in a passage, they will have adequately interpreted the passage-as-a-whole. Or it may involve students noting two or three alternative definitions of a term from a lexicon and proceeding to frame all of their subsequent interpretive work around support for one or another of these basic definitions. Such students need to recognize that statements mean more than the sum of the definitions of terms; statements communicate meaning through the dynamic relation of terms to one another in the clause or sentence (syntax) and through their function within their literary and historical/cultural contexts. The exegetical category of preliminary definition, which we previously described, is useful as a beginning point in interpretation, but one must not view it as the totality of interpretation or even as the frame into which all other evidence and inferences must fit.

ROOT FALLACY

Those who commit the root fallacy assume that the meaning of every occurrence of a word is finally determined by the original formation of the word (its *morphology*). In fact, words do not have inherent meanings that are set according to their original formation and necessarily carry those meanings throughout their use in the history of the language. Rather, the meanings of terms tend to develop over time and are always determined by their contexts.

(We discussed this fallacy briefly and gave a few examples related to etymology in "History of Terms" in chap. 14.)

James Barr, who coined the term *root fallacy*, gives an example from the prominent Old Testament scholar Norman Snaith:

> The first word of the first Psalm is Hebr. *'ašrê*, "blessed is . . . ," literally "happinesses of. . . ." This is related to words in various Semitic languages meaning "footstep," "go straight ahead, advance" and also to the Hebrew relative pronoun. Snaith concludes: "All this shows how apt is the use of the first word. The psalm tells of the true way as distinct from the false. The happy man is the man who goes straight ahead, because, as the last verse says, 'the Lord knoweth the way of the righteous,' while 'the way of the wicked shall perish.'" Thus a word is deemed to be unusually apt because other words from the same root existing in other languages, or existing in the same language but no longer having the etymological sense (e.g., the Hebrew relative pronoun), have or may be supposed to have had in the past a sense of "place" or "way," and the theme of the psalm as a whole is about ways, the right way and the wrong way. There is not the slightest evidence that these associations were in the mind of the poet, and indeed some of them were almost certainly unknown and unknowable to him and his contemporaries. The etymological associations are used without any inquiry whether they existed in the minds of those who used the poem.[3]

A New Testament example involves the word *hilaskomai*, which appears in several passages dealing with Christ's sacrificial atonement and is translated "expiate" or "propitiate." Some have noted that the verb came from the root *hileōs*, which means "gracious," and they have concluded that *hilaskomai* originally meant "to make gracious," or "to cause to be gracious." But students commit the root fallacy when, from this information regarding the root, they draw the conclusion that every occurrence of the term *hilaskomai* in the New Testament suggests that Christ's atonement caused or even forced a resistant God to become gracious toward us. The term as used in the New Testament does not necessarily carry the meaning bound up in its original formation.

As we mentioned previously, however, sometimes the root can be suggestive of the meaning of the term as used in its context. For example, the Greek term for "disciple," *mathētēs*, derives from the word *manthanō*, meaning "to learn"; this concern for learning corresponds to a significant aspect of the term *mathētēs* as employed in its New Testament contexts.[4]

3. Barr, *Semantics of Biblical Language*, 116.

4. Although by the time of the NT the term *mathētēs* had come to mean primarily a follower of a teaching or teacher rather than a learner per se, the notion of learning continued to be present in the concept according to its presentation in the NT. See Michael J. Wilkins, *Discipleship in the Ancient World and Matthew's Gospel*, 2nd ed. (Grand Rapids: Baker Academic, 1995).

FALLACY OF REVERSE ETYMOLOGY

We have seen that arguing for the meaning of a biblical term ultimately on the basis of the etymology, or original formation, of that Greek or Hebrew term is problematic. But a manifestly more fallacious choice is to interpret a term in a biblical passage on the basis of the etymology of the English word that certain translations use to render the original Greek or Hebrew term. Such would be the case, for example, if one were to interpret the word *gospel* in New Testament passages as "good tale" or "good story," according to the morphological development of the English word (from Old English—*gōd* [good] + *spell* [tale]). Another example is interpreting the biblical term *instruction* according to the etymology of that word, which derives from the Middle English and is formed from the Latin *instruere*, "to build."

FALLACY OF SEMANTIC ANACHRONISM

The fallacy of semantic anachronism involves interpreting Hebrew and especially Greek words in the Bible on the basis of contemporary English words that stem from the Greek or Hebrew term. An example one frequently encounters is that of interpreting the Greek word *dynamis* (might/power) according to the English word "dynamite," suggesting that *dynamis* carries with it the idea of potentially dangerous, explosive energy. Another example is the word translated "exile" in 1 Peter 1:17, which is *paroikia*, from which comes our English word "parish." But one would be committing the fallacy of semantic anachronism to interpret the Petrine passage in terms of the meaning of the English word "parish." While tracing the semantic development from a Hebrew or Greek word to the English may serve the heuristic function of causing one to recognize certain dimensions of the significance of the original term as employed in its biblical context, one should not allow such considerations to determine the sense of the biblical term. Language is dynamic; therefore one has every reason to expect significant differences between modern English words and their Hebrew or Greek derivations.[5]

FALLACY OF THEOLOGICAL ANACHRONISM

Closely related to semantic anachronism is the fallacy of theological anachronism, which involves assuming that a theological term in a biblical passage corresponds completely to the understanding of that term in the theological tradition of the church or the theological tradition of one's own faith community. When readers of biblical passages encounter such words as *sanctification*, *predestination*, *election*, or *atonement*, they naturally construe these words according to their own theological preunderstanding, and they often hold these preunderstandings deeply and cherish them fervently. This situation,

---

5. Because of the historical relationship between English and Greek, the English language contains many more cognates with Greek than it does with Hebrew.

therefore, requires probing self-reflection to identify exactly what one thinks these terms mean or what one wants these terms to mean, and it requires a determination to fairly consider alternative ways of construing these terms or concepts in the biblical text. We are not saying that the theological tradition of the church or of individual faith communities cannot inform and illumine the meaning of these terms in the Bible; certainly they can and should. But they can do so only insofar as one's understanding of these terms is confirmed by the biblical data as processed through proper exegetical practices.

Fallacy of Partial Evidence

Limitations of time or implicit commitment to a preunderstanding can cause the student to deal with only a part of the relevant evidence, leading to a skewed interpretation. If time is the issue, the selection of evidence may be random and arbitrary. If commitment to certain preunderstandings is the issue, this selectivity would be prejudicial. To be sure, all students deal with limitations of time, and the rich, deep nature of the biblical text means that full interpretation of almost any biblical passage requires more time than they can invest. But they should be committed to identifying the most critical evidence for interpreting a passage and then dealing with that evidence as thoroughly as time permits. The most effective antidote to prejudicial selectivity is a determination to consider alternative interpretations and actively to seek evidence for interpretations that one had not considered or to which one is resistant. Students must certainly account for opposing evidence and alternative explanations or interpretations.

Fallacy of Violation of Genre

As we mentioned in "Literary Forms" in chapter 14, literary form, or genre, involves an implicit agreement between author and readers that a given text should be read according to the expectations of its genre and over against other ways of reading and construing the passage. Thus students should identify the genre employed and interpret the passage according to the characteristics and expectations of that genre. Failure to do so involves the *violation of genre* and can lead to a gross misinterpretation.

The Bible itself contains accounts of persons who misunderstood communication because of a violation of genre. When Nathan told David the parable of the poor man and the ewe lamb, David mistook Nathan's parable for prose narrative (and more specifically, a judicial case), thereby failing to understand the prophetic communication until Nathan expressly said, "You are the man!" (2 Sam. 12:1–7). Moreover, many throughout the history of the church into the present day have been inclined to interpret passages that are prose narrative as if they were in the form of allegory. Such persons frequently recognize the form of these passages as historical story or description, but they use them as allegories to teach spiritual lessons. And although the lessons drawn from them are frequently true because they are based on a general awareness of the biblical message, they have no organic relation to the historical narratives under consideration. Such an approach may be enticing, but it is also deceptive. Often crossing the line of demarcation between prose-narrative interpretation and allegorical exposition is almost imperceptible. We often encounter this phenomenon while listening to preaching. A sermon on Israel's defeat of Jericho (Josh. 6) may probe, "What walls need to come down in our lives?" Or a sermon on Jesus at the well (John 4) may focus on "the Samaritans in our lives." In both cases the likelihood exists that the exposition behind these sermons is at least to some extent allegorical.[6]

FALLACY OF FRAGMENTATION

Fragmentary interpretation treats the Scriptures as if they are merely a collection of isolated verses, each of which is to be understood apart from its immediate and broad context. Such a practice is partly due to the rather arbitrary division of the Bible into chapters and verses. In addition, some students have a view of biblical inspiration that leads to a practically *oracular* understanding of the nature of the biblical text. According to this view, every individual statement from the Bible contains in itself absolute divine truth, and God speaks directly in each clause or sentence in isolation from the others. All of this fragmentation can lead to the neglect of the contextual setting of biblical statements.

Ministers are among the worst offenders in this connection. They frequently disregard the setting of the passage they take as a text. One of us recalls listening to a sermon in which he was surprised to hear the preacher take only half of one verse as his sermon text; he wondered why the preacher did not read at least the entire verse. But soon he realized that the preacher could not have preached the sermon he delivered if he had read the remainder of the verse. And if Christian ministers are guilty of such a practice, what can one expect of their parishioners who depend upon them for guidance in biblical interpretation?

PSYCHOLOGICAL FALLACY

Like several others in this list, the psychological fallacy was already mentioned, in our discussion of the psychological factor (chap. 14). Like these others, it bears additional mention at this point. The psychological fallacy occurs when one interprets a passage on the basis of emotional or psychological considerations when such data or indications are lacking within the passage or its context. The psychological fallacy may relate to claims made

6. See Robert A. Traina, *Methodical Bible Study: A New Approach to Hermeneutics* (New York: Ganis & Harris, 1952), 172–74, for a more detailed discussion of the allegorical approach.

regarding the psychological/emotional state of the author or about the inner state of characters described within passages.

An example is Bishop John Shelby Spong's suggestion that Paul's statements against homosexual behavior in the first chapter of Romans should be interpreted as a "homophobia" that masked Paul's own latent homosexual urges. Here the bishop commits the psychological fallacy involving the author, since (at least according to our study) there is no indication in the passage that the reader is invited to engage in a psychological analysis of Paul in order to ascertain the message of the passage. The argument of the passage does not depend upon and is not affected by Paul's alleged psychological condition.[7] This reading involves the imposition onto the text of complex modern psychological theory, fueled by contemporary social and political interests. When Oesterley and Robinson suggest that the account of Hosea's marriage to the harlot Gomer in the early chapters of his book indicates that "Hosea suffered from sex-obsession, which drove him into the thing of which he had the greatest horror,"[8] these scholars commit the psychological fallacy. And when a prominent preacher insists that David's sins of adultery with Bathsheba and the subsequent murder of Uriah (2 Sam. 11) were due to David's "midlife crisis," without citing any evidence that such is the perspective of the text, this preacher commits the psychological fallacy involving a character within the narrative.[9]

FALLACY OF ILLEGITIMATE TOTALITY TRANSFER

As we mentioned in "Word Usage" (chap. 14), the phrase "illegitimate totality transfer" was coined by James Barr and was used by him to refer to the practice of uncritically reading the connotations and associations of every occurrence of a word into the use of that term in a given biblical passage. In the discussion on word usage, we emphasized that students need to conduct a critical conversation between the term as employed in the passage being

---

7. John Shelby Spong, *Sins of Scripture: Exposing the Bible's Texts of Hate to Reveal the God of Love* (San Francisco: HarperSanFrancisco, 2005), 135–42; idem, *Living in Sin: A Bishop Rethinks Human Sexuality* (San Francisco: Harper & Row, 1988), 151. One may use such considerations in the evaluation of the passage (see chap. 17). But in our judgment, the evidence for Spong's assessment is sorely lacking.

8. W. O. E. Oesterley and Theodore H. Robinson, *An Introduction to the Books of the Old Testament* (New York: Meridian Books, 1958), 351–52.

9. We do not deny the legitimacy of exploring the psychological conditions of historical personages as a historical enterprise, but these proposals are not a primary means of interpreting a passage that lacks psychological or emotional references or any indication that the reader is to employ such considerations in the construal of the passage. Moreover, the reconstruction of the psychology or emotions of flesh-and-blood biblical authors and characters is a precarious operation because in almost all cases the only witness we have to them is the biblical text itself. If the biblical text lacks psychological or emotional references, the process of psychological reconstruction tends to be speculative.

interpreted within its literary context and every other occurrence of the word in order to assess whether, and if so, how, the other biblical occurrences might provide linguistic background that assists in interpreting the passage under consideration. The operative question is, What kind of linguistic background and understanding of this word does the implied author assume the implied reader has and will bring to bear in the construal of this word in this passage? Other occurrences may provide linguistic background filling out the context of the passage under interpretive consideration and suggesting what the implied author assumed his audience possessed and would use in the reading of his passage. But occurrences of the term elsewhere in the Bible may indicate other ways in which the word was used and understood, which are essentially different from the way the word is employed in the passage being studied. In such a case, the very difference can serve as a foil for the author's employment of the term and can illumine, by way of contrast, the specific concerns of the text being interpreted.

We would like to expand the notion of illegitimate totality transfer beyond linguistic (or word-usage) considerations to matters of *scriptural testimony* and *historical background*. As we discussed above, one aspect of scriptural testimony is locating other biblical passages that develop the concept that is found in the passage under consideration. But the same kind of critical interaction between the passage and other biblical passages that we just described for word usage pertains also to this type of scriptural testimony. Students must ask themselves, How does the concept as described in the other biblical passage relate to the kind of conceptual background that the implied author of this passage assumed his audience would possess and would bring to bear in the construal of this passage? To read uncritically into a given passage everything that all the other biblical writers say or suggest regarding the concept would be to commit the fallacy of illegitimate totality transfer.

Students will remember that a further type of scriptural testimony involves an examination of *other biblical passages* that are quoted or alluded to in the passage they are interpreting. Again, a critical conversation is required in order to ascertain what aspects of the passage quoted or alluded to are intended by the implied author to be brought to bear in the interpretation of his passage; then one can make use of the quoted or referenced passage according to indications given by the implied author of the passage being studied.

An additional type of scriptural testimony involves the consideration of *parallel passages*. It pertains, for example, to the ways in which a parallel account of the same event or teaching in another Gospel illumines the passage being interpreted. Here again, students should engage in a critical conversation so as to bring to bear, for the interpretation of the passage, only the specific information provided by the parallel accounts that the implied author of the passage assumed his readers would know and use in the interpretation of the passage.

The discussion in "Historical Background" (chap. 14) urges that students avoid a kind of overinterpretation that occurs when information pertaining to *historical background* of an event is read uncritically into a passage. Students should engage in a critical comparison between the contextual indicators of the passage under consideration and historical background in order to assess what background information the text (to personify the text for the moment) requires the reader to bring in order to interpret the passage accurately and fully, and they should accordingly make use of *only* that background information.[10] Doing anything more would involve a form of illegitimate totality transfer.[11]

Fallacies of Inferences

Some fallacies pertain not so much to evidence cited, that is, to premises, as they do to the process of drawing inferences, or conclusions, from evidence. Most of these fallacies involve hidden, or unstated, assumptions. The following are some of the more common fallacies of inferences.

FALLACY OF REFERENTIAL ANACHRONISM

The fallacy of referential anachronism involves the assumption that, as a general principle, biblical statements referred to events in the future; therefore their meaning is ultimately locked until it is made clear to those who actually experience the events. Those who practice this approach expound the Old Testament as if it at every point foreshadows the New Testament, and they direct every interpretive inference to fulfillment in Christ and the New Testament. They interpret even the minutest details in historical narratives as types

---

10. Samuel Sandmel refers to this uncritical citation and imposition of historical parallels as "parallelomania." See his Society of Biblical Literature presidential address: "Parallelomania," *JBL* 81 (1962): 2–13. Sandmel especially objects to uncritical assumptions of derivation, i.e., asserting that a given passage directly stems or derives from a certain other passage.

11. A specific form of this illegitimate totality transfer as it pertains to historical background is the "fallacy of irrelevant background," which involves citing background that is not relevant for the meaning of the passage understood as the communication conveyed by the implied author to the implied reader. For example, it would be illegitimate to interpret a passage in one of our Gospels by appeal to a reconstruction of Jesus's original Aramaic statement because none of the Gospels envisages a reader who knows Aramaic. This involves bringing in background information that the intended audience did not know and could not be expected to use in the construal of the passage. Such an appeal may be legitimate in terms of event or speech reconstruction in the process of historical criticism, but it would be overinterpretation and should not be used as the basis for interpreting the text in its final form. The same holds true for appeal to the meaning of the Hebrew term in an OT passage quoted by Luke or Hebrews. Luke and the writer of Hebrews apparently did not know Hebrew; and they certainly assumed that their readers would know not the Hebrew text but only the Septuagint. A further example would be the tendency on the part of Bultmann and some others to interpret the NT according to a full-blown gnosticism that actually emerged only in the second and third Christian centuries. See Rudolf Bultmann, *Theology of the New Testament*, trans. Kendrick Grobel, 2 vols. in 1, Scribner Studies in Contemporary Theology (New York: Scribner's Sons, 1955).

that are fulfilled in the New Testament. Such a view begins with the legitimate principle that the Old Testament is a preparation for the revelation of the New Testament. However, every detail of the Old Testament is not necessarily a type for New Testament events or persons, and even the details that are types for New Testament fulfillment have a basic meaning and significance in the historical context of those to whom the passages were originally directed. To understand the Old Testament this way is to violate two basic principles of exegesis: first, the need to understand passages in terms of their historical setting; and second, the need to expound passages in terms of the (implied) author's intention. One should be careful, therefore, not to draw inferences that necessarily assume typological significance for accidental resemblances between occurrences in the Old and New Testaments.

But this fallacy pertains not only to the insistence that every Old Testament passage be interpreted in terms of its realization in the New Testament; it also pertains to the tendency on the part of some readers to assume that the Bible, both Old Testament and New Testament, is replete with predictions of future events. They draw inferences that are intended to show how passages prognosticate major events that have subsequently occurred. This fallacy usually stems from the failure to differentiate between prophecy and pure prediction. In prophecy the aspect of foretelling is inevitably connected with the forthtelling; in fact, the primary purpose of foretelling is to support the prophet's message. Therefore the prophet's foretelling is relevant to the concrete historical situation in which and for which he spoke. Pure prediction, in contrast, may be totally unrelated to the historical setting in which it is made. The Scriptures, we believe, contain prophecies but not pure predictions, and when one overlooks this fact, one disregards the importance of the historical element in the Scriptures and therefore misinterprets them.

Fallacy of Composition

This fallacy involves the assumption that what is true of the part is necessarily true of the whole.[12] If one were to infer that because Luke presents some Samaritans as more generous (10:29–37) or grateful (17:11–19) than some Jews, he wants his audience to conclude that all Samaritans are morally superior to Jews, then one would be going well beyond the evidence and committing the fallacy of composition. The same would be the case if one were to infer from the story of the healing of the lame man at the Beautiful Gate in Acts 3:1–10 that Luke thereby teaches that all who are in need of physical healing will find it if they likewise place their faith in the name of Jesus. The fallacy of composition often surfaces in inferences that use the first-person plural: "This passage teaches that *we* can or that *we* should," suggesting that what is

12. Engel, *With Good Reason*, 93–94; Rudinow and Barry, *Invitation to Critical Thinking*, 281.

said to or about particular persons in particular situations necessarily pertains to everyone everywhere, or at least to all believers.[13]

FALLACY OF DIVISION

The fallacy of division is the opposite of the fallacy of composition. This fallacy involves the assumption that what is true of the whole is necessarily true of the part.[14] For example, when the book of Isaiah declares that the nation of Israel was sinfully rebellious in the time of Isaiah, one should not infer that every individual Hebrew was thus guilty. What was true of the nation as a whole was not necessarily true of every person within the nation. Such *may* be the case but is not necessarily so.

FALLACY OF HASTY GENERALIZATION

In the fallacy of hasty generalization, "an exceptional case is used as the basis for a general conclusion that is unwarranted."[15] One would commit this fallacy if one were to argue that because the Lord turned away from his intended judgment upon Israel on the basis of the earnest prayer of the prophet Amos (7:1–6), this passage teaches that God always turns away from his judgmental intentions when God's righteous minister implores him. The book of Amos may present the events of this passage as exceptional. Similarly, one would commit this fallacy if one were to argue from the fact that the book of Joel counts the locust plague as God's judgment upon the sin of Judah to the inference that the book of Joel teaches that natural disasters are always God's judgment upon the sins of nations. Again, the book of Joel may make no such claim but instead addresses only the judgmental divine purpose of this particular natural disaster.

FALLACY OF BIFURCATION

The fallacy of bifurcation[16] is sometimes labeled "the false Either-Or"[17] because it insists upon only two possible alternatives (either this or that) when, in fact, a third alternative is possible. Those who commit this fallacy take contraries to be contradictions. In contradictory statements, both propositions cannot be true and both cannot be false (a genuine either-or: either this is true or that is true); yet in contrary statements, both propositions

---

13. The issue as to whether the teaching of a passage legitimately applies to all persons, or at least to other persons in other places and other times, is a matter of evaluation and application, which we discuss in part 4.

14. Engel, *With Good Reason*, 94; Rudinow and Barry, *Invitation to Critical Thinking*, 281.

15. Engel, *With Good Reason*, 108; cf. Irving Copi, *Introduction to Logic*, 2nd ed. (New York: Macmillan, 1961), 64.

16. Engel, *With Good Reason*, 111–13.

17. Carson, *Exegetical Fallacies*, 90–92. Rudinow and Barry, *Invitation to Critical Thinking*, 312–13, refer to this error as the "fallacy of false dilemma."

cannot be true but both may be false. Thus a third alternative exists: neither is true.

One would commit the fallacy of bifurcation if one were to infer that because Gamaliel was not against the apostles in that he argued for their release (Acts 5:33–39), he must therefore have been for them, that is, he must have been a supporter of their cause. Here the following two propositions cannot be true at the same time: Gamaliel was for the apostles and Gamaliel was against the apostles. But they could both be false. Hence, a third possibility exists: according to the book of Acts, Gamaliel was neither against the apostles nor a supporter of the apostles.

To take a further example, one would fall into this fallacy if one were to infer that because the Old Testament does not condemn polygamy, it must advocate it. The Old Testament may neither condemn nor advocate polygamy but may simply concede the practice without making a clear judgment one way or the other.

FALLACY OF BEGGING THE QUESTION

In popular parlance, "begging the question" has come to refer to a situation that prompts, or poses, a question, but in logic "the fallacy of begging the question is committed when, instead of offering proof for its conclusion, an argument simply reasserts the conclusion in another form. Such arguments invite us to assume that something has been confirmed when in fact it has only been affirmed or reaffirmed."[18] In other words, in begging the question one states a conclusion in the form of a premise, and the so-called inference simply repeats the conclusion with which one began. Note the following example:

PREMISE	In Mark 7:27 Jesus takes a bigoted attitude toward Gentiles.
INFERENCE	Therefore Mark presents Jesus here as a bigot.

Here we see that the premise actually presents the interpretive conclusion (without providing evidence), and the inference simply repeats the conclusion already stated. It has yet to be argued, from evidence, that this passage expresses a bigoted position toward Gentiles. It begs the question of the meaning and character of Jesus's statement to the Syrophoenician woman.

Note a further example:

PREMISE	In Matthew 5:48 Jesus gives his disciples the impossible command to be perfect as their heavenly Father is perfect.
INFERENCE	Therefore, this command is an unrealizable ideal toward which disciples should strive but never expect to actualize.

18. Engel, *With Good Reason*, 114. See also Copi, *Introduction to Logic*, 65–66.

Here again, the premise contains the conclusion, which is simply repeated in slightly different terms. It begs the question of the meaning of *perfect*. The premise itself assumes its impossibility.

FALLACY OF ASSUMED PREMISE

Drawing inferences that go beyond the evidence cited by lacking sufficient evidentiary foundation is most often the result of unstated or assumed premises. It is critically important for students to make explicit all premises leading to inferences. Only in this way can students assess premises for their validity. Note the implicit, unstated premises in the following examples:

PREMISE	In 1 John 4:8 John declares that God is love.
INFERENCE	Therefore this passage teaches that God will never condemn anyone.

This inference assumes an unstated premise, that God's love is of such a nature that it necessarily excludes all condemnation.

PREMISE	In Mark 15:34 Jesus indicates that at the cross God has forsaken him.
INFERENCE	At the point of Jesus's death, God laid all the guilt and wrath of the world's sin upon Jesus.

This inference assumes several unstated premises: (1) that God actually did forsake Christ at the cross; (2) that God's forsaking involved a personal repudiation of Jesus over against, say, a functional decision not to intervene so as to deliver him from death on the cross; (3) that if a personal repudiation was involved, such repudiation was an expression of God's revulsion and horror at the sins of the world. These unstated premises may or may not be valid; but the interpretive process requires that they be expressed and tested by evidence.

FALLACY OF FALSE CAUSE

The fallacy of false cause[19] occurs if one asserts or assumes causality when one has not demonstrated such causality from the evidence or premises cited. The assumed causality may be either extratextual or intratextual.

The following is an example of *extratextual* assumed causality: Because Herod unfairly executed John the Baptist (Mark 6:14–29), therefore Herod's guilty conscience caused Herod to believe that Jesus was John raised from the dead (Mark 6:16). The text says nothing, at least explicitly, about Herod's guilty conscience, which is an extratextual psychological assessment, and the evidence cited does not bear the inference of causality. This causal connec-

19. Engel, *With Good Reason*, 132–37; Carson, *Exegetical Fallacies*, 133–34; Copi, *Introduction to Logic*, 64–65; Rudinow and Barry, *Invitation to Critical Thinking*, 321–22.

tion may be true, but the inference would be sound only if one cited specific evidence for this causality.

Intratextual assumed causality occurs when two elements are presented in the text and the student simply assumes that a causal relationship exists. Note this example:

PREMISE 1	Samuel was opposed to the emergence of the Israelite monarchy (1 Sam. 8:6).
PREMISE 2	Samuel pronounced judgment against the first Israelite king, Saul (1 Sam. 13:8–15; 15:10–33).
INFERENCE	Samuel pronounced judgment against Saul because of his personal distaste for the monarchy and his desire to sabotage it.

Here both premises are found in the text, but the text makes no causal connection between them (at least the premises do not present evidence of a causal connection). This inference lacks the evidence required for the causal connection.[20]

FALLACY OF APPEAL TO FEAR

The fallacy of appeal to fear[21] involves a way of drawing conclusions or inferences, based not on the fair appraisal of evidence, but on considerations of the likely effects that possible interpretation will have upon persons or institutions. This process of reasoning contains the unstated assumption that any conclusion, no matter how viable it is on the basis of the evidence cited, cannot be allowed to stand if it causes what the student considers to be unacceptable harm or distress.

One common form of the fallacy of appeal to fear is the *slippery-slope* argument,[22] which states that any interpretive conclusion that may eventually encourage persons to adopt other, more theologically (or ethically) dangerous conclusions should be avoided. In our opinion, no community and no person ultimately has anything to fear from the truth, so long as the truth is properly understood and presented.

Sometimes the fallacy of appeal to fear takes a more personal form: persons implicitly fear that if they adopt a given interpretation or set of interpretations, it could have serious negative consequences for them, such as loss of position or exclusion from their theological community.[23] We do not wish in

20. More specifically, this argument involves post hoc, ergo propter hoc (after this, therefore because of this): the assumption that an event that occurs *after* another event occurred *because of* that previous event.

21. Engel, *With Good Reason*, 190–94; Carson, *Exegetical Fallacies*, 106–8.

22. Rudinow and Barry, *Invitation to Critical Thinking*, 323–24.

23. James D. Weinland, *How to Think Straight* (Totowa, NJ: Rowman & Allanheld, 1963), 128–29.

any way to dismiss the potential pain that such a situation may entail, but we feel obligated to mention that it is precisely at such points that students of the Bible who are people of faith are confronted with the issue of whether they are prepared to submit to the authority of Scripture over their lives, with all the risk that such commitment necessarily carries.

AD HOMINEM FALLACY

Ad hominem fallacy[24] (*ad hominen* means "to or toward a person") refers to an argument made against a position, based not on the merits of the position itself but on the background or character of the person who advocates the position. In interpretation, this fallacy pertains especially to inferences made from the evidence of the *interpretation of others*. It involves dismissing or disparaging an interpretation because it has been offered by someone who is, from the perspective of the student, suspect. The student may infer that the interpretation and exegetical arguments put forward by a given scholar are not to be taken seriously because the scholar is, say, a Catholic, or a liberal, or a fundamentalist. Students need to judge exegetical arguments and conclusions on their own merits; in the final analysis, neither the background nor the commitments of the person who presents arguments have anything to do with the validity or lack of validity of the arguments themselves.

FALLACY OF APPEAL TO AUTHORITY

Usually the fallacy of appeal to authority[25] involves appeal to persons who lack competence in the area under consideration, for example, appealing to an attorney on matters of medicine. But we would like to employ this designation to refer to the practice of simply accepting the exegetical arguments and conclusions of a scholar because of the person of the scholar, shown through reputation, publications, or achievements.[26] In a sense, this is the opposite of the ad hominem fallacy because it involves a positive appeal to the background or character of the person advocating an argument or position without due regard to the merits of the arguments or positions themselves. Again, this fallacy involves especially the *interpretation of others* and pertains to the practice of simply citing the interpretations given by commentators or other scholars and drawing inferences that assume the legitimacy of these interpretations because they come from recognized scholars. But scholars have no independent interpretive authority. Students must judge the soundness of the interpretations of scholars by the same methods and standards that they use to judge their own evidence and inferences.

---

24. Engel, *With Good Reason*, 166–68; Copi, *Introduction to Logic*, 54–57.
25. Engel, *With Good Reason*, 183–88, 203; Carson, *Exegetical Fallacies*, 22–23; Copi, *Introduction to Logic*, 61–62.
26. Rudinow and Barry, *Invitation to Critical Thinking*, 19–20, 300–303.

FALLACY OF CONSENSUS OPINIO

Closely related to the fallacy of appeal to authority is the fallacy of appealing to the general scholarly consensus. In fact, the fallacy of *consensus opinio* is a specific form of the appeal to authority; this fallacy involves appeal to a certain type of authority, the authority of the group, in this case the scholarly group. It is true that one should take scholarly consensus seriously because none of us is able to explore exhaustively all the intricacies of every exegetical issue in even individual passages, as the community of scholars has done. Therefore, when students argue for an interpretation that contradicts the *consensus opinio*, they should realize that they bear the burden of showing, by citing specific evidence, exactly how the scholarly consensus is wrong and what is the basis for such an assessment. But there is nothing infallible about scholarly consensus; and the history of interpretation is replete with examples of "assured results" of scholarship that have been swept away by new evidence or more sound arguments.[27]

Fallacies of Orientation

We might label fallacies that describe mistaken perspectives toward the process of interpretation *fallacies of orientation*. These are all specific forms of the adoption of a deductive, or presuppositional, approach over against an inductive, or evidential, one.

FALLACY OF ILLEGITIMATE QUESTIONS

The fallacy of illegitimate questions[28] may involve interpretive questions that fail to emerge from the text itself and therefore those that the text is not prepared to answer. It may also involve questions that are framed in such a way as to assume an answer. We previously emphasized that proper interpretation involves answering questions that arise from observations of the text itself, so as to ensure that the interpretation accords with the agenda of the text. But the fallacy of the illegitimate question involves the process of interpreting passages by answering questions that the text does not raise and that thus diverge from the agenda of the text. The attempts to answer such questions will lead either to speculation or to irrelevance. Answers to such questions will be either flatly wrong from the perspective of the sense of the text, or manifestly beside the point.

The type of illegitimate question that assumes an answer is actually an interrogative form of begging the question; it is sometimes called a *loaded question* or *leading question*. Some examples are, Why does Ezekiel call Russia "Gog" in Ezekiel 38? Why does Paul describe the pretribulation rapture

---

27. Bockmuehl, *Seeing the Word*, 37–38.
28. Engel, *With Good Reason*, 122–25.

of the church as he does in 1 Thessalonians 4? These questions assume an interpretation, and any answer will necessarily confirm the presupposition of the question.

DOGMATIC FALLACY

Dogmatic fallacy involves the attempt to find support in the Scriptures for certain dogmas that have already been accepted. As a result, students explain the Bible in such a way as to support certain beliefs, and they promptly and arbitrarily reject all possible interpretations that may negate those beliefs. Such an approach often involves the fallacy of fragmentation, previously described, for it employs proof texts that are torn from their contexts in order to support certain dogmas. The dogmatic fallacy reflects the fact that the Scriptures can be used to prove anything.

The element of truth in the dogmatic fallacy is that, within the church, the Bible should be appealed to as the authority for Christian beliefs. Those who commit the dogmatic fallacy, however, fail to understand accurately the true meaning of the authority of the Scriptures. For the Scriptures are actually authoritative only if they are used as the basis for formulating one's beliefs and not if they are employed merely to support one's dogmatic presuppositions. The first approach begins with the Scriptures and moves to beliefs; the second begins with beliefs and moves to the Scriptures. In the first case, the Bible is the actual authority; in the second case, the authority has shifted to the theological presupposition with which one began. In brief, the first is doctrinal, for it seeks in the Scriptures the beliefs they contain. The second is dogmatic, for it involves the assertion of tenets for which substantiation is to be found in the Bible.

RATIONALISTIC FALLACY

The rationalist tries to expound the Scriptures in such a way as to make them acceptable to human reason. For example, the many "lives of Jesus" written by classic nineteenth-century liberals, such as David Friedrich Strauss, are replete with naturalistic explanations of Jesus's miracles offered to appease the rationalistic sensibilities of Victorian intellectuals.[29]

Such an emphasis has various causes. For example, the inability to believe certain biblical facts such as miracles often results in rationalistic interpretation. Rationalism reminds students that exegesis must involve the use of reason and that they should engage in a sincere attempt to comprehend the message of the Bible and to relate that message to the realities of the world, employing their best and most rigorous thinking in the process. But the rationalist

---

29. David Friedrich Strauss, *The Life of Jesus Critically Examined*, trans. Peter C. Hodgson from the 4th German ed. (1840), Lives of Jesus Series (Philadelphia: Fortress, 1972); cf. Albert Schweitzer, *The Quest of the Historical Jesus: The First Complete Edition*, ed. John Bowden (Minneapolis: Fortress, 2001).

needs to recognize the possibility that reason is finite and that reason itself may point to the limits of reason. Moreover, in order properly to interpret the message of the Bible, one needs to be open to the transcendent perspective of the text even if in the end one does not accept its perspective on the reality of the transcendent.

A specific manifestation of the rationalistic fallacy is the mythological approach to interpretation. Frequently, in order to remove what cannot be comprehended or accepted by reason, one will declare that certain events are myths, that is, fictional representations of reality, rather than actual historical occurrences. They are like the shell of a walnut and thus may be discarded as soon as the nut's meat—that is, the spiritual truth it conveys—is discovered.[30]

To a great extent, such an approach serves to negate the historical aspect of the Scriptures: it denies that an indispensable relation exists between history and the conveyance of spiritual truth. This opinion will often result in the position that the Gospels contain the Christ myth.[31] According to this view, the resurrection was not a real historical event. It was a myth whose purpose is to teach the supreme spiritual truth that though Jesus was slain, his spirit still lives.[32] When one learns this important spiritual lesson and participates in it existentially, one may then dismiss the *story* that was used to express it.

REDUCTIONISTIC FALLACY

The fallacy of the reductionistic approach to the Bible takes a certain aspect of the Bible's reality to be the totality of the Bible's character. One form of the reductionistic fallacy is the *panhistorical fallacy*. According to this view, the Bible should be studied almost exclusively as the history of certain peoples.[33] Such an approach fails to realize that the Scriptures contain more

30. A helpful clarification and description of myth, especially as it pertains to the OT, can be found in John N. Oswalt, *The Bible among the Myths: Unique Revelation or Just Ancient Literature?* (Grand Rapids: Zondervan, 2009).

31. John Hick, ed., *The Myth of God Incarnate* (London: SCM, 1977); Burton L. Mack, *The Myth of Innocence: Mark and Christian Origins* (Philadelphia: Fortress, 1988); cf. Michael Green, ed., *The Truth of God Incarnate* (Grand Rapids: Eerdmans, 1977).

32. Rudolf Bultmann, *Kerygma and Myth: A Theological Debate*, ed. Hans W. Bartsch (New York: Harper & Row, 1961); Marcus J. Borg and John Dominic Crossan, *The Last Week* (San Francisco: HarperSanFrancisco, 2006), 189–216.

33. E.g., Rainer Albertz, *A History of Israelite Religion in the Old Testament Period*, 2 vols., OTL (Louisville: Westminster John Knox, 1994); J. Alberto Soggin, *Joshua*, OTL (Philadelphia: Westminster, 1972); Gösta W. Ahlström, *The History of Ancient Palestine*, ed. Diana Edelman (Minneapolis: Fortress, 1993); Heikki Räisänen, *Beyond New Testament Theology: A Story and a Programme*, 2nd ed. (London: SCM, 2000); Jacques Berlinerblau, *The Secular Bible: Why Nonbelievers Must Take Religion Seriously* (Cambridge: Cambridge University Press, 2005). Of course, many historical studies are not *panhistorical*: instead, they attend seriously to narrative and/or theological issues, as does Bright, *History of Israel*; Iain Provan, V. Philips Long, and Tremper Longman III, *A Biblical History of Israel* (Louisville:

than history; they present history that is embedded in literary narrative and mediated through text, presented from the perspective of divine, transcendent purpose. The events that the Bible describes can be approached only through the literary/narrative framework that the biblical text provides. The historical study of the Bible is thus necessarily bound up with literary study and with theological study.[34] The historical narrative reveals the God of history. Therefore one cannot limit the process of exegesis to an examination of empirically verifiable historical events recorded there or to the bare historical facts of the documents' production.[35] The panhistorical view, however, reminds students of the important truth that the biblical message is first of all a witness to the God who acts in history, and that the biblical narrative almost always claims to present actual events on the plane of history.

Another form of the reductionistic fallacy is the *panliterary fallacy*. According to this view, the Bible can be reduced to literature. At one time in some circles, the study the Bible as great literature was quite popular.[36] Many of those who have examined the Scriptures from this standpoint have failed to take into account the fact that purpose is essential to greatness in literature: in some extreme cases, they searched the Bible merely for its euphonious phrases and picturesque images as if it were a purposeless collection of appealing expressions and no more. More recently, some, but by no means all, practitioners of certain forms of *literary criticism* have tended to reduce the Bible to its literary character.[37] They restrict the study of the Bible to its literary power to construct its own world of formative cognitive meaning in the process of reading, as all literature does, and they do so without attending to its histori-

---

Westminster John Knox, 2003); Ben Witherington III, *New Testament History: A Narrative Account* (Grand Rapids: Baker Academic, 2001); Gerd Theissen and Annette Merz, *The Historical Jesus: A Comprehensive Guide* (London: SCM, 1998); N. T. Wright, *The Resurrection of the Son of God* (Minneapolis: Fortress, 2003); Martin Hengel, *The Cross of the Son of God* (London: SCM, 1986).

34. Bockmuehl, *Seeing the Word*, 47.

35. To do so would be to commit the *genetic fallacy*: the false notion that the meaning of a reality is reducible to its beginnings. See Engel, *With Good Reason*, 170–73.

36. E.g., Leland Ryken, *The Literature of the Bible* (Grand Rapids: Zondervan, 1974). Ryken himself appreciates the theological genius of the Bible, and this recognition is reflected in most of his later works, including *Words of Delight: A Literary Introduction to the Bible*, 2nd ed. (Grand Rapids: Baker Academic, 1992).

37. Examples of literary critics who attend to the theological meaning and claims of the text include Robert Polzin, *Moses and the Deuteronomist: A Literary Study of the Deuteronomic History* (New York: Seabury, 1980); L. Daniel Hawk, *Every Promise Fulfilled: Contesting Plots in Joshua*, LCBI (Louisville: Westminster John Knox, 1991); Barry G. Webb, *The Book of Judges: An Integrated Reading*, JSOTSup 46 (Sheffield: JSOT Press, 1987); Sternberg, *Poetics of Biblical Narrative*; Kingsbury, *Christology of Mark's Gospel*; Mark Allan Powell, *God with Us: A Pastoral Theology of Matthew's Gospel* (Minneapolis: Fortress, 1995); idem, *Chasing the Eastern Star: Adventures in Biblical Reader-Response Criticism* (Louisville: Westminster John Knox, 2001); idem, *What Is Narrative Criticism?*

cal or theological claims.[38] But in biblical study, just as event cannot be known or thought about without narrative, so also event cannot be collapsed into narrative. Historical narrative bears witness to event and to the importance of event. Even as the panhistorical approach tends to focus on the historical to the exclusion of the literary, the panliterary approach tends to focus on the literary to the exclusion of the historical. Both of them tend to bracket out the question of the meaning and validity of the theological claims of the text. In fact, an inductive examination of the Bible may indicate that in the Bible the literary, historical, and theological are inextricably bound up together,[39] and interpreters cannot deal adequately with any one of these without attending to the others. Ultimately interpreters cannot deal adequately with any biblical passage without engaging the text in the complexity of its historical, literary, and theological matrix.

Example of Interpretation (2 Timothy 3:16)

The purpose of this example is to illustrate the process of inductive inferential reasoning rather than to resolve the issues raised. Likewise, the evidence cited is illustrative rather than exhaustive.

Interpreting graphē

Questions selected to be answered:

What is the meaning of *graphē*, "scripture," in 2 Timothy 3:16? To what does it refer?

A. "Sacred writings" and "scripture" are identical.
    Evidence: Context and inflections

Premise 1: Although "sacred writings" (*grammata*) in 2 Timothy 3:15 is plural and "scripture" (*graphē*) in 3:16 is singular;

---

38. To some extent this is true of the massive (and in many ways helpful) work by J. P. Fokkelman, *Art and Poetry in the Books of Samuel: A Full Interpretation Based on Stylistic and Structural Analysis*, 4 vols., Studia semitica neerlandica (Winona Lake, IN: Eisenbrauns, 1981–93), although this work implicitly contains some helpful theological insights; and Adele Berlin, *Poetics and Interpretation of Biblical Narrative*, BLS 9 (Sheffield: Almond, 1983), although at the end of the book she includes some brief reflections on the relationship between literary study and historical criticism. See also Shimon Bar-Efrat, *Narrative Art in the Bible*, JSOTSup 70, BLS 17 (Sheffield: Almond, 1989); Fewell and Gunn, *Compromising Redemption*; Hans Frei, *The Eclipse of Biblical Narrative* (New Haven: Yale University Press, 1974). See the corrective to the nonhistorical character of much NT narrative criticism in Peter Merenlahti, *Poetics for the Gospels? Rethinking Narrative Criticism* (London: T&T Clark International, 2002).

39. See also Wright, *New Testament and the People of God*, 47–166.

EVIDENCE: History of the term[40]

PREMISE 2: since both come from the same root (*graphō*), which means "to write";

EVIDENCE: Context

PREMISE 3: and since there seems to be no break between verses 15 and 16;

EVIDENCE: Context and inflections

PREMISE 4: and since "sacred writings" may refer to various parts of "scripture";

EVIDENCE: Inflection

PREMISE 5: and if "scripture" in verse 16 is a collective singular and refers to Hebrew scriptures in their entirety;

EVIDENCE: Syntax, word usage, and scriptural testimony[41]

PREMISE 6: and since *pasa* in verse 16 may be translated *all*;

INFERENCE: it may follow that "sacred writings" and "scripture" are identical.

B. "Sacred writings" (2 Tim. 3:15) and *graphē* (v. 16) are different.
EVIDENCE: Inflections

PREMISE 1: Because "sacred writings" is plural (v. 15), and "scripture" (v. 16) is singular;

EVIDENCE: Context and scriptural testimony

PREMISE 2: and because 2 Timothy 3:8 and Jude 14–15 contain references to material not found in Hebrew scripture;

INFERENCE: therefore the "sacred writings" may include more than "scripture."

---

40. Gottlob Schrenk, "γράφω, γραφή, γράμμα . . . ," in *TDNT* 1:749–73.
41. BDAG 782.

EVIDENCE: Scriptural testimony
(Rom. 9:15; 15:10; 1 Cor. 6:16; Gal. 3:16; Eph. 4:8; 5:14;
Matt. 19:4–5; Acts 4:24–25; 13:34–35; Heb. 1:6)

FURTHER PREMISE: However, since these statements are not introduced by the formulas commonly employed for citations from Hebrew scripture, such as "scripture says," "it says," "God says," and "it is written";

FURTHER INFERENCE: it may follow that such material may not be considered as being on the same level as Hebrew scripture.

C. Use of "scripture" (*graphē*) by Paul and others
EVIDENCE: Word usage and scriptural testimony
(Rom. 1:2; 4:3; 9:17; 10:11; 11:2; 15:4; Gal. 3:8, 22; 4:2)

PREMISE 1: Whereas Paul, the implied author of 2 Timothy, frequently uses a form of *graphē* to refer to Hebrew scripture(s);

EVIDENCE: Word usage and scriptural testimony
(Matt. 21:42; 26:54; Mark 12:10; 14:49; Luke 4:21; 24:27;
John 2:22; 7:42; Acts 1:16; 8:32)

PREMISE 2: and whereas other NT writers also use forms of *graphē* to refer to Hebrew scripture(s), with the possible exception of 2 Peter 3:16;

INFERENCE: consequently, "scripture" (*graphē*) probably refers to Hebrew scripture.[42]

D. Copies of Hebrew Scripture
EVIDENCE: Context and inflections

PREMISE 1: Whereas "are able" (*dynamena*) in 2 Timothy 3:15 is a participle in the present tense;

---

42. For the position that *graphē* may include extant written Christian traditions or even some apostolic writings, as may be suggested in 2 Pet. 3:16, see George W. Knight III, *Commentary on the Pastoral Epistles*, NIGTC (Grand Rapids: Eerdmans, 1992); William D. Mounce, *Pastoral Epistles*, WBC 46 (Nashville: Nelson, 2000). On the other hand, Philip H. Towner, *The Letters to Timothy and Titus*, NICNT (Grand Rapids: Eerdmans, 2006), holds that God-breathed *graphē* refers to the Hebrew Scriptures, but they need to be "understood and applied . . . within the hermeneutical framework provided by the Pauline gospel" (589).

PREMISE 2: and whereas the inferred forms of the copulas in verse 16 may be in the present tense: "All scripture *is theopneustos* and *is* useful";

EVIDENCE: Context, history of the text,
and historical background (v. 15)

PREMISE 3: and whereas the only versions of the Hebrew scripture extant in Paul's day and during the childhood and ministry of Timothy were *copies* of Hebrew scripture;

EVIDENCE: History of the text

PREMISE 4: and whereas there probably were some differences between the copies of Hebrew scripture and the original documents;

INFERENCE: therefore, the "scripture" to which the implied author refers probably includes some variations from the original texts.

E. Use of the Septuagint (LXX)
EVIDENCE: Scriptural testimony
(Rom. 3:10–18; 4:3; 9:15, 26; 2 Cor. 6:2; Gal. 3:10; 4:27; Heb. 1:5–12; 3:7–11; 3:15; 10:5–7) and interpretations of others

PREMISE 1: Since Paul and other NT writers may use the LXX even when it varies from the Hebrew text;[43]

EVIDENCE: See scriptural testimony above
(also Acts 2:16–21, 25–28, 34–35; 4:25–26; 7:42–43, 48–50;
Rom. 8:36; 15:9–12, 21)

PREMISE 2: and since they may use expressions such as "it is written," "God says," "the Holy Spirit says," or "it is said" to introduce these quotations;

INFERENCE: it may follow that at least parts of the LXX, along with copies of the original Hebrew text, are viewed as "scripture" by the implied writer.

43. The Masoretic Text is used as representative of the Hebrew text.

F. Use of paraphrases: Word or message versus words
EVIDENCE: Scriptural testimony
(Rom. 9:33; 1 Cor. 3:20; 2 Cor. 6:16–18; Gal. 3:10; 4:27)
and interpretation of others[44]

PREMISE 1: Whereas the implied author seems to paraphrase both the Hebrew text and the Septuagint;

PREMISE 2: and whereas he sometimes uses such expressions as "it is written" and "says the Lord" in introducing these apparent paraphrases;

INFERENCE: consequently, Paul may be more concerned with making clear the word or message of God in scripture than he is with citing its exact words.

Summary: At the end of this process, if more than one possibility emerges, it is necessary to indicate what the possibilities are, along with the lines of inferential reasoning apparently supporting each. If possible, a tentative decision then needs to be made regarding which possibility has the preponderance of support in its favor. If no interpretation seems to have such support, one should acknowledge that not even a tentative decision can be made.

Interpreting theopneustos

Questions selected to be answered:

What is the meaning of *theopneustos*, "God-inspired"?
To whom or to what does it refer?

A. Basic meaning of "God-inspired" (*theopneustos*)
EVIDENCE: Preliminary definition, etymology,
and interpretation of others[45]

PREMISE: Because the basic meaning of *theopneustos* may be simply "God-breathed,"

INFERENCE: it may follow that it is not possible to draw a specific description of the process of the "divine breathing" of "all scripture" (*pasa graphē*) from this expression.

---

44. Henry Barclay Swete, *An Introduction to the Old Testament in Greek*, rev. R. R. Ottley (Cambridge: Cambridge University Press, 1914), 381–405.
45. Eduard Schweizer, "θεόπνευστος," in *TDNT* 6:453–55.

B. "Scripture" as words spoken by God to the original authors
EVIDENCE: Inflection and interpretation of others[46]

PREMISE 1: Since *theopneustos* may be in the passive voice and may refer to the origin of "all scripture";

EVIDENCE: *pneō*;[47] scriptural testimony: "the word of the LORD came to" (Isa. 1:10; Jer. 1:2; Hosea 1:1; Amos 3:1; Mic. 1:1; Zeph. 1:12; Acts 9:10; 2 Pet. 1:19–21); and interpretations of others[48]

PREMISE 2: and since the second component of *theopneustos* may be derived from *pneō*;

EVIDENCE: Scriptural testimony:
"God says" or "said," "the Holy Spirit says" or "said" (Matt. 19:4–5; Acts 4:24–25; 13:34–35; Heb. 1:6; 3:7; see prophetic references above; John 10:34–35; 2 Pet. 1:19–21); and interpretation of others[49]

PREMISE 3: and since *pneō* may mean "breathed out";

INFERENCE: it may follow that *theopneustos* signifies God's speaking the words of scripture to the original authors, and thus that all scripture is spirated or verbally inspired.

C. God-inspired authors
EVIDENCE: Interpretation of others[50]

PREMISE 1: Because the second component of "God-inspired" may be derived from *pneō*;

EVIDENCE: Inflection and interpretation of others[51]

PREMISE 2: and because *theopneustos* may refer to the origin of "all scripture";

46. Raymond F. Collins, *I and II Timothy and Titus: A Commentary*, NTL (Louisville: Westminster John Knox, 2002), 264.

47. BDAG 449–50.

48. B. B. Warfield, *The Inspiration and Authority of the* Bible (Philadelphia: P&R, 1948), 133–40, 152–53; I. Howard Marshall, *Biblical Inspiration* (Grand Rapids: Eerdmans, 1983), 31–35.

49. Warfield, *Inspiration and Authority*, 135–40.

50. BDAG 449–50, 837–38.

51. I. Howard Marshall, *A Critical and Exegetical Commentary on the Pastoral Epistles*, ICC (Edinburgh: T & T Clark, 1999), 793–94.

EVIDENCE: Scriptural testimony

PREMISE 3: and because this use of *pneō* may reflect the analogy of Genesis 2:7, where God is said to breathe out into the nostrils of the man formed from the dust of the ground;

INFERENCE: it may follow that "God-inspired" means that God breathed out into those who wrote "all scripture," thus inspiring them in their authorial activity.

D. Divine source of "all scripture," not the manner of inspiration
EVIDENCE: Preliminary definition,
etymology, and interpretation of others[52]

PREMISE 1: Whereas *theopneustos* may simply refer to the divine source of the writing of Scripture;

INFERENCE: it may follow that one cannot draw a doctrine about the manner of divine inspiration from 2 Timothy 3:16.

E. Use of *pneō* versus use of words for speaking such as *legō* and *phēmi*
EVIDENCE: Word usage

PREMISE 1: Whereas *pneō* does not seem to be used for speaking in the New Testament;

EVIDENCE: Word usage and scriptural testimony

PREMISE 2: and whereas other words, such as *legō* and *phēmi*, are apparently used for speaking;

INFERENCE: it may follow that *theopneustos* does not refer to the spiration or speech of God.

F. Scripture extant in Paul's day is "God-inspired"
EVIDENCE: Syntax

PREMISE 1: Since 2 Timothy 3:16–17 is an elliptical statement lacking a main verb;

52. Eduard Schweizer, "θεόπνευστος," in *TDNT* 6:453–55.

PREMISE 2: and since the implied author could have used the past tense of the copula ("*was* God-inspired") to indicate that he was referring to the original writing of "all scripture";

↓

INFERENCE: it may follow that he was referring to the "theopneustic" (i.e., "God-inspired") quality of the scripture of his own day.

G. The Holy Spirit, power, and scripture
EVIDENCE: Context (2 Tim. 1:7–8, 12; 2:1; 3:5, 7, 9, 15)

PREMISE 1: Since the implied author seems to emphasize the powerlessness of false teachers;

EVIDENCE: See item D in the example "Interpreting *graphē* in 2 Timothy 3:16" above, which mentions *dynamena* ("are able") in 2 Timothy 3:15 (cf. 1:7–8; 3:5, 7, 9)

PREMISE 2: and since "sacred writings" in verse 15 may be equal to "all scripture" in verse 16;

EVIDENCE: Context, definition, and inflection[53]

PREMISE 3: and since in verse 15 the implied author uses a participial form of *dynamai* in the present tense (*dynamena*) to express the ability or power of the "sacred writings" available to Timothy from his childhood;

EVIDENCE: Word usage and scriptural testimony (Luke 4:14; Acts 1:8; Rom. 15:13; 1 Cor. 2:4; 1 Thess. 1:5; cf. John 6:63 and Eph. 6:17); interpretation of others[54]

PREMISE 4: and since such power seems to be associated with the breath or spirit of God;

↓

INFERENCE: it may follow that *theopneustos* refers to God's breathing his spirit into the "sacred writings" and "all scripture," thus making them *useful* and providing the reader with the existential power or ability to achieve the purposes stated in 2 Timothy 3:15 and 3:16b–17.

53. BDAG 261–62.
54. BDAG 262–63.

H. The function of scripture

EVIDENCE: Inflection

PREMISE: If the implied writer is using *theopneustos* in the active voice instead of the passive voice;

INFERENCE: it may follow that *theopneustos* means "God-inspiring," thus stressing the function and the intended effect of "all scripture" upon the reader.

Exercise: Interpretation

1. Following the suggestions in part 3, select one or two key questions from your detailed observation of Mark 15:33–39 and interpret the passage by answering that question through the use of evidential premises and inferences.

2. Following the suggestions in part 3, interpret Jonah 4:1–11 by answering key questions: What is the meaning of this dialogue between Jonah and God? How does it illumine the message of the book of Jonah? In the same way, interpret Mark 4:10–20 by answering a key question: What is the meaning of this parable?

Part 4

Evaluating and Appropriating

Having interpreted the text, readers must ascertain what values for thinking, character, and behavior they may derive from the interpretation of the text for the formation of contemporary personal and community life.[1] This process necessarily involves two phases, which we term *evaluation* and *application*, or better, *appropriation*.[2]

Discussion here about the many intricacies of this process is impossible. Moreover, the task of evaluation and appropriation is necessarily more open-ended than is the case with observation and interpretation. If observation and interpretation are not finally reducible to certain rules and techniques, such is even more the case with evaluation and appropriation. Therefore the purpose of the forthcoming presentation is to establish some essential principles and outline the main phases involved in evaluating and appropriating the biblical materials. Ultimately, students must work out the details for themselves in actual practice.

1. For a discussion of inductive biblical study as it relates to evaluation and appropriation, see Robert A. Traina, "Inductive Bible Study Reexamined in Light of Contemporary Hermeneutics II: Applying the Text," in McCown and Massey, *Interpreting God's Word for Today*, 85–109; Kuist, *These Words upon Thy Heart*, 133–58.

2. Many scholars now prefer the term *appropriation* to *application* because they say that application suggests a narrowly cognitive and behavioral focus, whereas appropriation more accurately describes the broadly formational character of the process of relating the text's values to contemporary existence. In order to avoid monotony, we use these terms interchangeably.

17

Description of Evaluation and Appropriation

Evaluation

According to *Webster's New College Dictionary*, *evaluate* means "to determine or fix the value of."[1] More specifically, one might say that to evaluate is to assess the worth of something, to appraise its excellence, relevance, and usefulness. Thus the process of evaluation involves answering questions such as these: Does the text actually fulfill the purpose for which it was written? Are the statements of the text valid or invalid? If valid, when and for whom and for what purposes are they valid? Clearly interpretation fundamentally informs the answering of these questions, and in the following pages students will repeatedly see that evaluation is closely related to interpretation. But because evaluation involves making value judgments, it is distinct from interpretation proper.

Students should carefully note the place of evaluation in an overall inductive study. They should realize, first, that evaluation must follow interpretation and not precede it or be simultaneous with it.[2] One can assess the meaning of the biblical text only after one has grasped that meaning. Students should also recognize that evaluation must precede appropriation proper. Contrary

1. *Webster's II New College Dictionary*, s.v. "Evaluate."
2. Kuist, *These Words upon Thy Heart*, 58; Birch and Rasmussen, *Bible and Ethics*, 170; Osborne, *Hermeneutical Spiral*, 440–41.

to common belief and practice, students are not ready to appropriate a passage as soon as they have discovered its meaning. In fact, in the process of appropriating passages, many students engage in evaluation only implicitly and subconsciously; consequently, they leave themselves vulnerable to all sorts of deductive assumptions that can creep into their thinking and determine their appropriation of the text. After interpreting a passage, students should pursue an intentional process of biblical assessment whereby they ascertain the worth and relevance of the text. Having engaged in biblical assessment, they should pursue an equally deliberate process of assessing the specific character of the contemporary situation and of establishing its connection to the biblical passage. For these reasons, one may well consider evaluation to be the major phase of the general process of appropriation.

One should not try to exempt the Bible from the process of assessing its worth and relevance, a process that has been labeled *judicial criticism*.[3] For, as we shall see, the Scriptures invite such critical assessment of the Bible-as-a-whole. Moreover, the Bible itself bears witness to the fact that individual parts of the Bible have varying degrees of pertinence and continuing value. This fact is confirmed when, with all readers, we recognize that if we could possess only certain books of the Bible, we would prefer some above others. People undoubtedly would have different opinions as to which books should be chosen, but the fact remains that readers would make a choice, and this act of choosing presupposes a variety of worth. Indeed, analysis of how readers use the Bible reveals that they always at least implicitly evaluate it. This constant implicit evaluation supports the claim that evaluation stems from the nature of the existence of the Bible.

General Evaluation

The evaluation of the biblical materials involves, first of all, the process of assessing the general validity and worth of the Scriptures-as-a-whole or large portions of them. Students pursue this matter by addressing the following questions: Is the Bible (or a major part of the Bible, such as the Old Testament) of any value for contemporary persons, or is it invalid and worthless? Does it have continuing value, and if so, what is the nature and extent of its value? Do the biblical materials have a purpose whose significance transcends the original production of these materials? If so, do the biblical materials fulfill these transcendent purposes? These questions are basic to all biblical evaluation and appropriation. If the Bible-as-a-whole or a large portion of

---

3. The expression *judicial criticism* is used in a neutral sense and in no way implies derogatory or destructive judgment. It is employed in this proper sense by Howard Tillman Kuist, who borrowed the expression from T. M. Greene. See Kuist, *These Words upon Thy Heart*, 58–59, 96, 107; Theodore Meyer Greene, *The Arts and the Art of Criticism* (Princeton, NJ: Princeton University Press, 1940).

it is of no value for contemporary life, the process of evaluation is at an end; and further, the possibility of appropriation has been removed because its presupposition is that biblical statements have value and therefore should be appropriated.

The process employed in answering these basic questions is too complex for detailed treatment in the present volume. In general, however, this process involves three elements: (1) identifying the primary purpose of the Bible, (2) assessing whether this primary purpose has any continuing relevance, and (3) ascertaining whether, and if so, to what extent, the Bible fulfills its primary purpose.[4] Students must address these issues for themselves on the basis of a reasonable examination of the text's evidence, and in light of the constant realities of human existence. Our own view, which we set forth as a tentative hypothesis, is that the primary purpose of the biblical materials is to bear testimony to the revelation of God, which comes through God's acts in history and through the explication of those acts as disclosures of God's purposes and will for God's creation, and especially his human creation. Such a purpose seems to be transcendent, by which we mean it is not limited to specific times and places but pertains to all persons everywhere and in all periods.

Because this tentatively stated purpose of the biblical materials involves both the acts of God on the plane of history and the purposes and will of God for (especially human) creation, the assessment of the Bible's fulfillment of these transcendent purposes (and thus the Bible's continuing validity) turns on two issues. The first issue is that of *historicity*. This issue addresses the following questions: Did these events, which are purportedly the actions of God, actually take place? And does the biblical claim of divine involvement in these events offer the most plausible explanation for them? The second issue is that of *theology*. This issue addresses the following question: Is the biblical understanding of God and God's relationship to the world, and especially to his human creation, convincing?

In the case of both issues, students must apply all the tests of truth and value that are pertinent in ascertaining the veracity and worth of any purportedly historical or theological statement. In relation to the first issue, historicity, one may use all the tests applied in a court of law to decide what events actually occurred and what is the best explanation for these events. At this point a truly inductive attitude is critically important in order to identify all philosophical

4. This process assumes that there is a primary purpose to the entire Bible. But in an inductive approach nothing should be assumed. The student should be open to the possibility that there is insufficient consistency among the various parts of the Bible to speak of an overall purpose. Such is not our position, but we recognize that some scholars are inclined toward such a conclusion. This conclusion of no overall purpose would actually mark the end of the process of *biblical* evaluation and appropriation, although one might hold this position for the Bible-as-a-whole while still allowing that only individual books or portions may be worthy of contemporary appropriation.

and ideological assumptions with which one comes to the historical evidence, with a view toward casting aside any assumptions that would stand in the way of an open and reasonable appraisal of the evidence.[5]

For example, if one approaches this question of historicity with the assumption of a closed universe that from the outset excludes the possibility of any transcendent divine involvement in the historical process, one is operating deductively and is not true to the spirit of open inquiry. But a person approaching the issue of historicity with the attitude that declares, "God said it; I believe it; and that settles it!" is also adopting a problematic position. Such an assertion is equally deductive and is unworthy of the courage with which the Bible casts its claims before the world.

In relation to the second issue, theology, tests include the test of congruity and the experiential test. The test of congruity tries to determine whether the various aspects of the biblical portrait of God and God's actions are coherent or are fundamentally contradictory. Of course, students should recognize the possible tensions in the biblical presentation of God and acknowledge that certain tensions are perhaps to be expected, given the complexity and transcendence of divine realities. Students will then need to ascertain whether underlying coherence exists that renders the biblical portrait of God internally consistent. The test of congruity also addresses the issue as to whether the biblical portrait of God, including God's actions and purposes, is coherent with what one knows otherwise of the realities of the world.[6] This test will determine whether the biblical portrait of God is externally consistent.[7]

5. For discussions on the general reliability of the OT, see Walter C. Kaiser Jr., *The Old Testament Documents: Are They Reliable and Relevant?* (Downers Grove, IL: InterVarsity, 2001); K. A. Kitchen, *On the Reliability of the Old Testament*, rev. ed. (Grand Rapids: Eerdmans, 2003); cf. William G. Dever, *What Did the Biblical Writers Know and When Did They Know It? What Archaeology Can Tell Us about the Reality of Ancient Israel* (Grand Rapids: Eerdmans, 2001). And for discussions on the reliability of the NT, see F. F. Bruce, *The Defense of the Gospel in the New Testament*, rev. ed. (Grand Rapids: Eerdmans, 1977); idem, *The New Testament Documents: Are They Reliable?* 6th ed. (Downers Grove, IL: InterVarsity, 2003); Paul Barnett, *Is the New Testament Reliable?* 2nd ed. (Downers Grove, IL: InterVarsity, 2004). For the historicity of the NT's presentation of the Jesus-history, compare N. T. Wright, *Jesus and the Victory of God* (Minneapolis: Fortress, 1996); John Dominic Crossan, *The Historical Jesus: The Life of a Mediterranean Jewish Peasant* (San Francisco: HarperSanFrancisco, 1991). For an excellent treatment of historicity for the resurrection, arguably the most significant event in biblical salvation history, see Richard R. Niebuhr, *Resurrection and Historical Reason: A Study of Theological Method* (New York: Scribner, 1957); cf. Marcus J. Borg and N. T. Wright, *The Meaning of Jesus: Two Visions* (San Francisco: HarperSanFrancisco, 1999).

6. The process of relating the biblical portrait to what one knows of the world's realities may bring into question the legitimacy of one's putative knowledge. In other words, it may cause one to recognize that what one thought one knew of the realities of the world may turn out to be only opinions that deserve to be challenged and perhaps overturned.

7. These questions pertain to the area of *Christian apologetics*. For a list of works on apologetics and a number of excellent articles, see Norman L. Geisler, ed., *Baker Encyclopedia of Christian Apologetics* (Grand Rapids: Baker Academic, 1999); W. C. Campbell-Jack, Gavin

The experiential test probes whether the biblical portrait of God's relationship to the world, and especially to his human creation, is a more compelling explanation of human experience of the world and life within the world than alternative interpretations offer. Existentialists and postmodernists sometimes assert that experience is the ultimate authority for persons, and especially persons in the contemporary world. But in fact, rather than experience itself, one's *interpretation* of experience must function as one's authority. For persons do not have direct cognition of their experience; their experience is always mediated to their consciousness through interpretive grids. The Bible presents a "strange new world," as Karl Barth describes it,[8] and this strange new world is actually the Bible's alternative interpretation of one's experience of the world and life within the world. In our judgment, the Bible presents this alternative interpretation as finally differing in significant ways from all other construals of human experience that have been offered in the history of the world.[9] The Bible, then, confronts persons with an ultimately different vision of reality and invites them to consider whether, at the end of the day, and with a genuine openness to new possibilities, this different vision turns out to be more convincing than the competing interpretations of human experience.[10]

Community participation has much to do with the shaping of persons' experiential interpretive grids; so a person raised in a Christian community will more likely find the Bible's construal of reality convincing than, say, an individual raised in a Muslim community. However, although community influence is powerful, it is not absolute. At any rate, perhaps part of persons' judgment regarding the validity of the biblical interpretation of reality ought to involve the authenticity that they experience in communities that attempt to be formed by the biblical vision over against the quality of other human communities, including religious ones.[11]

All serious students of the Bible—whether or not they are members of the community of faith and whether or not they accept the canonical authority

---

McGrath, and C. Stephen Evans, eds., *New Dictionary of Christian Apologetics* (Downers Grove, IL: InterVarsity, 2006).

8. Karl Barth, *The Word of God and the Word of Man*, trans. Douglas Horton ([Boston and Chicago?]: Pilgrim, 1928), 28–50.

9. Obviously the biblical *kerygma* and general human ways of thinking and understanding have some continuity between them, which involves the *preunderstanding* (discussed in chap. 2) that is necessary for persons to grasp even the basic message of the Bible. But we believe that the Bible presents its own perspective as one that in profound ways finally challenges generally accepted human ideologies and values.

10. For an excellent discussion of this experiential test, see Wright, *New Testament and the People of God*, 31–80. See also Richard B. Hays, *The Moral Vision of the New Testament: Community, Cross, New Creation* (San Francisco: Harper, 1996), 210–11.

11. As one applies this *community test*, however, one must realize that no community can perfectly embody the reality of the biblical message, no matter how committed that community is to such formation. See Dietrich Bonhoeffer, *Life Together* (San Francisco: Harper & Row, 1954).

of the Bible over their lives—have an obligation to assess the reliability of the Bible's testimonies and claims. The Bible itself invites such assessment, and intellectual honesty requires it. Of course, the degree to which this assessment is done and the ways in which it is pursued will vary from person to person. For example, professionals such as pastors will normally engage in a level of critical reflection that may not be necessary for typical laypersons. Likewise, some readers will be more troubled by doubts regarding the reliability of some of the Bible's claims than will be the case with certain other readers; the former will obviously be inclined to pursue these matters more vigorously. Then, too, some students will be confronted with questions raised by friends or acquaintances and find themselves in the position of needing to equip themselves to offer guidance or explanation.

The general biblical evaluation that students of the Bible are obliged to pursue may have certain stages. First, students should precisely identify the meaning and nature of the statement or testimony set forth within the Bible. One would be manifestly unfair in judging the Bible as deficient or unreliable on the basis of claims that the Bible does not actually make or positions it does not really adopt. This consideration points to the importance of sequence and especially to the principle that interpretation must precede evaluation.

Second, students should relate biblical statements or claims to the Bible's overall purpose. Scholars rightly recognize that any kind of judicial criticism must take into account the purpose for the writing.[12] For example, judging the reliability of a mathematics textbook on the basis of incidental psychological or sociological statements would be unfair. Not every statement made in the Bible may be equally significant in relationship to its purpose; therefore students should consider the relative significance of the various statements in the Bible for the fulfillment of the Bible's purpose and thus for the reliability and authority of the Bible. Granted, in principle, the Bible may present each of its statements as equally significant for the communication and validity of its message, but possibly the story of the floating axe head in 2 Kings 6:1–7, for example, does not operate on the same level within the Bible's theological structure as does the bodily resurrection of Jesus. Our purpose is not to indicate which of these alternatives is preferable; but we do insist that students have an obligation to decide, on the basis of their own inductive study of the Bible, whether the theological structure within the Bible renders certain claims more central to the Bible's purpose and hence more significant for the issue of the Bible's dependability than others. We further believe that students have an obligation to consider the consequences of that answer for their assessment of the Bible's reliability.

Third, students should acquaint themselves with all appropriate evidence for and against the Bible's claims, and they should fairly and reasonably weigh the

12. E.g., Mortimer Adler, *How to Read a Book*, rev. ed. (New York: Simon & Schuster, 1972), 137–67. See Traina, *Methodical Bible Study*, 210.

evidence, as much as possible setting aside unfounded assumptions.[13] Students may wish to keep in mind a few key principles when weighing the evidence.

1. Inductive reasoning does not allow for absolute certainty but for *degrees of probability* (see chap. 1). One must not insist, therefore, that evidence for the reliability of biblical statements or claims must render those statements absolutely certain. Such a standard is unrealistic. They must only be judged to be more probable or less probable.

2. Inductive reasoning always allows for the *possibility that additional evidence exists* that might be presently unavailable to us or may have been lost (see chap. 1). The appeal that if one only had more evidence, the Bible would be proved true would be unfair, but the recognition of the limits of evidence should cause one to be cautious in judging biblical statements or claims to be unreliable.

3. In the process of evaluation, one should *abstain from snap judgments*. One's appraisal should be characterized by deliberate decisions and a suspension of judgment whenever necessary. One should be more ready to doubt the value of one's own judgment than the value of the Scriptures. One can find significant historical reason to suspect that certain parts of the Bible have more reliability than sometimes meets the eye when one remembers that the Scriptures have undergone centuries of derogatory criticism. And they have not survived without sufficient cause. Their canonical status, for example, implies their worth to several generations of those within the community of faith in its beginnings and says something regarding their experiential value. The safest policy in appraising certain statements, then, is to be slow in judging them to be worthless.[14]

Specific Evaluation

Assuming that one's answer to the question of the general validity and worth of the Scriptures-as-a-whole is in the affirmative, one is confronted with the question of specific evaluation. Specific evaluation involves assessing the worth or value of individual biblical passages for their appropriation to

13. A practical suggestion for identifying evidence and arguments for and against biblical statements or claims is to begin by locating discussions by evangelicals or within books published by mainstream evangelical presses, such as Zondervan, InterVarsity, Baker Academic, and to some extent Eerdmans and Hendrickson. (Complete title lists for each of these publishing houses are available on their respective websites.) These discussions will typically not only present evidence and arguments for the reliability of the Bible or biblical statements and claims but will also cite scholars who argue for unreliability. (As a general rule, evangelical scholars tend to cite those who hold opposing points of view with greater regularity than do nonevangelical scholars.) Students should take these citations seriously and read for themselves the opposing points of view as presented by the scholars who hold them.

14. For the issue of apparent discrepancies in the Bible, see the discussion on substantial versus accidental and real versus apparent discrepancies in Traina, *Methodical Bible Study*, 212–13.

particular situations facing persons today. As such, it has two aspects: (1) *bibli-cal analysis*, which is the assessment of biblical passages for their continuing value for appropriation; and (2) *situational analysis*, which is the assessment of contemporary situations in order to determine the precise nature of a given situation to ascertain how, if at all, the teaching of a biblical passage relates to that situation.

BIBLICAL ANALYSIS

Biblical analysis is the process of assessing biblical statements or teach-ings in order to determine the legitimacy, scope, force, and degree of conces-sion of those statements or teachings for contemporary appropriation. Most scholars limit their discussions of specific biblical evaluation to matters of *legitimacy*. That is, they ask only whether the teaching of a specific biblical passage can legitimately be taken up and directly appropriated to situations in other times and places, or whether the teaching of the passage is so tied to its original historical situation that applying it directly in other times and places is no longer legitimate. While the question of legitimacy for appropriation is the most foundational issue in biblical analysis, it is by no means the only pertinent issue.

Once one determines that the teaching of a passage transcends its original historical situation so that one can legitimately appropriate it in other times and places, one must also determine the *scope* of its applicability. This in-volves asking whether the teaching of this passage applies to all persons in the world or only to certain persons, say, to those in the community of faith, or even more specifically only to leaders in the community of faith (e.g., 1 Tim. 3:1–13; Titus 2:1–10).

One must also determine the *force* of applicability: Some demands are absolutely required, so that one's acceptability to God is directly affected by compliance or noncompliance (e.g., Deut. 5:17; Mark 1:15). Some demands are highly recommended. They are part of the divine purpose but do not rise to the level that characterizes demands absolutely required (e.g., Luke 10:20; 2 Thess. 3:1). Others are only tactical suggestions. They constitute advice that may be helpful (e.g., Prov. 25:15–17; 2 Thess. 3:14).

Also one must determine the *degree of concession*, ascertaining whether a given biblical teaching or statement is an ideal accompanied by the concession that no one, or at least very few, can be expected to realize it;[15] or deciding

---

15. Note the disagreement over whether Jesus intended that his statements in the Sermon on the Mount are to be taken as ideals that no one can actually be expected to achieve or as require-ments that demand fulfillment. Reinhold Niebuhr takes Jesus's commands not to resist evil and to refuse to lend to one who desires to borrow (Matt. 5:39, 42) as "impossible possibilities." He insists that because of the sinfulness of humans and because humans necessarily function in an immoral society, the absolute love ethic of Jesus cannot be realized. Rather, one should make an attempt to approximate it by achieving justice. Thus the love ethic, though beyond one's

whether a biblical teaching or statement reflects a concession to frailty. In the case of concession to frailty, the divine will ideally involves a performance that surpasses what is actually described in the passage (e.g., 2 Kings 5:15–19).[16]

Twofold Nature of the Bible

Specific evaluation clearly belongs to an inductive approach to Bible study because the necessity for evaluation stems from the nature of the Bible itself. In general, one might say that the Bible has a twofold nature and, correspondingly, a twofold significance.

First, the Bible has certain *past-historical meanings*. All who read the Bible sense that they are hearing an author from the past. The text confronts them, then, as a communicative act that arises from the past and invites them to ask, What did the writer intend to say to those whom the text presents as the audience? The answering of this question falls under the domain of interpretation.[17]

Second, the Bible has certain *present-historical meanings*. All who read the Bible have the sense not only of the presence of an author but also of being addressed by the author. Modern readers may recognize that they are clearly

---

grasp, serves as a goal toward which one strives and a norm by which one judges all conduct (see Reinhold Niebuhr, *Interpretation of Christian Ethics* [1935; repr. with new preface, Cleveland: World, 1956]; idem, *Moral Man and Immoral Society* [New York: Scribner's Sons, 1932]). John Howard Yoder, in contrast, insists that these commands can and should be obeyed and that they pertain not only to individual ethics but to social ethics as well (*The Politics of Jesus* [Grand Rapids: Eerdmans, 1972], 12–13).

16. See William J. Webb, *Slaves, Women and Homosexuals: Exploring the Hermeneutics of Cultural Analysis* (Downers Grove, IL: InterVarsity, 2001), 58–66.

17. In past years the claim that the Bible is historical literature and should be interpreted as such would have hardly required substantiation. But in light of certain contemporary hermeneutical attempts to deny the significance of the past-historical reality of the biblical text, we believe we should mention briefly that this literature is profoundly historical in terms of its origins and its content. Its character as literature implies that it has historical origins; for all literature arose in the past and was addressed to others in the past. The meaning of texts at times may transcend their historical origins, but a realistic and holistic exegesis of these texts will attempt to tether any legitimate interpretation to the original circumstances of production, to the extent that one can identify them. The Bible is also historical in terms of its content: it witnesses to what it purports to be—God's acts in history. This historical testimony does not pertain only to the narrative portions of the Bible; for even biblical material that belongs to genres other than narrative, such as the Epistles, has a historical narrative substructure in that it assumes and indeed grows out of the salvation-historical meganarrative found in the Bible-as-a-whole. The Epistles have a double narrative substructure: the salvation-historical meganarrative and the implicit, and sometimes explicit, narrative of the history of the relationship between epistolary author and epistolary audience. In some epistles the salvation-historical meganarrative is the more prominent, while in other epistles the author-audience narrative is emphasized. See Ben Witherington III, *Paul's Narrative Thought World: The Tapestry of Tragedy and Triumph* (Louisville: Westminster John Knox, 1994); Marion L. Soards, "The Christology of the Pauline Epistles," in *Who Do You Say That I Am? Essays on Christology*, ed. Mark Allan Powell and David R. Bauer (Louisville: Westminster John Knox, 1999), 88–109.

different from the original intended audience inferred from the text (the implied reader); nevertheless, in some fashion modern readers are likewise addressed by the implied author of the text, precisely as a voice from the historical past. This sense of being addressed invites readers to ask, How does this text speak to me or to us in the present condition and circumstances? What value might this passage or book have for me or for others in my community or in our contemporary existence? The answering of these questions falls under the domain of evaluation and appropriation. The reality of present-historical meaning makes appropriation possible and obligatory. The fact that this present-historical meaning comes through past-historical communication makes evaluation necessary.[18]

Interpretation precedes evaluation. The recognition of this twofold nature of the Bible (past-/present-historical meanings) leads to certain broad implications. The first implication is that, as a general rule, interpretation should precede evaluation and the appropriation that stems from it. This principle we have mentioned before, but it bears repeating because in many quarters today it is challenged in both theory and practice. Within local church settings, this requirement regarding sequence is frequently challenged in practice. During Bible studies or discussions of biblical passages, one often hears participants casually declare, "This is what this passage is saying to me," and then talk about how the passage speaks to contemporary issues or problems in their lives. They assume that the ways in which they think the passage applies to them are coterminous with the meaning of the passage itself. In such a case, evaluation and appropriation precede and determine interpretation. One should be careful, however, not to be overly critical of laypersons who function this way, for they implicitly acknowledge the important truth that the study of the Bible is ultimately concerned with contemporary appropriation. They are right to emphasize contemporary appropriation, but the way they try to arrive at it may be unhelpful, ineffective, and indeed invalid.

This requirement of sequence is challenged also by certain persons in the biblical guild who on philosophical grounds deny the reality of stable meaning within texts and who instead insist that meaning resides entirely within the reader and that all interpretations are actually personal applications that readers project back into the text.[19] According to these scholars, appropriation *is* interpretation; any sense that one is engaging in biblical evaluation of

18. The Bible itself bears witness to the continuing relevance of its message. It has been pointed out by many scholars, most notably von Rad, *Old Testament Theology*, that the OT is largely a result of an ongoing process of applying earlier biblical materials to contemporary situations. Moreover, the Bible often explicitly mentions that certain of its statements have continuing relevance into the future. See Klein, Blomberg, and Hubbard, *Introduction to Biblical Interpretation*, 478.

19. See, e.g., Norman Holland, *The Dynamics of Literary Response* (New York: Norton, 1968); idem, *Five Readers Reading* (New Haven: Yale University Press, 1975).

the past-historical meaning of texts is an illusion. One finds this perspective in the more radical forms of reader-response criticism (see appendix B). The perspective stems ultimately from existentialism, which is the view that all knowledge is finally subjective: it exists within the subjective consciousness of the individual. This position has some truth. As we mentioned earlier in the discussion on the transjective character of biblical study (see chap. 2), readers' interpretation involves subjective as well as objective dimensions, and their applicatory concerns will often play a role in their construal of passages. But this position is finally a half-truth, for it ignores the reality that texts do have an existence outside of readers and that texts confront readers with the texts' own historical sociolinguistic constructs, which have the potential to direct readers' interpretations.

This reversal of the evaluation-interpretation sequence occurs whenever one uses a possible application as the basis for evaluating the legitimacy of an interpretation or as the basis for deciding between interpretations. Several years ago one of us participated in a seminar in which the speaker offered an interpretation of a biblical passage that clearly had nothing to do with the meaning of the passage as derived from the kinds of interpretive evidence that we discussed in part 3. When asked about the basis of his interpretation, the presenter replied that he based his interpretation upon "ethical" considerations. By this response he meant that he considered the applicatory consequences of a number of possible interpretations and chose the interpretation that would result in a contemporary application that was the most ethical, that is, the one that accorded best with his understanding of social justice.[20]

Evangelicals are certainly capable of this evaluation-interpretation reversal. We are aware of a presentation by an evangelical scholar in another discipline who declared that none of the interpretations of Jesus's threefold question to Peter in John 21 ("Do you love me more than these?") "helped" him; thus this scholar opted for an interpretation quite unique to himself, which he found to be of value to him in his contemporary life.

As we previously mentioned, the notion that interpretation should precede evaluation is a *general* principle; in actual practice one cannot rigidly separate interpretation from evaluation and appropriation. Applicatory potential is often the basis for pursuing the interpretation of passages in the first place, and readers cannot simply cast it out of their consciousness as they wrestle with the meaning of passages. Thus some elements of their application may find their way into the interpretive process. Likewise, the process of biblical

20. Yet his application might not have been the most ethical from the point of view of the Bible. He assumed either that his ethical perspective was the biblical one or that his ethical perspective was absolute and trumped the ethical authority of the Bible. At any rate, he adopted a hermeneutic that may well have prevented the ethical message of the particular passage he was interpreting from being heard.

evaluation and appropriation will often illumine aspects of the text's meaning that readers may have missed in the interpretation phase.

We cannot emphasize enough that the inductive process is ongoing and *spiracular*;[21] earlier stages in the process anticipate later ones, and later stages often require the student to return to the methodological concerns of earlier stages. The principle that interpretation precedes evaluation and appropriation refers to emphasis. One targets the process of ascertaining the passage's meaning in the interpretation stage, and one targets the process of assessing the potential of the passage's meaning for contemporary appropriation in the evaluation stage. Indeed, in a sense, one cannot fully understand the meaning of a passage until in life one has appropriated the passage's message. Richard Hays declares: "*Right reading of the New Testament occurs only where the Word is embodied.* We learn what the text means only if we submit ourselves to its power in such a way that we are changed by it."[22] Yet the careful interpretation of a passage may judge the applicatory concerns with which one approaches a passage and alert one that these concerns are invalid or unimportant.[23]

Interpretation proceeds toward evaluation. The second implication from the twofold nature of the Bible (past-/present-historical meanings) is that one must not stop at interpretation but must acknowledge that the work of evaluation and appropriation must be done. The nature of the Bible will not allow readers to consider interpretation as an end in itself. The second dimension of the twofold nature of the Bible, its present-historical aspect, must be pursued and given due weight.

This concern that interpretation must lead to evaluation and appropriation relates to what we may label the abortive character of commentaries; for most modern commentaries address exclusively the past-historical meaning of passages and say nothing about possible present-historical meanings.[24] Of course, in principle the fact that a given commentary focuses upon only certain aspects of the meaning of passages is not objectionable; writers, including commentators, have a right to limit their scope of inquiry. Moreover, no single commentary could attempt to give the full range of possible contemporary applications; yet it has become a part of the culture of commentary writing to limit discussion to the past-historical meaning, thus giving the impression that study of the text culminates not in evaluation and appropriation but in

21. See the introduction to this book.

22. Hays, *Moral Vision of the New Testament*, 305, emphasis original.

23. Thomas W. Ogletree, *The Use of the Bible in Christian Ethics* (Louisville: Westminster John Knox, 2003), 3–4.

24. Whereas most homiletic commentaries do not sufficiently attend to past-historical meaning as the basis for present-historical appropriation, so most exegetical commentaries fail to address the present-historical aspect of the text. See "Interpretation by Others" in chap. 14 regarding the use of homiletic commentaries for interpretive evidence.

interpretation. In fact, commentators could discuss certain key issues in the evaluation of passages and offer selective suggestions for contemporary appropriation without giving the impression that they have exhaustively considered the full range of applicatory possibilities.[25]

A tension exists between past-historical and present-historical meaning. The third implication that arises from the twofold nature of the Bible is that one must acknowledge a tension between the situation-embedded character of the Bible's past-historical meaning and the continuing significance of its present-historical meaning. This tension is expressed in the Bible's presentation of revelation. The content of the Bible is multifold: it contains history, geography, science, and so forth. But all of these things are incidental and tangential to the primary concern of the Bible, which simply is the revelation of God and of God's relationship with his creation, especially his human creation, centering on his chosen people Israel and later the church. Because God and his relationship to his (especially human) creation centering on his people have a constancy throughout history, the message of the Bible is as relevant for readers at the beginning of the twenty-first century as it was for the ancient Hebrews or the first-century church. God is still the same, and humanity, at least in terms of its deepest existence, remains the same. We recognize how constant is God's relationship with his chosen people Israel in the Old Testament period and with the church now through Jesus Christ, who is the ultimate fulfillment of God's purposes for Israel and the one to whom the church is joined by faith (e.g., John 5:39; 2 Cor. 1:20; Heb. 1:1–4). This principle of the continuity of divine revelation is the basis for the ongoing significance of the present-historical meaning of the text and makes contemporary appropriation possible.

However, when we say that the central burden of the Bible is the revelation of God and of God's relationship to his (especially human) creation, we speak in only the most general terms. When one examines the way in which the Bible presents this revelation, one finds that God has revealed himself to specific human beings at specific points in history, and in specific acts and specific speech. The revelation of God in the Bible is therefore not ahistorical or abstract but historical and specific. This principle of the specificity of divine revelation characterizes the past-historical meaning of the text and makes evaluation necessary.

Theologically speaking, this historical dimension of the revelation of God in the Bible relates to the doctrine of incarnation. According to the Bible, not

25. Some commentary series do include attention to evaluation and application. The attempt to evaluate passages in light of biblical revelation as a whole is made by the Word Biblical Commentary (WBC) series in the "Explanation" sections. In addition, the series Interpretation: A Bible Commentary for Teaching and Preaching (IBC), published by Westminster John Knox, and The NIV Application Commentary, published by Zondervan, both give specific attention to evaluation and appropriation. The quality and amount of attention given to the work of evaluation and appropriation in these commentaries varies greatly.

only has the revelation of God, that is, the Word of God, been incarnated in the flesh of Jesus; it has also been incarnated in historical acts and human speech. This principle of accommodation is divine adaptation to the human-historical situation. Christians tend to believe that their religion is superior to other religions in part because of its historical and incarnational nature, but this kind of revelation carries with it challenges of its own.

First comes the *situational* challenge. History and human speech are by nature situational. At times human speech can transcend the situation in which it was spoken, but it can never be entirely divorced from the situation. When one comes to the Scriptures, one finds a kind of *continuum of transcendence*. Certain statements of Scripture directly express more fundamental teachings, those that are less tied to the original situation into which they were spoken, than do others (see fig. 28).[26]

FIGURE 28
Continuum of transcendence

Situational/circumstantially	Transcendent statements
contingent statements	directly expressing
tied to original situation	trans-situational teachings

Most biblical passages stand somewhere between the two extremes on the continuum of transcendence, often because some aspects of their teaching are essentially transcendent while others are circumstantially contingent. Moreover, even the statements that belong on the transcendent end of the continuum are connected to some extent to the situation in which they were originally articulated. No statement can be entirely divorced from its original historical setting.[27]

An example of a statement that seems to directly express more fundamental teachings and to have only loose ties to the original situation is Galatians 6:10: "Whenever we have opportunity, let us work for the good of all, and especially for those of the family of faith." An example of a statement that seems to be closely tied to the original situation is 1 Timothy 5:23: "No lon-

26. The judgment regarding where a given passage falls on the continuum of transcendence—to what degree it expresses directly more fundamental teachings and is thus essentially transcendent, or to what degree it expresses teachings that are tied to the original situation and is thus circumstantially contingent—is made on the basis of the literary context and the entire biblical canon, as well as other types of evidence, which will be discussed below.

27. See Hays, *Moral Vision of the New Testament*, 299–300, who correctly notes that "every jot and tittle of the New Testament is culturally conditioned." His resistance to the separation of "timeless truth" from teachings that are "culturally conditioned," however, is overstated and turns especially on his objection to the notion of timelessness. We prefer to speak of *circumstantially contingent* versus *essentially transcendent*, rather than *culturally conditioned* versus *timeless*. See also David K. Clark's critique of "principlizing" as the practice of extracting timeless principles (*To Know and Love God: Method for Theology* [Wheaton, IL: Crossway, 2003], 91–98).

ger drink only water, but take a little wine for the sake of your stomach and your frequent ailments." Here the passage itself connects this instruction to the physical condition that Timothy was experiencing at the particular time, and no other passage in the biblical canon forbids the exclusive use of water or demands the consumption of wine. Yet situation-bound statements do not necessarily stand outside the possibility of contemporary appropriation, since they are often directly applicable today to essentially the same situations or parallel ones.[28]

Obviously readers could not take over and directly apply some passages no matter how much they might try to do so. Thus Deuteronomy 23:7 ("You shall not abhor any of the Edomites, for they are your kin") gives instruction regarding relationships to a people who no longer exist. The point is clear: One cannot simply assume that the surface meaning of any statement found in the Scriptures can be directly appropriated in today's contemporary setting.

At the same time, such a conclusion does not mean that passages one judges to be circumstantially contingent have no applicatory potential. Although usually one cannot legitimately appropriate the surface meaning of passages that are circumstantially contingent, one often finds that even these passages have underlying teachings that one can reasonably and legitimately appropriate. In such cases, one may not be able to appropriate the answers to the definitive question from one's interpretation, for the answers to the definitive questions tend to deal with the surface meaning of the text. But one may appropriate one's answers to the rational and implicational questions. The rational question probes the underlying reasons, or rationale, for the statement, and quite often at least some of these reasons that stand behind a circumstantially contingent statement are transcendent.[29] Answering the implicational question divulges the presuppositions and logical outgrowths of biblical passages. Generally the implications of a circumstantially contingent statement transcend the original situation. The identification of these underlying teachings in circumstantially contingent passages is what William J. Webb calls moving up the "ladder of abstraction."[30]

28. Klein, Blomberg, and Hubbard, *Introduction to Biblical Interpretation*, 491–93.

29. Webb, *Slaves, Women and Homosexuals*, 210, describes an analysis that identifies both the "ultimate" basis, or reason, which would be transcendent; and the "pragmatic" basis for a biblical statement, which would be situation-bound. The answer to the rational question in the interpretive process could lead to identifying both ultimate reasons/bases and pragmatic reasons/ bases. In such a case, the ultimate reasons/bases would be transcendent, while the pragmatic reasons/bases would be situation-bound. See also Klein, Blomberg, and Hubbard, *Introduction to Biblical Interpretation*, 487–88, 491–92; Charles H. Cosgrove, *Appealing to Scripture in Moral Debate: Five Hermeneutical Rules* (Grand Rapids: Eerdmans, 2002), 12–50.

30. Webb, *Slaves, Women and Homosexuals*, 54, 209–11. The language of "abstraction" suggests a *general* principle that lies behind the situation-bound statement; however, the issue is not general versus specific but circumstantially contingent versus transcendent. We therefore believe that the process is better described in terms of moving behind the surface meaning, or

A second challenge that arises from the historical and incarnational character of biblical revelation is the *progress of revelation*. The Bible-as-a-whole, particularly as it culminates in the New Testament, clearly indicates a progressive movement from the more primitive and incomplete revelation in the earlier periods toward the more complete revelation in the later periods, especially in Christ and his apostles. The Bible is not a flat book but a dynamic account of the revelation of God throughout a long history.

The progress of revelation involves two elements. For one, a development of revelation exists within the Old Testament-as-a-whole. Although this development is certainly historical, involving the constant readaptation of earlier biblical traditions by later Old Testament writers, one cannot assume the ability to trace this revelatory development in the Old Testament simply by tracking the theological and ethical ideas in the successive historical stages of the production of the Old Testament.[31] The major problem here is that even scholars cannot identify with assurance the specific historical development of traditions in the Old Testament. Scholars represent a wide divergence of thought about the dating of many Old Testament books. The result is that in several cases one cannot speak confidently about where a given Old Testament witness falls within the historical sequence.[32] Further, some Old Testament books give evidence of a more or less extended history of the development of traditions within them, so that vestiges of earlier theological and ethical ideas may stand alongside later ones in the same book.[33] Moreover, the dynamics of the entire canon, especially in its culmination in the New Testament, indicate that the progress of revelation in the Old Testament is not ultimately a matter

---

the definitive level, of situation-bound statements to underlying teachings at the rational and implicational levels. Such a process would allow the concretization of the underlying teaching to the situation in the situation-bound passage to provide specificity to the underlying teaching, even though the concretization itself would not be taken up and directly applied because of its situation-bound character. In all cases the goal should be to determine, as precisely as possible, the specific meaning of the transcendent teaching. See Klein, Blomberg, and Hubbard, *Introduction to Biblical Interpretation*, 500.

31. John Barton, *Understanding Old Testament Ethics* (Louisville: Westminster John Knox, 2003), 19–31.

32. To take just one example: the dating of the book of Joel has ranged from around 800 BC to around 300 BC. See Hans Walter Wolff, *Joel and Amos*, Hermeneia (Philadelphia: Fortress, 1977), 3–5.

33. This may be the case especially with the Pentateuch and the Deuteronomic history (Joshua–2 Kings) but might pertain also to some prophetic books, e.g., Hosea. See the discussions of these issues in the major OT introductions; a list of these introductions, with annotations, may be found in Bauer, *Annotated Guide to Biblical Resources*, 69–72. See also Blenkinsopp, *Pentateuch*; Sandra L. Richter, "Deuteronomic History," in *Dictionary of the Old Testament Historical Books*, ed. Bill T. Arnold and H. G. M. Williamson (Downers Grove, IL: InterVarsity, 2005), 219–30; Francis I. Andersen and David Noel Freedman, *Hosea*, AB (Garden City, NY: Doubleday, 1980); cf. A. A. Macintosh, *A Critical and Exegetical Commentary on Hosea*, ICC (Edinburgh: T&T Clark, 1997).

of historical sequence but of theological and ethical proximity to God's final revelation in Jesus Christ and the New Testament.

Thus most Christians have good reason to think that the revelation of God is less complete or developed in the accounts of the wars of extermination in Joshua, for example, than in the prophecies of God's gracious forgiveness of Judah in the book of Jeremiah. That assessment emerges finally not on the basis of historical sequence but out of an acknowledgment that the revelation of God's superabounding forgiveness in Jeremiah appears to be closer to the revelation of God in Jesus Christ than is the case with the wars of extermination in which God destroyed not only the leaders of the Canaanites but also voiceless women and children.[34]

All the same, to claim that some passages may contain relatively incomplete or imperfect revelation is not to suggest that these passages have no genuine revelatory significance. To say that the revelation of God is not as complete in the wars of extermination as in certain other portions of the Old Testament, such as the book of Jeremiah, is not to say that the wars of extermination contain no true revelation of God. The revelation of God may be less developed in the wars of extermination but is nevertheless real revelation; indeed, some aspects of God's character and purpose may be presented uniquely through the wars of extermination, so that one's understanding of God would be deficient if these accounts were absent from the canon. Still, such passages do not offer the final word regarding God's character and purpose, and any attempt to appropriate them must include a serious process of evaluation that identifies the situation-bound aspects that would be illegitimate for persons today, in light of the principle of the progress of revelation.

Yet the progress of revelation does not pertain only to development within the Old Testament. The second element involved in the progress of revelation is the relationship between the Old and New Testaments. This relationship has been a difficult problem since the beginning of Christianity. It is perhaps accurate to say that the overarching theological problem in the writings of the New Testament is the relationship between the covenants. One might even go so far as to say that this focus remains the fundamental issue in biblical theology and ethics and that almost every theological or ethical issue is related more or less directly to it. One's understanding of the relationship between the Testaments will make a difference in terms of one's evaluation and appropriation of biblical statements.

Throughout its history the church has clearly struggled with this issue of the relationship between the Testaments; consequently, we would be foolish

---

34. One should remember that although, in terms of historical progression, the exodus from Egypt took place before the wars of extermination, both the OT-as-a-whole and the NT consider the exodus to be a relatively more complete revelation of God than the wars of extermination. Yet one must grant that some of the same features are present in both, including the destruction of the (innocent) young; but they also have significant differences.

to insist that our view be adopted as the correct one. Every student has the responsibility to examine the biblical evidence inductively and on that basis to determine what seems to be the most plausible understanding of this relationship. It may be appropriate, however, for us to indicate one major possibility and to describe, in general terms, how that understanding of the relationship between the Testaments bears upon biblical evaluation.

We find that an examination of the Scriptures-as-a-whole indicates that the Old Testament relates to the New Testament in terms of preparation and fulfillment. The Old Testament prepares for the New Testament, and the New Testament fulfills the Old. Specifically, the two Testaments have a dialectical relationship between them because the notion of preparation-fulfillment involves *essential continuity* but with *some discontinuity*. Essential continuity exists because the concept of fulfillment implies a profound and fundamental connection with what preceded the fulfillment. But some discontinuity exists since the concept of fulfillment implies also that something has been added; it is not simply a continuation of what came before. We find an element of culminative, or climactic, disjuncture. In practice, altogether the New Testament sometimes confirms (e.g., 1 Pet. 1:16; James 4:6; Acts 17:24–25), sometimes corrects (e.g., Heb. 4:8; Mark 10:4–5; Gal. 5:6), sometimes expands the meaning of (e.g., Matt. 2:15; 5:21–30; Acts 2:25–28), and sometimes abrogates statements in the Old Testament (e.g., Matt. 5:38–45; Mark 7:14–23; Acts 10:1–48). The practical result is that one must allow the New Testament to determine what continues to be of value for direct appropriation in the Old Testament.[35]

The New Testament writers consistently affirm, both explicitly and implicitly, that the Old Testament is their authoritative Scripture. Indeed, they seem to consider that discontinuities between Old Testament and New Testament teaching actually arise out of a deeper and more profound understanding of the Old Testament revelation of God, and that this more profound understanding is made possible by the eschatological fulfillment to which the New Testament bears witness.

Moreover, the New Testament writers' affirmation of the continuing authority of the Old Testament Scriptures suggests both that they generally assume the ongoing validity of Old Testament teaching and that they wish their audience to accept the teaching of the Old Testament as authoritative except in the instances

35. This understanding of the relationship between the Testaments is a general description of the *covenantal* view. The two major competing views are dispensationalism, which emphasizes discontinuity between the period, or dispensation, of the OT and that of the NT; and theonomism, which insists on practically no discontinuity at all between the Testaments. For helpful presentations of these views, see Daniel P. Fuller, *Gospel and Law: Contrast or Continuum? The Hermeneutics of Dispensationalism and Covenant Theology* (Grand Rapids: Eerdmans, 1980); Greg L. Bahnsen, Walter C. Kaiser Jr., Douglas J. Moo, Wayne G. Strickland, and Willem A. VanGemeren, *Five Views on Law and Gospel* (Grand Rapids: Zondervan, 1996); John S. Feinberg, ed., *Continuity and Discontinuity: Perspectives on the Relationship between the Old and New Testaments* (Westchester, IL: Crossway, 1988).

in which they indicate a modification to the teaching of the Old Testament. In the absence of such indicators, then, readers of the New Testament should typically assume the continuing relevance of Old Testament teaching.

An example of this assumption of continuing relevance would be creation theology. With the exception of claims about Christ's role in creation and the new creation, the New Testament says relatively little about creation, compared to the much fuller treatment creation theology receives in the Old Testament. In the view of some scholars,[36] Protestants especially have at times focused so exclusively upon the New Testament that they have practically neglected whole areas of biblical theology and ethics that pertain to creation. Such neglect may in part lie behind the charge that Christians have all too often been neglectful of their stewardship of the environment.

NATURE OF BIBLICAL ETHICS

Thus far we have seen that the necessity for evaluative biblical analysis arises from the twofold nature of the Bible: it contains both past-historical meanings of passages and their present-historical significance, which emerges from the specific past-historical meaning. But the necessity for evaluative biblical analysis stems also from the nature of biblical ethics, which is occasional rather than systematic. The Bible contains neither a systematic theology nor a systematic code of ethics. Both the theological assertions and the ethical instructions of the Bible were occasioned by the situational demands that the biblical writers felt needed to be addressed. Thus in terms of ethics, the Bible is not a lawbook but a collection of occasional instructions. Therefore students must evaluate each biblical statement in terms of its role within the dynamic program of the presentation of good and bad, right and wrong, true and untrue in the Bible-as-a-whole.

To speak of a dynamic program of ethics within the Bible is to suggest the existence of a profound and implicit structure to the ethics of the Bible. Indeed, some sense of structure and of overarching dynamic connectedness between biblical ethical statements is necessary in order to talk at all about biblical ethics in the large. An inductive examination of the ethics of the Bible may reveal no overall structure to biblical ethics and that the various ethical instructions throughout the Scriptures involve essentially isolated, unrelated, and even contradictory moral counsel. But students are obliged to explore whether in fact the Bible has within it a structure of ethics, and if so, to identify the precise nature of this dynamic interconnectedness.

Almost all scholars who discuss biblical ethics either explicitly or implicitly adopt a structure of ethics that serves as the basis for their discussions.[37] Yet

36. E.g., Elizabeth Achtemeier, *Nature, God, and Pulpit* (Grand Rapids: Eerdmans, 1992).

37. For the necessity of some sort of overarching structure, see Birch and Rasmussen, *Bible and Ethics*, 59, 96, 180, who speak in terms of a "moral vision" that is concretized in individual

in spite of the fact that the various presentations of the structure of biblical ethics tend to have certain recurring emphases, at present the precise shape of this structure has no consensus. Therefore we would be highly presumptuous to insist that our understanding of this ethical structure is the only correct and proper one. Nevertheless, it may be helpful to indicate one possible way of understanding the overarching shape of biblical ethics and in the process to note certain features that scholars repeatedly mention in their discussion of biblical ethics in the large. The framework of biblical ethics depicted in figure 29 is based on our interpretation of numerous biblical passages and our reading of the Bible-as-a-whole. As such it is admittedly tentative, and we do not mean to present it as in any way definitive or final. We hope that it will at least be suggestive and illuminating. We will make no attempt to engage in the exhaustive task of supporting this framework or its major components by argument or extensive scriptural citation. Students who are familiar with the content of the Bible will be able to recall biblical evidence for this model and its major components.

As we mentioned previously, the purpose of the Bible may be to bear witness to the revelation of God and of God's relationship with his, especially human, creation; therefore the primary concern of the Bible is not ethical but theological, so ethics derives from the primary theological focus of the Bible. As such, any adequate understanding of the ethical structure of the Bible must emerge from the Bible's theological emphases.

We believe that the central theological concept in the Bible is the *lordship of God*;[38] the central affirmation is that God is actively at work to establish his lordship over the cosmos, and especially over his human creation. Therefore the center of biblical ethics, the human moral obligation, is to respond to God's lordship. This response involves the submission of selves to the dynamic and redemptive lordship of God. Every biblical instruction can perhaps be traced back to this ultimate expectation.

---

biblical passages. Hays, *Moral Vision of the New Testament*, 193–205, adopts a structure of NT ethics that involves the dynamic interplay between the focal images of community, cross, and new creation. And although W. J. Webb does not explicitly describe his understanding of the structure of biblical ethics, implicit in all that he does is the assumption of the overarching category of "redemptiveness." We believe that he might have strengthened his presentation by explicating the structure of ethics that constantly operates beneath the surface (Webb, *Slaves, Women and Homosexuals*, 30–36, 48, 50–54, 179–84, 240–42, 253–54).

38. The notion of the lordship of God is closely related to the kingdom or rule of God. But we find that lordship is preferable because it appears earlier and more comprehensively in the Bible. For the argument that the concept of the kingdom of God is central to the theological structure of the Bible, even though the phrase itself appears relatively infrequently throughout the Bible, see, e.g., John Bright, *The Kingdom of God: The Biblical Concept and Its Meaning for the Church* (Nashville: Abingdon, 1953); Herman Ridderbos, *The Coming of the Kingdom* (Philadelphia: P&R, 1962); George R. Beasley-Murray, *Jesus and the Kingdom of God* (Grand Rapids: Eerdmans, 1986).

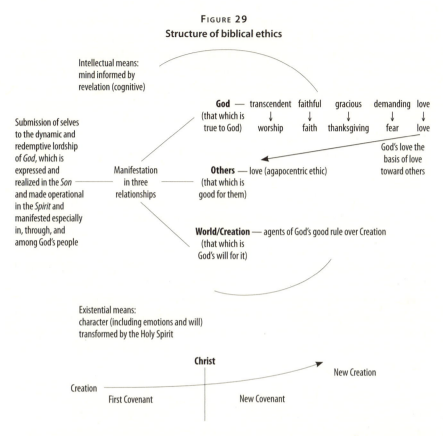

FIGURE 29
Structure of biblical ethics

The reference to the submission of *selves* is intentional. As we will mention later, we do not intend that this emphasis upon selves should diminish the vital role of community in ethics. Rather, by such an emphasis, we attempt to acknowledge the Bible's insistence that submission to the lordship of God involves a personal existential challenge to reject the claims that the self places upon persons, and especially the claim that persons have an ultimate obligation to the self (e.g., Gen. 3:1–7; Mark 8:34) rather than to God or to others (e.g., Matt. 22:15–22; Phil. 2:3–4; James 4:5–7).

Moreover, the Bible indicates that this submission of selves to the redemptive lordship of God is manifested in terms of relationships to the three major realities that confront all humans: God, others, and the world/creation.[39] Since from the biblical viewpoint God is the ultimate reality in the universe, including the universe of human lives, the primary relationship is with the Divine. According to the Bible, humans are to relate to God in terms of what is *true to God*. Because God is the transcendent creator, sustainer, and deliverer, hu-

39. See Martin Buber, *I and Thou* (New York: Scribner, 1970).

mans are to worship him. Because God is faithful or trustworthy, humans are to respond accordingly by placing their faith or confidence in God. Because God is gracious, providing good and withholding evil in ways that go far beyond what humans deserve, humans are to be grateful and offer thanks to God. Because God is demanding in his loving expectations and consequently renders judgment upon those who refuse to submit to his redemptive program, humans ought properly to fear him. And because God is love, humans can and should love him. Readers who are familiar with the biblical text will immediately recall scriptural passages that present these descriptions of God and these expectations of human response.

From the biblical viewpoint, this relationship with God is a first-order relationship that leads inexorably to a second-order relationship with others (e.g., Mark 12:28–31). Indeed, one's relationship with God inevitably expresses itself in relationship with others (e.g., Matt. 25:31–46; James 3:9; 1 John 4:16–21). According to the Bible, humans are to relate to others in terms of what is *good for them*, which is really love; for biblical love is "active well wishing," as James Moffatt describes it.[40] Thus many have argued that love is the center of biblical ethics.[41] However, a more accurate depiction says that love is the center, indeed the wellspring, of the ethics of human interpersonal relationships (Matt. 22:34–40). The Greek word the New Testament typically employs for love is *agapē*, so the model refers to ethical obligation toward others as an *agapocentric* ethic.

But the Bible attends also to humans' relationship to and responsibility toward the created order. According to the Bible, humans are to relate to creation as agents of God's good rule over creation and thus do what is *God's will for it*. Humans are, in a sense, God's vice-regents over creation (e.g., Gen. 1:26–30), called not to plunder creation but to care for it (e.g., 2:15).[42]

With regard to this model of biblical ethics, several emphases are worth noting. First, this is a *transcendent* model in that it acknowledges the initiation of God as the basis for both the possibility and obligation of ethics. Biblical ethics is, above all else, a response to what God is and what God has done

---

40. James Moffatt, *Love in the New Testament* (London: Hodder & Stoughton, 1929).

41. E.g., Anders Nygren, *Agape and Eros* (Philadelphia: Westminster, 1953), 48; Reinhold Niebuhr, *The Nature and Destiny of Man*, 2 vols. (New York: Scribner's Sons, 1941–43); Victor Paul Furnish, *The Love Command in the New Testament* (Nashville: Abingdon, 1972). Cf. Robert A. Traina, "Love," in *Baker's Dictionary of Christian Ethics*, ed. Carl F. H. Henry (Grand Rapids: Baker Books, 1973), 396–98. Hays, *Moral Vision of the New Testament*, 200–203, is quite right to critique the notion that love is the "unifying theme" of NT, or biblical, ethics. As this present model shows, love toward others hardly comprehends all biblical ethical obligations; humans have additional ethical obligations to God and to the world/creation. But from our perspective, all biblical expectations pertaining to persons' relationship with others is a manifestation of love.

42. Christopher J. H. Wright, *Old Testament Ethics for the People of God* (Downers Grove, IL: InterVarsity, 2004), 103–45.

(e.g., Exod. 20:2; 1 John 4:19). The model emphasizes transcendence also by acknowledging the role of the Son, through whom God expresses his lordship and through whom God brings his lordship to realization. God expresses his rule through the Son personally as the Son embodies God's kingdom. God also expresses his lordship through the Son instrumentally since the Son mediates the saving rule of God to others. And the model emphasizes transcendence in that it recognizes the role of the Spirit, who makes operational the lordship of God in the lives of individuals, communities, and ultimately the world.

Second, this is a *communal* model: it acknowledges that God intends to begin the process of manifesting his lordship in the world through his people, the community of faith. God called Israel, and now calls the church, to be the sphere where his lordship is particularly manifested through worship toward God, love among believers, and witness and service to the world.

Third, this is a *content-specific* model in that it allows for each of the categories herein described to be developed in terms of its presentation within particular passages throughout the Bible.[43] Students must make a vitally important decision not to treat these categories as broad abstractions whose content is provided by one's assumptions and personal predilections rather than by the data of the biblical passages, properly interpreted.

Fourth, this is a *developmental* model: it recognizes that the actions of God in establishing his redemptive lordship and the consequent ethical response on the part of humans are played out in a continuing historical process that begins with creation and culminates with the new creation. The Bible describes this progression from creation to new creation through the salvation-historical meganarrative that moves from the first covenant to the new covenant, with Jesus Christ at the center. The notion of historical progression is central, then, to one's understanding of biblical ethics. And the consideration of one's own historical situation is critical for one's deliberations regarding the appropriation of the biblical ethic.

Finally, this is a *holistic* model: it recognizes that biblical ethics include not merely behavior but also cognitive knowledge and transformed character. One can fulfill the biblical expectations only if one knows what those expectations are and what is involved in them; hence we refer to the intellectual means of a mind informed by revelation. But the intellectual means, though necessary, is not sufficient. The Bible is concerned not only with overt behavior but also with one's internal attitude and motive, in other words, with matters of character; hence we refer also to the existential means: to character, including emotions and will, transformed by the Holy Spirit.

TYPES OF EVIDENCE FOR BIBLICAL ANALYSIS

The discussion of the necessity and nature of specific evaluation has already introduced a number of principles that students should keep in mind as they

43. Hays, *Moral Vision of the New Testament*, 189–91.

engage in specific evaluation. At this point, however, focusing on the process of assessing the legitimacy, scope, degree of force, and degree of concession of biblical statements for contemporary appropriation is appropriate. An inductive approach requires that such assessment be made on the basis of the careful consideration of evidence.[44]

Four types of scriptural evidence may be relevant in evaluating a biblical statement. We described most of these while treating interpretation in part 3 above; here we wish to highlight their significance for evaluation. The examples will reveal that in many cases the line between interpretation and evaluation is difficult to draw. Often students will employ insights from the interpretation and use them for the evaluation of a passage. The examples will also demonstrate that in practice the various types of evidence have significant overlap; therefore, frequently two or more types of evidence may be used in tandem. Finally, the examples will show that evaluation pertains not only to the legitimacy of appropriating scriptural teachings in other times and places, but also to the degree of concession, the degree of force, and the scope of applicability.

Context. As in interpretation, so also in evaluation, context is generally the most significant type of evidence; for context involves authorial direction to the reader. Students should remember that context includes all evidence within the biblical book.[45]

According to Matthew 10:5–6, Jesus sent his disciples out on their missionary journey, charging them to "go nowhere among the Gentiles, and enter no town of the Samaritans, but go rather to the lost sheep of the house of Israel." In Matthew's Gospel the experience of the twelve disciples typically anticipates

44. For a thorough book-length discussion of various types of evidence, or criteria, used to determine situation-bound versus transcendent teachings within the Bible, see Webb, *Slaves, Women and Homosexuals.*

45. Three specific forms of contextual evidence may be mentioned here. One is *degree of sanction.* A greater degree of sanction, i.e., punishment, for noncompliance may suggest that the teaching is more likely transcendent, while a lesser degree of sanction, or no sanction at all, may suggest that the biblical writer is simply assuming or conceding an expectation that belongs to the broader culture at that time. The stating of significant judgmental consequences for an action may indicate a level of gravity and intentionality that tends to suggest transcendent force. A second type of specific contextual evidence is *serial comparison,* which draws on the likelihood of commensurability between the various elements mentioned in a series or list. Thus, as one is evaluating a certain statement or instruction in a given list, one might take note of other elements in that list in order to ascertain if one or more of these elements is clearly situation-bound or transcendent. Thus if other elements in the same list are clearly situation-bound, the statement or teaching being evaluated is more likely also to be situation-bound. A third specific form of contextual evidence is that of *divine comparison,* which points to the likelihood that a teaching is transcendent when instruction is based upon the character or actions of God (or Christ); see, e.g., Lev. 11:44–45; Eph. 4:32; 5:22–33. See Webb, *Slaves, Women and Homosexuals,* 172–79, 192–201, for a judicious and thorough discussion of these specific forms of contextual evidence, with helpful examples.

Part 5

Correlation

Correlation is the process of bringing together, or synthesizing, the interpretation (and appropriation) of individual passages so as to arrive at the meaning of larger units of biblical material. Correlation has two levels.

The first level of correlation is *literary*. Literary correlation is the synthesis of books that come from the same author.[1] When students are dealing with material from an author who has written more than one biblical book, as in the case of Paul, they can synthesize the meaning of individual books within the authorial body, or corpus, to arrive at the meaning of the corpus-as-a-whole. Thus students might wish to correlate the teaching of the various Pauline Epistles so as to develop an understanding of Pauline theology.[2]

The second level of correlation is *canonical*. Canonical correlation is the synthesis of canonical rather than authorial units. Students might synthesize the meaning of the various books of the Old Testament in order to develop

1. By *author* we mean the *implied author*, which as we mentioned (see chap. 4) is the author as he presents himself in the text and thus the portrait of the author that we infer from the text. Even if one agrees with many scholars that the Pastoral Epistles did not come from Paul but rather from one or more later writers representing the Pauline circle, one should recognize that Paul is the implied author of all thirteen NT Epistles that bear his name. We grant that at times distinguishing between implied authors and flesh-and-blood authors may have historical value. For this reason many critical scholars distinguish between the theology of Paul, which they derive from the so-called undisputed Pauline Epistles, and the theology of the later Pauline school, which they derive from the Pastorals.

2. One may infer a single author within collections of books, such as the Pentateuch or Deuteronomic history (i.e., Joshua–2 Kings). If so, literary correlation would pertain to the theology of these collections.

an Old Testament theology. Or they may synthesize the teachings of the Old and New Testaments so as to develop a biblical theology.[3]

At each of these levels, correlation may be either general or specific. Students engage in *general correlation* when they synthesize the entire teaching of an authorial corpus or a canonical unit. They pursue *specific correlation* when they synthesize the presentation of only one aspect or of a single topic. For example, students might undertake a general correlation of the writings of John by answering the question, What is the theology of the Johannine corpus? But they may choose to limit themselves to a specific correlation of the Johannine materials by answering the question, What is the meaning of divine judgment according to the writings of John?

---

3. One normally thinks of canonical units as pertaining to the OT, the NT, and the Bible-as-a-whole. But smaller canonical units exist within the two Testaments. For example, the Minor Prophets form a canonical unit within the OT, and the four Gospels form a canonical unit within the NT.

19

Character and Practice
of Correlation

Basis of Correlation

The possibility of correlation emerges from the consideration of both *unity* and *diversity* in the theological teachings of the Bible. If the Bible did not have diversity—difference in theological perspectives or emphases—students would have no occasion for synthesis. Conversely, if the Bible had no core of theological unity, students would have no foundation for synthesis.

Virtually all scholars grant the existence of theological diversity within the Bible. Historically, most scholars have also found a core of theological unity among the biblical witnesses. Many scholars, in fact, still affirm a profound theological unity among the biblical books.

In recent years, however, a growing number of scholars have insisted that the Bible has insufficient theological unity to make correlation possible. They argue that one may speak of the theology of Mark, or of Paul, but not of the New Testament. According to these scholars, biblical theology or even Old Testament or New Testament theology does not exist. Rather, the Bible presents only contradictory theological perspectives.[1] Many scholars who accept this viewpoint insist that readers of Scripture who think they find unity in biblical

1. For OT theologians who adopt this position, see Walter Brueggemann, *Theology of the Old Testament: Testimony, Dispute, Advocacy* (Minneapolis: Fortress, 1997); Erhard S. Gerstenberger, *Theologies in the Old Testament* (Minneapolis: Fortress, 2002). An example of a NT theologian who adopts this view is Georg Strecker, *Theology of the New Testament*, ed. Friedrich Wilhelm Horn (Louisville: Westminster John Knox, 2000).

teaching are actually imposing this unity upon the Bible. According to these scholars, attempts to correlate biblical teaching do not involve discovering dynamic theological coherence within the Bible itself but do involve importing theological unity from outside the Bible. Such unity, they say, typically reflects the theological traditions that readers bring to the text.[2]

Because an inductive approach remains open to all possibilities, those who practice inductive Bible study will acknowledge that scholars who reject any real theological unity within the Bible may be correct. But advocates of inductive Bible study should insist that such a claim emerge only from the serious examination of all the evidence. Moreover, the burden of proof is upon those who deny significant theological unity within the Bible, for both biblical and extrabiblical considerations point to the likelihood of essential theological unity.

In terms of biblical indications of theological unity within the Scriptures, critical scholarship has demonstrated that later biblical writers consistently adopted and adapted earlier biblical traditions. Thus critical scholars often speak of the growth of the biblical tradition, thereby suggesting a profound continuity from earlier to later biblical writers.[3] Extrabiblical indications of unity include especially the development of the biblical canon. The process of canonization, in which both Jewish and Christian communities of faith made judgments regarding which books should be included or excluded as Scripture, implies that these communities found a theological unity among the books that they accepted as canonical. These communities did not make canonical judgments quickly or easily. Rather, they reached their considered judgments over hundreds of years of discernment and reflection.[4]

Difficulty of Correlation

To say that reasons exist for postulating theological unity in the Bible as the basis for correlation is not to claim that the identification of that unity is simple or that the process of correlation is easy. In fact, the process of correlation tends to be complex and challenging. For one thing, correlation builds on the interpretation of many specific passages and books. Therefore one's correlation is only as valid as the accuracy of these multiple individual

2. See Peter Balla, *Challenges to New Testament Theology* (Peabody, MA: Hendrickson, 1998), for a discussion of scholars who hold this view and for a spirited defense of theological unity within the NT (and OT); cf. also John Goldingay, *Theological Diversity and the Authority of the Old Testament* (Grand Rapids: Eerdmans, 1987).

3. The constant readaptation of earlier canonical materials is emphasized by Gerhard von Rad. See esp. his *Old Testament Theology*. Cf. also Koch, *Growth of the Biblical Tradition*; Sanders, *Canon and Community*; idem, *From Sacred Story to Sacred Text*.

4. For discussions on the history of the development of the biblical canon, see Bauer, *Annotated Guide to Biblical Resources*, 12–15, 46–48, 182–83. Cf. also Balla, *Challenges to New Testament Theology*, 87–146.

interpretations. Moreover, correlation is the process of relating the meaning of individual passages and books. Therefore correlation involves a number of particular judgments regarding how the perspectives of individual passages and books properly interconnect. And the process of making these judgments pertaining to interconnections is not reducible to simple rules or formulas. The process of correlation resists the kind of step-by-step description that we have offered for observation and interpretation and, to some extent, evaluation and appropriation. Therefore correlation is especially vulnerable to subjective judgments and opinions.

However, correlation is not finally a matter of subjective individual judgments because correlation focuses on the objective data of the text. Like all phases of induction, correlation is transjective: it includes both objective and subjective aspects working together. Thus the process of correlation, which leads to biblical theology, is possible, but it may not be easy. Therefore correlation requires humility, recognition of tentativeness, and commitment to conversation with others, including those with whom the student may be inclined to disagree.

Importance of Correlation

As we mentioned in chapter 1, an inductive approach requires that the study of the Bible conform to the nature of the Bible itself. Thus the recognition that the Bible is a canonical collection and not simply a group of isolated books means that the goal of biblical study is the development of a biblical theology[5] that may form the basis for Christian faith and life.[6] Therefore

5. The discipline of biblical theology has received renewed attention over the past quarter century. In fact, scholars have debated much regarding the nature of biblical theology. James Barr, *The Concept of Biblical Theology* (Minneapolis: Fortress, 1999), notes that biblical theology has no agreed-upon definition. For major treatments on biblical theology, see Bauer, *Annotated Guide to Biblical Resources*, 33–36, 72–76, 212–16; cf. also the following recent treatments: Scott J. Hafemann and Paul R. House, *Central Themes in Biblical Theology: Mapping Unity in Diversity* (Grand Rapids: Baker Academic, 2007); James K. Mead, *Biblical Theology: Issues, Methods, and Themes* (Louisville: Westminster John Knox, 2007); Leo G. Perdue, Robert Morgan, and Benjamin D. Sommer, eds., *Biblical Theology: Introducing the Conversation*, Library of Biblical Theology (Nashville: Abingdon, 2009).

6. In our judgment, biblical theology is a description of the theological teachings of the writers of the Bible. For Christians, biblical theology is the basis for a biblically based systematic theology and Christian ethics. We thus agree with the fundamental distinction between biblical theology and systematic theology as originally set forth by Johann Philip Gabler in his famous 1787 essay, "An Oration on the Proper Distinction between Biblical and Dogmatic Theology and the Specific Objectives of Each," in *The Flowering of Old Testament Theology*, ed. Ben C. Ollenburger, Elmer A. Martins, and Gerhard F. Hasel (Winona Lake, IN: Eisenbrauns, 1992), 489–502; cf. John Sandys-Wunsch and Laurence Eldridge, "J. P. Gabler and the Distinction between Biblical and Dogmatic Theology," *Scottish Journal of Theology* 33 (1980): 133–88. This distinction was also made by, among others, Krister Stendahl, "Biblical Theology, Contempo-

readers must synthesize the meaning of individual passages and books so as to grasp the message of the Bible-as-a-whole.

The principle of the canon of Scripture implies that the Word of God is not reducible to individual passages or books read in isolation from the rest of the Bible. Rather, one encounters the Word of God as one studies the entire Bible in its dynamic complexity. Strictly speaking, claiming that a particular passage of Scripture, divorced from the rest of the canon, is the Word of God is inaccurate. Rather, specific passages function as the Word of God insofar as one understands these individual passages in light of the whole canon of Scripture.[7]

These considerations suggest that the concept of *sensus plenior* (fuller/ deeper meaning) may have value. *Sensus plenior* is the notion that God uses the interconnections between passages in the Bible to communicate a fuller meaning than the biblical authors themselves knew or intended.[8] Certainly the writers of the New Testament often posited a fuller significance to Old Testament passages than the original authors of those passages had in mind. The New Testament writers discerned this fuller significance through reading Old Testament passages in light of one another and in light of the Christ event. The historical character of biblical revelation suggests that this more comprehensive divine intention stands in continuity with the meaning of passages in their original historical and literary contexts. This fuller significance is an expansion of the original sense of passages. It does not contradict or stand in isolation from the original sense.[9] But it does move beyond the original sense. Readers may discern this fuller significance as they explore connections between biblical passages or as they consider ways in which earlier passages point ahead to later stages of the revelation of God within the flow of the biblical canon. In other words, readers may encounter this *sensus plenior*, this fuller sense, as they engage in correlation.

---

rary," in *The Interpreter's Dictionary of the Bible*, ed. George A. Buttrick (Nashville: Abingdon, 1962), 1:418–32; Raymond E. Brown, *Critical Meaning of the Bible*; I. Howard Marshall, *Beyond the Bible: Moving from Scripture to Theology* (Grand Rapids: Baker Academic, 2004). Many recent scholars have roundly criticized this distinction and the foundational character of biblical theology on the grounds that an objective synthesis of the theological teaching of the Bible is unrealistic. We recognize that any purely objective construal of biblical theology is impossible. Inevitably the theological perspectives and background of students will affect the way they understand the theology of the Bible. But we are saying that students should aim at grasping the theological witness of the biblical writers on the writers' own terms and that such a goal can be approximated.

7. Thus Vanhoozer, *Is There a Meaning in This Text?* 263–65, suggests that we might properly understand God to be the author of the whole canon: God is the *implied author* of the text read as a canonical whole.

8. See Raymond E. Brown, *The "Sensus Plenior" of Sacred Scripture* (1955; repr., Eugene, OR: Wipf & Stock, 2008); Douglas J. Moo, "The Problem of *Sensus Plenior*," in *Hermeneutics, Authority, and Canon*, ed. D. A. Carson and John D. Woodbridge (Grand Rapids: Zondervan, 1986), 179–211.

9. Brown, *"Sensus Plenior" of Sacred Scripture*, 313–14.

Types of Correlation

Up to this point we have focused on the synthesis of teachings within the biblical canon, or *internal correlation*, but one should also pursue *external correlation*. External correlation is the process of relating the teachings of Scripture to realities that one discovers in the world and outside the Bible.

Wilbert Webster White, perhaps the foremost pioneer in the development of inductive Bible study, rightly emphasizes that all truth is one. Therefore intellectual honesty requires that students continually relate one aspect or component of truth to others. Learning necessarily involves the acquisition of perspective and breadth.[10]

But the necessity of external correlation arises not only from educational goals and intellectual integrity; it arises also from the nature of the Bible. The Bible makes claims regarding the realities of the world. Thus the Bible invites, and indeed requires, that readers explore connections between the teachings of Scripture and the facts of the world as one encounters them.

---

10. Eberhardt, *Bible in the Making of Ministers*, 143–59. Many philosophers and theologians have also emphasized the unity of truth, perhaps most notably Wolfhart Pannenberg: see esp. his *Basic Questions in Theology*; idem, *Systematic Theology*, 3 vols. (Grand Rapids: Eerdmans, 1991–93).

20

Implementing Correlation

Process of Correlation

Although correlation builds on interpretation and appropriation, one cannot wait until one has interpreted and appropriated every passage in the Bible before beginning the process of correlation. Otherwise, the student would never begin to correlate, for it would require a lifetime to probe the meaning of every biblical passage.

Moreover, correlation is so critical for understanding the biblical message that one must give serious attention to correlation from the very beginning of scriptural study. Students should thus pursue the process of correlation with each passage they interpret and appropriate. Having studied the meaning of any passage, the student should consider ways in which the passage may relate to other biblical passages and may contribute to the entire biblical witness.

In addition, developing a biblical theology is a highly complex and comprehensive enterprise, and students must pursue this task incrementally. Indeed, the student will never complete the process of correlation. The insights that emerge with the study of biblical passages will constantly feed into the student's understanding of biblical teaching and theology.

Students may employ two broad procedures for synthesizing the teachings of Scriptures with each other and with the facts they encounter in the world: formal association and informal association.

Formal Association

Formal association is correlation according to topics or categories. One may study the way in which the Bible presents certain themes or topics, such as soteriology (salvation), pneumatology (the Spirit), ecclesiology (the community of faith/church), and anthropology (humanity). The topics just listed come from systematic theology, and understandably students usually think of biblical theology in terms of categories drawn from systematics or dogmatics. But one should not limit the teachings of Scripture, or biblical theology, to categories associated with systematic theology or systematic ethics.[1] The Bible's teachings concern a broad range of matters, including topics pertaining to pastoral care[2] and theological categories not usually discussed in dogmatic theology, such as covenant or promise. One may also employ this broad range of topics to relate the Bible to extrabiblical realities. For example, a recent book compares the Bible's presentation of disability to contemporary attitudes and findings regarding disabilities.[3]

Formal association carries the advantage of helping students understand discrete themes or ideas discussed in the Scriptures, but one must recognize that the Bible dynamically relates individual themes to one another. Thus one should avoid artificial compartmentalization.

Moreover, formal association requires that students not only identify and examine the themes or topics contained in the Bible as students construct a biblical theology. They must also pay attention to the relative emphasis that the Bible gives to each of these topics or themes.

In addition, students must attend to the ways in which each topic or theme finds development within the Bible-as-a-whole. The primary development within the Bible is the progression between the Old Testament and the New Testament. The New Testament concept of *fulfillment* requires that students take seriously the progression from preparation to fulfillment, keeping in mind the combination of continuity and discontinuity that is implicit within the notion of fulfillment. Indeed, this relationship between the Testaments is the central issue in biblical theology. Therefore students must consider carefully how each Testament bears its own witness to God's revelation, especially as that revelation comes to final expression in Jesus Christ.[4]

1. See Balla, *Challenges to New Testament Theology*, 21–23.
2. Several authors have emphasized pastoral care in interpreting individual biblical books or writers: Powell, *God with Us*; James W. Thompson, *Pastoral Ministry according to Paul: A Biblical Vision* (Grand Rapids: Baker Academic, 2006); regarding the role of the entire Bible in pastoral practice, also compare Paul Ballard and Stephen R. Holmes, eds., *The Bible in Pastoral Practice: Readings in the Place and Function of Scripture in the Church* (Grand Rapids: Eerdmans, 2005).
3. Hector Avalos, Sarah Melcher, and Jeremy Schipper, eds., *This Abled Body: Rethinking Disabilities and Biblical Studies* (Atlanta: Society of Biblical Literature, 2007).
4. The concept of the Christian canon suggests significant limitations in ultimately separating OT and NT theology. The distinction may be valid; but in the final analysis each is incomplete, and one cannot engage in theological synthesis of one Testament in isolation from the other. For helpful ways of relating OT and NT theology, see Childs, *Biblical Theology of the Old and New Testaments*; and Peter Stuhlmacher, *How to Do Biblical Theology* (Allison Park, PA: Pickwick Publications, 1995), who speaks not of "New Testament Theology" but of "Biblical Theology of the New Testament"; see idem, *Biblische Theologie des Neuen Testaments*, 2 vols. (Göttingen: Vandenhoeck & Ruprecht, 1992–99).

Informal Association

Informal association involves correlating teachings that do not belong to the same specific topic but that nevertheless complement or complete one another. For example, students may correlate the teachings of Micah 6:8; Matthew 4:17; Romans 6:1–14; and 1 John 1:5–2:11. The first passage describes certain basic requirements for God's people: "What does the LORD require of you but to do justice, and to love kindness, and to walk humbly with your God?" The three New Testament passages together indicate how this requirement can be realized: It is accomplished through a radical change in the orientation of the person (i.e., repentance) that comes by placing faith in God's act of establishing his end-time rule in his Son, Jesus Christ, resulting in personal communion with God through Jesus Christ. We could cite many additional examples. For instance, students may correlate passages describing God's love with those depicting divine judgment, or passages speaking of God's gracious forgiveness with those demanding obedience.[5]

Informal association arises from the consideration that all truth and life is finally unified. Each specific truth or aspect of life has a vital connection with every other truth or aspect of life. Therefore the student is encouraged to probe all such connections in order to try to grasp truth in its entirety.

But students must be careful to allow the specific sense of each individual passage to be heard and thereby avoid creating connections where they do not actually exist. In this way students will also avoid simply collapsing the meaning of distinct passages into one another. Rather, they will be able to capture the robust and dynamic *conversation* between the biblical passages they examine.

Fallacies of Correlation

Students may encounter several fallacies, or potential errors, as they engage in correlation. Some of them are indicated here. These fallacies occur when students overemphasize certain aspects of correlation to the denial or neglect of other equally significant aspects.

Fallacy of Overgeneralization

The fallacy of overgeneralization emphasizes general connections at the expense of particular content. This fallacy occurs when students give exclusive

---

5. These examples indicate that informal association is possible only when a general thematic connection between the teachings of the various passages exists. That is, the various passages must have a common general concern lying behind them in order for students to relate them to each other in the process of informal association. Thus the distinction between formal and informal association is a matter of degree of topical specificity. Formal association involves correlating passages that deal explicitly with the same specific topics.

attention to identifying broad principles or teachings and neglect the ways in which individual passages provide specific content to these broad principles or teachings. The result will be discussions of broad topics that lack any specific content, or discussions of broad topics into which students pour their own specific content. Such content emerges from the student's own presuppositions rather than from the data of the biblical text. For example, students may speak of the general biblical topic of God's love while neglecting the specific scriptural concern for divine demand and accountability, which is a critical component of the biblical presentation of God's love.

This fallacy surfaces in extrabiblical synthesis when students make only broad and superficial connections between biblical teaching and the realities they encounter in the world. Students thereby fail to relate the specifics of the biblical presentation to the particular insights that belong to extrabiblical studies and perspectives.

Fallacy of Invalid Separation

The fallacy of invalid separation emphasizes diversity at the expense of unity. This fallacy involves the failure to make connections when they may in fact exist, in favor of separating biblical truths into isolated and perhaps even competing categories. For example, many readers of the Bible fail to see any real connection between God's gracious offer of forgiveness and God's demand for righteous obedience, or the connection between God's love and divine judgment.

This fallacy may apply also to extrabiblical synthesis. Students may overemphasize the differences between the biblical presentation of a topic or issue and extrabiblical perspectives, with the result that students keep them essentially separate. They thus fail to discern the dynamic interaction between biblical and extrabiblical perceptions and insights, discerning only discontinuity while failing to identify points of connection between them. The result may be a bifurcated, or split, understanding of the realities of the world. This tendency may come to expression, for example, in the neglect of any connection between the biblical understanding of the created world and the modern discoveries of natural science.

Fallacy of Total Uniformity

The fallacy of total uniformity emphasizes unity at the expense of diversity. This fallacy involves the assumption that correlation requires absolute agreement between passages. It confuses theological consistency with theological uniformity. It allows for no difference in presentation or perspective between biblical passages dealing with the same or similar topics. Rather, it insists that all the relevant passages say essentially the same thing and does not allow for differences of perspective or emphasis among passages dealing with a common topic or theme. The result is a combination of eisegetical interpretation and shallow correlation. It leads to eisegesis because it tends to read the meaning of certain passages into other passages. And it results in shallow correlation because it excludes the peculiar contribution that each passage makes to the entire biblical presentation. On the other hand, robust theological consistency is not threatened but enhanced by the distinctive perspectives and differences in emphasis that each passage offers.

Fallacy of the Flat Book

The fallacy of the flat book is a specific form of the fallacy of total uniformity. This fallacy involves the denial of any real development within the Bible. It refuses to recognize that there may be a progression in presentation and understanding of various themes and topics from earlier revelation to later stages of revelation within the Bible. The Bible itself indicates that such progression exists, especially between the Old and New Testaments. As we mentioned above under "Evaluating and Appropriating" (see sec. 4), later stages of biblical revelation may clarify and even correct earlier stages. There is a real possibility, for example, that a development exists within the biblical view of the role of Israel in relation to God's redemption. The refusal to acknowledge such a possibility would be an expression of following a flat-book presupposition.

This consideration does not mean that passages belonging to the earlier stages make no real contribution to the final, comprehensive biblical understanding of the theme or topic. Yet it does mean that one must discern the contribution of each passage in light of the role that passage plays in the development of the theme or topic within the Bible-as-a-whole.

Example of Correlation (2 Timothy 3:15–17)

The following is a suggestive example of correlation that centers on the implied author's apparent appeal to the authority and value of Hebrew scripture mentioned in 2 Timothy 3:15–17. The correlative process as illustrated involves three stages. First, we explore the appeal to Hebrew scripture in the Pastoral Epistles, namely, 1 and 2 Timothy and Titus. Second, we explore the appeal to Hebrew scripture in the Pauline corpus. In the third and final stage we peruse the use of Hebrew scripture throughout the New Testament.

Hebrew Scripture in the Pastoral Epistles

As we have seen, the strong appeal to Hebrew scripture in 2 Timothy 3:15–17 appears in the context of Timothy's being prepared to deal with certain people in the "last days"; these are described in 3:2–9 and are characterized as "wicked people" and "impostors" in 3:13. Their problems are both doctrinal and ethical, and they stand in stark contrast to Timothy's exemplar Paul (3:10–12) and to his early teachers as a child (3:14; cf. 1:5). But most of all, the pastor reminds Timothy that the scriptural writings that had formed the sound foundations of his firm, longstanding faith are sacred, because they are theopneustic (that is, inspired by God) and essential for achieving the personal and ministerial goals that are indispensable for Timothy's future.

In 1 Timothy 1:3–11 the implied writer discusses the law in a favorable light and criticizes would-be teachers of the law who have no understanding of what they are saying. He proceeds to call the law "good" and to indicate that the law is addressed to those who are disobedient. He thus presents himself as having a proper understanding of and respect for the Mosaic law.

At the same time the implied author invokes other sources of authority, such as his own teaching and conduct (2 Tim. 3:10–12; 4:6–8). He includes, in addition, appeals to Christ Jesus (1 Tim. 1:2; 2:7; 5:11; 2 Tim. 1:2; 2:1, 3, 8, 10; Titus 1:1, 4; 2:13–14; 3:6), to his apostolic authority (1 Tim. 1:1; 2 Tim. 1:1; Titus 1:1), and to the gospel as proclaimed by him (1 Tim. 1:11; 2 Tim. 1:8, 10; 2:8).

In his admonitions regarding various groups of persons, Paul does use some quotations from Hebrew scripture, such as in 1 Timothy 5:18; and in other cases he alludes to Hebrew scripture, such as in 1 Timothy 6:4, 7, 8, 9, 15, and 16. In most cases, however, his admonitions appear to be solely the expression of his apostolic authority apart from reference to particular passages in the Hebrew scriptures.

The implied author also alludes to other material that is not found in Hebrew scripture, such as the statements in 2 Timothy 2:11–13 where he quotes a "sure saying"; in 1 Timothy 2:5–6 where he cites a statement emphasizing the oneness of God and the mediatorial role of Christ Jesus; and in 1 Timothy 3:16 where he describes the great "mystery of our religion," namely, the incarnation. And when he urges Timothy to "proclaim the message" (2 Tim. 4:2), he apparently has in mind more than the Hebrew scripture, since he has emphasized the importance of the gospel and of his own teaching.

All of these considerations raise the question of the relationship between these various appeals to authority. As we have previously stated, if the old covenant set forth in the Hebrew scripture is preparation for its fulfillment in the new covenant, then there is continuity between them; one cannot comprehend or proclaim the one without reference to the other. However, as previously stated, fulfillment also requires discontinuity, since more of the same cannot meet the requirement of transcendence that is essential for fulfillment. It is therefore important that Timothy, both in his personal life and in his ministry, keep this distinction in mind in order to carry out his ministry fully (2 Tim. 4:5).

Hebrew Scripture in the Pauline Corpus

Throughout the Pauline epistles there is clear evidence of the implied author's high respect for the Hebrew scriptures, though in most cases the LXX is used instead of translations of the Hebrew text. The two Pauline books in which the use of Hebrew scriptures plays the most dominant role are the letters to the Romans and to the Galatians.

The salutation of the epistle to the Romans seems to suggest two of the primary bases for the implied writer's authority: namely, his apostleship and the prophetic promises found in the holy scriptures that are fulfilled in the gospel (Rom. 1:1–7). Early in the Roman epistle Paul refers to a statement found in the prophet Habakkuk to support his main theme, namely, that justification is by faith (Rom. 1:16–17; Hab. 2:4). He later reinforces this motif by alluding to the justifying experiences of Abraham and David (Rom. 4:1–5, 6–8). The implied writer appeals to Hebrew scripture to support other emphases, including the universality of sin (3:9–18); the fatherhood of Abraham in relation to all believers, both circumcised and uncircumcised (4:9–12, 16–25); the effect of Adam's disobedience upon the entire human race (5:12–21); the character and role of Mosaic law (7:1–25); the decay and redemption of creation (8:19–22); God's election (9:6–18); the exclusion of disobedient Israel and the inclusion of believing Gentiles (9:24–33; 10:1–11:22; 15:7–21); the future deliverance of Israel (11:23–36); and love as a fulfillment of the law (13:8–10).

At the same time, he seems to part with the spirit of the imprecatory psalms, such as 58:6 and 137:8–9, and prefers the teachings of Jesus when he urges his readers not to repay evil with evil (12:14–21; cf. Matt. 5:43–48). Thus, though Paul has high regard for the authority of Hebrew scriptures, he recognizes that at times the gospel of Jesus Christ transcends them in order to fulfill them. The ultimate authority, then, is the gospel of Jesus Christ, of which the implied writer is an apostle.

With respect to the letter to the Galatians, Paul again emphasizes his apostolic authority (Gal. 1:1–2). He underlines this authority by claiming that he did not receive his gospel from other humans but by divine revelation, whose circumstances he takes pains to describe (1:11–17). He consequently opposes some in Jerusalem whom he characterizes as "false believers" (2:1–10, esp. v. 4). He subsequently differed with his fellow apostles Peter and perhaps James on the matter of table separation between Jewish Christians and uncircumcised Gentile Christians; he thus questioned the need for believing Gentiles to follow Mosaic dietary laws. In other words, he objected to the view that Gentiles had to become practicing Jews in order to be Christians and insisted that the view of certain Jerusalem apostles involved an insincere return to justification by law-works and a repudiation of justification by faith alone (2:11–3:5).

The implied writer of Galatians then returns to the justification of Abraham by faith and to the thesis that he is the father of all who are justified by faith (3:6–9; cf. Gen. 12:3). He further claims that all believing Gentiles have thereby become heirs of the promise made to Abraham (3:6–29). As to the law, it is a pedagogue who leads all to have faith in Jesus Christ and to the realization of divine sonship (3:19–29; 4:1–31). This sonship sets believers free from the Mosaic law in order to follow the "law of love" and to walk after the spirit and not after the flesh (5:1–26); thereby they all become members of the new "Israel of God" (6:1–16).

In his other epistles, such as the Corinthian letters, he frequently makes use of Hebrew scriptures and shows great respect for their authority; but at the same time, he always treats them as preparatory and not as ultimate. If and when the gospel, of which the implied writer claims to be an apostle (1 Cor. 1:1; 2 Cor. 1:1), transcends its preparation, Paul is not hesitant to give primacy to the gospel (e.g., 1 Cor. 5:6–8; 6:12–20; 7:17–19; 8:8–9; 9:20–21; 10:23–11:1; 2 Cor. 3:12–18; 5:14; 10:3–6).

Hebrew Scripture in the New Testament

We have already begun, to a certain extent, the process of examining correlation with regard to the use of Hebrew Scripture throughout the entire New Testament. The focus here will be upon the Gospels, including Luke-Acts and the Johannine corpus, consisting of John, 1–3 John, and the Revelation of John. Other books deserve attention, such as the non-Pauline epistles, but time and space will not permit such an exploration here.

The Gospel according to Matthew makes profuse use of citations from Hebrew scripture, more than any other book or group of books in the New Testament. It contains more than sixty such citations. Perhaps this phenomenon suggests that the implied author felt a strong need to stress the concurrence between the two covenants. He seems to agree strongly with the view regarding Hebrew scripture expressed in 2 Timothy 3:15–17.

The author's use of "fulfill" (*pleroō*) provides a key to understanding the relationship between the Christ event and the Hebrew scripture. The first use occurs in connection with the announcement of the virgin birth, based upon Isaiah 7:14 (Matt. 1:23). In this instance "fulfill" is used in relation to the purported realization of a prophetic prediction. In this case and in many others, the author uses passages from the Hebrew scriptures to provide testimony on behalf of Jesus.

In describing the ministry of John the Baptizer, preference is given to the LXX version, which indicates that the wilderness is the locale of John's ministry rather than the locale of the preparation (Mark 1:3; cf. Isa. 40:3). Thus, though there is obvious respect for the Hebrew scripture, the implied writer has no qualms about departing from its exact language in order to present support for the Christ event.

Another kind of fulfillment involves the relationship between a past event, namely, the deliverance of Israel from Egypt, and the flight of the holy family from Egypt (Matt. 2:15 and Hos. 11:1). In this case the latter event involving the Son of God brings to its highest culmination the deliverance of Israel as God's son. Still another kind of fulfillment is found in the Sermon on the Mount, where Jesus is quoted as saying, "Do not think that I have come to abolish the law or the prophets; I have come not to abolish but to fulfill" (Matt. 5:17). Perhaps "fulfill" in this context is not tantamount to obeying every iota or dot of the law, but rather realizing its purpose in the highest sense, that is, by achieving a righteousness that exceeds that of the legalistic scribes and Pharisees (5:19–20). Accordingly, Jesus subsequently parts with the law's view of oaths (5:33–37) and with its lex talionis (5:38–42).

Likewise, Jesus broke with strict adherence to the law of the sabbath, as a result of which he was persecuted by the scribes and Pharisees (Matt. 12:1; cf. Mark 2:23–28; 3:1–6; Luke 6:2, 9; John 5:9–18). Jesus's claim to be "Lord of the sabbath" made him superior to the Mosaic law as the Son of Man.

The Gospel according to Matthew and the other three Gospels make use of Isaiah 6:9–10 to emphasize judicial ignorance as one of the main reasons for the rejection of Jesus (Matt. 13:14–15; cf. Mark 4:12; John 12:36b–41). In the Synoptics, Jesus is said to compare his opponents to the Israelites of old; he likens them to the hard soil of the path, where the seed of the kingdom could not germinate. This condition was probably due to spiritual atrophy and was God's judgment upon persistent evil. The prophet Isaiah stated that the stubborn refusal of his countrymen to obey God resulted in their transposing values, so that they called evil good and good evil, and put darkness for light, and light for darkness, and put bitter for sweet and sweet for bitter (Isa. 5:20). As a result, said Isaiah, they were without understanding, and had unseeing eyes and unhearing ears. It was a similar condition that in some cases accounted for the opposition to Jesus that led to the crucifixion.

The three Synoptics use the parable of the wicked tenants as another way of explaining the crucifixion of Jesus (Matt. 21:33–46; Mark 12:1–12; Luke 20:9–19). The parable employs the well-known image of the vineyard to teach its lesson (cf. Isa. 5). Its primary structural law is the stark contrast between, on the one hand, the intention of the Father in sending the prophets and finally his Son and, on the other hand, the reaction of the wicked tenants. Instead of heeding the appeal to give God his due, the wicked tenants decided to kill the Son and heir in order to usurp his inheritance.

Another recognition of the authority of Hebrew scriptures in the Synoptics is their focus on love as the fulfillment of the great commandment (Matt. 22:34–40; Mark 12:28–34; Luke 10:27; cf. Deut. 6:4–5; Lev. 19:18). In answer to the question posed by a lawyer regarding the greatest commandment in the law, Jesus appeals to the Shema to answer: "You shall love the Lord your God with all your heart, and with all your soul, and with all your mind." He then added, appealing to a Levitical command, "You shall love your neighbor as yourself." Jesus indicates his attitude toward the full sweep of the Hebrew scriptures by stating, "On these two commandments hang all the law and the prophets."

The implied writer of the First Gospel also emphasizes Jesus as the son of King David. He mentions it in the very first verse of his writing and subsequently returns to it a number of times; the Gospel according to Luke also stresses this relationship. In addition, there is a recurring emphasis on the "kingdom of heaven," which is found a number of times in the other Synoptics as the "kingdom of God." The Matthean Jesus appeals to Psalm 110:1 to indicate the superiority of Jesus over David, in that David, "inspired by the Spirit," called him "Lord" (Matt. 22:44; cf. Mark 12:36; Luke 20:42–43).

Jesus's respect for Mosaic law is emphasized in his urging the cleansed leper to show himself before a priest and to make the offering for his cleansing that Moses commanded (Matt. 8:1–4; cf. Mark 1:44; Luke 5:12–16; Lev. 13:49). In the matter of divorce, however, Matthew reports Jesus as challenging the law on divorce by explaining it as a divine concession to the hardness of human hearts ("cardiosclerosis"; Matt. 19:3–9; cf. Mark 10:2–9), and indicating a preference for the orders of creation described in Genesis 2:24.

Perhaps the account of Jesus's temptations indicates most strikingly the high regard in which Jesus, as presented by the evangelists, held Hebrew scripture. In the Matthean account, for example, each response of Jesus begins with the expression "it is written," followed by a quotation from the Hebrew scripture (Matt. 4:4, 7, 10; cf. Luke 4:1–13). In this most critical hour, when Jesus's ministry was at stake, he chose to rely on Hebrew scripture as the primary means for defeating the devil.

Although we have already indicated some of the uses of Hebrew scripture in the Markan Gospel, a few others are noteworthy. The statement regarding John the Baptizer, for example, is attributed solely to Isaiah the prophet, although Mark 1:2 obviously cites Malachi 3:1. Some scribes apparently became aware of this discrepancy and replaced "the prophet Isaiah" with "the prophets." What accounts for this confusion is not clear, although one can understand how oral tradition might be responsible for this merging. Both Matthew and Luke restrict themselves to quoting from Isaiah alone.

Probably Mark's most significant appeal to the Hebrew scriptures is the utilization of the suffering servant motif of Isaiah 53. The key statement in this regard is found in Mark 10:45, where Jesus says, "For the Son of Man came not to be served but to serve, and to give his life a ransom for many." He urges his disciples to follow the same path of servanthood (Mark 10:43–44).

This appeal is Mark's answer to the scandal of the cross. One of the evangelists' main tasks was to convince their audience to accept as Lord and Savior one who was brutally crucified by his enemies. The one who was presented as the great deliverer and conqueror was killed at the hands of his evil opponents (cf. 1 Cor. 1:18–25). Even Peter, his own disciple, rebuked the one whom he had confessed to be the Christ when Jesus announced his forthcoming death (Mark 8:31–33). To counter this objection, the Markan Jesus reminded his disciples, and thereby the early church, that ancient Israel had made the same mistake. According to Isaiah, they despised and rejected the servant of Yahweh because he was a man of sorrows (Isa. 53:2–3), not realizing that he had borne their griefs and carried their sorrows, and that he was wounded for their transgressions (Isa. 53:4–5). The transfiguration that follows Jesus's first announcement of his forthcoming death confirms this view by the appearance of the prophet Elijah and the lawgiver Moses, along with the voice of the Father, who proclaimed, "This is my Son, the Beloved; listen to him!" (Mark 9:7).

The implied author of Mark reports the response of Jesus to certain Pharisees and scribes who criticized his disciples for eating with unwashed hands, which they considered defiled (7:1–23). Jesus appeals to the prophecy of Isaiah, which is used to charge those who made such accusations with being hypocrites, since they merely paid lip service to God and were devoid of a genuine concern for his commandments (7:6–8; Isa. 29:13). In fact, they chose to obey human traditions even though in the process they rejected God's commandments (Mark 7:9). They had an external view of defilement, while ignoring true defilement, which issues from within, that is, the heart (7:14–23).

It is important to note that the implied author of Mark inserts an editorial comment regarding the implication of Jesus's remarks: "Thus he declared all foods clean"(7:19b; cf. Acts 10:15; Rom. 14:14, 20). Assuming that this comment is not a gloss, it seems to represent a clear departure from Hebrew scripture, since food taboos were an important part of purity laws. Among the foods considered unclean were those that contained blood (Gen. 9:4; Lev. 17:14–15; Deut. 12:16, 23); beasts that did not have divided hooves and that chewed the cud (Lev. 11:3–7; Deut. 14:6–8); and even all foods eaten by Gentiles (Hos. 9:3).

The Olivet Discourse, sometimes called "the little apocalypse," takes seriously the "desolating sacrilege" mentioned in the apocalyptic material in the latter chapters of the book of Daniel (Mark 13:14; Matt. 24:15; Luke 21:20; cf. Dan. 9:27; 11:31; 12:11). In Mark and in the other Synoptics it is discussed in relation to the prediction of the destruction of Jerusalem and of the temple. This event, which occurred in AD 70, may be considered the end of the era represented by the Hebrew scripture. Both Jesus and his early followers were transitional figures, since on the one hand they broke with some of the practices enjoined under the old covenant, while at the same time they followed other practices, including temple worship. With the destruction of the temple, the fulfillment described in the book of Hebrews was the only genuine alternative.

According to the Synoptic Gospels, the cleansing of the temple occurred during passion week and was perhaps one of the chief reasons for the violent opposition to Jesus resulting in his crucifixion (Mark 11:15–19; Matt. 21:12–17;

Luke 19:45–48). In the Fourth Gospel the cleansing is recounted early in the record of Jesus's public ministry (John 2:13–22). In all cases the common thread is reference to what is written in Hebrew scripture as the reason for Jesus's action (see Isa. 56:7; Jer. 7:11; and Ps. 69:9).

The institution of the Lord's supper, based upon a reinterpretation of the Passover meal, is another significant instance of the respect paid to Hebrew scripture (Mark 14:12–25; Matt. 26:26–29; Luke 22:14–23). We note, in addition, Jesus's statement that he would be betrayed "as it is written" (Mark 14:21; Matt. 26:20–25; Luke 22:14, 21–23).

Jesus's cry of dereliction is a quotation from Psalm 22:1a (Mark 15:34; Matt. 27:46). The antecedents of the pronouns in the psalm along with the aspects of the verbs seem to indicate that the psalmist is describing his own experience. Jesus appears to quote it because he considers it to be appropriate to the crisis he is undergoing. The implied authors of both Gospels give the saying in the original language, followed by a translation into Greek. The apparent reason is to explain why the bystanders thought he was calling Elijah.

Moving now to the Luke-Acts corpus, the introduction to the Third Gospel makes it clear that the implied author has carefully examined accounts of those who are described as "eyewitnesses" and that he agrees with those accounts (Luke 1:1–4). It seems therefore proper to infer that he accepts their understanding of the Hebrew scripture and its fulfillment in Jesus Christ. The explicit evidence in the Gospel seems to support this inference, some of which we now cite.

Early in the Gospel the implied author includes a genealogy of Jesus as the presumed son of Joseph (Luke 3:23–38). Though his genealogy differs in some ways from the one found in Matthew (1:1–17), both rely upon data contained in Hebrew scripture. It is interesting to note that the Lukan genealogy is in reverse order of the one found in Matthew, and that it closes by describing Adam as the "son of God." Luke then proceeds to focus on the role of the Holy Spirit in the life and ministry of Jesus by emphasizing that it was the Spirit who led him into the wilderness and who was active in his return to Galilee (4:14). Upon Jesus's return to a synagogue in Nazareth, he used the occasion to read the following from the prophet Isaiah: "The Spirit of the Lord is upon me . . ." (4:18). Jesus then is reported as saying, "Today this scripture has been fulfilled in your hearing" (4:21). And when the people from his hometown demanded that he duplicate the miracles he had done in Capernaum, Jesus is reported as indicating that no prophet is acceptable in his own country. The implied author goes on to record faithfully the somewhat lengthy response of Jesus, using the example of Elijah (4:25–27).

There is much more evidence that the implied author of Luke had substantial knowledge of and great respect for the scripture of the Hebrew people. Among such evidence is the recurring use of such expressions as "it is written" and allusions to various persons mentioned in the Hebrew scripture, such as Abel, Abraham, Isaac, Jacob, Moses, Solomon, the prophets, Jonah, and Zechariah.

Since the implied author of the Book of the Acts is the same as that of the Third Gospel, it is not surprising that the attitude toward the Hebrew scripture just described is found also in the Acts. One of the first indications of this attitude is the statement that "the scripture had to be fulfilled, which the Holy Spirit through David foretold concerning Judas . . ." (Acts 1:16). In connection with the name of the field that was purchased by Judas and that became the place of his demise, the text reports that it was called "Hakeldama, that is, Field of Blood" (1:19). The reason cited in verse 20 is a statement in Psalm 69:25, though there are differences between the citation in Acts and the statement in the Hebrew scripture.

A similar phenomenon occurs with regard to the citation from Joel in connection with Pentecost (Acts 2:16–21; Joel 2:28–32). Though the citation is introduced as "what was spoken by the prophet Joel," there are clear differences between the statement here and what is found in Joel. However, as in the previous case, the differences do not affect the essence of the citations.

One of the considerations that needs to be taken into account is that the implied author of the book of Acts uses the LXX throughout. It does not follow that there is any lack of respect for Hebrew scripture, since the LXX was the Bible of the day and was commonly used by biblical writers as well as by their implied readers. Even when Hebrew scriptures were used, it was necessary to translate them into Greek.

One of the striking passages in Acts includes accusations against Stephen and his response. Stephen was charged with speaking blasphemous words against Moses and God (Acts 6:11). He was then brought before the council, where false witnesses accused him of "saying things against this holy place and the law" (6:13). According to the account, Stephen proceeded to make a lengthy statement reviewing the acts of God on behalf of the Hebrew people, beginning with Abraham and closing with the construction of the temple under Solomon (7:2–50). He then turned the tables on his accusers by describing them as a "stiff-necked people, uncircumcised in heart and ears . . ." who always resisted the Holy Spirit, who persecuted and killed the prophets as did their fathers, and who did not keep the law that had been delivered by angels (7:51–53). Stephen's adversaries became enraged and proceeded to stone him to death (7:54–8:1).

The inclusion of this passage indicates not only the implied author's awareness of the history recorded in the Hebrew scripture but also his acceptance of it and high regard for it. A number of other references to Hebrew scripture that support this understanding are sprinkled throughout the book of Acts, such as in 8:32–33; 10:12–14; 13:16–22, 33–35, 47; 15:5; 17:2–3; 21:26; 23:3; 24:14; and 28:25–27.

Moving now to the Johannine corpus, which consists of the Gospel according to John, 1–3 John, and the book of Revelation, we see that the implied author of the Fourth Gospel begins his prologue by referring to the opening verses of the creation narrative in Genesis 1. He interprets the creative speech-acts of Elohim as involving the divine Logos, who is later said to have become incarnate and lived among us (John 1:1–5, 14). Since the word for "lived" literally means "tabernacled," the use of "glory" ("we have seen his glory") may reflect the event reported in Exodus 40:34, where the "glory" of the Lord is said to have filled the tabernacle. In addition, the implied author of the Gospel later states that whereas the law came through Moses, grace and truth came through Jesus Christ (1:17).

In contrast to the Synoptics, the implied author reports the witness of John the Baptist in which he describes Jesus as "the Lamb of God" (1:29, 36). The lamb is the principal sacrifice used in connection with Passover (Exod. 12:1–13) and in the Levitical cult. In John 1:29, the Lamb of God is described as taking away the sin of the world.

Later in John 1, Philip is reported as telling Nathanael: "We have found him about whom Moses in the law and also the prophets wrote, Jesus son of Joseph from Nazareth" (v. 45). Nathanael is later said to address Jesus as "the king of Israel" (v. 49), after which Jesus describes what Nathanael will see by alluding to Jacob's ladder (v. 51; Gen. 28:12).

One of the main features of the Johannine account is the description of Jesus's public ministry (chaps. 1–12) in relation to the various Jewish festivals found in the Hebrew scriptures. Whereas in the Synoptics only the final Passover is highlighted, in the Fourth Gospel the implied author mentions feasts numerous times (2:13, 23; 5:1; 6:4; 7:2, 8, 11, 14, 37; 11:56; 12:12, 20) in addition to the final Passover (13:1, 29).

It is interesting to note that some of the signs Jesus performed and some of the claims he made regarding himself are associated with his activities at the Jewish festivals. For example, it is in connection with the Passover feast that he feeds the five thousand and subsequently is reported as saying, "I am the bread of life" (6:4–14, 35). And it is in relation to the Feast of Tabernacles that Jesus says, "I am the light of the world" (7:2; 8:12). This claim is repeated in connection with the healing of the man born blind (9:5).

The implied writer of John's Gospel includes appeals by Jesus to Abraham and to Moses on various occasions, viewing them both in a favorable light (5:46; 8:39, 56). Regarding Moses, the supposed hero of the opposition, Jesus is reported to have made the following claim to those who insisted they were followers of Moses: "Do not think that I will accuse you before the Father; your accuser is Moses, on whom you have set your hope. If you believed Moses, you would believe me, for he wrote about me" (5:45–46). At the same time, the implied writer is not hesitant to include statements by Jesus indicating his superiority to these two great figures in salvation history (6:32; 8:58).

Thus, although the implied writer of John's Gospel uses few quotations introduced by the formula "as it is written," he presents Jesus as having high regard for Hebrew scripture. Jesus is reported as freely using Hebrew scripture to answer his unbelieving opponents.

As to 1 and 2 John, again there are few citations from Hebrew scriptures introduced by a formulaic statement such as "it is written." At the same time, though, the emphasis upon loving one another accords with the Old Testament injunction to love one's neighbor that is emphasized in the Synoptic Gospels (Matt. 22:39; Mark 12:33; Luke 10:27; cf. Lev. 19:18; 2 John 5) On the other hand, the implied author calls attention to the words of Jesus: "I give you a new commandment, that you love one another. Just as I have loved you, you also should love one another" (John 13:34; cf. 1 John 2:8; 4:21). This new, superior commandment fulfills the one found in Hebrew scripture, which emphasizes loving one's neighbor as one loves oneself.

By way of contrast, the implied writer urges his readers not to be like Cain, who is "from the evil one" and who "murdered his brother"(1 John 3:12a). The reason cited for Cain's evil act was that "his own deeds were evil and his brother's righteous"(3:12b; cf. Gen. 4:8). Thus the implied writer relies on the text of Hebrew scripture to underline the difference between the "children of God" and the "children of the devil" (3:10).

We now turn to the book of Revelation, which uses the apocalyptic genre found in the latter chapters of Daniel. Although expressions such as "it is written," found so frequently in discursive and even narrative material, are lacking, numerous allusions to the Hebrew scriptures appear throughout the book. Among them are multiple references to the Lamb, which are reminiscent of the witness of John the Baptist recounted in the Fourth Gospel, and references to angels. In addition, the implied author mentions the following: a kingdom of priests and a holy nation (Rev. 1:6; cf. Exod. 19:6); seven golden lampstands (Rev. 1:12, 20; 2:1; cf. Exod. 25:31–40); the description of the one like the son of man (Rev. 1:13–14; cf. Dan. 7:9, 13); Balaam and Balak (Rev. 2:14; cf. Num. 25:1–2); hidden manna (Rev. 2:17; cf. Ps. 78:24; Isa. 56:3–5; 62:2; 65:15); the Son of God (Rev. 2:18; cf. Dan. 10:6); Jezebel (Rev. 2:20; cf. 1 Kings 18:4); the temple (Rev. 3:12; 21:22); the new Jerusalem (Rev. 3:12; 21:2, 10); the call of the seraphim (Rev. 4:8; cf. Isa. 6:3); the scroll (Rev. 5:1; cf. Dan. 12:4); the 144,000 servants sealed from the twelve tribes of Israel (Rev. 7:4–8); the Lion of the tribe of Judah and the Root of David (Rev. 5:5); the Creator (Rev. 10:7); the four beasts (Rev. 13:1–2; cf. Dan. 7:2–8); Sodom and Egypt as prototypes of the Roman Empire (Rev. 11:8); the plagues (Rev. 9:18); harlotry (Rev. 17:5; cf. Hos. 2:5; 4:15; Amos 7:17); the new Jerusalem (Rev. 21:9–22); and the river of life and the tree of life (Rev. 22:1–2).[6]

---

6. It is proper in the process of correlation to work first with the biblical material and then to interact critically with secondary sources that pertain to matters covered in correlation. In this

By way of summarizing the foregoing observations about the use of Hebrew scripture in the New Testament, then, we offer a few concluding remarks. First, in a broad sense the Hebrew scripture may be described as the "Bible" of Jesus and of the early church. In most cases it is the translation of the LXX that is used. In addition, the implied authors often seem to be more concerned with essential meanings than with precise language.

Second, the implied authors of the New Testament thus exhibit a reverence for the Hebrew scriptures that holds them up as "sacred" (*hieros*; 2 Tim. 3:15), both in their origins and in their extant form (2 Tim. 3:16–17). "Sacred" writings are those associated with God, in contrast with those that are purely human. Accordingly, Paul describes the scriptures as "holy" (Rom. 1:2).

The Hebrew scriptures are also viewed by New Testament authors as being theopneustic. The implied author of Ephesians, for example, describes the word of God as the sword of the Spirit (Eph. 6:17). The prophets are described as being led by the Spirit of Christ when predicting his sufferings and his coming glory (1 Pet. 1:11). Perhaps it is valid to say that the word of God and the Spirit of God are inseparable. Whenever the word of God goes forth, it is always accompanied by his Spirit.

Third, at the same time, the implied authors of the New Testament do not accept the Hebrew scriptures as God's final, eschatological word. They look forward to a new and greater covenant that fulfills them. Thus the relationship between the old and the new is dialectical: the main relationship is that of continuity, but there is also by necessity some discontinuity. Accordingly, Jesus urges his disciples to obey certain Mosaic laws, such as the commandments against murder and adultery, while at the same time telling them to deviate from statements in the Hebrew scriptures regarding oath-taking (Matt. 5:33–37; cf. Exod. 20:7; Lev. 19:12; Num. 30:2; Deut. 23:21) and the practice of lex talionis (Matt. 5:38–42). Likewise, the implied writer of Romans reflects the spirit and teaching of Jesus in his exhortations in 12:14–21. Thus he understands that the statements of the imprecatory psalms, such as those found in Psalms 55:15; 58:6; 69:28; 109:29; and 137:8–9, are not to be followed by disciples of Jesus Christ. At the same time he states that "whatever was written in former days was written for our instruction, so that by steadfastness and by the encouragement of the scriptures we might have hope" (Rom. 15:4).

---

abridged example of correlation we limit ourselves to the direct examination of biblical data, but one could go on to interact with such works as Steven Moyise, *Paul and Scripture: Studying the New Testament Use of the Old Testament* (Grand Rapids: Baker Academic, 2010); Bill T. Arnold, "Luke's Characterizing Use of the Old Testament in the Book of Acts," in *History, Literature and Society in the Book of Acts*, ed. Ben Witherington III (Cambridge: Cambridge University Press, 1996), 300–323; and Richard Bauckham, *The Climax of Prophecy: Studies in the Book of Revelation* (Edinburgh: T&T Clark, 1993). Bauckham argues that Revelation is intended, in large part, to bring to a climax the Hebrew scriptures around the figure of the suffering and exalted Christ.

There are a number of passages in the New Testament that use Hebrew scripture to achieve the purposes stated in 2 Timothy 3:15–17. The implied author of Romans and Galatians appeals to Abraham and to David to instruct his implied readers "for salvation through faith in Christ Jesus" (Rom. 4; Gal. 3:6–9, 14, 16, 29; 2 Tim. 3:15b). And though the implied author of the book of Hebrews views "faith" in a somewhat different way from the implied author of the Pauline epistles, he uses the roll of faith, taken in large part from Hebrew scripture, as part of a "cloud of witnesses" to encourage his readers to persevere and to realize doctrinal and ethical purposes similar to those cited in 2 Timothy 3:16–17 (Heb. 11; 12:1–21).

Exercise: Correlation

Following the suggestions in part 5, correlate your interpretation and appropriation of Jonah 4:1–11; Mark 4:10–20; and Mark 15:33–39 with the rest of the Scriptures, showing how each of these passages may contribute to a biblical theology of the themes or issues emphasized in the passage.

Epilogue

The main purpose of this book is to encourage reflection, dialogue, and experimentation. We make no claim that it sets forth the only way or necessarily the best way to do inductive biblical study. Instead, it is a testimonial regarding what we have found meaningful in both study and teaching.

We have established a website for comments and questions at http://www .inductivebiblicalstudy.com and would encourage readers to make use of it. We have also included there video presentations on inductive Bible study and a number of studies on specific passages and books. We look forward to your responses.

Appendix A

General Discussion of Induction and Deduction

A lengthy discussion of the technical issues that logicians pursue in their disputations regarding induction and deduction is beyond the purpose of this present volume. In short, both induction and deduction pertain to premises and the inferences drawn causally from them.[1] But the specific meaning of induction and deduction and the relation between them has been understood in three ways.

Models of Induction/Deduction

The Expansive Model

For some theoreticians, induction is the movement from *particular premises* or data, which are derived from observations and thus constitute evidence, to inferences that are in the form of *general principles*. Induction and deduction are defined most commonly in this way, which we dub the expansive model. Thus *Webster's New International Dictionary of the English Language* begins the entry for *induction* by describing it as an "act or process of reasoning from part to the whole, from particulars to generals, or from the individual to the universal." The entry on *deduction* includes this statement: "*Deduction* proceeds from general principles to other general principles or to particulars; *induction* seeks to establish general principles or laws by examination of

---

1. Because an assertion is made or posited (premise), a conclusion can be drawn (inference). Thus the connection between premises and inferences is expressed by *therefore* or its equivalent.

particular cases."[2] This understanding of induction pertains especially to the sciences (both natural and human), with their concern to identify general laws or patterns, and stands as the foundation of the scientific method as set forth paradigmatically by Francis Bacon.[3] According to this understanding, induction moves from particular observed data to expansive general conclusions; so one might refer to this view as the *expansive* model of induction.

The Essential Model

In the essential model, induction is the movement from premises that are unknown to persons until they are discovered through a process of observation (and thus become evidence) to inferences that form probable knowledge of other realities. Deduction, in contrast, involves already-known premises because they are a priori assumptions or presuppositions, or because all data have been examined and a comprehensive statement can be made on the basis of an earlier inductive examination, and then moves onward to inferences that necessarily follow from the premises.

According to this understanding, induction differs from deduction in two ways: in terms of premises and in terms of inferences. Inductive premises are those based upon evidence that derives from observation, whose validity is determined by the quality and adequacy of observation; whereas deductive premises are principles or claims that are simply assumed to be true and thus function as uncontested presuppositions. Inductive inferences are always probable, never absolutely certain, because from premises they extrapolate conclusions that involve matters beyond those included in the premises themselves, whereas deductive inferences are presented as certainties because they are logically necessary conclusions from the premises in that they address matters implicit within the premises themselves.[4] The quintessential form of deductive reasoning is the *syllogism*,[5] as in this example:

2. *Webster's New International Dictionary of the English Language, Unabridged*, 2nd ed., s.v. "Induction"; s.v. "Deduction."

3. Francis Bacon, *Novum Organum*; cf. Robert Audi, ed., *Cambridge Dictionary of Philosophy* (Cambridge: Cambridge University Press, 1995), 60–61; Paul Edwards, ed., *The Encyclopedia of Philosophy* (New York: Macmillan, 1967), 1:235–40.

4. This distinction between induction and deduction on the basis of the probability versus certainty in conclusions is often noted. For example, *Webster's New International Dictionary* (2nd ed., s.v. "Deduction") declares: "*Deduction* as contrasted with *induction* is distinguished by the fact that the conclusion is certain and necessary if the premises are." And Edward Craig, ed., *Routledge Encyclopedia of Philosophy* (London: Routledge, 1998), 2:755, describes induction: "It is now generally allowed that there are many other patterns of inference that can also provide reasonable grounds for believing their conclusions, even though their premises do not guarantee the truth of their conclusions. In current usage, it is common to call all such inferences inductive. It has been widely thought that all knowledge of matters of fact that we have not observed must be based on inductive inferences from what we have observed." See also Engel, *With Good Reason*, 7–9.

5. A syllogism begins with a general premise that must be accepted for deductive logic to work. The general premise must be all-inclusive, comprehensive, and absolute, a given such as an

MAJOR PREMISE/PRESUPPOSITION	All men are mortal.
MINOR PREMISE/PRESUPPOSITION	John is a man.
CONCLUSION	Therefore John is mortal.

Of course, to say that the syllogism is the quintessential form of deductive reasoning is not to say that it is the exclusive form of deduction. Any mode of reasoning that begins with uncontested presuppositions and construes data accorded to these uncontested presuppositions is deductive.

The quintessential form of inductive reasoning, however, is the *hypothesis*, a tentative conclusion that invites additional evidence for confirmation or correction, as in this example:

PREMISE/EVIDENCE	Matthew typically employs the imperatival future tense when quoting or alluding to an Old Testament passage.
CONCLUSION	Therefore this evidence implies that the imperatival future in Matthew 5:48 may indicate that this passage is a quotation or allusion to an Old Testament passage.

One might refer to this second view as the *essential* model of induction because it represents the essence of inductive reasoning: the movement from premises established through observation to probable or hypothetical inferences/conclusions. This essential model is actually implicit within the expansive model. The expansive model also embraces a process that moves from premises established on the basis of observation onward to probable or hypothetical inferences. Both of these models are evidential in that they insist on the movement from evidential premises to conclusions. But the expansive model assumes that the premises are particular cases that lead to inferences regarding general principles or laws, while the essential model insists that sometimes it is necessary or appropriate to argue from particular premises or data to equally particular conclusions.

According to both of these views of induction/deduction just presented (expansive and essential), induction and deduction are antithetical, contradictory, and mutually exclusive.[6] In any given instance, one must reason either

---

a priori, presupposition, axiom, mathematical theorem, or a theological or philosophical belief. A syllogism has three components: (1) a general statement concerning a certain class, (2) the specific identification of an individual case included in this class, and (3) the application of the general statement to the individual case. See Weinland, *How to Think Straight*, 62–87.

6. According to the essential and expansive models of induction/deduction, the only way to avoid conflict or contradiction between induction and deduction is to base the general premise of a modified form of deductive reasoning on a general inference from a process of inductive reasoning. For example, after observing that various humans die, one could inductively conclude that many or even most humans die. However, no one could possibly observe every human being who ever lived. Therefore, an inductive conclusion based on the particular instances of human death could never be all-inclusive, comprehensive, or absolute. A deductive premise based on this

inductively or deductively. A third understanding of induction/deduction, however, views them as complementary.

The Foundational Model

The foundational model uses the term *induction* to refer to the establishment of a premise on the basis of observation; it uses *deduction* to refer to the process of drawing inferences from the premise. This third construal is represented in the definition of *deduce* from *The Compact Edition of the Oxford English Dictionary*: "to derive by process of reasoning or inference; to infer."[7] If *deduce* means "to infer" or "to conclude," then all inferential reasoning must include deduction. In popular speech, of course, *deduction* is often used to refer to any logical conclusion, even one in the form of an inference drawn from observed evidence. Thus, for example, Sir Arthur Conan Doyle repeatedly presents his character Sherlock Holmes as a master of "deductive reasoning,"[8] even though the great detective employs a process of logic that moves from observed evidence to (probable) hypotheses. According to the essential understanding of induction herein described, that would be an example of inductive reasoning. One might refer to this third view as the *foundational* model of induction because it equates induction with the foundation or first component of the inferential process: the premise.

Models of Induction/Deduction and Inductive Bible Study

We use *inductive/induction* in Bible study according to the second view presented above: the *essential* understanding of induction. Although many theoreticians, especially since Hume, have registered philosophical problems with the expansive understanding of induction,[9] the purview of the present discussion does not include the exploration of the issues surrounding these philosophical problems. We want, however, to make the vital point that the expansive view of induction is not utilizable when dealing with the interpretation of texts. The goal of interpretation is essentially to understand the sense of the text rather than to extrapolate grand systems, patterns, or laws from the examination

---

kind of inductive inference would need to read: Many or most human beings are mortal. And the conclusion could not go beyond the *probability* that a particular human being is mortal. Thus a deductive movement from general to particular is valid if the premises are verified inductively by the evidence. In this case, where inductive inferences go on to constitute the general premises from which deduction proceeds, one can speak of deduction and induction as complementary. Cf. Eberhardt, *Bible in the Making of Ministers*, 130–31.

7. *The Compact Edition of the Oxford English Dictionary* (Oxford: Oxford University Press, 1971), 1:666, s.v. "Deduce."

8. Doyle, *Complete Sherlock Holmes*.

9. See especially the discussion on "problem of induction," in Audi, *Cambridge Dictionary of Philosophy*, 651–52.

of individual passages.[10] As previously indicated, the expansive understanding of induction might work well with a scientific model that assumes a more or less consistent causality such as exists in the natural and human sciences and can thus project comprehensive patterns from individual instances. But it does not accord with the nature of texts that express the dynamic of human communication, which is characterized by at least a significant element of individuality, freedom, play, and serendipity.[11]

We also find problems with the foundational model of induction. Most problematic is the consideration that this view does not even try to address the critical issue of the distinctive modes of reasoning involved in induction over against deduction; instead, it simply points out the obvious fact that the reasoning process always has two operative components: premises and inferences. Moreover, because lexicographers often define not only *deduce* but also *induce* as the logical drawing of inferences or conclusions, this view of induction tends to make induction and deduction virtually identical, thus rendering the distinction between induction and deduction meaningless.

The foundational model of induction has been put forward many times as the form of induction employed in inductive Bible study. According to this view, induction is coterminous with the direct observation of the text and the establishment of evidential premises, and deduction is coterminous with the process of drawing interpretive inferences and conclusions. This position is held by those who say that one engages in inductive Bible study when one is examining the biblical text directly but then moves into deductive Bible study at the point where one consults secondary sources. In this view, inductive Bible study is synonymous with the direct study of the text (where observation and the development of premises occur) while deductive Bible study is synonymous with the consultation of commentaries (where conclusions and inferences are presented). When one consults a commentary, it is claimed, one leaves the realm of inductive observations (premises) and moves into the realm of deductive conclusions (inferences).

This understanding of inductive Bible study has led to two practical consequences. First, it has led many to adopt a truncated view of inductive Bible

10. Most persons study biblical passages with a view toward finally developing a constructive and comprehensive theology, such as a theology of God. But this process (discussed in part 5 under "Correlation") involves the synthesis of the teaching of individual passages throughout the Bible and is distinct from the expansive understanding of induction, which could involve extrapolating grand schemes or comprehensive systems from one or two individual passages.

11. Many advocates of inductive Bible study have described induction in terms of this expansive model: from particular premises to general conclusions. But within their writings one looks in vain for any development of this notion as it pertains to biblical interpretation or any practical explication of induction in Bible study as a process from particular to general. One suspects that they have simply repeated this common definition of induction and affirmed it in theory while in practice they have operated with the essential model of induction. See, e.g., Eberhardt, *Bible in the Making of Ministers*, 130; Kuist, *These Words upon Thy Heart*, 61.

study: they insist that any holistic study of the Bible must include not only induction (direct observation of the text/premises) but also deduction (a concern for inferences/interpretive conclusions, including the use of commentaries, etc.). Thus these practitioners believe that all proper Bible study must be both inductive and deductive.[12] The problem with this view is that it entirely misses the critical hermeneutical point: induction involves an orientation toward the text that seeks to allow the text to speak on its own terms in such a way as to be free from the imposition of the reader's alien agenda.[13] The issue does not concern *what* is studied (the text itself versus books about the text) but *how* study is conducted. One should study with radical openness to the evidence pertaining to the meaning of the text, wherever such evidence might be found or whatever form it might take, rather than expressing an inclination to force one's presuppositions onto the meaning of the text. Obviously, one could engage in a kind of direct reading of the text itself that involves the crassest form of agenda imposition. Likewise, one could employ commentaries in such a way as to discern critically the proper assistance that commentaries can give in presenting evidence to ascertain accurately and precisely the sense of the text.[14]

In addition to a truncated view of inductive Bible study, this foundational understanding of induction has led to an unrealistically restrictive view of inductive Bible study. Sometimes advocates of inductive Bible study assume that the only thing necessary in the study of the Bible is the observation of the text itself. This perspective is represented in inductive Bible study manuals or workbooks that ask only after the facts of the text, for example, Who is speaking in Mark 1:7–8? What claims does he make about the coming one? Obviously, such a superficial orientation to the text cannot serve as an ade-

---

12. This view is put forward by Eberhardt, *Bible in the Making of Ministers*, 129–41, where he argues that the necessity of a deductive complement to an inductive approach was implicit within the thinking of W. W. White. Cf. Kuist, *These Words upon Thy Heart*, 60–61. See the discussion of this understanding of the relationship between induction and deduction within the history of inductive Bible study in Traina, "Inductive Bible Study Reexamined in Light of Contemporary Hermeneutics I: Interpreting the Text," in McCown and Massey, *Interpreting God's Word for Today*, 74–77. For an example of this understanding of inductive Bible study from someone outside the inductive Bible study movement, see Osborne, *Hermeneutical Spiral*, 40: "An inductive approach normally means an intensive, personal study of a text without recourse to other study aids or tools like commentaries."

13. This concern to avoid imposing one's own views onto the message of the biblical text is clearly the primary concern of those in the history of the inductive Bible study movement, who appealed to the principle of induction.

14. As we mention elsewhere (esp. in chap. 5), inductive Bible study insists on the priority of direct study of the text itself: one should place stress on the direct study of the text and, as a general principle, should begin with the study of the text itself before examining secondary sources. But we insist that the essential view of induction requires that all evidence, of whatever type and wherever it might be found, should be used to form inductive premises, including evidence derived from secondary sources.

quate basis for the serious scholarly examination of biblical passages that is required of Christian leaders. But this kind of focus on the basic facts of the text clearly cannot in itself supply even laypersons with a real sense of the meaning of the text. In an attempt, then, to address the desire for a theologically consequential reading of the text, those who produce such manuals will often impose, or at least suggest, theological interpretations, and they will do so without citing any biblical evidence for these interpretations. Those who use such manuals often implicitly construe the basic facts of the text according to their own preconceived notions and thus engage in a presupposition-imposing process while convinced that their study is truly inductive.

The second understanding of induction, the essential model, properly addresses the critical issues involved in biblical interpretation, especially the key issue of process toward interpretive goal: *What kind of reasoning process is required by the goal of interpretation—namely, the ascertainment of textual sense?* The essential model of induction insists that the difference between induction and deduction has to do with the mode or direction of reasoning. In an inductive approach, one moves from evidential premises to (hypothetical/ tentative) conclusions. In a deductive approach, one moves from assumptions or presuppositions to an examination of data, with a view toward construing the data ultimately according to the assumptions with which one began.[15] As employed by inductive Bible study, then, induction is evidential, and deduction is presuppositional.

15. There has been much discussion in some philosophical circles of late regarding *abduction*, otherwise known as "inference to best explanation." Abduction involves putting forth a number of possible explanations for data or phenomena and making a judgment as to which of these explanations best accords with all of the factors involved in the data or phenomena. Some consider abduction to be an alternative to both induction and deduction, such as Vanhoozer, *Is There a Meaning in This Text?* 333–34. But Vanhoozer proceeds to describe abduction in terms of (1) hypotheses and (2) probability over against absolute proof, both of which are central to induction. The view of Gilbert Harman is preferable: inductive inferences are, or should be, inferences to best explanation, that is, abductive. Abduction analyzes the imaginative, rational, and psychological processes involved in the discovery of inductive inferential possibilities and the selection of the inductive possibility that best explains the entirety of the data. See Gilbert Harman, "The Inference to the Best Explanation," *Philosophical Review* 74 (1965): 88–95; Peter Lipton, *Inference to Best Explanation*, 2nd ed. (London: Routledge, 2004); cf. Ted Honderich, ed., *Oxford Companion to Philosophy* (Oxford: Oxford University Press, 1995), 407–8; Audi, *Cambridge Dictionary of Philosophy*, 1.

Appendix B

Presuppositions
in Contemporary
Hermeneutical Discussion

How does inductive Bible study relate to the hermeneutical movements that insist on the thoroughgoing, definitive role of preunderstandings/presuppositions in biblical interpretation? From an inductive Bible study perspective, what can a critical assessment of these views reveal about the nature of the study of the Bible, the demands of the interpretive process, and especially the objective/subjective dialectic that we describe as transjective? We present here a brief assessment of those who would advocate for a determinative role for an *existential preunderstanding* and for *ecclesial preconceptions*.

Description of Existential Preunderstanding

Some insist that the Bible must be interpreted according to an existential preunderstanding. This contemporary existential view of preunderstanding was influenced by Friedrich Schleiermacher through Wilhelm Dilthey, who emphasizes the interpersonal nature of hermeneutics. Dilthey holds that through literary expressions the interpreter (I) relives and reenacts empathically the experience, both cognitive and transcognitive, of the writer (Thou). Such discovery of the I in the Thou is possible, says Dilthey, because of a preunderstanding of the immanence of God based on the commonality of human personality and of lived experience. The interpreter as a historical being is innately equipped to understand historical documents. In fact, this apprehension is often on an intuitive, nonrational level that Dilthey calls "divination."[1]

Martin Heidegger, whose philosophy was very significant in the development of existentialist hermeneutics, echoes the view of Dilthey. The only possible beginning for understanding is the preunderstanding of the concrete existence of the I (*Dasein*). In hermeneutics, the self cannot be escaped.[2]

Rudolf Bultmann, who has greatly influenced contemporary biblical hermeneutics, took his cue from Dilthey and Heidegger. He answers the question raised by his essay "Is Exegesis without Presuppositions Possible?" in the negative.[3] The interpreter cannot go to the Scriptures with an empty head. Exegesis inevitably is affected by the makeup and the cultural existence of the interpreter. In fact, understanding the biblical text is not possible without interrogating that text. The questions asked, which determine the meanings found, are inevitably informed by one's self-understanding. For example, the biblical concept of fear cannot be understood without a preunderstanding of fear from lived experience. A point of contact is needed between the biblical text and the interpreter concerning fear if understanding is to take place. Thus Bultmann agrees with Dilthey's distinction between the objective study of the physical sciences and the subjective nature of the study of history.[4] Though supporters of the New Hermeneutic, represented by Ernst Fuchs and Gerhard Ebeling, have some differences with Bultmann regarding the necessity and possibility of discovering the historical Jesus, they essentially agree with Bultmann regarding an existential approach to hermeneutics.[5]

In following Dilthey and Heidegger, Bultmann's and the New Hermeneutic's emphasis on the role of preunderstanding in hermeneutics is reasonable. What makes Bultmann's view problematic is the particular theological preunderstanding that he brings to the text and his refusal to subject his preunderstanding to the judgment of the text. He approaches the biblical text with a naturalistic and positivistic view of history that decides in advance how the sense of the text should be understood.

Bultmann insists that, for a modern scientific person, the physical world is a closed causal continuum that does not allow for divine miracle.[6] Consequently, Bultmann argues that these modern people consider biblical data to be *myths*, which their preunderstanding will not allow them to accept. Bultmann characterizes these myths as ways of describing God in physical and human

1. See Wilhelm Dilthey, *Gesammelte Schriften* (Stuttgart: Teubner, 1962), 7:201–2, 236; cf. H. A. Hodges, *The Philosophy of Wilhelm Dilthey* (London: Routledge & Kegan Paul, 1952), 119.

2. Cf. Martin Heidegger, *Being and Time* (Oxford: Blackwell, 1962), 62.

3. See Rudolf Bultmann, *Existence and Faith: Shorter Writings of Rudolf Bultmann* (Cleveland: World, 1960), 289–96.

4. Rudolf Bultmann, *Jesus and the Word* (London: Collins, 1958), 11.

5. Ernst Fuchs, "The New Testament and the Hermeneutical Problem," in *The New Hermeneutic*, ed. James M. Robinson and J. B. Cobb Jr., New Frontiers in Theology 2 (New York: Harper, 1964), 111–45; Gerhard Ebeling, *Word and Faith* (London: SCM, 1963).

6. See Bultmann, *Existence and Faith*, 291–93.

terms, the otherworldly in terms of the this-worldly. They are attempts, he says, to explain the unusual in terms of supernatural invasion.[7]

In dealing with such materials, Bultmann uses a hermeneutic of *demythologizing* to discover the existential meaning of these myths. He operates on the basis that an event (*Historie*) and its existential value (*Geschichte*) have no necessary connection. Modern scientific people, Bultmann says, cannot accept the miracle of the bodily resurrection of Christ; the resurrection myth means that Christ's death is salvific and that Christ indeed is Lord. The objective-historical is thus transformed into something subjective-historical.[8] As a consequence, Bultmann's *Theology of the New Testament* reads more like Bultmann's theology than the theology of the New Testament.[9]

Evaluation of Existential Preunderstanding

Many of Bultmann's hermeneutical insights are valid and helpful, especially his insistence that we must always understand the text in relation to ourselves and that we must always process our understanding of the biblical object in relation to our preunderstandings/presuppositions. His insights emphasize a point that all readers of the Bible should acknowledge: the reason why the interpretations of some readers are superficial and unsatisfying is that they themselves are shallow people. They have not developed the potential depth of their own humanity. Bultmann is right to call for an engagement between the reader in his/her experience and the biblical text, but he fails to sufficiently take into account that this engagement is in the form of an encounter in which the voice of the biblical text is dominant.

In the structure of the communicative model of texts, readers as they interpret are addressed as *hearers*; they are not approached as *speakers*. In other words, by the very nature of the case, the text-reader engagement gives no opportunity for the reader to speak back to the text[10] in any way that the text (or the authorial presence encountered in the text) will hear. The fact that readers are addressed as hearers, whose role is to listen, rather than as speakers, whose role is to talk, suggests that readers should give priority to the intentional attempt to listen to the text on its own terms, according to its own horizon.[11]

---

7. See Bultmann, *Kerygma and Myth*, 10–11.
8. Ibid., 15–16.
9. See Bultmann, *Theology of the New Testament*.
10. The only possible exception to this rule would be something such as the rhetorical question: an assertion in question form that is intended to draw from the reader an answer (e.g., Matt. 6:25). However, this example is actually no exception at all, for the rhetorical question *requires* agreement with the assertion that is implicit within the rhetorical question.
11. In one sense an appropriate approach is to think of the reader-text engagement as a conversation. But it is properly an inner conversation that the reader has about the meaning and possible appropriation of the text: it is an internal conversation or dialogue in reaction to the text. It is not the kind of conversation in which the text hears and can be transformed, but

But Bultmann's embrace of existentialism, and especially his insistence on adopting a hermeneutic so fully dependent upon the philosophy of Heidegger and of neo-Kantianism, leads him to assimilate the horizon of the biblical text into his own horizon as a contemporary reader, with the result that he is unable fully to hear and appropriate the text in its otherness. He thus adopts a religious model of extreme individualism that is oblivious to the communal dimensions of New Testament theology. Also, he is compelled to adopt a canonical reductionism, in practice ignoring all those biblical traditions and themes that do not fit his emphasis on existential encounter. Ironically, in his attempt to read the text in such a fashion that it would seriously connect with the subjective experience of the contemporary reader, Bultmann's collapse of the message of the text into his own preunderstanding prevents the text from engaging the subjective experience of the modern reader in truly new and revolutionary ways. Thiselton declares:

> *Only if we respect the distinctiveness of the horizons of the text* as against the distinctiveness of our own reader-horizon can a creative and productive interaction of horizons occur. The distance between the reader and the text performs a positive hermeneutical function. *Premature* assimilation into the perspectives projected by the horizons of readers leaves the reader trapped within his or her own prior horizons. Worse, in such a case the reader may stand under the illusion that the texts have fully addressed him or her.[12]

Although the existentialist program as developed by Bultmann is adopted in its pure form by few scholars today,[13] the notion of the necessity and appropriateness of a presuppositionally determined construal of the Bible is very much alive. N. T. Wright points out that Bible study conducted by conservative and pietistic laypeople often works from a purely subjective model that asks only, What is this text saying to me? thereby collapsing the "horizon of the text" into the readers' own horizon.[14] The result of this purely subjective approach is that the subject is impoverished; for the distinctive and often challenging message of the text is largely silenced in favor of a circular process, according to which one reads one's own contemporary concerns into the text, only to read them out again.

---

one in which the reader, by using self-conversation about the meaning of the text, can come to a greater understanding, with the potential result of transformation.

12. Thiselton, *New Horizons in Hermeneutics*, 8, emphasis original; Vanhoozer, *Is There a Meaning in This Text?* 435, reminds us of the subjective freedom and liberation in objectivity: "Reading Scripture also frees us from the tyranny of the present. The text contains a 'dangerous memory' [Karl Barth] that has the potential to liberate us from the confines of our epoch and to orient our action, in hope, to the future."

13. See Neill and Wright, *Interpretation of the New Testament*, 237–51; John K. Riches, *A Century of New Testament Study* (Valley Forge, PA: Trinity Press International, 1993), 199–232; Meyer, *Reality and Illusion*, 70; Stuhlmacher, *Historical Criticism and Theological Interpretation*, 51–55.

14. Wright, *New Testament and the People of God*, 60.

Indeed, we have recently talked to a leader of a prominent international evangelical ministry to college and university students who summarizes the most common response that staff members hear from university students concerning Bible studies in essentially this way: "The claim that a passage has this or that meaning to communicate is ridiculous. Everyone comes to a passage with one's own experiences, concerns, and agenda, which do not merely affect or condition one's construal of the passage but absolutely determine it. Therefore a passage means whatever a person takes it to mean, and construal is entirely the result of the kinds of questions or concerns the reader brings to the passage out of the reader's own experience." Clearly the spirit of existentialism can take many shapes and forms.

A version of the existentialist approach has recently emerged in the form of the insistence that the specific nature of the community in which reading is done determines how persons within that community, and the community as a whole, will understand texts, including the biblical text. Every interpretive community has its own ethos, concerns, traditions, expectations, and purposes; this dynamic matrix of community experience leads each community to adopt its own way of reading the text (reading strategy) that effectively predetermines how the text will be construed.[15] This view is now widely held regarding the study of literature in general, and it has been given impetus by such scholars as the philosopher Richard Rorty[16] and the literary critic Stanley Fish.[17] But it has also been adopted specifically in biblical studies by a number of scholars, including Daniel Patte[18] and Stanley Hauerwas.[19]

15. Vanhoozer, *Is There a Meaning in This Text?* 113, refers to hermeneutical theory of both personal and communal existentialism as "the general relativity thesis": "what interpreters observe in a text is wholly dependent on the interpreter's 'trajectory' (e.g., prejudices, aims, interests), and 'position' (e.g., gender, race, class)."

16. See Richard Rorty, *The Linguistic Turn* (Chicago: University of Chicago Press, 1967); idem, *Philosophy and the Mirror of Nature* (Princeton, NJ: Princeton University Press, 1979); idem, *Consequences of Pragmatism* (Minneapolis: University of Minnesota Press, 1982); idem, *Contingency, Irony, and Solidarity* (Cambridge: Cambridge University Press, 1989).

17. Stanley Fish, *Is There a Text in This Class? The Authority of Interpretive Communities* (Cambridge, MA: Harvard University Press, 1980); idem, *Doing What Comes Naturally: Change, Rhetoric, and the Practice of Theory in Literary and Legal Studies* (Oxford: Clarendon, 1989).

18. Daniel Patte, *Discipleship according to the Sermon on the Mount: Four Legitimate Readings, Four Plausible Views of Discipleship, and Their Relative Values* (Valley Forge, PA: Trinity Press International, 1996); idem, *The Challenge of Discipleship: A Critical Study of the Sermon on the Mount as Scripture* (Harrisburg, PA: Trinity Press International, 1999); Cristina Grenholm and Daniel Patte, eds., *Reading Israel in Romans: Legitimacy and Plausibility of Divergent Interpretations* (Harrisburg, PA: Trinity Press International, 2000); Gary A. Phillips and Nicole Wilkinson Duran, eds., *Reading Communities, Reading Scripture: Essays in Honor of Daniel Patte* (Harrisburg, PA: Trinity Press International, 2002).

19. Stanley Hauerwas, *Unleashing the Scripture: Freeing the Bible from Captivity to America* (Nashville: Abingdon, 1993).

As in all major hermeneutical approaches, much in this understanding of the role of interpretive communities is legitimate and helpful. These scholars have identified and analyzed a feature that is important in all interpretive work, a feature that has often been overlooked. Much of what we assume to be natural and inevitable in the interpretive process is, in fact, due to our socialization within the community to which we belong. But the problem lies with the extreme position that this school of thought holds: it emphasizes the social-subjective component of the understanding process largely to the exclusion of the potentially determinative role of the biblical text with its own horizon.

Empirically, social history reveals that whole cultures and subcultures have been changed through the power of texts, received as a distinct and challenging word. The horizons of individual readers and of reading communities are capable of shifting on the basis of the message of texts; indeed, these horizons constantly change as communities experience and respond to all sorts of realities, including textual realities, outside of their own communal structures of thought.[20]

With this sole emphasis upon the power of distinct reading strategies within particular communities, a further practical problem is that textual understanding is transmogrified into community understanding. The focus is now upon understanding community experience and community dynamics over against understanding the text itself. The process of understanding the text, in any real sense and on its own terms, is deemed to be a useless and pointless exercise. Ironically, this kind of emphasis upon community interpretation actually robs the interpretive process of its genuine communal character, broadly conceived; for according to many who hold this view, communities cannot engage in a discourse with other communities that will lead them to arrive at a fuller understanding of the meaning communicated by texts. Each community has its own reading strategy and corresponding textual construals, and any discussion of the meaning of texts with other reading communities inevitably involves their talking about themselves and even past each other. All that is left is what Kevin J. Vanhoozer calls "'comparative hermeneutics': the analysis and criticism of the way various cultures see and interpret."[21]

Description of Ecclesial Preconceptions

In addition to the existentialist approach, some insist that the Bible must be interpreted according to ecclesial preconceptions. Many Christian scholars hold

---

20. Meyer, *Reality and Illusion*, 49–53, speaks of the power of "new ascertainments" to change or modify horizons; cf. Max Turner, "Historical Criticism and Theological Hermeneutics," 58–59; Thiselton, *New Horizons in Hermeneutics*, 31–54, 170.

21. Vanhoozer, *Is There a Meaning in This Text?* 103.

that the Bible as Scripture must properly be interpreted according to the faith confession and faith experience of the church as the community of believers, meaning that the theological tradition of the church is a presupposition with which one must come and construe the text. Drawing upon certain insights from those who insist upon the determinative character of *community inter-pretation* described previously, some scholars who advocate this ecclesial view argue that the Bible can be, and has been, studied in a variety of ways, and that the way in which the Bible is read and consequently understood depends upon the community that is doing the reading. These scholars insist, then, that those in the church should read the biblical text according to the realities that shape the church as the community of faith.

But these scholars go further. They argue that because the biblical materials arose from the community of faith (Israel and the church) and were directed to the community of faith, and because they come in the form of canon, which orients their existence toward the community of faith, the church is *the proper sphere* within which these writings should be interpreted.[22] The Bible really belongs to the church. Robert W. Wall thus asserts that "Scripture's legal address is the worshiping community,"[23] and "a biblical writing is canonical property."[24]

As far as these thinkers are concerned, historical-critical scholarship in the modern period has essentially taken the Bible from the church and placed it in the hands of modernity's skepticism, secularism, and cynicism. The study of the Bible in the academy is not only "uninterested in promoting theological understanding and redemptive results as a strategic part of the church's mission in the world," but it is also committed to "problematize Scripture," with the purpose of advocating the Bible's "inherent unreliability in matters of faith and life."[25] By adopting modern historicism, the academic biblical guild approaches the biblical text as a window that is "darkened" by theological conjecture; it tries to purge the study of the text of its theological character by focusing upon the historical background that gave rise to the biblical writings or to find the real Jesus within his own historical setting, believing that truth is communicated through speculatively reconstructed history, not through theological texts.[26] This historical criticism may then be appropriate to the ethos, traditions, and purposes of the academy, but it does not accord with the proper function of canonical Scripture in the

22. Hauerwas, *Unleashing the Scripture*, 9, thus says, "The Bible is not and should not be accessible to merely anyone, but rather it should only be made available to those who have undergone the hard discipline of existing as part of God's people."

23. Robert W. Wall, "Reading the Bible from within Our Traditions," in Green and Turner, *Between Two Horizons*, 90.

24. Ibid., 93.

25. Ibid., 90.

26. Ibid., 92.

church, which is to nurture the church's spiritual life and to foster Christian formation.

The proper focus for the interpretation of the Bible within the church, these scholars maintain, is not some speculative reconstruction of a history behind the text, but the plain sense of the final form of the canonical text.[27] The proper framework for the interpretation of the Bible within the church is not the modern historical model (critical orthodoxy) of the guild but the theology of the church, a theology that finds expression especially in the church's rule of faith (*regula fidei*).

The multiplicity of possible interpretations of Scripture that surfaced in the church's struggle against heretical groups led the early church to insist that the Bible must be interpreted according to the rule of faith. Indeed, it is asserted that in the church "a critical engagement with the biblical text requires the interpreter to test theological claims by the Rule,"[28] and the church's interpretation must "constrain" the theological teaching of the text by the church's rule of faith.[29] For these scholars, the rule of faith is not synonymous with Scripture but is prior to Scripture, or at least is based on what was prior to the writing of the Christian Bible, in that it was fashioned by the life and teaching of Jesus. It is, really, the essence of the gospel, whose proclamation by Jesus preceded the writing of the New Testament (Luke 24:13–35, 44–49). The rule of faith summarizes the heart of the Christian faith with a view toward serving as a "boundary marker" for Christian identity. One should, perhaps, speak of the "*rules* of faith," for the attempt to capture the sum of the Christian faith was made by several church fathers: although their statements contain common theological and christological beliefs, these various fathers expressed their beliefs differently and fitted them together by different grammars.[30] A representative attempt to articulate the rule of faith comes from Tertullian:

> Now with regard to this rule of faith, . . . it is, you must know, that which prescribes the belief that there is only one God, and that he is none other than the creator of the world, who produced all things out of nothing through his own word, first of all sent forth. The word is called his son, and under the name of God, was seen in diverse manners by the patriarchs, heard at all times in the prophets, and at last brought by the Spirit and power of the Father down into the virgin Mary. He was made flesh in her womb, and being born of her, went forth as Jesus Christ. Thereafter, he preached the new land and the new promise of the kingdom of heaven, and he worked miracles. Having been crucified, he rose again on the third day. Having ascended into the heavens, he sat at the right hand of the Father. He sent in place of himself the power of the Holy Spirit to lead

27. Ibid., 93, 96. See also Hart, "Tradition, Authority, and a Christian Approach," 196; Wall, "Canonical Context and Canonical Conversations," 168, 170–71.

28. Wall, "Reading the Bible from within our Traditions," 102.

29. Ibid., 88, 90.

30. Ibid., 89.

those who believe. He will come with glory to take the saints to the enjoyment of everlasting life and of the heavenly promises and to condemn the wicked to everlasting fire. This will take place after the resurrection of both these classes, together with the restoration of their flesh. This rule . . . was taught by Christ, and raises among us no other questions than those which heresies introduce, and which make people heretics.[31]

In spite of some slight differences, these expressions of the rule of faith from the fathers are summaries of the salvation-historical meganarrative found in the Bible. Everything here is taught as an emphasis in the Bible, and the summaries relay the broad strokes of the biblical narrative. Indeed, Irenaeus himself, who first introduced the notion of the rule of faith, recognized it to be a biblical summary, a synthesis of biblical passages interpreted contextually, that is, a summary of biblical teaching arrived at by responsible exegesis.[32]

These scholars maintain that although the Bible is the church's preeminent authority,[33] the interpretation of the Bible within the church is profoundly influenced by its communal and theological life, which is informed not only by the biblical text but also by the church's great ecumenical creeds, hymns, the testimonies of its saints, and the theological writings of its faithful.[34] According to these scholars, persons in the church need to acknowledge this situation as the actual reality of the church's life,[35] and the church needs to recognize that it is called to pursue a continual dialogue between the biblical text and its theological tradition, a dialogue in which the biblical text informs the church's theological tradition, and conversely, the church's theological tradition informs the church's interpretation of the biblical text. However, for most of these scholars, the role of Scripture is primary; thus Trevor Hart describes this dialogue as a "progressive hermeneutical spiral," which is characterized by "a constant return to the text of Scripture itself," for the Bible is "the primary source and norm for Christian faith and the fashioning of Christian identity."[36]

31. Tertullian, *Prescription against Heretics* 90, quoted in ibid., 88.

32. Hart, "Tradition, Authority, and a Christian Approach," 187–88, 190.

33. Ibid., 184: the Bible is the Church's "primary authority for the formation of Christian identity at every level."

34. See William J. Abraham, *Canon and Criterion in Christian Theology: From the Fathers to Feminism* (Oxford: Oxford University Press, 1998).

35. Hart, "Tradition, Authority, and a Christian Approach," 184–85, says, "Theological concerns (in the guise of tradition) are always present and always important in any approach to the text of the Bible as Scripture. Theology, that is to say, is something we bring with us to the text as well as something the raw materials for which we quarry from it. . . . Many voices shape our interpreting, but theological tradition is important among these. There is nothing to be gained and everything to be lost by pretending otherwise—that is, to allege either that this influence is not there or that we are immune to it."

36. Ibid., 190–91.

Evaluation of Ecclesial Preconceptions

These scholars have raised a number of critical issues, and their arguments have highlighted some of the most prominent dimensions of the existence and function of the Bible. For one thing, they have quite properly attacked the claim of historical critics that their method is objective because it operates as purely historical and is not tainted by the necessarily subjective character of theological assertions and convictions. They have rightly pointed out, as we previously indicated, that pure objectivity does not exist; everyone has presuppositions, and these presuppositions are often related to the culture or community of which one is a part.

But an inductive approach would go further by noting that the issue of a theological reading of the text over against one that is essentially historical-critical is not purely a matter of community preference but is also a matter of the nature of the biblical text itself. The text of the Bible is preeminently theological. No study of this text, no matter who does it or in what context it is performed, is fully adequate unless the text's primarily theological character is embraced in the process of its interpretation. Of course, the Bible contains various kinds of data and relates to many different aspects of reality; it can therefore legitimately be studied in order to illumine the history of religions, to reconstruct the history of Israel or the life of Jesus, or even to illustrate the psychological insights of Carl Jung. But anyone who engages in these kinds of studies of the biblical text should acknowledge that the text is quintessentially theological in its material content (above all, it concerns God, and its primary purpose from beginning to end is to make proclamatory claims regarding divine realities). Thus any study of these ancillary matters should be pursued through the prism of the text's theological obsession, and for that matter its concern for the ecclesial community.

Given this preeminently theological character of the text, even the biblical guild in its own work should typically emphasize the theological meaning of the text. Ben F. Meyer states, "Religious literature calls for interpretation alert to religious meanings and values. The issue is the utterly basic one of catching on, or not."[37] Indeed, the attempt to reject or even just to ignore the theological dimension in the study of the Bible is itself a theological decision; as Adolf Schlatter pointed out a century ago, to reject (in practice) the

---

37. Meyer, *Reality and Illusion*, 149. Meyer draws a distinction between "interpretation" and "analysis." Interpretation is the ascertaining of the "intended sense" of a document. Because these documents are religious/theological, this interpretation involves their theological meaning. Analysis is the exploration of issues behind the text (e.g., sources, redactions, historical reconstructions). Meyer contends that interpretation comes logically and practically prior to analysis; the guild, then, cannot do its work of historical-critical reconstruction without first attending to the (theological) meaning of the text.

significance of the theological claims of a theological document is to make a theological judgment.[38]

This consideration that the theological character of the biblical text, at least to some extent, can and should be engaged by *all* who read the Bible, raises a serious question about the claim that the Bible can be properly interpreted as a theological witness only by those who are in the community of faith and come to the text from the perspective of faith.

We acknowledge that the Bible was produced from within the faith community and was directed primarily to others within the faith community; it deals with theological and spiritual realities that are, to at least some significant extent, embodied in the faith community from generation to generation.[39] And the New Testament itself speaks of the role of the Holy Spirit (who dwells preeminently in the church) in leading Christians into deeper understanding of the truth (e.g., John 16:5–15). All of these considerations lead to the conclusion that, in general, persons within the church should have greater capacity to understand the profundities and fullness of the biblical message than those who lack such theological background or ecclesially informed faith experience.

But even this claim may require a measure of qualification since no individual Christian or Christian community experiences biblical faith perfectly, and all have some tendency toward theological and/or spiritual dysfunction,

38. See Adolf Schlatter, "Atheistische Methoden in der Theologie," *Beiträge zur Förderung christlicher Theologie* 9, no. 5 (1905): 229–50. For the English translation, see Adolf Schlatter, "Atheistic Methods in Theology," trans. David R. Bauer, *Asbury Theological Journal* 51 (Fall 1996): 45–57. This article was reprinted as an appendix in the English translation of Werner Neuer's short biography of Schlatter: "Appendix D: Adolf Schlatter on Atheistic Methods in Theology," in *Adolf Schlatter: A Biography of Germany's Premier Biblical Theologian*, trans. Robert W. Yarbrough (Grand Rapids: Baker Academic, 1995), 211–25. Peter Stuhlmacher (*Historical Criticism and Theological Interpretation*, 83–91) makes the same general case: he calls for a "hermeneutics of consent" that involves biblical scholars attending to the history of effects of the text, that is, entering into critical dialogue with the theological tradition of the church (the principle of "hearing"), while being open to the possibility of divine transcendence, to which the biblical text bears witness. The scholar is not necessarily a person of faith and will not necessarily ever become a person of faith, but the scholar should be an "advocate of a listening intellect who is open to the Christian tradition and the possibility of address through the biblical *kerygma*, without himself [necessarily] being able to rise to faith in the truth of this message" (89–90).

39. Note Luther's principle of *Sache und Sprache* (thing and speech): "Whoever does not understand the things cannot draw the sense from the words." Quoted in Meyer, *Reality and Illusion*, 91. Marcel Dumais points out that the implied reader of at least most of the NT documents is a member of the community of faith (as is true of the OT as well). See Marcel Dumais, "Sens de l'Écriture: Réexamen à la lumière de l'herméneutique philosophique et des approches littéraires récentes," *NTS* 45 (1999): 325. For the English translation, see Marcel Dumais, "The Sense of Scripture Re-Examined in Light of Philosophical Hermeneutics and Recent Literary Approaches," trans. David R. Bauer, *The Asbury Journal* 63, no. 1 (2008): 53–74. Cf. Bockmuehl, *Seeing the Word*, 70–71, 92, 113.

which could distort rather than enable understanding of the text's theological message.[40] In addition, the notion that the church's theology is ultimately and absolutely determinative for its scriptural understanding could lead to a kind of reading in which the message of the text is simply assimilated to the church's theology.[41] Thiselton gives the following warning:

> Yet when we look at the history of biblical interpretation, we can see that too often a theological pre-understanding has brought about a premature and uncritical understanding of the text, in which the text was forced to say only what was required by a given theological tradition. . . . The general tendency [in the medieval period] was to interpret the New Testament in such a way that it merely spoke back the current tradition of the church. In Gadamer's language, it could not bring new truth to speech.[42]

This kind of assimilation is theologically and spiritually destructive for the church's life: it prevents the Bible from functioning as the means of God's correction for the thought and life of the church (and of Christians). Gerhard Ebeling reminds us: "According to Luther, the word of God always comes as *adversarius noster*, our adversary. It does not simply confirm and strengthen us in what we think we are, and in what we wish to be taken for. . . . This is the way, the only way, in which the word draws us into concord and peace with God."[43] Indeed, one should note that almost every biblical book assumes an attitude of confrontation and challenge toward the community of faith to

40. Meyer, *Reality and Illusion*, 93–94.

41. Some argue that the insistence upon a construal of scriptural passages that is determined by the Christian reader's contemporary faith position is based on the use of the OT Scriptures within the NT, for the NT is typically not interested in the "original significance" of OT passages but assigns new meaning to OT passages in light of the NT's own fresh theological convictions. But we should be very careful here, for the hermeneutical and theological issues involved in the use of the OT within the NT are extremely complex. Drawing quick and hasty conclusions becomes easy and dangerous. One thing seems certain to most scholars: The major theological and hermeneutical basis for rereading OT passages in the NT is the NT's Christology, eschatology, and salvation history. The conviction that all of salvation history finds its eschatological fulfillment in Jesus Christ and his work of salvation and of forming the end-time people of God led the NT writers to read the OT as witness to the revelation of God in Jesus Christ. This emphasis suggests that the hermeneutical trajectory culminates precisely and necessarily in the historical revelation of Jesus Christ, which is proclaimed in the NT; therefore use of the OT in the NT does not in itself warrant a Christian rereading of biblical passages (both OT and NT) on the basis of post-NT Christian reflection or experience. See esp. Richard N. Longenecker, *Biblical Exegesis in the Apostolic Period*, 2nd ed. (Grand Rapids: Eerdmans, 1999); Donald Juel, *Messianic Exegesis: Christological Interpretation of the Old Testament in Early Christianity* (Philadelphia: Fortress, 1988); cf. Hays, *Echoes of Scripture*.

42. Thiselton, *Two Horizons*, 316; cf. Hauerwas, *Unleashing the Scripture*, 23, who says, "You do not have or need 'a meaning' of the text when you understand that Church is more determinative than text."

43. Quoted in Thiselton, *Two Horizons*, 319.

which it is addressed; rather than simply confirming or adopting the "what is" of the theology or lifestyle of the community, these writings typically offer that which is, at least to some extent, an alternative version in the form of "what ought to be different."

Moreover, the tendency on the part of those in the faith community to uncritically bring their theological assumptions to the reading of the text can dull the sharp and challenging message that biblical passages were originally intended to communicate to the faithful. Thus Walter Wink describes such a reading of the parable of the Pharisee and tax collector (Luke 18:9–14) on the part of those who have been socialized into the conceptual world of the Christian faith. These readers bring a set of what are now Christian assumptions to the parable: the assumption that Pharisees are evil, self-righteous, murderous hypocrites; and that tax collectors are receptive, humble, trusting seekers after truth. But this set of assumptions is exactly opposite to the kinds of assumptions that this parable expects its readers will bring to it. In order that the parable might have its intended effect of profoundly undoing and radically reversing whole clusters of cherished beliefs, the implied author anticipates that readers will approach the parable with the working assumptions that Pharisees are paragons of moral and religious virtue, and tax collectors are unspeakably vile. As Thiselton indicates, "A parable which originally had the function of unsettling the hearer and overturning his values now serves to confirm him in the values which he already has."[44]

Further, Christians are in danger of misunderstanding the sense of biblical passages when they uncritically interpret these passages in light of theological formulations or disputes that have arisen in the course of the history of the church. They are making a serious mistake when they assume, for example, that every Pauline passage that mentions election directly addresses the issue of unconditional election as it has been debated in the Western church from the time of Augustine and especially Calvin and Arminius.

An additional problem is that to speak of the church's theology, according to which Christians ought to interpret the text, is to speak in a most general way. As we discussed, the rule of faith, as articulated by the fathers, is very broad and basic, essentially a summary of scriptural teaching reflecting the overall biblical narrative; thus the rule of faith (*regula fidei*) is closely related to, though not entirely identical with, the analogy of faith (*analogia fidei*).[45] If one wished to talk about the church's rule of faith as that which contains more specific content, one would be compelled to admit that there is, and always has been, a lack of consensus on a vast number of particular issues.

44. Ibid., 15.

45. The claim that the rule of faith is not completely synonymous with Scripture is true because any summary of the biblical story is a selective abstraction of the biblical text itself, and any selective abstraction will be informed to a greater or lesser extent by ideological or theological convictions.

Markus Bockmuehl posits that the fathers up to around AD 150 had unique access to the apostolic faith through first- or second-person acquaintance with the apostles themselves and should be granted a privileged role in Christian interpretation; yet even Bockmuehl acknowledges that on certain critical issues the fathers disagreed among themselves.[46] In another passage, Bockmuehl laments that many "ecclesial readings" are general and anemic.[47]

One is forced, then, either to reject the notion of the rule of faith as imposing from the outside any sort of specific interpretive content or to understand the rule of faith as essentially a reading of the biblical story, that is, of the canon in its entirety and in its structure, especially as it comes to culmination in the New Testament. This reading would be conducted within the broad contours of the church's theological convictions, which the church itself considers to be preeminently scriptural.[48] In this latter case, the claim that one ought to interpret individual passages in light of the rule of faith is tantamount to insisting that one should faithfully interpret Scripture in light of Scripture, within the canonical context, and from the perspective of the church's experience and articulation of the Christian faith, which themselves have been shaped by Scripture canonically read. In practice, the rule of faith employed inductively in the interpretation of the Bible would involve above all a heuristic function in that it would point to and illumine certain aspects of the text's

46. Bockmuehl, *Seeing the Word*, 223–25.

47. Ibid., 60.

48. W. W. White and The Biblical Seminary in New York seemed to have affirmed this principle of correlating the faith of the church generally and the basic affirmations of the Bible read canonically. White was concerned that the Bible should be handled "in such a way as to avoid provoking the spirit of controversy and to foster unity among all students by concentrating . . . upon fundamental principles that express the teaching of Scriptures-as-a-whole and therefore tend to unite on a common basis all devout and Bible-loving Christians." Elsewhere the statutes of The Biblical Seminary in New York indicated that its purpose was to prepare Christian leaders who would be "positive, constructive, non-disputatious . . . [and who would] concentrate on the indubitable certainties of historic Christianity as declared in the Christian Scriptures, and . . . be loyal to the historic faith of the Church as held in common by evangelical Christians." These statements are taken from the statutes of The Biblical Seminary in New York, as quoted in Eberhardt, *Bible in the Making of Ministers*, 215–16. White saw the Apostles' Creed as a comprehensive statement of the truth of the Bible-as-a-whole and as providing "the doctrinal foundation of the Seminary." According to him, "it admirably and concisely summarizes the essential doctrines of Christianity as set forth in the Scriptures." He found this creed especially appealing because "it had been not arrived at deductively . . . and then promulgated *ex cathedra*. Rather, it had been derived inductively and was originally the precipitate, not the postulate, of Christian experience" (quoted in ibid., 212). Moreover, the seminary's doctrinal position consisted of the following brief statement: "The seminary shall acknowledge the authority of the Holy Scriptures as the only infallible rule of faith and practice and shall assert the right and responsibility of the individual to interpret Scripture as he is led by the Holy Spirit. All teaching shall be based upon a belief in the deity of Christ, his atoning sacrifice as the sole ground of men's salvation, and the associated elements of apostolic and evangelical Christianity" (quoted in ibid., 215–16).

meaning (both individual passages and the Bible-as-a-whole) that would be missed if one did not come to the Scriptures informed by the church's faith as experienced through ecclesial participation. Thus Richard B. Hays declares: "Tradition must be heard and weighed; it carries indispensable insights both about the meaning of Scripture and about matters that Scripture does not address explicitly. Nonetheless, the tradition must be constantly resubmitted to critical scrutiny in light of the New Testament [and we might say biblical] texts. (Indeed, Christian tradition itself witnesses to the authoritative primacy of Scripture.) Otherwise, tradition can smother the text or co-opt its radical challenges."[49]

Yet the Bible exists not only in the church but also in the world. Even if it was directed primarily to the faith community, its content has significance for the world community.[50] It does not address readers with anything like a code, available only to those in the faith community. And in terms of empirical evidence, we know that it has been the means by which millions of persons who did not have faith or any prior connection with the church have come to faith through reading its pages. Indeed, the church has always held that the Bible has an evangelistic function and potential. Thus Ernst Fuchs perceptively asks how we can claim that the biblical writings can *create* Christian faith if we also insist that an understanding of them *presupposes* faith?[51]

The best conclusion to draw from this entire discussion is that participation in the Christian faith experience and faith community is not necessary for a *basic* understanding of the theological message of the Bible, yet such participation is potentially greatly advantageous for grasping the theological message of the Bible in its depth and richness. But it is potentially helpful to come to the text with a faith perspective only if one is prepared to submit that faith perspective to the corrective judgment of the text.

49. Hays, *Moral Vision of the New Testament*, 296–97.

50. As even Francis Watson concedes: see his *Text, Church, and World*, 11, 19–29, 236–40.

51. Ernst Fuchs, *Zum hermeneutischen Problem in der Theologie*, Gesammelte Aufsätze 1 (Tübingen: Mohr, 1959), 9–10, quoted in Thiselton, *Two Horizons*, 18.

Appendix C

Selectivity

The Meaning and Significance of Selectivity

Goethe is reported to have said, "The artist is known by selection." Someone else has observed that much had to be excluded from the biblical record in order for some to be included. Both of the preceding statements imply the same thing: *Purposive selectivity characterizes the books of the Bible.* In other words, biblical authors had definite purposes that motivated their writings, and they chose their materials and utilized them in such a way as to best accomplish their purposes.

The factor of selectivity, then, is basic to the work of biblical writers. It is, however, also important for the work of observers. They are ultimately searching for the implied author's purpose, which is disclosed both by what is included and by what is excluded. Consequently, an awareness of the principle of purposeful selection is just as significant for the observer as it was for the biblical writer.

Kinds of Selectivity

There are two kinds of selectivity. The first is *quantitative* or *proportionate selectivity*. This type of selectivity utilizes the element of mass or quantity. It entails the choice of a series of similar events or ideas, whose sheer weight impresses certain facts on the reader's mind.

Readers discover the presence and importance of quantitative selectivity by applying the law of proportion. The law of proportion is the principle that an author typically devotes the greatest quantity of material proportionately to what he feels is most significant and helpful in conveying his message. Consequently, the observer often becomes aware of quantitative selectivity by determining the ratio between the amount of material concerned with certain facts and the time span covered by those facts, and by comparing that ratio with a corresponding one in regard to other materials. For example, perhaps ten chapters are devoted to events covering one year, and one chapter is given to events covering a hundred years. When one compares the two ratios of material to time, one may conclude that the author considers the events that happened in the one year to be much more important for his purposes than those that occurred in the hundred-year span.

The book of Genesis affords an excellent illustration of proportionate selectivity. Chapters 12–50, that is, thirty-nine chapters, are occupied with events that span a period of only four generations. On the other hand, the first eleven chapters cover a period of many generations. Apparently the author is calling particular attention to the Hebrew nation and especially to the patriarchs, and he may suggest that what is contained in chapters 12–50 is more directly significant for the realization of his purpose than the material in chapters 1–11. This notation provides the observer with an insight that can be invaluable in the discovery of the aim and message of a book or passage.[1]

But the chronological element is not essential to observing proportion. In the logical type of literature, such as one finds in the Epistles, quantitative selectivity may simply involve devoting a greater amount of space to one idea or factor than to others. For instance, in John 17 about two-thirds of Jesus's prayer is given to indicating the bases for Jesus's petitions, whereas only one-third of the prayer is concerned with stating the actual petitions. This observation may well afford the grounds for using the law of proportion in the interpretation of John 17.

One should also note that quantitative selectivity does not necessarily point to importance or lead the reader to conclude that the author gives the greatest space (or extent of attention) to what he considers to be the most important. The book of Joel indicates, for example, that although the writer gives relatively less space to the day of the Lord as future cosmic judgment and salvation (2:28–3:21) than he does to the day of the Lord reflected in present-historical events in Judah and Jerusalem (1:2–2:27), he is still moving his book to a high point of culmination in his description of the day of the Lord as future event. In other words, other considerations lead to the conclusion that quantitative selectivity in this instance does not necessarily relate to the issue of importance. But considering proportion does cause readers

---

1. For extended, helpful discussions of quantitative selectivity, see Chatman, *Story and Discourse*, 62–79; Genette, *Narrative Discourse*, 77–115.

to ask themselves why a writer gives relatively more space to one issue, or feature, than to others.[2]

The second type of selectivity is *qualitative selectivity*. It arises from the recognition that any writer chooses or selects what to include and what to exclude. The event recorded in Genesis 12:10–20 may serve as an example of this kind of selectivity. It is not one of many similar occurrences. In its context it stands as a singular event. It pictures a self-reliant Abraham, whereas the preceding and following events depict a man of faith. Now, in Genesis 20 one finds almost an exact duplicate of this incident. In its immediate setting, however, it is peculiar.

Regarding this type of event or idea, the observer should ask, Why did the implied author include this particular event or idea? Why is it where it is? What does it contribute to the whole in view of its relations to the surrounding events or ideas? If these and similar questions are answered, one will discover the purpose implicit in this kind of selectivity.

2. A similar exception to the principle of greater quantity as indicating importance is found in the book of Jude, where the writer gives much more space to his description of the opponents (vv. 5–16) than he does to exhortations toward his readers (vv. 3, 17–23). As Richard Bauckham demonstrates, the structure of Jude indicates that the emphasis lies with the exhortations rather than with the description of the troublers. Apparently Jude needs to develop the description of the troublers quite fully as grounds for what was most significant for him: instructions to his readers. See Richard J. Bauckham, *Jude, 2 Peter*, WBC 50 (Waco: Word, 1983), 4; idem, "The Letter of Jude: An Account of Research," *Aufstieg und Niedergang der römischen Welt: Geschichte und Kultur Roms im Spiegel der neueren Forschung* (New York: de Gruyter, 1988), 2.25.5:3800–3808.

Appendix D

The Use of Original-Language Resources

A knowledge of the original biblical languages—Hebrew and Greek—is essential for the fullest measure of rich, penetrating, and precise interpretation. Therefore, students who have the opportunity should do everything possible to gain mastery of the biblical languages. But students who do not know Hebrew or Greek can do much to make use of Hebrew and Greek resources. A number of specific processes allow such students to make use of significant original-language works. Students can employ most major Bible software programs to pursue original-language preliminary definition and word usage. Students who lack proficiency in the languages should consult the instruction manuals or specialists in these software programs to determine precisely how to effectively use particular software programs.

The process we present here represents just one possible means whereby students without facility in the biblical languages might make use of certain published resources for preliminary definition and word usage (and context, insofar as context involves occurrences of the word elsewhere within the biblical book). The process is quite simple and relatively inexpensive.

The Use of Hebrew Resources

Preliminary Definitions for All Words except Verbs

PROCESS

For preliminary definition of all Hebrew words except verbs (e.g., nouns, adjectives), we suggest the following:

1. Read the passage being interpreted in the King James Version and identify the way in which the KJV has translated the passage, specifically
   noting the English word the KJV has used to translate the term being
   pursued for preliminary definition.
2. In *Strong's Exhaustive Concordance*, find the entry for the word as
   translated in the KJV and locate within that entry the specific passage.
   At the end of the line will be a number; that number is the *Strong's*
   number for the Hebrew word that stands in the passage.[1]
3. Take the *Strong's* number and go to *A Hebrew and English Lexicon of
   the Old Testament*, by F. Brown, S. R. Driver, and C. A. Briggs (BDB;
   use an edition that is indexed to *Strong's*).[2] There the student may note
   the basic definition of the word.

EXAMPLE: HOSEA 9:10

But [Israel] came to Baal-peor, and consecrated themselves to a thing of shame,
and became detestable like the thing they loved.

To pursue a preliminary definition of "a thing of shame," begin by noting
how that word is translated by the KJV: the KJV renders the word as "shame," as
does the NRSV. Then look up "shame" in *Strong's Exhaustive Concordance*, find
within that entry Hosea 9:10, and note the number at the end of that line: 1322.
Next consult an edition of BDB that is indexed to *Strong's*. Go to the index at
the back of the lexicon, find the number 1322, and locate the page in the lexicon
where that word is defined. On finding that page and seeing the number 1322, the
student will encounter the definition of the Hebrew word, which happens to be
bōšet (pronounced *bōsheth*), that stands behind "shame" in Hosea 9:10.

Preliminary Definitions for Verbs

PROCESS

The process is slightly different for Hebrew verbs because Hebrew verbs
appear in various *stems*, and the meaning of a verb in one stem may be different from the meaning of the verbal root in another stem. The following is
the process for Hebrew verbs:

1. Find the word in the KJV and note how it is translated there.
2. Look up the word in *Strong's Exhaustive Concordance*, find the reference
   to the verse within the entry, and note the number at the end of the line.

---

1. *Strong's* numbers may also be obtained through searching the KJV online at http://www
.blueletterbible.org/.
2. An edition of BDB with *Strong's* numbering has an index at the back of the volume
giving the page number in the lexicon where the entry corresponding to the *Strong's* number
is found.

3. Take that number and go to *The Englishman's Hebrew Concordance of the Old Testament* by George Wigram (use an edition that is numerically coded to *Strong's*). Each entry will have a *Strong's* number. Find the entry that corresponds to the number of the word you are looking for, locate the passage being interpreted, and note the stem under which the passage is found.

4. Then go to BDB (an edition coded to *Strong's* numbers), look up the *Strong's* number in the index at the back of the lexicon, find the entry with the *Strong's* number, and within the entry note the definition for the verb in the stem that the student identified from *The Englishman's Hebrew Concordance*. That will be the preliminary definition for the Hebrew word in the passage.

EXAMPLE: JOSHUA 1:6
Be strong and courageous.

To interpret "courageous," first find the word in the KJV, which translates it "of good courage." Then look up "courage" in *Strong's Concordance*, find Joshua 1:6, and identify the number 553. Take that number and find the entry under 553 in *The Englishman's Hebrew Concordance*, and note that Joshua 1:6 appears there under the stem "Kal." Then go to the index at the back of BDB, identify the page in the lexicon where the entry for that word is found, and locate the entry for that word in the lexicon. There the student will find the discussion for that word, which happens to be *'amēṣ* (pronounced *'amēts*), under "Kal" (or "Qal").

Word Usage

We suggest the following for word usage of all Hebrew words:

1. Find the word in the KJV and note how it is translated there.
2. Locate the word in *Strong's Exhaustive Concordance*, find within the entry the reference to the passage being interpreted, and note the number at the end of that line.
3. Go to *The Englishman's Hebrew Concordance*, find the numbered entry, and identify all the passages in the Hebrew Bible where that word occurs. If the word in question is a verb, one would identify first all the passages where the verb in that stem appears and would give priority in context and word usage to the verb in that stem. If one had time, one could also explore the occurrences of the verb in other stems, realizing that those are, as a rule, relatively less significant than occurrences of the verb in the same stem.[3]

---

3. In addition to using *Strong's* numbers to determine preliminary definitions and word usage, those who employ the history of terms interpretive determinant (discussed above in

The Use of Greek Resources

Preliminary Definitions

For the preliminary definition of Greek words, we suggest the following:

1. Identify how the word is translated in the King James Version.
2. Look up that word in *Strong's Exhaustive Concordance*.
3. Locate the passage in question in the entry in *Strong's* and note the number at the end of the line.
4. Take that number to the *Greek-English Lexicon of the New Testament: Coded with the Numbering System from Strong's Exhaustive Concordance of the Bible*, by Joseph Henry Thayer. There find the definition for the Greek word.[4]

Word Usage

For word usage of Greek words, we suggest the following:

1. Identify how the word is translated in the KJV.
2. Look up that word in *Strong's Exhaustive Concordance*.
3. Locate the passage in question in the entry in *Strong's* and note the number at the end of the line.
4. Take that number to *A Concordance to the Greek Testament*, by W. F. Moulton and A. S. Geden (use an edition that is coded to *Strong's*). There find all occurrences of the word in the New Testament.

Example (Matthew 1:1)

An account of the genealogy of Jesus the Messiah. (Matt. 1:1)

While interpreting "genealogy," note that the KJV translates that word as "generation"; thus find "generation" in *Strong's* and note that the number at the end of the line featuring Matthew 1:1 is 1078. Then find 1078 in Thayer's *Greek-English Lexicon* for preliminary definition and in Moulton and Geden's *Concordance* for word usage.

---

chap. 14) may also use *Strong's* numbers to locate discussions of Greek and Hebrew terms in certain OT and NT theological dictionaries or wordbooks, which offer in-depth studies of major biblical terms.

4. It is also possible to work through the above steps by using the resources available at http://www.blueletterbible.org/.

Appendix E

Critical Methods in Inductive Bible Study

Inductive Bible study focuses on the meaning of the final form of the text, and each of the major critical methods discussed below can contribute to one's understanding of the meaning of the text in its final form.

Contributions of Critical Methods

Historical criticism can fill in details and offer both a comprehensive and specific historical context. In these ways historical criticism may assist students as they pursue evidence under the *historical background*. Moreover, the biblical narratives in general point to the salvation-historical significance of the events they describe, implying the importance of knowing as much as possible about these events. Acquiring such knowledge is precisely the purpose of historical criticism.

Source criticism can alert readers to the existence of various written sources behind the text and can thereby explain certain features within a book or passage. Most scholars agree, for example, that the early chapters of Genesis contain two accounts of creation that probably existed independently of each other and were brought together by a later writer or redactor without a great deal of internal harmonization. Consequently, the two have certain tensions between them (1:1–2:3 and 2:4–3:24). One notes, for instance, that the first account describes creation in seven days while the second seems to indicate that creation took place on one day. One also finds that although the first account indicates that humans were created after the animals, the second account describes the creation of the man before the animals. These tensions were allowed to continue in the final text and apparently were not considered problematic by either the writer/redactor or the community of faith that recognized Genesis as authoritatively formational and ultimately as officially canonical Scripture. The relevant point here is that these differences or tensions within the final text are explainable on the basis of source criticism.[1]

This example from the first chapters of Genesis illustrates one of the essential contributions of source criticism. It is foundational for an examination of the redactional activity of a writer. Clearly the identification of sources is a prerequisite for the analysis of the writer's editing of sources into a final document so as to communicate his theological message according to his (pastoral) purpose. Here, then, one finds that the redactor of Genesis may have combined these two independent accounts, and in so doing he created something of a tertium quid: a new, third account that is greater than the sum of the two original accounts. By combining these two accounts as he has, the writer is inviting his audience to read them together as part of a comprehensive narrative. The very tensions that the writer has allowed to stand contribute in their own way to the reader's construal of the narrative-as-a-whole.

Form criticism can also be helpful in the interpretation of the final text. Recognizing the presence of certain stereotypical features that belong to the form, or genre, can alert one to the role that these features normally played and the function they performed in such genres. One is able to interpret these features and their arrangement in the text according to the genre expectations that the writer quite possibly assumed his readers would share. This construal would involve interpreting the passage on the basis of *typicality*, but certain stereotypical features may, in a given passage, be conspicuous by their absence or may be presented in an order that differs from the usual and expected order. A given passage may even include certain features that are not usually included in this genre at all. In such a case, the writer may be encouraging the reader to take note of these unique features and probe what might be the significance of these departures from the norm for the meaning of the specific passage. This analysis would involve interpreting the passage on the basis of its *peculiarities*, its departures from the formal norm.[2]

---

1. One could argue that this discussion is circular. The recognition of tensions leads to postulating two sources, and this postulation is then employed to explain the tensions. But the fact remains that such tensions can perhaps best be explained by the existence of originally separate documents.

2. Yet at this point one must be careful to remember that most individual passages do not conform to all the ideal features of a formal genre. One of the characteristics of genre is that individual instances tend to vary to a greater or lesser extent from the ideal form. Nevertheless, at times these departures from the typical ideal may point toward unique emphases in a given passage.

However, the critical method that generally has the most direct bearing upon the interpretation of the final text is *redaction criticism*. Redaction criticism involves the analysis of the final writer's editorial decisions in the service of his attempt to communicate his message to his readers.[3] For example, in Acts 2:17–21, Luke (through the speech of Peter) cites Joel 2:28–32, but in the process he introduces a number of changes to that original Old Testament passage. This redactional activity suggests that Luke, through the speech of Peter, wishes the implied reader of Acts[4] to note the alterations to the original wording of this prophetic passage and to consider the significance of these alterations for the meaning of Acts 2.[5]

Redaction criticism assumes that the reader can identify the source (or precursor) text (*Vorlage*) and thus analyze the specific editorial changes that have been made. At times students may have difficulty knowing for certain whether a writer is making use of, and redacting, a particular passage. This difficulty has led some scholars, such as Richard Hays, to identify criteria upon which to base decisions regarding an author's use of or allusion to another passage.[6]

As we mentioned previously, redaction criticism is often based on earlier decisions regarding source theories. If one concludes, as is almost certainly the case, that Chronicles employed the Deuteronomic history (Joshua–2 Kings) as a principal source, then one has a relatively firm basis for the redactional analysis of passages in Chronicles.[7] Redaction criticism of the Gospels clearly depends upon the source theory one adopts for the literary relationship between the Synoptic Gospels. The general, but by no means absolute, consensus regarding the sources of the Synoptic Gospels is the "two-source hypothesis,"[8]

3. Although redaction criticism normally deals with the editorial activity of the final writer, sometimes the focus is upon the editorial activity of writers responsible for the development of earlier written sources. Pentateuchal studies, e.g., sometimes include a concern to trace the redactional activity and tendencies of those responsible for the Yahwist source or the Elohist source.

4. The implied reader of Acts knows the OT and is expected to recognize quotations and allusions from the OT.

5. For the sake of redactional analysis, it is inconsequential whether one concludes that Luke was primarily responsible for the speech in Acts 2 or that he was simply reporting verbatim Peter's remarks on that historical occasion. By including it in his book, Luke is taking ultimate responsibility for all redaction of OT passages quoted by any (reliable) characters in the book of Acts.

6. Hays, *Echoes of Scripture in the Letters of Paul*. See the broader application of Hays's principles to NT writers other than Paul by Powell, "Expected and Unexpected Readings in Matthew."

7. See, e.g., Steven L. McKenzie, *The Chronicler's Use of the Deuteronomistic History*, Harvard Semitic Monographs 33 (Atlanta: Scholars Press, 1985); Sara Japhet, *The Ideology of the Book of Chronicles and Its Place in Biblical Thought*, 2nd ed., Beiträge zur Erforschung des Alten Testaments und des Antiken Judentums 9 (Frankfurt: Peter Lang, 1997); Steven S. Tuell, *First and Second Chronicles*, IBC (Louisville: John Knox, 2001).

8. See B. H. Streeter, *The Four Gospels: A Study in Origins* (London: Macmillan, 1924); Stein, *Synoptic Problem*.

which postulates that Matthew and Luke used two principal sources for their Gospels: Mark, which would thus be the earliest of the Gospels, and a hypothetical sayings-source called Q.[9] If one accepts this *consensus opinio*,[10] then one might examine Matthew's use of Mark and Q in order to discern Matthew's theological purpose in individual passages throughout his Gospel as well as the theological *tendencies* of the Gospel of Matthew in the large.[11] One might note, for example, that Matthew may have edited, or redacted, Mark 10:2–9 by adding the clause "except for unchastity" (Matt. 19:9), and one might go on to consider the significance of this change for Matthew's understanding of divorce and remarriage.[12]

Limitations of Critical Methods

This discussion has emphasized the potential contributions of these critical methods for the interpretation of the biblical text, but one must acknowledge two qualifications. The first qualification is that each of these critical processes involves moving behind the final form of the text, which is the

9. So named because Q is the first letter of the German word for source: *Quelle*. Some scholars accept the notion of Markan priority and affirm that Matthew and Luke used Mark but reject the existence of Q, arguing instead that Luke knew Matthew and used not only Mark but also Matthew in the composition of his Gospel.

10. Almost all redaction criticism of the Synoptic Gospels has been based on the two-source hypothesis. Although for years scholars considered the theory to be one of the "assured results of higher criticism," it has been vehemently challenged over the past forty years by advocates of the Griesbach hypothesis, which argues that the literary relationship of the Synoptic Gospels involves the order Matthew-Luke-Mark. W. R. Farmer has argued for the Griesbach hypothesis in his book *The Synoptic Problem: A Critical Analysis* (New York: Macmillan, 1964), and also subsequently produced a study that develops the significance of adopting the Griesbach hypothesis for Gospel history and interpretation; see W. R. Farmer, *Jesus and the Gospel: Tradition, Scripture, and Canon* (Philadelphia: Fortress, 1982). See also David B. Peabody, Lamar Cope, and Allan J. McNichol, eds., *One Gospel from Two: Mark's Use of Matthew and Luke* (London: SCM, 2001); and Sherman E. Johnson, *The Griesbach Hypothesis and Redaction Criticism* (Atlanta: Scholars Press, 1991).

11. An example of a meticulous and sustained redaction-critical interpretation of Matthew's Gospel by an evangelical scholar is Robert H. Gundry, *Matthew: A Commentary on His Handbook for a Mixed Church under Persecution* (Grand Rapids: Eerdmans, 1994); see also the important series of early redaction-critical studies collected in Günther Bornkamm, Gerhard Barth, and Heinz Joachim Held, *Tradition and Interpretation in Matthew*, trans. Percy Scott, NTL (Philadelphia: Westminster, 1963).

12. This addition does not necessarily mean that Matthew *created* this saying. One possibility is that Jesus actually gave this exception and that Matthew incorporated it from another source (either oral or written). The determination as to whether the historical Jesus uttered this exception, and in what circumstances, is a matter for historical criticism. But whatever the ultimate basis for Matthew's inclusion of this "exception clause," he has incorporated it into a passage that he took over from Mark (on the assumption of the two-source hypothesis); this fact renders it a redactional act on Matthew's part and invites an exploration of his purpose in incorporating this exception clause as he has and where he has it in his Gospel.

only text we have, or the only text that presently actually exists. Any move to reconstruct putative realities behind the present text necessarily involves at least some degree of speculation; yet one must be careful not to paint with a broad brush, for some of these critical reconstructions are much more speculative than others. Nevertheless, an element of speculation is always present; therefore one must always be more or less tentative when working behind the text, whether such work involves the reconstruction of events (historical criticism), oral traditions (form criticism), written sources (source criticism), or editorial intentions on the part of flesh-and-blood writers (redaction criticism).

The second qualification involves certain tensions between the perspective of these critical methods and that of the final form of the biblical text. As we previously mentioned, the interpretation of the text focuses upon the sense, or meaning, that the implied author wishes the implied reader to seize from the text. The central questions in interpretation, then, are these: How does the implied author wish the implied reader to approach the text and thus to derive meaning from the text? What kind of implied reader does the implied author have in mind? What kind of process of reading does the implied author assume? Each of these critical methods assumes a reader and reading process that is different from what the implied authors of the biblical materials expected. Therefore these methods offer real but only indirect aid in the reading process. They do not provide data that are finally determinative for the essential construal of the meaning of the text in its final form.

For its part, *historical criticism* presents alternative historical narratives that necessarily differ from those the biblical writers presented to the implied readers in the biblical text.[13] These alternative narratives are actually scholarly constructs that reflect the concerns and ideology of the contemporary world, and especially the contemporary academic world.[14] Although historical critics sometimes succumb to the fantasy that their reconstructed narratives are purely objective over against the allegedly tendentious biblical narratives that are colored by the religious perspective and even propagandistic purposes of the biblical writers, the fact remains that the reconstructed narratives that histori-

13. These historical narratives are not necessarily *contradictory* to those presented in the biblical text. But even the historical critics who accept the historical reliability of the biblical text place these events in another narrative construct in the very process of describing or discussing them. See, e.g., Wright, *Jesus and the Victory of God*; idem, *Resurrection of the Son of God*.

14. John P. Meier, *A Marginal Jew: Rethinking the Historical Jesus*, ABRL (New York: Doubleday, 1987–2001), 1:1, incisively points out that the reconstructed "historical Jesus" is a "scientific construct, a theoretical abstraction that does not and cannot coincide with the full reality of Jesus of Nazareth as he actually lived and worked in Palestine during the 1st century of our era." Meier's trenchant comments about the quest by historical criticism for the historical Jesus obtain for historical criticism of the Bible generally.

cal criticism offers are themselves necessarily informed by the philosophical and theological views of the scholars who create them.[15] And much contemporary historical study—being heir to the modern historical consciousness that tries to bracket out all transcendence, or divine involvement, from historical explanation—adopts a perspective that is at odds with that of the biblical writers, whose biblical perspective holds that the ultimate key to meaning in history is the action of God.[16]

Source criticism involves the reconstruction of written documents that have themselves been absorbed into the final form of the text. The identification of earlier sources, then, actually involves the reversal of the literary process that created the text in its present form, yet this present form is the vehicle of communication between the implied author and the implied reader. And insofar as *form criticism* tries to reconstruct the oral stage of the tradition, it shares in the same reversal of the process of tradition development that is characteristic of source criticism.[17]

At first blush, *redaction criticism* seemingly focuses upon the text in its final form and thus relates directly to the implied reader, who is addressed by the final text. However, redaction criticism does not, precisely speaking, deal with the final form of the text but seeks to reconstruct the intentions of the flesh-and-blood author that lie behind the text and that find expression in the author's editorial process.[18] The image of the readers in redaction criticism is that of persons who have the biblical text in front of them with sources that the author used to develop his text on either side of the biblical text; they are constantly comparing the biblical text with the sources in order to ascertain the intentions of the writer as derived from changes the writer has made to

15. It cannot be otherwise; for the philosophy of history has increasingly recognized that history inherently involves *interpreted* events and that it is impossible for historians to present or discuss events without at the same time communicating, at least implicitly, their understanding of the significance of these events. See, e.g., the influential discussion of R. G. Collingwood, *The Idea of History*, rev. ed. (Oxford: Oxford University Press, 1993); cf. Wright, *New Testament and the People of God*, 81–118.

16. For all practical purposes, this is the case even with someone like John Bright, who accepts the general historical reliability of the OT accounts; see Bright, *History of Israel*.

17. Both source criticism and form criticism have been criticized for a tendency to atomize or fragment the text, dicing the text into bits and pieces and thereby destroying the unity of the final text. This fragmentation may leave readers with isolated pieces that lack any context except what the scholars themselves construct.

18. This description is especially true of early redaction critics, who focused almost exclusively upon changes made to received tradition, with the corollary that they tended to consider as irrelevant the elements that the editors simply took over from their sources. Later redaction critics give greater attention to the redactors' decisions to include earlier material without alteration and to the complete compositions that these redactors have created. In other words, more recently redaction criticism has tended to treat these redactors as real authors rather than as mere editors; this more recent form of redaction criticism is thus sometimes called *composition criticism*.

his sources. In our judgment, no biblical text envisages this kind of reader or reading process.[19]

But even if redactional changes may not be conclusive for the interpretation of the text, such changes may serve a heuristic or confirmational function. They may serve a heuristic function in that these redactional considerations can, at times, draw attention to certain features that belong to the text in its final form, features that one might otherwise miss or tend to ignore. And these redactional considerations may serve to confirm or validate the significance of certain elements within the final text.[20]

For example, one may note that Matthew introduces his version of the parable of the mustard seed by speaking of a grain of mustard seed that "a man took and sowed in his field" (13:31 RSV), which echoes the same phrase that introduces the immediately preceding parable, the parable of the weeds in 13:24 ("The kingdom of heaven may be compared to a man who sowed good seed in his field" [RSV]), where the field represents "the world" (13:38). Immediate context suggests, then, that in Matthew's parable of the mustard seed, the growth of the grain of mustard seed refers to the kingdom's growth or enlargement in the world. But readers might wonder if in this case one could put too much weight on the repetition of this phrase in the immediate context of Matthew 13. After all, later the Matthean Jesus will use this very same image of a grain of mustard seed to represent faith in the heart of disciples (17:20). Perhaps, then, the growth of the mustard seed in this parable refers to the growth of faith in an individual's heart. But here redaction criticism may help readers to confirm their inclination to give the greater weight to the repetition of the phrase in the immediate context.

According to the two-source hypothesis, Matthew has edited the Markan parable by replacing Mark's phrase "as if a man should scatter seed upon the

19. The original intended readers of certain biblical books may have been acquainted with sources that lay behind these books. For example, assuming the two-source hypothesis, one might plausibly believe that not only did Luke know Mark and Q but that his readers did as well. Still, the text gives no indication that the writer invites his readers to construe the meaning of his Gospel by hunting for editorial changes, nor does the student have any reason to believe that Luke assumed his audience would thus read his Gospel.

20. Redaction criticism normally focuses upon the interpretive significance of redactional activity for the passage that bears the marks of redaction, the later redacted passage. But in fact redaction criticism can illumine the precursor text, the earlier passage that is the basis of redaction. For example, the Chronicler's redaction of a passage from the Deuteronomic history may not only illumine the meaning of the text of Chronicles but may also shed light on the passage from the Deuteronomic history. The Chronicler's use of the Deuteronomic history (including editorial modifications) may be regarded as the first chapter in the history of interpreting the Deuteronomic history. Such redactional activity, then, may be examined by the student under the rubric of the interpretation of others. This use of redactional adaptation for the interpretation of others would be especially warranted if one understands the interpretation of others to include the broad history of influence, or history of the reception of the text, as in the approach of *Wirkungsgeschichte*. See comments under "Nature and Importance of Communal Study" in chap. 7.

ground" (Mark 4:26 RSV) with "a man who sowed good seed in his field" (Matt. 13:24 RSV).[21] This redactional change indicates a significant level of authorial attention to the phrase "a man who sowed good seed in his field" (Matt. 13:24 RSV) in the parable of the weeds and its connection to the similar "a grain of mustard seed which a man took and sowed in his field" (13:31 RSV) in the next parable; this attention leads to the explanation of "field" as referring to "the world," which follows (13:38).[22]

In an example from the Old Testament, according to the Deuteronomic history, the Lord in his anger incited David to number Israel (2 Sam. 24:1), but the Chronicler has redacted his Deuteronomic source by stating that Satan thus incited David. This redactional change draws the attention of the reader of Chronicles to satanic initiation over against divine initiation in this action of David. A consideration of this editorial change may lead the reader to interpret the Chronicles passage by probing the significance of assigning this action to Satan over against the alternative notion of the divine origin of David's actions.[23]

21. The parable of the weeds does not appear in Mark; it is found only in Matthew. Luke's version of the parable of the mustard seed reads, "which a man took and sowed in his garden" (Luke 13:19 RSV).

22. As mentioned previously, the target of interpretation is the intention of the implied author rather than that of the flesh-and-blood author because the implied author is the only author actually accessible and because the focus of biblical interpretation is the text itself. But we also mentioned that readers normally, and necessarily, assume continuity between the implied author and the flesh-and-blood author. When redaction criticism brings to the reader's attention what appears to be deliberate editorial activity on the part of the writer, the reader is implicitly invited to employ that information in order to confirm or clarify issues that are found within the final form of the text. The problem occurs when readers use redactional changes to draw interpretive meaning that in principle is not discernible from a sensitive reading of the text itself.

23. These examples reveal that this use of redaction criticism may be a more specific form of the heuristic examination of parallel passages as discussed under "Scriptural Testimony" in chap. 14.

Appendix F

Logical Outlines

Use of Logical Outlines

In view of the description of a logical outline (see "Interpretive Integration" in chap. 15), this type of outline is especially helpful in studying the ideological type of literature, such as what one finds in the Epistle to the Romans or the Epistle to the Hebrews.

One should be aware that this type of outline is merely a *means* of coming to grips with the logic of a unit of literature. Its use does not imply that the author of a passage or book had an outline in mind that he slavishly followed in his writing. It simply serves as a tool by which to trace logical development, to discover how various thoughts are related to each other, to determine what is primary and what is secondary, and to ascertain the conclusion toward which the author is moving.

One should also note that the logical outline is an *imperfect* means. It has its shortcomings, as one soon discovers when one uses it to any great degree. However, it seems to be the best instrument for bringing one face-to-face with the development and force of a logical passage.

Suggestions for Making Logical Outlines

The following suggestions are designed to assist in making logical outlines:

1. Use the sentence form of outlining because the force of an argument can be conveyed only by full statements.

2. Analyses in terms of purpose, basis, result, and so forth may be placed in parentheses after the various statements of the outline. They should not in themselves constitute the points of the outline.

3. Indicate clearly and cogently the *relations* between ideas in one or both of the following ways: first, by position because, for example, a subordinate position indicates a subordinate idea; and second, by connectives and connections, such as *therefore, for, because, for this reason,* or dependent and independent clauses. These relations should be expressed so as to result in actually proving what the author is proving.

4. At the head of each outline, state in proposition form the theme of the passage. Among other things, such a theme should reveal the logical relation of the passage to its immediate context and its purpose in the movement of the book-as-a-whole. Sometimes such a theme is explicitly stated, and in other instances it is implied. In both cases the theme should be discovered and noted. One should be careful that the theme is found through induction and not superimposed on the passage. The outline should demonstrate the logical steps that the biblical writer follows in substantiating his theme.

5. As was indicated in the preceding suggestion, a logical outline must include both what is explicit and what is implicit in a unit. One must read between the lines if one is to catch the full force of the argument of a logical passage. However, one must be careful to base one's conclusions on objective data and not on pure imagination.

6. Follow the order of the text so as to avoid the danger of altering its logic. Sometimes it makes no substantial difference if one varies the order of the text. At other times serious changes may result. Therefore the safe practice is to follow the exact arrangement of the passage.

7. Be thorough in your outlining: the thoughts of certain portions of Scripture are so closely knit together that to omit one thought would cause a serious gap in the argument. It is better to be too thorough, if that is possible, than not to be thorough enough.

8. Use the regular outline form: I, A, 1, a, (1), (a), etc. Do not use a "I" unless it is followed by a "II," an "A" unless followed by a "B," etc. Outlining involves setting down two or more aspects of one thing. If there are not at least two aspects of the idea being considered, then it should not be outlined. If, for example, one places an "A" under an "I" without a corresponding "B," one should combine the "A" with the "I."

9. Use your own language. Avoid merely repeating the terminology of the text.

10. A logical outline should serve two purposes: synthesis and analysis. The major points, especially "I" and "A," should be synthetic. For example, the Roman numerals should represent the greatest possible synthesis of similar ideas in relation to a certain theme. On the other hand, the more minor points should represent the analytical aspect of the outline. They should contain the

individual arguments that are woven together so as to support the more major arguments and the theme. (Note: A summary outline is an abbreviated form of logical outline that can be a helpful tool in describing and tracing only the major movements of a passage. See example from Rom. 2:1–3:8 below.)

11. Avoid dividing statements into too many small parts because of the danger of losing the element of continuity. On the other hand, avoid combining too many ideas into one statement because of the danger of missing the importance of each.

12. Indicate chapter-and-verse references after your major points.

13. Prepare an outline only after thorough study, and let it be a means of summarizing your study. If one has studied a passage well, it ought to fall into an outline of its own accord. One should not be concerned about outlining as such during the process of interpretation.

Examples of Logical Outlines

Example of a Detailed Outline (Romans 1:18–32)

Theme: The Gentiles need the gospel of salvation because, having the truth about God through revelation, they deliberately suppressed it because of their disrespect for God and are therefore the objects of God's wrathful and just judgment. (v. 18)

    I. For they have the truth about God as God has plainly revealed it to them; they are therefore without the excuse of ignorance. (vv. 19–20—*revelation—consequent responsibility*)

        A. For what can be learned about God, namely, his existence and nature, can be discerned by them; God has consciously and clearly shown it to them. (v. 19—*fact of revelation*)

            1. This has been true ever since the foundation of the world, since creation is the means by which God has disclosed himself to them. (v. 20a—*substantiation—time and means of revelation*)

            2. For through creation, which may be seen, the unseen character of God, that is, his everlasting might and other-than-humanness, has been made plainly visible. (v. 20b—*further substantiation—content of revelation*)

        B. Because of this plain manifestation of God's existence and nature, they cannot excuse their actions on the basis of a lack of knowledge. (v. 20c—*purpose and outcome of revelation—responsibility*)

    II. Because, although they were given a conspicuous revelation of the truth about God, they deliberately repressed it and refused to act in accordance with it. (vv. 21–23—*rejection and retrogression*)

A. Instead of paying the admiration due to God because of his manifested grandeur, and instead of being grateful to him for his provisions, they refused to worship him or give him thanks. (v. 21a—*contrast—lack of worship—first step in decline*)

B. They rather became ineffectual in their thinking because they tried to reason without postulating the Divine. The result was utter confusion in their innermost beings. (v. 21b—*contrast—darkened intellect and heart—second step in decline*)

C. As a consequence, they were completely self-deceived, claiming to be wise whereas they were actually fools, and the depth of their folly is shown by the fact that they exchanged the majestic splendor of the true, incorruptible God for the mere likenesses of corruptible men, birds, four-footed beasts, or even creeping things. (vv. 22–23—*result—false worship—third step in decline*)

III. Because they had a plain revelation of God and deliberately suppressed it, he judged them by removing the restraining power of conscience and reason and surrendering them to their own corrupt desires and depraved minds. (vv. 24–32—*retribution—result*)

A. God delivered them to the power of the lusts of their hearts. (vv. 24–25—*result*)

   1. This behavior resulted in uncleanness, specifically involving the mistreatment of their bodies among themselves. (v. 24—*subsequent result*)

   2. God's surrender of them to their desires together with its consequences, I repeat, came about because they exchanged the true God, the God of everlasting power and divinity, for gods who have no corresponding realities; and because they adored and served the creature rather than the Creator, who alone deserves praise. (v. 25—*repetition of reason*)

B. Because they exchanged the true God for false gods and creatures for the Creator, God delivered them to the power of their shameful passions. (vv. 26–27—*repetition of reason and further result*)

   1. As a consequence, their women exchanged normal for abnormal sexual practices. (v. 26b—*result*)

   2. Similarly, men too engaged in unbridled and ignominious acts of homosexuality, the results of which constituted their rightful judgment. (v. 27—*similar result*)

C. And again, I repeat, because they deliberately refused to approve and admit God in their thinking, God also delivered them to the power of a reprobate and degenerate mind and thereby to all manner of irrational and unfit conduct, both personal and social. (vv. 28–32—*repetition of reason and further result*)

1. They were thus filled with all kinds of injustice, wickedness, covetousness, malignity. They are full of envious discontent, mortal hatred, contentiousness, falsity, evilness of mind. They are whisperers, false accusers and backbiters, scorners of God, despiteful, arrogant, braggarts, inventors of injurious things, disobedient to parents, without understanding, agreement breakers, heartless, ruthless. (vv. 29–31—*result and particularization*)
2. In fact, so utterly depraved are they that, knowing well God's decree that those who deliberately commit these sins will inevitably and justly be condemned to death, they not only do these things themselves, but even clap their hands when others practice them. (v. 32—*further result and particularization*)

Example of a Summary Outline (Romans 2:1–3:8)

Theme: The Jews also need the gospel of salvation. For judgment is universally based on actual character and deeds; and because the Jews—although having great privileges and claiming thereby to be teachers—are so morally deficient that the Gentiles blaspheme God because of them, and because they cannot be exempted through physical circumcision or self-justification, they too are under God's condemnation.

I. Judgment is *universally* based on *actual character* and *actions*. (2:1–16—*general principle*)

II. Because judgment is *universally* grounded on *actual character* and *actions*, and you Jews, although having great privileges and because of them being certain that you are able to teach others, are so morally corrupt that the Gentiles blaspheme God because of you, you too, I say, are under divine condemnation. (2:17–24—*specific application*)

III. *Being guilty and under judgment*, you will not be delivered from wrath by appealing either to the physical rite of circumcision or to any amount of intellectual evasion and rationalization. (2:25–3:8—*rebuttal to anticipated objections*)

Bibliography

Abraham, William J. *Canon and Criterion in Christian Theology: From the Fathers to Feminism*. Oxford: Oxford University Press, 1998.

Abrams, Meyer Howard. *A Glossary of Literary Terms*. 4th ed. New York: Holt, Rinehart & Winston, 1981.

Achtemeier, Elizabeth. *Nature, God, and Pulpit*. Grand Rapids: Eerdmans, 1992.

———. *Preaching from the Old Testament*. Louisville: Westminster John Knox, 1989.

———. "The Relevance of the Old Testament for Christian Preaching." In *A Light unto My Path: Old Testament Studies in Honor of Jacob M. Myers*, edited by H. N. Bream, Ralph Daniel Heim, and Carey A. Moore, 3–24. Philadelphia: Temple University Press, 1974.

Adeyemo, Tokunboh, ed. *Africa Bible Commentary: A One-Volume Commentary Written by Seventy African Scholars*. Grand Rapids: Zondervan, 2006.

Adler, Mortimer. *How to Read a Book*. Rev. ed. New York: Simon & Schuster, 1972.

Ahlström, Gösta W. *The History of Ancient Palestine*. Edited by Diana Edelman. Minneapolis: Fortress, 1993.

Aland, Barbara. "Welche Rolle spielen Textkritik und Textgeschichte für das Verständnis des Neuen Testaments? Frühe Leserperspektiven." *New Testament Studies* 52 (July 2006): 303–18.

Aland, Kurt, ed. *Synopsis of the Four Gospels: Completely Revised on the Basis of the Greek Text of Nestle-Aland, 26th Edition, and the Greek New Testament, 3rd Edition*. New York: United Bible Societies, 1985.

———, ed. *Vollständige Konkordanz zum griechischen Neuen Testament*. 2 vols. Berlin: de Gruyter, 1975–83.

Aland, Kurt, and Barbara Aland. *The Text of the New Testament: An Introduction to the Critical Editions and to the Theory and Practice of Modern Textual Criticism*. Translated by Erroll F. Rhodes. 2nd ed. Grand Rapids: Eerdmans, 1989.

Albertz, Rainer. *A History of Israelite Religion in the Old Testament Period.* 2 vols. Old Testament Library. Louisville: Westminster John Knox, 1994.

Allen, Willoughby C., and L. W. Grensted. *Introduction to the Books of the New Testament.* 3rd ed. Edinburgh: T&T Clark, 1929.

Alter, Robert. *The Art of Biblical Narrative.* New York: Basic Books, 1981.

———. *The Art of Biblical Poetry.* New York: Basic Books, 1985.

Andersen, Francis I., and David Noel Freedman. *Hosea.* Anchor Bible. Garden City, NY: Doubleday, 1980.

Armerding, Carl E. *The Old Testament and Criticism.* Grand Rapids: Eerdmans, 1983.

Armstrong, Paul B. *Conflicting Readings: Variety and Validity in Interpretation.* Chapel Hill: University of North Carolina Press, 1990.

Arnold, Bill T. "Luke's Characterizing Use of the Old Testament in the Book of Acts." In *History, Literature and Society in the Book of Acts,* edited by Ben Witherington III, 300–323. Cambridge: Cambridge University Press, 1996.

Arnold, Bill T., and John H. Choi. *A Guide to Biblical Hebrew Syntax.* Cambridge: Cambridge University Press, 2003.

Audi, Robert, ed. *Cambridge Dictionary of Philosophy.* Cambridge: Cambridge University Press, 1995.

Aune, David E. *The New Testament in Its Literary Environment.* Library of Early Christianity. Philadelphia: Westminster, 1987.

———. *The Westminster Dictionary of New Testament and Early Christian Literature and Rhetoric.* Louisville: Westminster John Knox, 2003.

Avalos, Hector, Sarah Melcher, and Jeremy Schipper, eds. *This Abled Body: Rethinking Disabilities and Biblical Studies.* Atlanta: Society of Biblical Literature, 2007.

Bachmann, H., and W. A. Slaby, collaborating eds. *Computer Concordance to the Novum Testamentum Graece.* Edited by the Institute for New Testament Textual Research and the Computer Center of Münster University. Berlin: de Gruyter, 1985.

Bacon, Benjamin Wisner. "The 'Five Books' of Matthew against the Jews." *Expositor* 15 (1918): 56–66.

———. *Studies in Matthew.* New York: Henry Holt, 1930.

Bacon, Francis. *Novum Organum.* 1620. Reprint, Oxford: Clarendon, 1888.

Bahnsen, Greg L., Walter C. Kaiser Jr., Douglas J. Moo, Wayne G. Strickland, and Willem A. VanGemeren. *Five Views on Law and Gospel.* Grand Rapids: Zondervan, 1996.

Bailey, James L. "Genre Analysis." In *Hearing the New Testament: Strategies for Interpretation,* edited by Joel B. Green, 197–221. Grand Rapids: Eerdmans, 1995.

Bailey, James L., and Lyle D. Vander Broek. *Literary Forms in the New Testament: A Handbook.* Louisville: Westminster John Knox, 1992.

Baker, David W., and Bill T. Arnold. *The Face of Old Testament Studies: A Survey of Contemporary Approaches.* Grand Rapids: Baker Academic, 1999.

Balla, Peter. *Challenges to New Testament Theology*. Peabody, MA: Hendrickson, 1998.

Ballard, Paul, and Stephen R. Holmes, eds. *The Bible in Pastoral Practice: Readings in the Place and Function of Scripture in the Church*. Grand Rapids: Eerdmans, 2005.

Barbour, Ian. *Issues in Science and Religion*. London: SCM, 1966.

Bar-Efrat, Shimon. *Narrative Art in the Bible*. Journal for the Study of the Old Testament: Supplement Series 70. Bible and Literature Series 17. Sheffield: Almond, 1989.

Barnett, Paul. *Is the New Testament Reliable?* 2nd ed. Downers Grove, IL: InterVarsity, 2004.

Barr, James. *The Concept of Biblical Theology*. Minneapolis: Fortress, 1999.

———. *Fundamentalism*. Philadelphia: Westminster, 1978.

———. *The Semantics of Biblical Language*. London: SCM, 1983.

Barrett, C. K. *The Gospel according to St. John: An Introduction with Commentary and Notes on the Greek Text*. 2nd ed. Philadelphia: Westminster, 1978.

Barth, Karl. *The Word of God and the Word of Man*. Translated by Douglas Horton. [Boston and Chicago?]: Pilgrim, 1928.

Barton, John. *Holy Writings, Sacred Text: The Canon in Early Christianity*. Louisville: Westminster John Knox, 1997.

———. *Reading the Old Testament: Method in Biblical Study*. Rev. ed. Louisville: Westminster John Knox, 1996.

———. *Understanding Old Testament Ethics*. Louisville: Westminster John Knox, 2003.

Bauckham, Richard J. *The Climax of Prophecy: Studies in the Book of Revelation*. Edinburgh: T&T Clark, 1993.

———. *Jude, 2 Peter*. Word Biblical Commentary 50. Waco: Word, 1983.

———. "The Letter of Jude: An Account of Research." *Aufstieg und Niedergang der römischen Welt: Geschichte und Kultur Roms im Spiegel der neueren Forschung*. Part 2, *Principat* 25.5:3800–3808. New York: de Gruyter, 1988.

Bauer, David R. *An Annotated Guide to Biblical Resources for Ministry*. Peabody, MA: Hendrickson, 2003.

———. *The Structure of Matthew's Gospel: A Study in Literary Design*. Journal for the Study of the New Testament: Supplement Series 31. Bible and Literature Series 15. Sheffield: Almond, 1988.

Bauer, W., F. W. Danker, W. F. Arndt, and F. W. Gingrich. *A Greek-English Lexicon of the New Testament and Other Early Christian Literature*. 3rd ed. Based on the 6th ed. of Walter Bauer's *Griechisch-deutsches Wörterbuch zu den Schriften des Neuen Testaments und der frühchristlichen Literatur*. Chicago: University of Chicago Press, 2000.

Beasley-Murray, George R. *Jesus and the Kingdom of God*. Grand Rapids: Eerdmans, 1986.

———. *John*. Word Biblical Commentary 36. Waco: Word, 1987.

Beekman, John, John Callow, and Michael Kopesec. *The Semantic Structure of Written Communication*. 5th ed. Dallas: Summer Institute of Linguistics, 1981.

Bendavid, Abba. *Maqbilôt ba-Miqra* [*Parallels in the Bible*]. Jerusalem: Carta, 1972.

Berkouwer, G. C. *Holy Scripture*. Studies in Dogmatics. Grand Rapids: Eerdmans, 1975.

Berlin, Adele. *Poetics and Interpretation of Biblical Narrative*. Bible and Literature Series 9. Sheffield: Almond, 1983.

Berlinerblau, Jacques. *The Secular Bible: Why Nonbelievers Must Take Religion Seriously*. Cambridge: Cambridge University Press, 2005.

Biddle, Mark Edward. "Redaction Criticism, Hebrew Bible." In *Dictionary of Biblical Interpretation*, edited by John H. Hayes, 2:373–76. Nashville: Abingdon, 1999.

Birch, Bruce C., and Larry L. Rasmussen. *Bible and Ethics in the Christian Life*. Rev. ed. Minneapolis: Augsburg, 1989.

Black, David Alan. *It's Still Greek to Me: An Easy-to-Understand Guide to Intermediate Greek*. Grand Rapids: Baker Academic, 1998.

Black, David Alan, and David S. Dockery, eds. *Interpreting the New Testament: Essays on Methods and Issues*. Nashville: Broadman & Holman, 2001.

Black, Max. "Metaphor." In *Philosophical Perspectives on Metaphor*, edited by Mark Johnson, 63–82. Minneapolis: University of Minnesota Press, 1981.

Blass, F., and A. Debrunner. *A Greek Grammar of the New Testament and Other Early Christian Literature*. Translated and edited by Robert W. Funk. Chicago: University of Chicago Press, 1961.

Blenkinsopp, Joseph. *Ezra-Nehemiah: A Commentary*. Old Testament Library. Louisville: Westminster John Knox, 1988.

———. *The Pentateuch: An Introduction to the First Five Books of the Bible*. Anchor Bible Reference Library. New York: Doubleday, 1992.

Blomberg, Craig L. *Interpreting the Parables*. Downers Grove, IL: InterVarsity, 1990.

Bockmuehl, Markus. *Seeing the Word: Refocusing New Testament Studies*. Grand Rapids: Baker Academic, 2006.

Bonhoeffer, Dietrich. *Life Together*. San Francisco: Harper & Row, 1954.

Booth, Wayne. *The Rhetoric of Fiction*. Chicago: University of Chicago Press, 1961.

Borg, Marcus J., and John Dominic Crossan. *The Last Week*. San Francisco: HarperSanFrancisco, 2006.

Borg, Marcus J., and N. T. Wright. *The Meaning of Jesus: Two Visions*. San Francisco: HarperSanFrancisco, 1999.

Bornkamm, Günther, Gerhard Barth, and Heinz Joachim Held. *Tradition and Interpretation in Matthew*. Translated by Percy Scott. New Testament Library. Philadelphia: Westminster, 1963.

Botterweck, G. Johannes, Helmer Ringgren, and Heinz-Josef Fabry, eds. *Theological Dictionary of the Old Testament*. Translated by J. T. Willis et al. 15 vols. Grand Rapids: Eerdmans, 1974–2006.

Braun, Francis. *English Grammar for Language Students: Basic Grammatical Terminology Defined and Alphabetically Arranged*. Ann Arbor, MI: Ulrich's Books, 1947.

Brawley, Robert L. *Centering on God: Method and Message in Luke-Acts*. Literary Currents in Biblical Interpretation. Louisville: Westminster John Knox, 1990.

———, ed. *Character Ethics and the New Testament: Moral Dimensions of Scripture*. Louisville: Westminster John Knox, 2007.

Bright, John. *The Authority of the Old Testament*. Nashville: Abingdon, 1967.

———. *A History of Israel*. 4th ed. Louisville: Westminster John Knox, 2000.

———. *The Kingdom of God: The Biblical Concept and Its Meaning for the Church*. Nashville: Abingdon, 1953.

Bromiley, Geoffrey W., ed. *The International Standard Bible Encyclopedia*. Rev. ed. 4 vols. Grand Rapids: Eerdmans, 1979–88.

Brooks, James A., and Carlton L. Winbery. *Syntax of New Testament Greek*. Lanham, MD: University Press of America, 1979.

Brotzman, Ellis R. *Old Testament Textual Criticism: An Introduction*. Grand Rapids: Baker Academic, 1994.

Brown, Colin, ed. *New International Dictionary of New Testament Theology*. 4 vols. Grand Rapids: Zondervan, 1975–79.

Brown, Francis, S. R. Driver, and Charles A. Briggs. *A Hebrew and English Lexicon of the Old Testament*. 1907. Reprint, Peabody, MA: Hendrickson, 1979, 1996, with *Strong's* numbering.

Brown, Raymond E. *The Critical Meaning of the Bible*. New York: Paulist Press, 1981.

———. *The "Sensus Plenior" of Sacred Scripture*. 1955. Reprint, Eugene, OR: Wipf & Stock, 2008.

Brown, William P., ed. *Character and Scripture: Moral Formation, Community, and Biblical Interpretation*. Grand Rapids: Eerdmans, 2002.

Bruce, F. F. *The Canon of Scripture*. Downers Grove, IL: InterVarsity, 1988.

———. *The Defense of the Gospel in the New Testament*. Rev. ed. Grand Rapids: Eerdmans, 1977.

———. *The New Testament Documents: Are They Reliable?* 6th ed. Downers Grove, IL: InterVarsity, 2003.

Brueggemann, Walter. *First and Second Samuel*. Interpretation: A Bible Commentary for Teaching and Preaching. Louisville: John Knox, 1990.

———. *Theology of the Old Testament: Testimony, Dispute, Advocacy*. Minneapolis: Fortress, 1997.

Buber, Martin. *I and Thou*. New York: Scribner, 1970.

Bultmann, Rudolf. *Existence and Faith: Shorter Writings of Rudolf Bultmann*. Cleveland: World, 1960.

———. *Jesus and the Word*. London: Collins, 1958.

———. *Kerygma and Myth: A Theological Debate*. Edited by Hans W. Bartsch. New York: Harper & Row, 1961.

———. *Theology of the New Testament*. Translated by Kendrick Grobel. 2 vols. in 1. Scribner Studies in Contemporary Theology. New York: Scribner's Sons, 1955.

Burridge, Richard A. *What Are the Gospels? A Comparison with Graeco-Roman Biography*. Cambridge: Cambridge University Press, 1992.

Caird, George B. *The Language and Imagery of the Bible*. Philadelphia: Westminster, 1980.

———. *New Testament Theology*. Edited by L. D. Hurst. Oxford: Clarendon, 1994.

Calvin, John. *Institutes of the Christian Religion*. Edited by John T. McNeill. Translated by Ford Lewis Battles. Philadelphia: Westminster, 1960.

Cameron, Lynne, and Graham Low, eds. *Researching and Applying Metaphor*. Cambridge Applied Linguistics. Cambridge: Cambridge University Press, 1999.

Campbell-Jack, W. C., Gavin McGrath, C. Stephen Evans, eds. *New Dictionary of Christian Apologetics*. Downers Grove, IL: InterVarsity, 2006.

Carroll R., M. Daniel, and Jacqueline E. Lapsley, eds. *Character Ethics and the Old Testament: Moral Dimensions of Scripture*. Louisville: Westminster John Knox, 2007.

Carson, D. A. *Exegetical Fallacies*. 2nd ed. Grand Rapids: Baker Academic, 1996.

———. *New Testament Commentary Survey*. 6th ed. Grand Rapids: Baker Academic, 2007.

Carter, Charles E. "Opening Windows onto Biblical Worlds: Applying the Social Sciences to Hebrew Scripture." In *The Face of Old Testament Studies: A Survey of Contemporary Approaches*, edited by David W. Baker and Bill T. Arnold, 421–51. Grand Rapids: Baker Academic, 1999.

Case, Shirley Jackson. *The Social Origins of Christianity*. Chicago: University of Chicago Press, 1923.

Chatman, Seymour. *Story and Discourse: Narrative Structure in Fiction and Film*. Ithaca, NY: Cornell University Press, 1978.

Childs, Brevard S. *Biblical Theology in Crisis*. Philadelphia: Westminster, 1970.

———. *Biblical Theology of the Old and New Testaments: Theological Reflection on the Christian Bible*. Minneapolis: Fortress, 1992.

———. *Introduction to the Old Testament as Scripture*. Philadelphia: Fortress, 1979.

———. *The New Testament as Canon: An Introduction*. Philadelphia: Fortress, 1985.

Clark, David K. *To Know and Love God: Method for Theology*. Wheaton, IL: Crossway, 2003.

Classen, Carl Joachim. *Rhetorical Criticism of the New Testament*. Leiden: Brill, 2002.

Clines, David J. A. "The Arguments of Job's Three Friends." In *Art and Meaning: Rhetoric in Biblical Literature*, edited by David J. A. Clines, David M. Gunn, and Alan J. Hauser, 199–214. Sheffield: JSOT Press, 1982.

————. *The Theme of the Pentateuch*. 2nd ed. Journal for the Study of the Old Testament: Supplement Series 10. Sheffield: JSOT Press, 1997.

Coggins, R. J., and J. L. Houlden, eds. *A Dictionary of Biblical Interpretation*. London: SCM, 1990.

Coleridge, Samuel Taylor. *Biographia Literaria: Biographical Sketches of My Literary Life and Opinions and Two Lay Sermons*. London: Bell & Daldy, 1880.

Collingwood, R. G. *The Idea of History*. Rev. ed. Oxford: Oxford University Press, 1993.

Collins, John J. *The Apocalyptic Imagination: An Introduction to Jewish Apocalyptic Literature*. 2nd ed. Biblical Resources Series. Grand Rapids: Eerdmans, 1998.

Collins, Raymond F. *I and II Timothy and Titus: A Commentary*. New Testament Library. Louisville: Westminster John Knox, 2002.

Cone, James H. *A Black Theology of Liberation*. Philadelphia: Lippincott, 1970.

————. *God of the Oppressed*. Rev. ed. Maryknoll, NY: Orbis Books, 1997.

Conzelmann, H., and A. Lindemann. *Arbeitsbuch zum Neuen Testament*. Tübingen: Mohr, 1975.

Coogan, Michael D., ed. *The Oxford History of the Biblical World*. New York: Oxford University Press, 1998.

Copi, Irving. *Introduction to Logic*. 2nd ed. New York: Macmillan, 1961.

Cosgrove, Charles H. *Appealing to Scripture in Moral Debate: Five Hermeneutical Rules*. Grand Rapids: Eerdmans, 2002.

————, ed. *The Meanings We Choose: Hermeneutical Ethics, Indeterminacy, and the Conflict of Interpretations*. Journal for the Study of the Old Testament: Supplement Series 411. The Bible in the Twenty-First Century Series 5. London: T&T Clark, 2004.

Cotterell, Peter, and Max Turner. *Linguistics and Biblical Interpretation*. Downers Grove, IL: InterVarsity, 1989.

Craig, Edward, ed. *Routledge Encyclopedia of Philosophy*. London: Routledge, 1998.

Crossan, John Dominic. *The Historical Jesus: The Life of a Mediterranean Jewish Peasant*. San Francisco: HarperSanFrancisco, 1991.

Culpepper, R. Alan. *Anatomy of the Fourth Gospel: A Study in Literary Design*. Foundations and Facets. Philadelphia: Fortress, 1983.

Dahood, Mitchell. *Psalms*. 3 vols. Anchor Bible. Garden City, NY: Doubleday, 1965–70.

Dana, H. E., and Julius R. Mantey. *A Manual Grammar of the Greek New Testament*. New York: Macmillan, 1927.

Darr, John. *On Character Building: The Reader and the Rhetoric of Characterization in Luke-Acts*. Literary Currents in Biblical Interpretation. Louisville: Westminster John Knox, 1992.

Davidson, Benjamin. *The Analytical Hebrew and Chaldee Concordance*. 2nd ed. Peabody, MA: Hendrickson, 1990.

Deissmann, Adolf. *Light from the Ancient East*. Translated by Lionel R. M. Strachan. New York: Doran, 1927. Originally published as *Licht vom Osten* (1908).

deSilva, David A. *Honor, Patronage, Kinship and Purity: Unlocking New Testament Culture*. Downers Grove, IL: InterVarsity, 2000.

———. *Perseverance in Gratitude: A Socio-Rhetorical Commentary on the Epistle "to the Hebrews."* Grand Rapids: Eerdmans, 2000.

Dever, William G. *What Did the Biblical Writers Know and When Did They Know It? What Archaeology Can Tell Us about the Reality of Ancient Israel*. Grand Rapids: Eerdmans, 2001.

Dewey, Joanna. *Markan Public Debate: Literary Technique, Concentric Structure, and Theology in Mark 2:1–3:6*. Society of Biblical Literature Dissertation Series 48. Chico, CA: Scholars Press, 1980.

Dewey, John. "Method." In *Cyclopedia of Education*, edited by Paul Monroe, 4:204–5. New York: Macmillan, 1913.

Dibelius, Martin. *A Commentary on the Epistle of James*. Revised by Heinrich Greeven. Hermeneia: A Critical and Historical Commentary on the Bible. Philadelphia: Fortress, 1975.

———. *From Tradition to Gospel*. Translated by Bertram Lee Woolf. Cambridge, UK: James Clarke, 1971. Originally published as *Die Formgeschichte des Evangeliums* (1919).

Dillard, Raymond B., and Tremper Longman III. *An Introduction to the Old Testament*. Grand Rapids: Zondervan, 1994.

Dilthey, Wilhelm. *Gesammelte Schriften*. Vol. 7. Stuttgart: Teubner, 1962.

Dodd, C. H. *According to the Scriptures: The Sub-Structure of New Testament Theology*. London: Nisbet, 1952.

Doyle, Arthur Conan. *The Complete Sherlock Holmes*. Garden City, NY: Doubleday, [1930?].

Dozeman, Thomas B., and Konrad Schmid, eds. *A Farewell to the Yahwist? The Composition of the Pentateuch in Recent European Interpretation*. Atlanta: Society of Biblical Literature, 2006.

Drane, John. *Introducing the Old Testament*. Rev. ed. Oxford: Lion, 2000.

Dumais, Marcel. "Sens de l'Écriture: Réexamen à la lumière de l'herméneutique philosophique et des approches littéraires récentes." *New Testament Studies* 45 (1999): 325.

———. "The Sense of Scripture Re-Examined in Light of Philosophical Hermeneutics and Recent Literary Approaches." Translated by David R. Bauer. *The Asbury Journal* 63, no. 1 (2008): 53–74.

Dynes, Wayne R., and Stephen Donaldson, eds. *Homosexuality in the Ancient World*. New York: Garland, 1992.

Ebeling, Gerhard. *Word and Faith*. London: SCM, 1963.

Eberhardt, Charles R. *The Bible in the Making of Ministers: The Scriptural Basis of Theological Education; The Lifework of Wilbert Webster White*. New York: Association Press, 1949.

Eco, Umberto. *Interpretation and Overinterpretation*. Edited by S. Collini. Cambridge: Cambridge University Press, 1992.

———. *The Role of the Reader: Explorations in the Semiotics of Texts.* London: Hutchinson, 1981.

Edwards, Paul, ed. *The Encyclopedia of Philosophy.* Vol. 1. New York: Macmillan, 1967.

Ehrman, Bart D. *Misquoting Jesus: The Story behind Who Changed the Bible and Why.* San Francisco: HarperSanFrancisco, 2005.

Elliott, John H. *1 Peter.* Anchor Bible. New York: Doubleday, 2000.

———. *What Is Social-Scientific Criticism?* Guides to Biblical Scholarship. Minneapolis: Fortress, 1993.

Ellis, E. E. "Quotations in the New Testament." In *The International Standard Bible Encyclopedia*, edited by Geoffrey W. Bromiley, 4:18–25. Grand Rapids: Eerdmans, 1988.

Endres, John C., William R. Millar, and John Barclay Burns, eds. *Chronicles and Its Synoptic Parallels in Samuel, Kings, and Related Biblical Texts.* Collegeville, MN: Liturgical Press, 1998.

Engel, S. Morris. *With Good Reason: An Introduction to Informal Fallacies.* 2nd ed. New York: St. Martin's Press, 1982.

Epp, Eldon Jay, and Beverly Roberts Gaventa. *Junia: The First Woman Apostle.* Minneapolis: Fortress, 2005.

Epp, Eldon Jay, and George W. MacRae, eds. *The New Testament and Its Modern Interpreters.* Philadelphia: Fortress, 1989.

Erickson, Richard J. *A Beginner's Guide to New Testament Exegesis: Taking the Fear out of Critical Method.* Downers Grove, IL: InterVarsity, 2005.

Eslinger, Lyle M. "Viewpoints and Point of View in 1 Samuel 8–12." *Journal for the Study of the Old Testament* 26 (1983): 61–76.

Evans, Craig A., and Stanley E. Porter, eds. *Dictionary of New Testament Background.* Downers Grove, IL: InterVarsity, 2000.

Even-Shoshan, Abraham. *A New Concordance of the Old Testament.* Jerusalem: Kiryat Sepher, 1977–80; Grand Rapids: Baker Academic, 1984.

Farmer, W. R. *Jesus and the Gospel: Tradition, Scripture, and Canon.* Philadelphia: Fortress, 1982.

———. *The Synoptic Problem: A Critical Analysis.* New York: Macmillan, 1964.

Fee, Gordon D. "Textual Criticism of the New Testament." In *Studies in the Theory and Method of New Testament Textual Criticism*, edited by Eldon J. Epp and Gordon D. Fee, 3–16. Studies and Documents 45. Grand Rapids: Eerdmans, 1993.

Fee, Gordon D., and Douglas Stuart. *How to Read the Bible for All Its Worth.* 2nd ed. Grand Rapids: Zondervan, 1993.

Feinberg, John S., ed. *Continuity and Discontinuity: Perspectives on the Relationship between the Old and New Testaments.* Westchester, IL: Crossway, 1988.

Ferguson, Everett. *Backgrounds of Early Christianity.* 2nd ed. Grand Rapids: Eerdmans, 1993.

Fewell, Danna Nolan, and David M. Gunn. *Compromising Redemption: Relating Characters in the Book of Ruth*. Literary Currents in Biblical Interpretation. Louisville: Westminster John Knox, 1990.

Fiorenza, Elisabeth Schüssler. *Bread Not Stone*. Boston: Beacon, 1995.

——. *In Memory of Her: A Feminist Theological Reconstruction of Christian Origins*. New York: Crossroad, 1983.

Fischer, David Hackett. *Historians' Fallacies: Toward a Logic of Historical Thought*. New York: Harper & Row, 1970.

Fish, Stanley. *Doing What Comes Naturally: Change, Rhetoric, and the Practice of Theory in Literary and Legal Studies*. Oxford: Clarendon, 1989.

——. *Is There a Text in This Class? The Authority of Interpretive Communities*. Cambridge, MA: Harvard University Press, 1980.

Fletcher, Joseph. *Situation Ethics: The New Morality*. Philadelphia: Westminster, 1966.

Fokkelman, J. P. *Art and Poetry in the Books of Samuel: A Full Interpretation Based on Stylistic and Structural Analysis*. 4 vols. Studia semitica neerlandica. Winona Lake, IN: Eisenbrauns, 1981–93.

Fowl, Stephen E. *Engaging Scripture: A Model for Theological Interpretation*. Malden, MA: Blackwell, 1998.

——. "The Role of Authorial Intention and the Theological Interpretation of Scripture." In *Between Two Horizons: Spanning New Testament Studies and Systematic Theology*, edited by Joel B. Green and Max Turner, 71–87. Grand Rapids: Eerdmans, 2000.

Fox, Michael. "The Uses of Indeterminacy." *Semeia* 71 (1995): 173–92.

France, R. T. "The Formula-Quotations of Matthew 2 and the Problem of Communication." *New Testament Studies* 27 (1980–81): 233–51.

Freedman, David Noel, ed. *The Anchor Bible Dictionary*. 6 vols. New York: Doubleday, 1992.

Freedman, William. "The Literary Motif: A Definition and Evaluation." *Novel* 4, no. 2 (1970–71): 123–31.

Frei, Hans. *The Eclipse of Biblical Narrative*. New Haven: Yale University Press, 1974.

Fretheim, Terence E., Lloyd R. Bailey Sr., and Victor P. Furnish, eds. *Deuteronomic History*. Interpreting Biblical Texts. Nashville: Abingdon, 1983.

Frye, Northrop. *Anatomy of Criticism: Four Essays*. Princeton, NJ: Princeton University Press, 1957.

Fuchs, Ernst. "The New Testament and the Hermeneutical Problem." In *The New Hermeneutic*, edited by James M. Robinson and J. B. Cobb Jr., 111–45. New Frontiers in Theology 2. New York: Harper, 1964.

Fuller, Daniel P. *Gospel and Law: Contrast or Continuum? The Hermeneutics of Dispensationalism and Covenant Theology*. Grand Rapids: Eerdmans, 1980.

Furnish, Victor Paul. *The Love Command in the New Testament*. Nashville: Abingdon, 1972.

Gabler, Johann Philip. "An Oration on the Proper Distinction between Biblical and Dogmatic Theology and the Specific Objectives of Each." In *The Flowering of Old Testament Theology*, edited by Ben C. Ollenburger, Elmer A. Martins, and Gerhard F. Hasel, 489–502. Winona Lake, IN: Eisenbrauns, 1992.

Gadamer, Hans-Georg. *Truth and Method*. New York: Crossroad, 1988.

Gasque, W. Ward. *A History of the Interpretation of the Acts of the Apostles*. Peabody, MA: Hendrickson, 1975.

Geisler, Norman L., ed. *Baker Encyclopedia of Christian Apologetics*. Grand Rapids: Baker Academic, 1999.

———. *Options in Contemporary Christian Ethics*. Grand Rapids: Baker Academic, 1981.

Genette, Gerard. *Narrative Discourse: An Essay in Method*. Ithaca, NY: Cornell University Press, 1980.

———. "Time and Narrative." In *Aspects of Narrative*, edited by J. Hillis Miller, 181–99. New York: Columbia University Press, 1970.

Gerstenberger, Erhard S. *Theologies in the Old Testament*. Minneapolis: Fortress, 2002.

Gibbs, Raymond. *The Poetics of Mind: Figurative Thought, Language, and Understanding*. Cambridge: Cambridge University Press, 1994.

Girdlestone, Robert B. *Synonyms of the Old Testament: Their Bearing on Christian Doctrine*. 1897. Reprint, Grand Rapids: Eerdmans, 1976.

Goldingay, John. *Models for Interpretation of Scripture*. Grand Rapids: Eerdmans, 1995.

———. *Theological Diversity and the Authority of the Old Testament*. Grand Rapids: Eerdmans, 1987.

Gottwald, Norman K. "Domain Assumptions and Societal Models in the Study of Pre-Monarchic Israel." In *Community, Identity, and Ideology: Social Science Approaches to the Hebrew Bible*, ed. Charles E. Carter and Carol L. Meyers, 170–81. Sources for Biblical and Theological Study 6. Winona Lake, IN: Eisenbrauns, 1996.

———. *The Tribes of Israel: A Sociology of the Religion of Liberated Israel*. Maryknoll, NY: Orbis Books, 1979.

Green, Joel B., ed. *Hearing the New Testament: Strategies for Interpretation*. Grand Rapids: Eerdmans, 1995.

———. "The Practice of Reading the New Testament." In *Hearing the New Testament: Strategies for Interpretation*, edited by Joel B. Green, 411–27. Grand Rapids: Eerdmans, 1995.

Green, Michael, ed. *The Truth of God Incarnate*. Grand Rapids: Eerdmans, 1977.

Greene, Theodore Meyer. *The Arts and the Art of Criticism*. Princeton, NJ: Princeton University Press, 1940.

Greenlee, J. Harold. *Introduction to New Testament Textual Criticism*. Rev. ed. Peabody, MA: Hendrickson, 1995.

Grenholm, Cristina, and Daniel Patte, eds. *Reading Israel in Romans: Legitimacy and Plausibility of Divergent Interpretations.* Harrisburg, PA: Trinity Press International, 2000.

Grimes, Joseph E. *The Thread of Discourse.* Janua linguarum, series minor 207. Berlin: Mouton, 1975.

Gundry, Robert H. *Matthew: A Commentary on His Handbook for a Mixed Church under Persecution.* Grand Rapids: Eerdmans, 1994.

———. *The Use of the Old Testament in St. Matthew's Gospel with Special Reference to the Messianic Hope.* Novum Testamentum Supplements 18. Leiden: Brill, 1967.

Gunkel, Hermann. *Introduction to Psalms: The Genres of the Religious Lyric of Israel.* Completed by Joachim Begrich. Translated by James D. Nogalski. Mercer Library of Biblical Studies. Macon, GA: Mercer University Press, 1998. Originally published as *Einleitung in die Psalmen* (1933).

———. *The Psalms: A Form-Critical Introduction.* Translated by Thomas M. Horner. Facet Books Biblical Series 19. Philadelphia: Fortress, 1967. Originally published as *Die Religion in Geschichte und Gegenwart* (2nd ed., 1930).

Gunton, Colin E. *Enlightenment and Alienation: An Essay towards a Trinitarian Theology.* Contemporary Christian Studies. Basingstoke, UK: Marshall, Morgan & Scott, 1985.

Gustafson, James. "The Place of Scripture in Christian Ethics." *Interpretation* 24 (1970): 435–38.

Guthrie, Donald. *New Testament Introduction.* 4th ed. Downers Grove, IL: InterVarsity, 1990.

Hafemann, Scott J., and Paul R. House. *Central Themes in Biblical Theology: Mapping Unity in Diversity.* Grand Rapids: Baker Academic, 2007.

Handy, Lowell K. *Jonah's World: Social Science and the Reading of Prophetic Story.* Oakville, CT: Equinox, 2007.

Hanson, Paul D. *Old Testament Apocalyptic.* Interpreting Biblical Texts. Nashville: Abingdon, 1987.

Harman, Gilbert. "The Inference to the Best Explanation." *Philosophical Review* 74 (1965): 88–95.

Hart, Trevor. "Tradition, Authority, and a Christian Approach to the Bible as Scripture." In *Between Two Horizons: Spanning New Testament Studies and Systematic Theology,* edited by Joel B. Green and Max Turner, 183–204. Grand Rapids: Eerdmans, 2000.

Hatch, Edwin, and Henry A. Redpath. *A Concordance to the Septuagint and Other Greek Versions of the Old Testament.* 2 vols. Oxford: Clarendon, 1897–1906.

Hauerwas, Stanley. *Community of Character: Toward a Constructive Social Ethic.* Notre Dame, IN: University of Notre Dame Press, 1981.

———. *The Peaceable Kingdom: A Primer in Christian Ethics.* Notre Dame, IN: University of Notre Dame Press, 1983.

———. *Unleashing the Scripture: Freeing the Bible from Captivity to America.* Nashville: Abingdon, 1993.

Hawk, L. Daniel. *Every Promise Fulfilled: Contesting Plots in Joshua*. Literary Currents in Biblical Interpretation. Louisville: Westminster John Knox, 1991.

Hayes, John H. *An Introduction to Old Testament Study*. Nashville: Abingdon, 1979.

—————, ed. *Old Testament Form Criticism*. San Antonio: Trinity University Press, 1974.

Hays, Richard B. "The Conversion of the Imagination: Scripture and Eschatology in 1 Corinthians." *New Testament Studies* 45 (July 1999): 391–412.

—————. *Echoes of Scripture in the Letters of Paul*. New Haven: Yale University Press, 1989.

—————. *The Faith of Jesus Christ: An Investigation of the Narrative Substructure of Galatians 3:1–4:11*. Society of Biblical Literature Dissertation Series 56. Chico, CA: Scholars Press, 1983.

—————. *The Moral Vision of the New Testament: Community, Cross, New Creation*. San Francisco: HarperSanFrancisco, 1996.

Heidegger, Martin. *Being and Time*. Oxford: Blackwell, 1962.

Hengel, Martin. *The Cross of the Son of God*. London: SCM, 1986.

Henry, Matthew. *Commentary on the Whole Bible*. 6 vols. 1706. Reprint, New York: Revell, [1983?].

Hick, John, ed. *The Myth of God Incarnate*. London: SCM, 1977.

Hirsch, E. D., Jr. *The Aims of Interpretation*. Chicago: University of Chicago Press, 1976.

—————. *Validity in Interpretation*. New Haven: Yale University Press, 1967.

Hodges, H. A. *The Philosophy of Wilhelm Dilthey*. London: Routledge & Kegan Paul, 1952.

Hodges, John C., and Mary E. Whitten, with Suzanne S. Webb. *Harbrace College Handbook*. 10th ed. San Diego: Harcourt Brace Jovanovich, 1986.

Holladay, William L. *A Concise Hebrew and Aramaic Lexicon of the Old Testament*. Grand Rapids: Eerdmans, 1971.

Holland, Norman. *The Dynamics of Literary Response*. New York: Norton, 1968.

—————. *Five Readers Reading*. New Haven: Yale University Press, 1975.

Holmberg, Bengt. *Sociology and the New Testament: An Appraisal*. Minneapolis: Fortress, 1990.

Holmes, Michael W. "Textual Criticism." In *Interpreting the New Testament: Essays on Methods and Issues*, edited by David Alan Black and David S. Dockery, 46–73. Nashville: Broadman & Holman, 2001.

Honderich, Ted, ed. *Oxford Companion to Philosophy*. Oxford: Oxford University Press, 1995.

Horrell, David G. *Social-Scientific Approaches to New Testament Interpretation*. Edinburgh: T&T Clark, 1999.

House, Paul R. *The Unity of the Twelve*. Journal for the Study of the Old Testament: Supplement Series 97. Sheffield: Almond, 1990.

Huck, Albert. *A Synopsis of the First Three Gospels with the Addition of the Johannine Parallels.* Revised by Heinrich Greeven. 13th ed. Grand Rapids: Eerdmans, 1982.

Iser, Wolfgang. *The Act of Reading: A Theory of Aesthetic Response.* Baltimore: Johns Hopkins University Press, 1978.

———. *The Implied Reader: Patterns of Communication in Prose Fiction from Bunyan to Beckett.* Baltimore: Johns Hopkins University Press, 1975.

Jackson, Timothy P. *The Priority of Love: Christian Charity and Social Justice.* Princeton, NJ: Princeton University Press, 2003.

Jakobson, Roman. "Linguistics and Poetics." In *Style in Language*, edited by T. A. Sebeok, 350–77. Cambridge, MA: MIT Press, 1960.

Janzen, Waldemar. *Old Testament Ethics: A Paradigmatic Approach.* Louisville: Westminster John Knox, 1994.

Japhet, Sara. *The Ideology of the Book of Chronicles and Its Place in Biblical Thought.* 2nd ed. Beiträge zur Erforschung des Alten Testaments und des antiken Judentums 9. Frankfurt: Peter Lang, 1997.

Jewett, Robert. *Romans.* Hermeneia: A Critical and Historical Commentary on the Bible. Minneapolis: Fortress, 2007.

Johnson, Elliott E. *Expository Hermeneutics: An Introduction.* Grand Rapids: Academie Books, 1990.

Johnson, Luke Timothy. *James.* Anchor Bible. New York: Doubleday, 1995.

———. *The Writings of the New Testament: An Interpretation.* Rev. ed. Minneapolis: Fortress, 1999.

Johnson, Sherman E. *The Griesbach Hypothesis and Redaction Criticism.* Atlanta: Scholars Press, 1991.

Joüon, Paul, and T. Muraoka. *A Grammar of Biblical Hebrew.* 2 vols. Subsidia biblica 14.1–2. Rome: Biblical Institute Press, 1991.

Juel, Donald. *Messianic Exegesis: Christological Interpretation of the Old Testament in Early Christianity.* Philadelphia: Fortress, 1988.

Kaiser, Walter C., Jr. *The Old Testament Documents: Are They Reliable and Relevant?* Downers Grove, IL: InterVarsity, 2001.

———. *Toward an Exegetical Theology: Biblical Exegesis for Preaching and Teaching.* Grand Rapids: Baker Academic, 1981.

Kaiser, Walter C., Jr., and Moisés Silva. *An Introduction to Biblical Hermeneutics: The Search for Meaning.* Rev. ed. Grand Rapids: Zondervan, 2007.

Kautzsch, E., ed. *Gesenius' Hebrew Grammar.* 2nd ed. Revised in accord with the 28th German ed. by A. E. Cowley. Oxford: Clarendon, 1909.

Kee, Howard Clark. *Knowing the Truth: A Sociological Approach to New Testament Interpretation.* Minneapolis: Fortress, 1989.

Keener, Craig S. *The IVP Bible Background Commentary: New Testament.* Downers Grove, IL: InterVarsity, 1994.

Kennedy, George A. *New Testament Interpretation through Rhetorical Criticism.* Chapel Hill: University of North Carolina Press, 1984.

Kingsbury, Jack Dean. *The Christology of Mark's Gospel*. Philadelphia: Fortress, 1983.

———. *Matthew: Structure, Christology, Kingdom*. Philadelphia: Fortress, 1975.

Kitchen, K. A. *Ancient Orient and Old Testament*. Chicago: InterVarsity, 1966.

———. *On the Reliability of the Old Testament*. Rev. ed. Grand Rapids: Eerdmans, 2003.

Kittel, Gerhard, and Gerhard Friedrich, eds. *Theological Dictionary of the New Testament*. Translated by Geoffrey W. Bromiley. 10 vols. Grand Rapids: Eerdmans, 1975–76.

Klein, William W., Craig L. Blomberg, and Robert L. Hubbard Jr. *Introduction to Biblical Interpretation*. 2nd ed. Nashville: Nelson, 2004.

Knight, Douglas A., and Gene M. Tucker, eds. *The Hebrew Bible and Its Modern Interpreters*. Chico, CA: Scholars Press, 1985.

Knight, George W., III. *Commentary on the Pastoral Epistles*. New International Greek Testament Commentary. Grand Rapids: Eerdmans, 1992.

Koch, Klaus. *The Growth of the Biblical Tradition: The Form-Critical Method*. New York: Scribner, 1969.

Kohlenberger, John R., III. *The Hebrew-English Concordance to the Old Testament: With the New International Version*. Grand Rapids: Zondervan, 1998.

———. *Zondervan NIV Nave's Topical Bible*. Grand Rapids: Zondervan, 1992.

Köhler, Ludwig, and Walter Baumgartner. *The Hebrew and Aramaic Lexicon of the Old Testament*. Revised by Walter Baumgartner and Johann Jakob Stamm. 3rd ed. 5 vols. Leiden: Brill, 1994–2000.

Kraft, Charles. *Christianity in Culture: A Study in Dynamic Biblical Theologizing in Cross-Cultural Perspective*. Maryknoll, NY: Orbis Books, 1979.

Krentz, Edgar. *The Historical-Critical Method*. Guides to Biblical Scholarship. Philadelphia: Fortress, 1975.

Kroeger, Richard Clark, and Catherine Clark Kroeger. *I Suffer Not a Woman: Rethinking 1 Timothy 2:11–15 in Light of Ancient Evidence*. Grand Rapids: Baker Academic, 1992.

Kuhn, Thomas S. *The Structure of Scientific Revolutions*. 2nd ed. Chicago: University of Chicago Press, 1970.

Kuist, Howard Tillman. *These Words upon Thy Heart: Scripture and the Christian Response*. Richmond: John Knox, 1947.

Kümmel, Werner Georg. *Introduction to the New Testament*. Rev. ed. Nashville: Abingdon, 1975.

———. *The New Testament: The History of the Investigation of Its Problems*. Nashville: Abingdon, 1972.

Lakoff, George, and Mark Johnson. *Metaphors We Live By*. Chicago: University of Chicago Press, 1980.

Lakoff, George, and Mark Turner. *More Than Cool Reason: A Field Guide to Poetic Metaphor*. Chicago: University of Chicago Press, 1989.

Lane, William L. *Hebrews*. 2 vols. Word Biblical Commentary 47A–B. Dallas: Word, 1991.

Lanser, Susan Sniader. *The Narrative Act: Point of View in Prose Fiction*. Princeton, NJ: Princeton University Press, 1981.

Larson, Mildred L. *Meaning-Based Translation: A Guide to Cross-Language Equivalence*. 2nd ed. Lanham, MD: University Press of America, 1998.

Lawrence, Louise Joy. *An Ethnography of the Gospel of Matthew: A Critical Assessment of the Use of the Honour and Shame Model in New Testament Studies*. Wissenschaftliche Untersuchungen zum Neuen Testament, 2nd ser., 165. Tübingen: Mohr Siebeck, 2003.

Lewis, C. S., and E. M. W. Tillyard. *The Personal Heresy: A Controversy*. Oxford: Oxford University Press, 1939.

Liddell, Henry George, and Robert Scott. *A Greek-English Lexicon*. Revised and augmented by Henry Stuart Jones and Roderick McKenzie. Oxford: Clarendon, 1940.

Lipton, Peter. *Inference to Best Explanation*. 2nd ed. London: Routledge, 2004.

Lonergan, Bernard. *Method in Theology*. New York: Herder & Herder, 1972.

Longacre, Robert E. *The Grammar of Discourse*. New York: Plenum, 1983.

Longenecker, Richard N. *Biblical Exegesis in the Apostolic Period*. 2nd ed. Grand Rapids: Eerdmans, 1999.

Longman, Tremper, III. *Old Testament Commentary Survey*. 4th ed. Grand Rapids: Baker Academic, 2007.

Louth, Andrew. *Discerning the Mystery: An Essay on the Nature of Theology*. Oxford: Clarendon, 1983.

Louw, Johannes P. *Semantics of New Testament Greek*. Philadelphia: Fortress, 1982.

Louw, Johannes P., and Eugene A. Nida, eds. *Greek-English Lexicon of the New Testament Based on Semantic Domains*. 2nd ed. 2 vols. New York: United Bible Societies, 1989.

Luc, Alex. *New International Dictionary of Old Testament Theology and Exegesis*. Edited by Willem A. VanGemeren. Grand Rapids: Zondervan, 1997.

Lund, Nils W. *Chiasmus in the New Testament: A Study in the Form and Function of Chiastic Structures*. 1942. Reprint, Peabody, MA: Hendrickson, 1992.

Luz, Ulrich. *Matthew: A Commentary*. Vol. 1, *Matthew 1–7*. Hermeneia: A Critical and Historical Commentary on the Bible. Philadelphia: Fortress, 1989.

———. *Matthew: A Commentary*. Vol. 2, *Matthew 8–20*. Hermeneia: A Critical and Historical Commentary on the Bible. Minneapolis: Fortress, 2005.

———. *Matthew: A Commentary*. Vol. 3, *Matthew 21–28*. Hermeneia: A Critical and Historical Commentary on the Bible. Minneapolis: Fortress, 2005.

Macintosh, A. A. *A Critical and Exegetical Commentary on Hosea*. International Critical Commentary. Edinburgh: T&T Clark, 1997.

Mack, Burton L. *The Myth of Innocence: Mark and Christian Origins*. Philadelphia: Fortress, 1988.

————. *Rhetoric and the New Testament*. Guides to Biblical Scholarship. Minneapolis: Fortress, 1990.

Malina, Bruce J. *Christian Origins and Cultural Anthropology: Practical Models for Biblical Interpretation*. Atlanta: John Knox, 1986.

————. *The New Testament World: Insights from Cultural Anthropology*. 3rd ed. Louisville: Westminster John Knox, 2001.

Malina, Bruce J., and John J. Pilch. *Social-Science Commentary on the Letters of Paul*. Minneapolis: Fortress, 2006.

Malina, Bruce J., and Richard L. Rohrbaugh. *Social-Science Commentary on the Synoptic Gospels*. Minneapolis: Fortress, 2003.

Marshall, I. Howard. *Beyond the Bible: Moving from Scripture to Theology*. Grand Rapids: Baker Academic, 2004.

————. *Biblical Inspiration*. Grand Rapids: Eerdmans, 1983.

————. *A Critical and Exegetical Commentary on the Pastoral Epistles*. International Critical Commentary. Edinburgh: T&T Clark, 1999.

————, ed. *New Testament Interpretation: Essays on Principles and Methods*. Grand Rapids: Eerdmans, 1977.

Martin, Dale. "Heterosexism and the Interpretation of Romans 1:18–32." *Biblical Interpretation* 3 (1995): 332–55.

Martin, Ralph P. *New Testament Foundations*. Rev. ed. 2 vols. Grand Rapids: Eerdmans, 1986.

Martyn, J. Louis. *Galatians*. Anchor Bible. New York: Doubleday, 1997.

Matthews, Victor H., and Don C. Benjamin. *Social World of Ancient Israel, 1250–587 B.C.E.* Peabody, MA: Hendrickson, 1993.

Mayes, A. D. H. *The Old Testament in Sociological Perspective*. London: Pickering, 1989.

Mays, James Luther. *The Lord Reigns: A Theological Handbook to the Psalms*. Louisville: Westminster John Knox, 1994.

————. "The Place of the Torah Psalms in the Psalter." *Journal of Biblical Literature* 106 (1987): 3–12.

————. *Psalms*. Interpretation: A Bible Commentary for Teaching and Preaching. Louisville: John Knox, 1994.

McCann, J. Clinton, Jr. *The Shape and Shaping of the Psalter*. Journal for the Study of the Old Testament: Supplement Series 159. Sheffield: JSOT Press, 1993.

————. *A Theological Introduction to the Book of Psalms*. Nashville: Abingdon, 1993.

McCarter, P. Kyle. *Textual Criticism: Recovering the Text of the Hebrew Bible*. Guides to Biblical Scholarship. Philadelphia: Fortress, 1986.

McConville, J. Gordon. *Grace in the End: A Study in Deuteronomic Theology*. Studies in Old Testament Biblical Theology. Grand Rapids: Zondervan, 1993.

McCown, Wayne, and James Massey, eds. *Interpreting God's Word for Today: An Inquiry into Hermeneutics from a Biblical Theological Perspective*. Wesleyan Theological Perspectives 2. Anderson, IN: Warner, 1982.

McKenzie, Steven L. *The Chronicler's Use of the Deuteronomistic History*. Harvard Semitic Monographs 33. Atlanta: Scholars Press, 1985.

McKenzie, Steven L., and Stephen R. Haynes. *To Each Its Own Meaning: An Introduction to Biblical Criticisms and Their Application*. Louisville: Westminster John Knox, 1993.

McKnight, Edgar V. "Presuppositions in New Testament Study." In *Hearing the New Testament: Strategies for Interpretation*, edited by Joel B. Green, 278–300. Grand Rapids: Eerdmans, 1995.

———. *What Is Form Criticism?* Guides to Biblical Scholarship. Philadelphia: Fortress, 1969.

McLay, R. Timothy. *The Use of the Septuagint in New Testament Research*. Grand Rapids: Eerdmans, 2003.

McNeile, Alan Hugh. *The Gospel according to Matthew*. London: Macmillan, 1938.

Mead, James K. *Biblical Theology: Issues, Methods, and Themes*. Louisville: Westminster John Knox, 2007.

Meier, John P. *A Marginal Jew: Rethinking the Historical Jesus*. 3 vols. Anchor Bible Reference Library. New York: Doubleday, 1987–2001.

Mendenhall, George H. *Law and Covenant in Israel and in the Ancient Near East*. Pittsburgh: The Biblical Colloquium, 1955.

Merenlahti, Peter. *Poetics for the Gospels? Rethinking Narrative Criticism*. London: T&T Clark International, 2002.

Metzger, Bruce M. *The Canon of the New Testament: Its Origin, Development, and Significance*. Oxford: Clarendon, 1987.

———, ed. *A Textual Commentary on the Greek New Testament*. 2nd ed. Stuttgart: United Bible Societies, 1994.

Metzger, Bruce M., and Bart D. Ehrman. *The Text of the New Testament: Its Transmission, Corruption, and Restoration*. 4th ed. Oxford: Oxford University Press, 2005.

Meyer, Ben F. *Reality and Illusion in New Testament Scholarship: A Primer in Critical Realist Hermeneutics*. Collegeville, MN: Michael Glazier, 1994.

Meyers, Carol L., and Eric M. Meyers. *Haggai, Zechariah 1–8*. Anchor Bible. New York: Doubleday, 1987.

———. *Zechariah 9–14*. Anchor Bible. New York: Doubleday, 1993.

Miller, Donald G. *The Way to Biblical Preaching: How to Communicate the Gospel in Depth*. Nashville: Abingdon, 1957.

Miller, J. Maxwell. *The Old Testament and the Historian*. Guides to Biblical Scholarship. Philadelphia: Fortress, 1976.

Mills, Watson E., ed. *Bibliographies for Biblical Research*. New Testament Series. 21 vols. Lewiston, NY: Mellen Biblical Press, 1993–2002.

Minear, Paul S. *New Testament Apocalyptic*. Interpreting Biblical Texts. Nashville: Abingdon, 1981.

Mittmann, Siegfried, and Götz Schmitt, eds. *Tübinger Bibelatlas*. Stuttgart: Deutsche Bibelgesellschaft, 2001.

Moffatt, James, ed. *Letters of Principal James Denney to His Family and Friends.* London: Hodder & Stoughton, [1922?].

———. *Love in the New Testament.* London: Hodder & Stoughton, 1929.

Moltmann, Jürgen. *Theology of Hope.* San Francisco: HarperSanFrancisco, 1991.

Moo, Douglas J. "The Problem of *Sensus Plenior*." In *Hermeneutics, Authority, and Canon,* edited by D. A. Carson and John D. Woodbridge, 179–211. Grand Rapids: Zondervan, 1986.

———. *Romans.* New International Commentary on the New Testament. Grand Rapids: Eerdmans, 1996.

Moore, Stephen D. *Literary Criticism and the Gospels: The Theoretical Challenge.* New Haven: Yale University Press, 1989.

Morgan, G. Campbell. *The Study and Teaching of the English Bible.* Revised by E. D. De Rusett. London: Hodder & Stoughton; New York: Fleming H. Revell, 1910. Also available online at http://www.gcampbellmorgan.com/studyteach.html.

Morson, Gary Saul, and Caryl Emerson. *Mikhail Bakhtin: Creation of a Prosaics.* Palo Alto, CA: Stanford University Press, 1990.

Moulton, James Hope, and George Milligan. *The Vocabulary of the Greek Testament Illustrated from the Papyri and Other Non-Literary Sources.* Grand Rapids: Eerdmans, 1930.

Moulton, W. F., and A. S. Geden. *A Concordance to the Greek Testament.* Edited by I. Howard Marshall. 6th ed. New York: Continuum, 2002.

Mounce, William D. *Pastoral Epistles.* Word Biblical Commentary 46. Nashville: Nelson, 2000.

Mowinckel, Sigmund. *The Psalms in Israel's Worship.* Translated by D. R. Ap-Thomas. 2 vols. Nashville: Abingdon, 1963. Originally published as *Offersang og sangoffer* (1951).

Moyise, Steven. *Paul and Scripture: Studying the New Testament Use of the Old Testament.* Grand Rapids: Baker Academic, 2010.

Muilenburg, James. "Form Criticism and Beyond." *Journal of Biblical Literature* 88 (1969): 1–18.

Mulholland, M. Robert. "Sociological Criticism." In *Interpreting the New Testament: Essays on Methods and Issues,* edited by David Alan Black and David S. Dockery, 170–86. Nashville: Broadman & Holman, 2001.

Murphy, Roland E. *Wisdom Literature: Job, Proverbs, Ruth, Canticles, Ecclesiastes, and Esther.* Forms of Old Testament Literature 13. Grand Rapids: Eerdmans, 1981.

Neill, Stephen, and Tom Wright. *The Interpretation of the New Testament, 1861–1986.* 2nd ed. New York: Oxford University Press, 1988.

Nelson, Richard D. "The Anatomy of the Book of Kings." *Journal for the Study of the Old Testament* 40 (1988): 39–48.

Newman, Barclay. *A Concise Greek-English Dictionary of the New Testament.* Stuttgart: United Bible Societies, 1993.

Neyrey, Jerome H. *2 Peter, Jude.* Anchor Bible. New York: Doubleday, 1993.

Nicholson, Ernest. *The Pentateuch in the Twentieth Century: The Legacy of Julius Wellhausen*. Oxford: Clarendon, 1998.

Nida, Eugene A. *Exploring Semantic Structures*. International Library of General Linguistics 11. Munich: Wilhelm Fink, 1975.

Niebuhr, Reinhold. *Interpretation of Christian Ethics*. 1935. Reprint with new preface, Cleveland: World, 1956.

———. *Moral Man and Immoral Society*. New York: Scribner's Sons, 1932.

———. *The Nature and Destiny of Man*. 2 vols. New York: Scribner's Sons, 1941–43.

Niebuhr, Richard R. *Resurrection and Historical Reason: A Study of Theological Method*. New York: Scribner, 1957.

Noth, Martin. *The Deuteronomistic History*. Journal for the Study of the Old Testament: Supplement Series 15. Sheffield: JSOT Press, 1981.

Nygren, Anders. *Agape and Eros*. Philadelphia: Westminster, 1953.

Oesterley, W. O. E., and Theodore H. Robinson. *An Introduction to the Books of the Old Testament*. New York: Meridian Books, 1958.

Ogletree, Thomas W. *The Use of the Bible in Christian Ethics*. Louisville: Westminster John Knox, 2003.

Osborne, Grant R. *The Hermeneutical Spiral: A Comprehensive Introduction to Biblical Interpretation*. 2nd ed. Downers Grove, IL: InterVarsity, 2006.

Oswalt, John N. *The Bible among the Myths: Unique Revelation or Just Ancient Literature?* Grand Rapids: Zondervan, 2009.

Overholt, Thomas W. *Cultural Anthropology and the Old Testament*. Guides to Biblical Scholarship. Minneapolis: Fortress, 1996.

Pannenberg, Wolfhart. *Basic Questions in Theology*. 2 vols. Philadelphia: Fortress, 1970–71.

———. *Systematic Theology*. 3 vols. Grand Rapids: Eerdmans, 1991–93.

Patte, Daniel. *The Challenge of Discipleship: A Critical Study of the Sermon on the Mount as Scripture*. Harrisburg, PA: Trinity Press International, 1999.

———. *Discipleship according to the Sermon on the Mount: Four Legitimate Readings, Four Plausible Views of Discipleship, and Their Relative Values*. Valley Forge, PA: Trinity Press International, 1996.

Peabody, David B., Lamar Cope, and Allan J. McNichol, eds. *One Gospel from Two: Mark's Use of Matthew and Luke*. London: SCM, 2001.

Perdue, Leo G., Robert Morgan, and Benjamin D. Sommer, eds. *Biblical Theology: Introducing the Conversation*. Library of Biblical Theology. Nashville: Abingdon, 2009.

Perrin, Norman. *What Is Redaction Criticism?* Guides to Biblical Scholarship. Philadelphia: Fortress, 1969.

Perschbacher, Wesley J., ed. *The New Analytical Greek Lexicon*. Peabody, MA: Hendrickson, 1990.

Petersen, David L. *Haggai and Zechariah 1–8*. Old Testament Library. Philadelphia: Westminster, 1984.

———. *Zechariah 9–14 and Malachi*. Old Testament Library. Louisville: Westminster John Knox, 1995.

Petersen, David L., and Kent Harold Richards. *Interpreting Biblical Poetry*. Guides to Biblical Scholarship. Minneapolis: Fortress, 1992.

Phillips, Gary A., and Nicole Wilkinson Duran, eds. *Reading Communities, Reading Scripture: Essays in Honor of Daniel Patte*. Harrisburg, PA: Trinity Press International, 2002.

Pierce, Claude Anthony. *Conscience in the New Testament: A Study of "Syneidēsis" in the New Testament*. Studies in Biblical Theology 15. Chicago: Allenson, 1955.

Pinnock, Clark. "Climbing out of the Swamp: The Evangelical Struggle to Understand the Creation Texts." *Interpretation* 43 (April 1989): 143–55.

Piper, John, and Wayne Grudem, eds. *Recovering Biblical Manhood and Womanhood: A Response to Evangelical Feminism*. Wheaton, IL: Crossway, 1991.

Polzin, Robert. *Moses and the Deuteronomist: A Literary Study of the Deuteronomic History*. New York: Seabury, 1980.

Porter, Stanley E. *Handbook of Classical Rhetoric in the Hellenistic Period (330 B.C.–A.D. 400)*. Leiden: Brill, 1977.

Powell, Mark Allan. "Characterization on the Phraseological Plane in the Gospel of Matthew." In *Treasures New and Old: Contributions to Matthean Studies*, edited by David R. Bauer and Mark Allan Powell, 161–77. Atlanta: Scholars Press, 1996.

———. *Chasing the Eastern Star: Adventures in Biblical Reader-Response Criticism*. Louisville: Westminster John Knox, 2001.

———. "Expected and Unexpected Readings in Matthew: What the Reader Knows." *Asbury Theological Journal* 48, no. 2 (1993): 31–52.

———. *God with Us: A Pastoral Theology of Matthew's Gospel*. Minneapolis: Fortress, 1995.

———. *Jesus as a Figure in History: How Modern Historians View the Man from Galilee*. Louisville: Westminster John Knox, 1998.

———. *What Are They Saying about Acts?* New York: Paulist Press, 1991.

———. "What Is Literary about Literary Aspects?" In *Society of Biblical Literature 1992 Seminar Papers*, edited by Eugene H. Lovering Jr., 41–48. Atlanta: Scholars Press, 1992.

———. *What Is Narrative Criticism?* Guides to Biblical Scholarship. Minneapolis: Fortress, 1990.

Priest, John F. "Sociology and Hebrew Bible Studies." In *Dictionary of Biblical Interpretation*, edited by John H. Hayes, 2:483–87. Nashville: Abingdon, 1999.

Provan, Iain V., Philips Long, and Tremper Longman III. *A Biblical History of Israel*. Louisville: Westminster John Knox, 2003.

Rad, Gerhard von. *Biblical Interpretations in Preaching*. Nashville: Abingdon, 1977.

———. *Old Testament Theology*. 2 vols. New York: Harper & Row, 1962–65.

Rainey, Anson F., and R. Steven Notley, eds. *The Sacred Bridge: Carta's Atlas of the Biblical World*. Jerusalem: Carta, 2006.

Räisänen, Heikki. *Beyond New Testament Theology: A Story and a Programme*. 2nd ed. London: SCM, 2000.

Rast, Walter E. *Tradition History and the Old Testament*. Guides to Biblical Scholarship. Philadelphia: Fortress, 1972.

Ratzsch, Del. *Science and Its Limits: The Natural Sciences in Christian Perspective*. 2nd ed. Downers Grove, IL: InterVarsity, 2000.

Rendtorff, Rolf. *The Old Testament: An Introduction*. Philadelphia: Fortress, 1986.

———. *Das überlieferungsgeschichtliche Problem des Pentateuch*. Beihefte zur Zeitschrift für die alttestamentliche Wissenschaft. Berlin: de Gruyter, 1992.

Resseguie, James L. *Narrative Criticism of the New Testament: An Introduction*. Grand Rapids: Baker Academic, 2005.

———. *The Strange Gospel: Narrative Design and Point of View in John*. Leiden: Brill, 2001.

Riches, John K. *A Century of New Testament Study*. Valley Forge, PA: Trinity Press International, 1993.

Richter, Sandra L. "Deuteronomic History." In *Dictionary of the Old Testament Historical Books*, edited by Bill T. Arnold and H. G. M. Williamson, 219–30. Downers Grove, IL: InterVarsity, 2005.

Ricoeur, Paul. *Interpretation Theory: Discourse and the Surplus of Meaning*. Fort Worth: Texas Christian University Press, 1976.

Ridderbos, Herman. *The Coming of the Kingdom*. Philadelphia: P&R, 1962.

Robertson, A. T. *A Grammar of the Greek New Testament in Light of Historical Research*. Nashville: Broadman, 1934.

Rodd, Cyril S. "Sociology and Social Anthropology." In Coggins and Houlden, *Dictionary of Biblical Interpretation*, 635–39.

Rohrbaugh, Richard L., ed. *The Social Sciences and New Testament Interpretation*. Peabody, MA: Hendrickson, 1996.

Romer, Thomas C. *The Deuteronomistic History: A Social-Science Commentary*. New York: Continuum, 2000.

Rorty, Richard. *Consequences of Pragmatism*. Minneapolis: University of Minnesota Press, 1982.

———. *Contingency, Irony, and Solidarity*. Cambridge: Cambridge University Press, 1989.

———. *The Linguistic Turn*. Chicago: University of Chicago Press, 1967.

———. *Philosophy and the Mirror of Nature*. Princeton, NJ: Princeton University Press, 1979.

Rudinow, Joel, and Vincent E. Barry. *Invitation to Critical Thinking*. 5th ed. Belmont, CA: Wadsworth/Thomson, 2004.

Russell, D. S. *The Method and Message of Jewish Apocalyptic, 200 BC–AD 100*. Old Testament Library. Philadelphia: Westminster, 1964.

Ryken, Leland. *The Literature of the Bible*. Grand Rapids: Zondervan, 1974.

———. *Words of Delight: A Literary Introduction to the Bible*. 2nd ed. Grand Rapids: Baker Academic, 1992.

Sailhamer, John H. *The Pentateuch as Narrative: A Biblical-Theological Commentary*. Grand Rapids: Zondervan, 1992.

Sakenfeld, Katharine Doob, ed. *The New Interpreter's Dictionary of the Bible*. 5 vols. Nashville: Abingdon, 2006–2009.

Sanders, James. *Canon and Community: A Guide to Canonical Criticism*. GBS. Philadelphia: Fortress, 1984.

———. *From Sacred Story to Sacred Text: Canon as Paradigm*. Philadelphia: Fortress, 1987.

———. *Torah and Canon*. Philadelphia: Fortress, 1972.

Sandmel, Samuel. "Parallelomania." *Journal of Biblical Literature* 81 (January 1962): 2–13.

Sandys-Wunsch, John, and Laurence Eldridge. "J. P. Gabler and the Distinction between Biblical and Dogmatic Theology." *Scottish Journal of Theology* 33 (1980): 133–88.

Scanzoni, Letha D., and Virginia R. Mollenkott. *Is the Homosexual My Neighbor? A Positive Christian Response*. 2nd ed. San Francisco: HarperCollins, 1994.

Schlatter, Adolf. "Appendix D: Adolf Schlatter on Atheistic Methods in Theology." In *Adolf Schlatter: A Biography of Germany's Premier Biblical Theologian*, by Werner Neuer, 211–25. Translated by Robert W. Yarbrough. Grand Rapids: Baker Academic, 1995.

———. "Atheistic Methods in Theology." Translated by David R. Bauer. *Asbury Theological Journal* 51 (Fall 1996): 45–57.

———. "Atheistische Methoden in der Theologie." *Beiträge zur Förderung christlicher Theologie* 9, no. 5 (1905): 229–50.

Schmeller, Thomas. "Sociology and New Testament Studies." In *Dictionary of Biblical Interpretation*, edited by John H. Hayes, 2:487–92. Nashville: Abingdon, 1999.

Schmidt, Werner H. *Old Testament Introduction*. 2nd ed. Louisville: Westminster John Knox, 1995.

Schweitzer, Albert. *The Quest of the Historical Jesus: The First Complete Edition*. Edited by John Bowden. Minneapolis: Fortress, 2001.

Segundo, Luis. *The Liberation of Theology*. Maryknoll, NY: Orbis Books, 1976.

Seters, John van. *The Pentateuch: A Social-Science Commentary*. London: T&T Clark, 2004.

Shuler, Philip L. *A Genre for the Gospels: The Biographical Character of Matthew*. Philadelphia: Fortress, 1982.

Sider, John W. "Rediscovering the Parables of Jesus: The Logic of the Jeremias Tradition." *Journal of Biblical Literature* 102 (1983): 61–83.

Sider, Ronald L. "Toward a Biblical Perspective on Equality: Steps on the Way toward Christian Political Engagement." *Interpretation* 43 (1989): 156–69.

Silva, Moisés. *Biblical Words and Their Meaning: An Introduction to Lexical Semantics*. Grand Rapids: Zondervan, 1983.

Smith, W. Robertson. *Lectures on the Religion of the Semites*. London: Black, 1889.

Soards, Marion L. "The Christology of the Pauline Epistles." In *Who Do You Say That I Am? Essays on Christology*, edited by Mark Allan Powell and David R. Bauer, 88–109. Louisville: Westminster John Knox, 1999.

Soggin, J. Alberto. *Joshua*. Old Testament Library. Philadelphia: Westminster, 1972.

Soskice, Janet Martin. *Metaphor and Religious Language*. Oxford: Clarendon, 1985.

Soulen, Richard N., and R. Kendall Soulen. *Handbook of Biblical Criticism*. 3rd ed. Louisville: Westminster John Knox, 2001.

Spicq, Ceslaus. *Agape in the New Testament*. Translated by Marie Aquinas McNamara and Mary Honoria Richter. 3 vols. St. Louis: Herder, 1963–66.

Spina, Frank. "Canonical Criticism: Childs versus Sanders." In McCown and Massey, *Interpreting God's Word for Today*, 165–94.

Spong, John Shelby. *Living in Sin: A Bishop Rethinks Human Sexuality*. San Francisco: Harper & Row, 1988.

———. *Sins of Scripture: Exposing the Bible's Texts of Hate to Reveal the God of Love*. San Francisco: HarperSanFrancisco, 2005.

Spurgeon, Charles H. *The Treasury of David*. 3 vols. 1869. Reprint, Grand Rapids: Zondervan, 1966.

Steen, Gerard. *Understanding Metaphor in Literature: An Empirical Approach*. London: Longman, 1994.

Stein, Robert H. *The Synoptic Problem: An Introduction*. Grand Rapids: Baker Academic, 1987.

Steinberg, Naomi. "Social-Scientific Criticism." In *Dictionary of Biblical Interpretation*, edited by John H. Hayes, 2:478–81. Nashville: Abingdon, 1999.

Stendahl, Krister. "Biblical Theology, Contemporary." In *The Interpreter's Dictionary of the Bible*, edited by George A. Buttrick, 1:418–32. Nashville: Abingdon, 1962.

Sternberg, Meir. *Expositional Modes and Temporal Ordering in Fiction*. Baltimore: Johns Hopkins University Press, 1978.

———. *The Poetics of Biblical Narrative: Ideological Literature and the Drama of Reading*. Bloomington: Indiana University Press, 1987.

Stott, John R. W. *Baptism and Fullness: The Work of the Holy Spirit Today*. 2nd ed. Downers Grove, IL: InterVarsity, 1976.

Stowers, Stanley K. *Letter Writing in Greco-Roman Antiquity*. Library of Early Christianity. Philadelphia: Westminster, 1986.

Strauss, David Friedrich. *The Life of Jesus Critically Examined*. Translated by Peter C. Hodgson from the 4th German ed., 1840. Lives of Jesus Series. Philadelphia: Fortress, 1972.

Strecker, Georg. *Theology of the New Testament*. Edited by Friedrich Wilhelm Horn. Louisville: Westminster John Knox, 2000.

Streeter, B. H. *The Four Gospels: A Study in Origins*. London: Macmillan, 1924.

Stronstad, Roger. *The Charismatic Theology of St. Luke*. Peabody, MA: Hendrickson, 1984.

———. *The Prophethood of All Believers: A Study of Luke's Charismatic Theology*. Grand Rapids: Zondervan, 1993.

Stuhlmacher, Peter. *Biblische Theologie des Neuen Testaments*. 2 vols. Göttingen: Vandenhoeck & Ruprecht, 1992–99.

———. *Historical Criticism and Theological Interpretation of Scripture*. Philadelphia: Fortress, 1977.

———. *How to Do Biblical Theology*. Allison Park, PA: Pickwick Publications, 1995.

Swete, Henry Barclay. *An Introduction to the Old Testament in Greek*. Revised by R. R. Ottley. Cambridge: Cambridge University Press, 1914.

Tate, W. Randolph. *Biblical Interpretation: An Integrated Approach*. Rev. ed. Peabody, MA: Hendrickson, 1996.

Taylor, Vincent. *The Formation of the Gospel Tradition*. London: Macmillan, 1960.

Terry, Milton S. *Biblical Hermeneutics*. Rev. ed. New York: Methodist Book Concern, 1911.

Thayer, Joseph Henry. *Greek-English Lexicon of the New Testament: Coded with the Numbering System from Strong's Exhaustive Concordance of the Bible*. Peabody, MA: Hendrickson, 1996.

Theissen, Gerd, and Annette Merz. *The Historical Jesus: A Comprehensive Guide*. London: SCM, 1998.

Thiselton, Anthony C. "'Behind' and 'In Front Of' the Text: Language, Reference, and Indeterminacy." In *After Pentecost: Language and Biblical Interpretation*, edited by Craig Bartholomew, Colin Greene, and Karl Möller, 97–120. Scripture and Hermeneutics Series 2. Grand Rapids: Zondervan, 2001.

———. *The First Epistle to the Corinthians*. New International Greek Testament Commentary. Grand Rapids: Eerdmans, 2000.

———. *New Horizons in Hermeneutics: The Theory and Practice of Transforming Biblical Reading*. Grand Rapids: Zondervan, 1992.

———. *The Two Horizons: New Testament Hermeneutics and Philosophical Description*. Grand Rapids: Eerdmans, 1980.

Thomas, John Christopher. *Footwashing in John 13 and the Johannine Community*. Sheffield: JSOT Press, 1991.

———. *The Spirit of the New Testament*. Leiden: Deo, 2005.

Thompson, David L. *Bible Study That Works*. Rev. ed. Nappanee, IN: Evangel Publishing House, 1994.

Thompson, James W. *Pastoral Ministry according to Paul: A Biblical Vision*. Grand Rapids: Baker Academic, 2006.

Thomson, Ian H. *Chiasmus in the Pauline Letters*. Sheffield: Sheffield Academic Press, 1995.

Throckmorton, Burton H. *Gospel Parallels: A Comparison of the Synoptic Gospels*. 5th ed. Nashville: Nelson, 1992.

Tov, Emanuel. *Textual Criticism of the Hebrew Bible*. 2nd ed. Minneapolis: Fortress, 2001.

Towner, Philip H. *The Letters to Timothy and Titus*. New International Commentary on the New Testament. Grand Rapids: Eerdmans, 2006.

Traina, Robert A. "Inductive Bible Study Reexamined in Light of Contemporary Hermeneutics I: Interpreting the Text." In McCown and Massey, *Interpreting God's Word for Today*, 53–84.

———. "Inductive Bible Study Reexamined in Light of Contemporary Hermeneutics II: Applying the Text." In McCown and Massey, *Interpreting God's Word for Today*, 85–109.

———. "Love." In *Baker's Dictionary of Christian Ethics*, ed. Carl F. H. Henry, 396–98. Grand Rapids: Baker Books, 1973.

———. *Methodical Bible Study: A New Approach to Hermeneutics*. New York: Ganis & Harris, 1952.

Trench, Richard C. *Synonyms of the New Testament: Studies in the Greek New Testament*. 1880. Reprint, Grand Rapids: Eerdmans, 1953.

Trible, Phyllis. *Rhetorical Criticism: Context, Method, and the Book of Jonah*. Guides to Biblical Scholarship. Minneapolis: Fortress, 1994.

Tucker, Gene M. *Form Criticism of the Old Testament*. Guides to Biblical Scholarship. Philadelphia: Fortress, 1971.

———. "Prophetic Speech." In *Interpreting the Prophets*, edited by James Luther Mays and Paul J. Achtemeier, 27–40. Philadelphia: Fortress, 1987.

Tuckett, Christopher, ed. *The Messianic Secret*. Issues in Religion and Theology 1. Philadelphia: Fortress, 1983.

Tuell, Steven S. *First and Second Chronicles*. Interpretation: A Bible Commentary for Teaching and Preaching. Louisville: John Knox, 2001.

Turner, Max. "Historical Criticism and Theological Hermeneutics of the New Testament." In *Between Two Horizons: Spanning New Testament Studies and Systematic Theology*, edited by Joel B. Green and Max Turner, 44–70. Grand Rapids: Eerdmans, 2000.

Uspensky, Boris. *A Poetics of Composition: The Structure of the Artistic Text and Typology of a Compositional Form*. Berkeley: University of California Press, 1973.

VanGemeren, Willem A., ed. *New International Dictionary of Old Testament Theology and Exegesis*. 5 vols. Grand Rapids: Zondervan, 1997.

Vanhoozer, Kevin J. *Is There a Meaning in This Text? The Bible, the Reader, and the Morality of Literary Knowledge*. Grand Rapids: Zondervan, 1998.

———. "The Reader in New Testament Interpretation." In *Hearing the New Testament: Strategies for Reading*, edited by Joel B. Green, 301–28. Grand Rapids: Eerdmans, 1995.

Vannutelli, Primus. *Libri synoptici veteris testamenti seu librorum regum et chronicorum loci paralleli*. Rome: Pontifical Biblical Institute Press, 1931–34.

Vaux, Roland de. *Ancient Israel: Its Life and Institutions*. 2 vols. New York: McGraw-Hill, 1965.

Wagner, Günter, ed. *An Exegetical Bibliography of the New Testament*. Macon, GA: Mercer University Press, 1983–.

Wald, Oletta. *The Joy of Discovery in Bible Study*. Rev. ed. Minneapolis: Augsburg, 1975.

Wall, Robert W. "Canonical Context and Canonical Conversations." In *Between Two Horizons: Spanning New Testament Studies and Systematic Theology*, edited by Joel B. Green and Max Turner, 165–82. Grand Rapids: Eerdmans, 2000.

———. "1 Timothy 2:9–15 Reconsidered (Again)." *Bulletin for Biblical Research* 14, no. 1 (2004): 81–103.

———. "Reading the Bible from within Our Traditions." In *Between Two Horizons: Spanning New Testament Studies and Systematic Theology*, edited by Joel B. Green and Max Turner, 88–107. Grand Rapids: Eerdmans, 2000.

Wallace, Daniel B. *Greek Grammar beyond the Basics: An Exegetical Syntax of the New Testament*. Grand Rapids: Zondervan, 1996.

Waltke, Bruce K., and M. O'Connor. *An Introduction to Biblical Hebrew Syntax*. Winona Lake, IN: Eisenbrauns, 1990.

Walton, John H., Victor H. Matthews, and Mark Chavalas. *The IVP Bible Background Commentary: Old Testament*. Downers Grove, IL: InterVarsity, 2000.

Warfield, B. B. *The Inspiration and Authority of the Bible*. Philadelphia: P&R, 1948.

Watson, Duane Frederick. *The Rhetoric of the New Testament: A Bibliographic Survey*. Tools for Biblical Study 8. Blandford Forum, UK: Deo, 2006.

Watson, Francis. *Text, Church, and World: Biblical Interpretation in Theological Perspective*. Grand Rapids: Eerdmans, 1994.

Webb, Barry G. *The Book of Judges: An Integrated Reading*. Journal for the Study of the Old Testament: Supplement Series 46. Sheffield: JSOT Press, 1987.

Webb, William J. *Slaves, Women and Homosexuals: Exploring the Hermeneutics of Cultural Analysis*. Downers Grove, IL: InterVarsity, 2001.

Weber, Max. *Ancient Judaism*. Translated by Hans H. Gerth and Don Martindale. Glencoe, IL: Free Press, 1952. Originally published as *Antike Judentum* (1920).

Weeden, Thomas J., Sr. *Mark: Traditions in Conflict*. Philadelphia: Fortress, 1971.

Wegner, Paul D. *A Student's Guide to Textual Criticism of the Bible*. Downers Grove, IL: InterVarsity, 2006.

Weinland, James D. *How to Think Straight*. Totowa, NJ: Rowman & Allanheld, 1963.

Wellhausen, Julius. *Prolegomena to the History of Israel: With a Reprint of the Article "Israel" from the Encyclopaedia Britannica*. Edinburgh: A. & C. Black, 1885.

Westcott, Brooke Foss, and Fenton John Anthony Hort. *The New Testament in the Original Greek*. Vol. 1, *The Text Revised*. . . . Vol. 2, *Introduction and Appendix*. New York: Harper & Brothers, 1881–82.

Westermann, Claus. *Basic Forms of Prophetic Speech*. Louisville: Westminster John Knox, 1991.

———. *Roots of Wisdom: The Oldest Proverbs of Israel and Other Peoples*. Louisville: Westminster John Knox, 1994.

Wigram, George V. *The Englishman's Hebrew Concordance of the Old Testament*. Peabody, MA: Hendrickson, 1996.

Wilkins, Michael J. *Discipleship in the Ancient World and Matthew's Gospel*. 2nd ed. Grand Rapids: Baker Academic, 1995.

Wilson, Robert R. *Sociological Approaches to the Old Testament*. Guides to Biblical Scholarship. Philadelphia: Fortress, 1984.

Wimsatt, W. K., and Monroe Beardsley. "The Intentional Fallacy." In *The Verbal Icon: Studies in the Meaning of Poetry*, edited by W. K. Wimsatt, 3–18. Lexington: University of Kentucky Press, 1954.

Winter, Bruce W. *After Paul Left Corinth: The Influence of Secular Ethics and Social Change*. Grand Rapids: Eerdmans, 2001.

Winter, Bruce W., and Andrew D. Clarke, eds. *The Book of Acts in Its First Century Setting*. Vol. 2., *The Book of Acts in Its Ancient Lieterary Setting*. Grand Rapids: Eerdmans, 1993.

Witherington, Ben, III. *The Jesus Quest: The Third Search for the Jew of Nazareth*. Downers Grove, IL: InterVarsity, 1995.

———. *New Testament History: A Narrative Account*. Grand Rapids: Baker Academic, 2001.

———. *New Testament Rhetoric: An Introductory Guide to the Art of Persuasion in and of the New Testament*. Eugene, OR: Cascade, 2009.

———. *Paul's Narrative Thought World: The Tapestry of Tragedy and Triumph*. Louisville: Westminster John Knox, 1994.

Wold, Donald J. *Out of Order: Homosexuality in the Bible and the Ancient Near East*. Grand Rapids: Baker Academic, 1998.

Wolff, Hans Walter. *Joel and Amos*. Hermeneia: A Critical and Historical Commentary on the Bible. Philadelphia: Fortress, 1977.

Wolters, Al. "The Text of the Old Testament." In *The Face of Old Testament Studies: A Survey of Contemporary Approaches*, edited by David W. Baker and Bill T. Arnold, 19–37. Grand Rapids: Baker Academic, 1999.

Wolterstorff, Nicholas. *Divine Discourse: Philosophical Reflections on the Claim That God Speaks*. Cambridge: Cambridge University Press, 1995.

———. "The Promise of Speech-Act Theory for Biblical Interpretation." In *After Pentecost: Language and Biblical Interpretation*, edited by Craig Bartholomew, Colin Greene, and Karl Möller, 73–90. Scripture and Hermeneutics Series 2. Grand Rapids: Zondervan, 2001.

Wrede, William. *The Messianic Secret*. Translated by J. C. G. Greig. Library of Theological Translations. Cambridge, UK: James Clarke, 1971. Originally published as *Das Messiasgeheimnis in den Evangelien* (1901).

Wright, Christopher J. H. *An Eye for an Eye: The Place of Old Testament Ethics Today*. Downers Grove, IL: InterVarsity, 1983.

———. *Old Testament Ethics for the People of God*. Downers Grove, IL: InterVarsity, 2004.

Wright, N. T. *Jesus and the Victory of God*. Minneapolis: Fortress, 1996.

———. *The New Testament and the People of God*. Minneapolis: Fortress, 1992.

———. *The Resurrection of the Son of God*. Minneapolis: Fortress, 2003.

Würthwein, Ernst. *The Text of the Old Testament: An Introduction to the Biblia Hebraica*. Translated by Erroll F. Rhodes. Rev. ed. Grand Rapids: Eerdmans, 1995.

Yamasaki, Gary. *Watching a Biblical Narrative: Point of View in Biblical Exegesis*. New York: T&T Clark, 2007.

Yoder, John Howard. *The Politics of Jesus*. Grand Rapids: Eerdmans, 1972.

Author Index

433

Subject Index